COMMUNAL LAND OWNERSHIP IN CHILE

Para Max Emiliano, el más amado

Para mis padres, eternos amantes de su pueblo Canela Baja y para todos aquellos que como ellos emigraron al Norte de Chile buscando un futuro major para sus hijos

También para todos aquellos comuneros que quedaron empeñados en su lucha por sobrevivir en su terruño

Finalmente, para Bernardo Silva y Juan de Dios Ogalde que pagaron con su vida el defender la teirra

Communal Land Ownership in Chile
The agricultural communities in the commune of Canela, Norte Chico (1600–1998)

GLORIA L. GALLARDO FERNÁNDEZ
Swedish University of Agricultural Sciences, Sweden

LONDON AND NEW YORK

First published 2002 by Ashgate Publishing

Reissued 2018 by Routledge
2 Park Square, Milton Park, Abingdon, Oxon OX14 4RN
711 Third Avenue, New York, NY 10017, USA

Routledge is an imprint of the Taylor & Francis Group, an informa business

Copyright © Gloria L. Gallardo Fernández 2002

All rights reserved. No part of this book may be reprinted or reproduced or utilised in any form or by any electronic, mechanical, or other means, now known or hereafter invented, including photocopying and recording, or in any information storage or retrieval system, without permission in writing from the publishers.

Notice:
Product or corporate names may be trademarks or registered trademarks, and are used only for identification and explanation without intent to infringe.

Publisher's Note
The publisher has gone to great lengths to ensure the quality of this reprint but points out that some imperfections in the original copies may be apparent.

Disclaimer
The publisher has made every effort to trace copyright holders and welcomes correspondence from those they have been unable to contact.

A Library of Congress record exists under LC control number: 2001099961

ISBN 13: 978-1-138-71831-9 (hbk)
ISBN 13: 978-1-138-71829-6 (pbk)
ISBN 13: 978-1-315-19591-9 (ebk)

Contents

List of Figures		*vi*
List of Tables		*vii*
Preface		*x*
List of Abbreviations		*xiii*
List of Equivalences and Measures		*xvi*
PART 1: GENERAL INTRODUCTION		1
1	Introduction	3
2	Overview of the Chilean Land Tenure Structure and the Socio-Economic Setting of the Study Object	60
3	On Agricultural Communities and their Geographical Setting	98
PART 2: THE HISTORICAL PAST		131
4	Land Tenure Formation in Colonial Chile	133
5	The Hacienda El Totoral and the Agricultural Community of Canela Baja: a Common Introduction	186
6	The Hacienda El Totoral: the Development Path of Private Property	214
7	Historical Formation of the Agricultural Community Canela Baja: a Reconstruction	250
PART 3: CONTEMPORARY HISTORY		299
8	The Agricultural Community Canela Baja and the Struggle for Espíritu Santo	301
9	Fundos and Communities Ending the 1900s	329
10	The Common Denominator	364
Primary Sources and Literature		*406*
Appendix 1: Present surnames in the community Canela Baja		*422*
Appendix 2: Short description of the survey		*425*
Appendix 3: Other services in the commune of Canela		*429*
Index		*436*

List of Figures

Figure 1.1	Agricultural communities of Region IV	38
Figure 1.2	Settlements in the Canela Commune	46
Figure 3.1	The communes of Region IV (Coquimbo)	100
Figure 3.2	Types of climate in the Canela Commune	102
Figure 3.3	Land areas of the agricultural communities of Canela Commune	109
Figure 3.4	Land exploitation in the agricultural communities of Canela Commune	114
Figure 3.5	Land ownership in the agricultural communities	118
Figure 5.1	Pedro Cortes Monroi's descent	190
Figure 5.2	The boundaries of *Estancia* La Canela at 1679	192
Figure 6.1	The subdivision of *Hacienda* El Totoral: 1890-1990 (44,180 ha)	248
Figure 7.1	The *Estancias* La Canela and Mincha (~1605-1726)	257
Figure 7.2	The *Estancias* La Canela and Mincha (~1739-1753)	266
Figure 7.3	The sub-division of *Estancia* Canela Baja: 1679-1974	288
Figure 7.4	The sub-division of *Estancia* Mincha: 1605-1979	297

List of Tables

Table 1.1	Agricultural communities in Chile	21
Table 1.2	Agricultural properties in Chile, according to origin, land ownership form and 'ethnic' composition	22
Table 1.3	Distribution of the agricultural communities by communes in the Norte Chico	36
Table 1.4	Sub-areas of the agricultural community Canela Baja	43
Table 2.1	Development of land tenure in Chile (1924-1985)	67
Table 2.2	The structure of land tenure in Chile (1985)	68
Table 2.3	Types of agricultural enterprise, number, percentage and total area in Chile, 1989	69
Table 2.4	Categories of peasant exploitation in Chile, 1989	70
Table 2.5	Total population in the agricultural communities, number of *comuneros* with rights, of resident *comuneros*, and of families of non *comuneros*, according to CBR of Illapel (1986), IREN (1977) and number of *comuneros* according to the communities (1979) in the Canela commune	74
Table 2.6	The total area of the agricultural communities	77
Table 2.7	Fundos and reserves of the Canela Commune, including only those properties of over 500 ha	79
Table 2.8	Distribution of all forms of agricultural estates by size in the Canela commune, 1983	80
Table 2.9	Total number of estates in the Canela commune, 1988-89	81
Table 2.10	Total number of estates in the Mincha commune (now Canela), 1929	82
Table 2.11	Population by gender in the Canela commune and its main urban villages, 1982	84

Table 2.12	Population by age groups in the Canela commune, 1982	87
Table 2.13	Population of 15 years of age and more, according to occupational situation (occupied-vacant) in the Canela commune, 1982	88
Table 2.14	Occupied by economic branch in the Canela commune, 1982	89
Table 2.15	Cattle existence in the agricultural communities of the Canela commune, 1986	96
Table 3.1	The classes and soils and need for vegetation proposed by IREN in the agricultural communities of the Canela Commune, by area	108
Table 3.2	Types of land in the Canela commune	112
Table 3.3	Land ownership in an agricultural community of Norte Chico before 1993	115
Table 4.1	The percentage indigenous population with respect to the Province of Coquimbo at the beginning of the 1800s	163
Table 6.1	Average annual value of the Chilean peso in terms of £ sterling, 1830-1925 (in pence of £, rounded to nearest penny)	221
Table 6.2	The *fundo* El Totoral: 1890-1972	224
Table 6.3	The *fundo* Las Palmas: 1890-1939	230
Table 6.4	The *fundo* Puerto Oscuro: 1890-1972	236
Table 7.1	List of marriages in Mincha Parish, 1689-1714	260
Table 7.2	Land sales in the *Estancias* Canela Baja and Alta, 1805-1868	282
Table 8.1	List of the *comuneros* of Espíritu Santo, 1893	313
Table 8.2	The *fundo* Espíritu Santo, 1853-1972	314
Table 9.1	Land ownership in an agricultural community of Region IV from 1993	361

Table A1	List of the present ten most common surnames among the *comuneros* of the agricultural community Canela Baja	423
Table A2	List of the present two/three most common surnames among the *comuneros* of the agricultural community Canela Baja by sub-areas	423
Table A3	Sub-areas agricultural community Canela Baja and the sample	427
Table A4	Weekly sales of newspapers in the village Canela Baja	431

Preface

The idea for this dissertation was born in 1987. I was travelling from Santiago to the copper mine enclave Chuquicamata, in the Chilean desert, where my parents used to live, when the bus passed near my village Canela Baja, 300 km. north of Santiago, where I was born. After having been abroad almost half of my life, living in Poland, Sweden and Mexico, I was returning to Chile with the intention of putting down roots in my country. Reflecting then on my village and its communal land ownership – about which I discovered I knew practically nothing – the first, theoretical, question arose: how to conceive the 'persistence' or 'survival' of this form of ownership and agrarian production within a framework that, in my opinion, most would view as mainly capitalist, taking place in the country as a result of the changes that the Chilean agrarian structure has undergone since the 1960s.

These changes had not only modernised agriculture, but more importantly had destroyed the *latifundium*, for centuries the economic base of the national oligarchy. During the same period, paradoxically, the legal recognition of the agricultural communities, until then without any defined legal status, started to take form. Of these two social institutions – the *latifundium* and the agricultural communities – both rooted in the colonial period, the one that at the end of the 1900s was still 'surviving' was that of the agricultural communities. In this way, the 'endurance' of the agricultural communities became the 'disconfirming evidence' or empirical 'phenomenon' that appeared 'problematic' to me. Although I tried in my Master thesis to criticise the use of the theory of mode of productions, which in Latin-America drew its inspiration from Marx, yet long and largely by way of Althusser, I was still trying to analyse my village with the concepts of this theory, so fascinating but so sterile if not concerned with the study of concrete societies, societies that do not belong to the classical core of the European nations.

After I had formulated the first question, it followed that scientific curiosity about the origin of this type of community, would later provide me with my second question. I soon discovered that these communities had their origin in the colonial land grants and since these evolved into private property, I had an example of an 'inverted' transition between 'modes of productions'. The second question became how to conceive the transition from private property to the semi-communal ownership within this theory. This example came to reconfirm for me that while the theory about capitalism's development accounts for the general tendency, it is the study of specific cases that can help to determine in what circumstances and to which extent the requisites prescribed by the theory are fulfilled in a given social reality. Moreover, the study of 'deviant cases' at the micro level could help to refine the theoretical structure and avoid its oversimplification.

The investigation then took form with two sociologically relevant, empirical issues: historically, the development of semi-communal land ownership formed out of private property and presently, the reproduction of this form of semi-communal land ownership. In pursuing to treat these issues and trying to apprehend the questions they gave birth to, I included in the original thesis an overview of the different approaches about the small peasantry and its survival, passing through an overview of the theory of modes of production and what I considered was its inability to conceptualise particular cases which do not fit into the theory. I illustrated this with my case study applied both to the colonial and post-colonial period. Stevenson's approach on communal land ownership was thought to be an alternative and a complement to the Marxist approach.

As the study developed, however, the question of the form of the semi-communal land ownership became more and more dominant. When the case study was fully developed, the communal form and its historical development had become the central question. While my two original issues remained central, the two questions born from them became superfluous. Consequently, my intention to use them to highlight through particular cases the shortcomings of extrapolating the theory of modes production automatically to other historical contexts and material conditions also disappear.

Capitalism is however, the dominant mode of production and we cannot disregard that other forms of production are all related to it. Therefore, it is still valid in rhetorical terms to present communal land ownership as a paradox. As Marx might say, paradoxes are, however, apparent.

Many people have, in one way or another way, made this study possible. Among them I thank my advisers Docent Mats Franzén and PhD Mekuria Bulcha at the Department of Sociology as well as my second reader, Professor Björn Eriksson.

I would like to acknowledge in second place all those *comuneros* who shared their information about the agricultural communities with me. The list of *comuneros* and non *comuneros* is interminable. I constantly disturbed many people, starting with the priest, passing through the police to the Mayors in charge. I want, however, especially to thank among the *comuneros*, Pedro Carvajal, Joel Muñoz and Emiliano Cortés. Many other people contributed in different ways to this thesis during the years. Among them I thank for their tutorial supports during my time in Chile, the sociologists Sergio Gómez and Marcelo Charlin and the assistant Carmen Gloria, all from FLACSO, and the anthropologist Rigoberto Rivera from GIA in Santiago. I also thank here both José Joaquín Brunner and Norbert Lechner for opening the doors of FLACSO, giving me the chance to get in touch with Sergio and Marcelo. I am indebted to my friend, the journalist Patricia Moscoso, who rendered me many services from Chile during those years, as well as with my friends and cousins Editha Valencia and Miryam Ollarzú. My gratitude to all those who helped me to carry out the survey during several days climbing hills up and down, including Camilo, the driver. I am also in debt to both the Archivo Nacional and Biblioteca Nacional and their staff in Santiago. I spent many days there.

The list of friends and colleagues that encouraged me is long, but I want to mention ultimately my Ghanaian friend and colleague PhD Dan-Bright Dzorgbo for both rich intellectual and editing questions. I cannot forget Robert Dixon-Gough from the Land Management Research Unit, School of Surveying, University of East London, for the editing of the book and for Cheryl Wheeler, also from the School of Surveying, for redrawing the maps. I alone am responsible, however, for this dissertation. Its shortcomings belong to me.

Gloria L. Gallardo Fernández

Department of Rural Development Studies
Swedish University of Agricultural Sciences, Uppsala
September 2001

List of Abbreviations

[ ]	my parenthesis
AGRARIA	Consultorías Profesionales Agrarias (Agrarian Professional Consulting)
AJ	Archivo Judicial (Judicial Archive)
AN	Archivo Notarial (Notarial Archives)
ANCH	Archivo Nacional de Chile (Chile's National Archive)
AP	Archivos Parroquiales (Parochial Archives)
CAS	Commision Asistencia Social (Social Assistance Commission)
CBR	Conservador de Bienes Raíces (Conservatory of Real Estate)
CCA	Caja de Crédito Agrario (Agrarian Credit Bank)
CCH	Caja de Crédito Hipotecario (Mortgage Credit Bank)
CEDECOM	Centro de Desarrollo Comunitario Económico y Social (Communitarian Centre of Economic and Social Development)
CEPAL	Comisión Económica para America Latina (ECLA, United Nations Economic Commission for Latin-America)
CESOC	Centro de Estudios Sociales (Centre of Social Studies)
CIDA	Comité Interamericano de Desarrollo Agrícola (ICAD, Inter-American Committee for Agricultural Development). ICAD is formed by the following international organisations: CEPAL (ECLA), FAO, BID (IDB), OEA and IICA
CIDERE	Comisión Regional de Ganado Caprino (Regional Commission of Cattle Goat)
CIREN	(former IREN), Centro de Investigación de Recursos Naturales (Research Centre of Natural Resources)
CODELCO	Corporación Nacional del Cobre
CONAF	Corporación Nacional Forestal (National Forestry Corporation)
CORA	Corporación de Reforma Agraria (Agrarian Reform Corporation)
CORFO	Corporación de Fomento (Development Corporation)
DFL	Decreto con Fuerza de Ley (Decree with Legal Power)
ETA	Estudios y Trabajos Agrícolas (Agricultural Studies and Work)

FAO/PAF – CHILE	Organización de las Naciones Unidas para la Agricultura y la Alimentación/Plan de Acción Forestal para Chile (United Nations Organisation for Agriculture and Alimentation/Action Plan for Reafforestation, Chile)
FIDA	Fondo Internacional de Desarrollo Agrícola (International Fund of Agricultural Development)
FLACSO	Facultad Latinoamericana de Ciencias Sociales (Latin American Faculty of Social Sciences)
GIA	Grupo de Investigaciones Agrarias (Agrarian Research Group)
HRB	Héctarea de Riego Básico (Irrigated Basic Hectare)
ICAD	See CIDA
ICIRA	Instituto de Capacitación e Investigación de Reforma Agraria (Agrarian Reform's Institute for Capacity and Investigation)
IER	Instituto de Educación Rural (Institute of Rural Education)
IGM	Instituto Geográfico Militar (Militar Geographic Institute)
INDAP	Instituto de Desarrollo Agropecuario (Development Institute for Agriculture and Cattle Raising)
INE	Instituto Nacional de Estadísticas (National Statistics Institute)
INFOR	Instituto Forestal, filial de CORFO (Forestal Institute)
INIA	Instituto de Investigaciones Agropecuarias (Investigation Institute of Agriculture and Cattle Raising)
INPROA	Instituto de Promoción Agraria (Institute of Agrarian Promotion)
IPC	Indice de Precios al Consumidor (Retail Price Index)
IREN	See CIREH
JUNDEP	Juventudes Para El Desarrollo y La Producción (identidad asociada FAO), (Youths for Development and Production, unit associated to FAO)
MC	Municipalidad de Canela (Canela Municipality)
MM	Municipalidad de Mincha (Mincha Municipality)
NGO	Non Government Organisation
OBN	Oficina de Bienes Nacionales (Office of National Estates)
ODENA	Oficina de Normalización Agraria (Office of Agrarian Standardisation)
RA	Rol de Avalúos (Valuation Roll)
RCCBR	Rol de Cobro-Contribuciones de Bienes Raíces (Roll of Collection-Contributions of Real Estates)

REA	Rol Extracto Agrícola (Agricultural Extract Roll)
RP	Registro de propiedad (Real Estate Register)
s.a.	*Sine anno* (non date)
SAG	Servicio Agrícola Ganadero (Agricultural Grazer Service)
SHALOM	Círculo de Profesionales Cristianos para el Desarrollo (Circle of Christian Professionals for Development)
SII	Servicio de Impuestos Internos (Internal Tax Service)
s.l.	*Sine loco* (without place)
SNGM	Servicio Nacional de Geología y Minera de Chile (Chile's National Service for Geology and Mining)
SNS	Servicio Nacional de Salud (National Health Service)
UF	Unidad de Fomento (Fomentation Unit)

List of Equivalences and Measures

Cuadras	three *cuadras* are equivalent to approximately five hectares
Escudos (E°)	the middle exchange in 1970 was E° 12 per dollar. "The dollars from 1975 are equivalent 1.39 times those from 1970" (Cortázar and Downey, 1977:700)
Fanega	grain measure equivalent to 1.60 bushel
Legua	one Spanish league equals 5,572 meters or approximately 5.5 kilometres
Peso ($)	the value of the Chilean *peso* was in March 1991, 355.38 per 1 US-dollar. In February 1998 it was 455 *pesos*
Quintal	a qq or quintal is a metric unit of weight, equal to 100 kilograms
Unidades de Fomento (UF)	UF's value in 1979 was of 640 *pesos ($)*, in 9 October 1990 was of 6,427.58 *pesos*
Vara	unit of length, about 2.8 feet

PART 1
GENERAL INTRODUCTION

1 Introduction

Purpose of the study

Since the earliest discovery of agriculture, it has been the basic way of obtaining the means for survival and reproduction of humankind. The pivotal means for that survival and reproduction has predominantly been the land. As such, land can be the object of some, though limited, forms of ownership. Except for the socialist experiences in different parts of the world, and of public or state ownership, there are at present roughly two forms of land ownership: communal and private, with some forms that are combination of both. The trend has undeniably been throughout the nineteenth century towards private property. Nonetheless, marginal but global, communal land ownership still exists in different parts of the world.

A form

The purpose of this study is to investigate the historical origin, emergence and present reproduction of the communal, or more specifically, semi-communal land ownership, of the Norte Chico region in Chile. This will be through a case study of the agricultural community Canela Baja and its colonial predecessor, the *estancia* La Canela in the commune with the same name, in the province of Choapa. The study object represents an example among 200 such agricultural communities existing in the Norte Chico. For the sake of clarity, it is important not to confuse the agricultural community Canela Baja with the commune of Canela. Within the Chilean political-administrative division of the country, the communes correspond to the minor units. They are followed, in ascendant order, by the provinces and the regions. Region IV, has three provinces: Elqui, Limarí and Choapa. I will be mostly referring to Norte Chico as this region is known historically. The latter has four communes: Illapel, Salamanca, Los Vilos and Canela.

Although agricultural communities, organised under communal land ownership, may be found in different parts of Chile, it is only in the Norte Chico (or Region IV) that this peculiar form of land ownership, even for

Chile, is widespread, occupying approximately 1 million hectares (or 25% of the region's land area). According to CIPRES (1992:2), this form of land ownership is also to be found in Regions III (Atacama), V (Valparaíso) and the Metropolitan Region (Santiago). Any further information is given about how many they are and what their legal status is. Nonetheless, it is only in Region IV that these are common. This relation in the Canela commune is much higher, covering approximately between 50-70% of its area. In this commune 24 of the 26 agricultural communities of the province of Choapa are concentrated (see Table 1.3). Here semi-communal land ownership is the predominant land property form.

The Norte Chico of Chile is peculiar both within a national and a Latin-American context not only because of its current land tenure structure, but also because it presents the development of semi-communally owned property out of private property. Here the colonial institution of *mercedes de tierra*, or land grants, did not simply evolve into a structure of *latifundium* and *minifundium*, as it mainly did in the rest of Chile. The semi-communal land ownership of the agricultural communities developed, alongside the *latifundium*, becoming a hybrid, neither *latifundium* nor *minifundium* but in, I would suggest a form of its own. The concepts of *latifundium*, *hacienda* or *fundo* are commonly used in Chile indistinctly to denote a large landed estate. The concept of *minifundium* refers to small landed estates. Historically the *minifundium* has its roots mainly in the *latifundium* (see Chapter 4).

In spite of that, being as old as the *latifundium*, it was not until quite recently that the form became legally recognised. Notwithstanding that recognition, as a form, it has been an unattended one. It has not been fully understood, and still lacks a theoretical foundation, which would give a framework to the hitherto 200 existing agricultural communities, together constituting the regional phenomena of semi-communal land ownership so characteristic for the Norte Chico.

However, communal land exists not only in Chile, but in different parts of the world, for example in Switzerland, South Africa or Mexico, and hence in different socio-political contexts and material conditions. Paraphrasing Braudel (1981, Vol. 1:111), I would say that the variations about the same form of property, i.e., communal land ownership, are numerous, but they are always imposed by local conditions; material and geographical, mountainous in some cases, but not in others.

Introduction

What then is communal land ownership? As a first definition, in the case that I will be examining here, it can be characterised by the coexistence of communal and (semi) private land property within the limits of one bigger landed unit. In a permanent and undivided form this belongs to all the *comuneros* (commoners) registered in that community. It is the specific inter-weaving into one unit of two forms of properties, which together could be conceived as contradictory, that gives shape to the singular socio-economic organisation that conforms to this institution; what is known in Chile as an agricultural community. I subscribe here to the difference between the concepts of institution and organisation discussed by Brante and Norman (1995:33-43). Institutions are defined as rules and habits that govern our behaviour and thinking, supplying individuals with conventions, norms and etiquette, but also with motives, preferences and goals. To institutions belong also ideology, i.e., values and ideas about how reality is and should be. Institutions contain self confirming and self producing mechanisms. Institutions not only standardise our behaviour but also our thinking and perception of the world. When institutions become systematised and formalised in law, they become organisations.

The most basic element of the agricultural communities is, however, the communal land being its most specific feature, distinguishing it, as a form of property, both from private property and open access. The latter, in fact, stands not for property, but for the absence of it (Stevenson, 1991:52).

As Hendricks (1990:19) has argued:

> land tenure does not exist in a vacuum. Particular forms of land holding are intimately connected with different modes of social relations.

Communal land ownership is not just a form of owning the land, but also a way to produce and reproduce the peasantry. Thus, ownership itself is always attached to social subjects, constituting, as a form of agricultural social production, a socio-economic organisation or institution. An agricultural community is, in this way, an institution organised under the form of communal, or semi-communal land ownership, whose multiple members are landowners.

As such, this institution, is part of a heterogeneous agrarian structure comprising different land tenure systems, or forms, which conform to that agrarian structure. By land tenure system, Stavenhagen (1970) understands the distribution of property and usufruct rights to land. The land tenure system conditions the economic and social relations, on the one hand, between different kinds of landowners and, on the other, between owners and labourers.

> Around these basic pivots (man-land and man-man relationships) have arisen legal norms, stratification hierarchies, patterns of social behaviour and political power systems, all of which, taken as a whole, are subsumed under the term 'agrarian structures' (Stavenhagen, 1970: X, emphasis original).

Similar to Stavenhagen's concept is CIDA's definition of land structure as:

> the combination of the land tenure systems and the relationships that occur between them and that characterise a given region (Comité Interamericano de Desarrollo Agrícola (CIDA) or Inter-American Committee for Agricultural Development (ICAD), 1966: VI-VII).

As land tenure, CIDA understands the traditional relationships and legal rules given between individuals, groups and institutions that regulate and determine the rights, as well as obligations concerning the use of the land, its transfer and the usufruct of its products (CIDA, 1966: VI-VII).

To structure the discussion, I will for analytical purposes, distinguish between two main dimensions regarding land tenure, to use a broader term than property; the form of land ownership, and its historical development. The concept of tenure is broader than the concept of ownership. Tenure does not necessarily involve property, but the access to it. Therefore, when I refer to the general agrarian structure, tenure is more appropriate, as it includes the access to land by other ways than direct ownership. However, the concept of property is here the appropriate one when dealing not only with the agricultural communities, but also the *latifundia* and *minifundia* as it deals in fact with ownership, and not only access. Within the agricultural communities and from their perspective, both historical factual, and legally, the concept of tenure is also appropriate (see Chapters 3 and 9). Tenure will also be used when, for example, it is not possible to define with certainty that it is ownership, or when the legal definition is not very clear. See also Stavenhagen's and CIDA's previous definition on land tenure or agrarian structure.

Introduction

This investigation deals with the form and its development, and attempts to answer *what* is the form, and *how* it has developed. The exposition of this work will, however, follow the inverse way, i.e., it will first show how, through the empirical case, the form has developed, and thereafter answer what is the form from a theoretical perspective, differentiating it both from private property and open access.

However, because the form has to develop out of something before it becomes established, it is possible to conceptually separate form, origin and emergence, even though they are inseparable in reality. Firstly I will deal with the question of the form, and thereafter origin and emergence, as well as what is, in my opinion, the difference between them.

As a form of property, the agricultural communities of the Norte Chico share many characteristics with other communities in different countries. This is first of all the common land ownership/tenancy and the characteristics and prerogatives it allows, as compared to both estates and small peasantry. I will return below in a more detailed form to this, exemplifying it, specifically with the *latifundium* and *minifundium* in Latin America. The individual plots of land within the communal land are another such characteristic. With some exceptions, the exploitation of both the communal and private production spheres is usually individual. The communal form is the common denominator.

Regarding the historical origin of the form, I will suggest that the agricultural communities of the Norte Chico differ in a special way. Here we find their historical peculiarity, and another neglected problem; the knowledge about the origin of this peculiar institution is still precarious.

To illustrate the global form of the Norte Chico's agricultural communities, but also their specificity regarding the question of the origin, I will draw some contrasting comparisons in these two respects with some other examples of agricultural communities. These will comprise the Mexican, the South African, the Mapuche and Aymara Chilean communities, the Swiss Alps and also the now extinct English open field system.

Regarding the form, which all communities share, they also diverge historically in their origin and emergence. Although it is not easy to distinguish between origin and emergence, since they are interwoven, it is possible to identify the origin as the 'starting point' of a community. In the case of emergence, this should be taken as the development process during which the community is constituted or formed. This would point out the many and varied circumstances that led to the shaping of the form. In other words, I would suggest that there is a difference between the question of the origin and the emergence of the form. Some examples of present communal land ownership are, against what one may commonly believe, not residues or remnants of a pre-colonial or pre-capitalist period, or some type of 'original' American or African forms of land ownership. They are quite the opposite, the result of political factors. Other examples of communal land ownership, on the contrary, are the result of long historical processes.

However, the difference between the origin and emergence of the form may be of importance to the stability of the form in time, and therefore, in relation to how the individual involved may perceive it. A communal land ownership which is a result of a spontaneous developing process, in comparison to an imposed form, should, as a social institution, have more solid grounds than an imposed one, and therefore a major stability as a form over time. We could also make a distinction between imposed and spontaneous forms. The fact that some forms are imposed, however, highlights another aspect; the imposed forms are not so much communities, as reserves or homelands.

Within the imposed form, the way this is imposed may also be important for how production is organised, and how the access to land is perceived by the individuals. Seen from their point of view, the actors may experience the imposed form, either by force or as a result of a legal decree which can be beneficiary for them, or not.

So having on one hand, the form of communal land ownership as the common denominator, we have on the other the social aspect resulting from their particular history. The implications of such aspects are not only psychological or political, but also of importance for the ecological environment, and, thus, for all of us. See for instance *Twenty Years to Nowhere. Property Rights, Land Management and Conservation in Ethiopia*, Yeraswork Admassie, 1995, where the author takes the importance of property rights conditions for (failure) soil and afforestation programs in Ethiopia as a result of diverse state policy (capitalist and socialist) and how the peasants perceived them.

Due to theoretical and practical purposes in this chapter, I will deal with the Mexican, South African, Mapuche and Aymara Chilean communities, saving the Swiss Alps and the now extinct English open field system to the last chapter. Theoretically, with the help of the Swiss and

English examples, the question of what is the form will, following Stevenson (1991) be partially empirically exemplified. Practically, since because the Chilean Norte Chico's agricultural communities historically show more resemblance with the last two cases, this will become clear after Part 2, when I demonstrate, through my case study, the long and lethargic development process of semi-communal land ownership in Chile's Norte Chico. Only then, will communal land as a form be theoretically approached and systematically compared, both with private property and open access arriving to Stevenson's formal definition.

Conversely, since I am postulating that the agricultural communities of the Norte Chico diverge regarding origin, with both the Mexican and the South African examples of agricultural communities and also from other Chilean agricultural communities (once this has been established and the differences pointed out) then we can leave these cases behind. In other words, for these cases it is not necessary to follow the whole historical process, as their 'starting point' is quite clear, by which they differ from those communities where communal land ownership is the result of a long and spontaneous historical process.

Before continuing, I have to stress a methodological consideration regarding this issue. When using the term contrast, I do not mean I am performing a proper comparison in the sense of following all the aspects, step by step, in every example of community, but rather that I am taking those that are relevant from the point of view of my study purpose. Therefore, it is important to understand that in taking the case of South Africa, I am not looking for the most representative example of communal land ownership in the African continent, but of an example that serves to incorporate the political dimension, the imposition of the form, into the question of the origin and emergence of some forms of communal land ownership.

While the Mexican and South African examples represent the Third World context, those of Chile will represent the national context. Before proceeding to the former examples, let me here develop some of the mentioned characteristics and prerogatives that communal land ownership allows, exemplifying this specifically with the agricultural communities of Norte Chico and the *latifundium* and *minifundium* in Latin America. In this way, common as well as disparate elements will be illustrated.

It is necessary to keep in mind the referred analytical distinction between form and history. While some of the differences between communal and private land ownership refer to the form, our common sociological denominator, others refer to history, the same being valid for the similarities. As form, origin and emergence are in reality inseparable, it is not always easy to differentiate between them in the examples given below, the reason being that many may be juxtaposed against each other.

As suggested, communal land ownership is different both from the *latifundium, haciendas* or *fundos*, and the *minifundium* in Latin America. These are all private properties. However, as a hybrid form of property, the agricultural communities also share aspects with both of them, one of the most important being a common origin through the colonial *mercedes de tierras*.

Theoretically, the form of communal land attached to diverse, peasant agricultural communities is commonly conceived as a 'remnant' of the past, or as an example of the small peasantry, more or less synonymous with a reservoir of labour force, either for the rural estates or the urban zones. The borderlines between these conceptions of 'pre-capitalist', 'small peasantry' or a 'labour reservoir' is not very clear. It is clearer that communal land ownership is commonly conceived in a rudimentary way and without empathy for its own peculiarity. I would suggest that it is not only theoretically and empirically, a relatively abandoned form, but also a misunderstood one.

Cardoso (1982:100), indicates that it is common to find how the existence of pre-capitalist modes of production are qualified as residues or anomalies, when, for Marx, these 'anomalies' would not be sub-products of capitalism's historical evolution, but on the contrary, they would rather designate the natural limits of said process. This position that sees the existence of non capitalist relations of production as vestiges, abnormalities or accidents within capitalism, reveals, according to Cardoso, a vision that postulates a form of evolution that is considered normal. How could the survival of pre-capitalist modes of production be residues, questions Cardoso, when the rural structures were always perfectly adapted to the needs of the peculiar development that characterises the Latin-American peripheral capitalism. Cardoso argues that capitalism has a disintegrating effect on the existing modes of production, but as autonomous and differentiated modes of production, maintaining features that could be integrated to peripheral capitalism.

Mostly, the agricultural communities in Latin-America are included within the *minifundium* (Gómez, 1989:6, see Table 2.4). Rivera

(1988a:45), for example, includes the Mapuche communities, within it. So also do Astorga (1985:100) and Pucciarelli (1985:56) with the communal land ownership of the Mexican *ejido*. Bengoa (1988:192) is also in broad agreement with this concept. Referring to the tradition of common grassland in Chile, he identifies the agricultural communities of the Norte Chico with the *minifundium*, when he affirms that in that region the small peasants have maintained the hills as common since colonial times. As we shall see in Chapter 4, these authors adhere to a line already drawn by Borde and Góngora (1956).

By the small peasantry, in the Latin American case *minifundium*, I mean firstly, the group of agrarian producers that, principally, due to scarcity of land, base their production and reproduction mainly but not exclusively, on subsistence agriculture. This is a primitive agriculture, which often has:

> a minimum of potential development for the agriculture in commercial scale (Baraona *et al*, 1961:178).

The peasant and his family dedicate most of their active time to produce for their own consumption (Stavenhagen, 1979:207-208). Securing the sustenance of the small peasantry and their families is difficult due to the lack of irrigated land. Added to this, other factors come into play; the traditional and precarious techniques and conditions of production, which reflect a poor development of the productive forces, its marginality and dependency on the urban centres of economical and political power. Being the *minifundia* in the neighbourhood of the *latifundia*, or other strong types of large enterprise (agricultural or not), often in control of credit, commercial exchange and the local authorities, the small property exists in a tight relation with them. They serve commonly, but not always, as a reservoir of labour in a position of subordination (a more extensive discussion on this concrete matter, referring specifically to the agricultural communities, is developed in Chapter 6). Furthermore, they are often subjected to the hostility of these stronger types of properties in the struggle for land or water (Borde and Góngora, 1956; Baraona *et al*, 1961; Albala *et al*, 1967). Most of the characteristics belonging to the *minifundium* are also peculiar to the agricultural communities. This is not to say that the agricultural communities are *minifundia*.

Considering the land possessions of the *comuneros* of the agricultural communities of the Norte Chico individually, they could be considered as *minifundia*. Yet this is only possible if we ignore their most specific feature, the communal land.

If individual size was the one criterion used to include the agricultural communities within the *minifundium*, in their totality many of them would definitively be bigger than the neighbouring *haciendas* or *fundos*. However, there is among the agricultural communities, large-scale differences ranging from 37.5 to 102,312 ha. Of a total of 158 communities about which IREN reports in 1977, 17.7% had up to 1,000 ha, 72.7% between 1,000 and 10,000 and 9.5% over 10,000 ha (IREN, 1978: Vol I:39. See also IREN, 1977 (2) Catastro, 23-27). Obviously, the size should be put in relation to the number of *comuneros* belonging to the community. In the named examples there are 7 and 200 *comuneros*, which give 5.3 and 511.5 ha *per capita*, respectively. However, the issue of the size relates to a very central matter; that the agricultural communities, keeping their territorial integrity in a permanent, undivided form, historically avoided conversion into *minifundium*.

Many agricultural communities have also remained large productive units, not totally dissimilar to that of the *haciendas*, which many of them, in fact, originally were. Therefore, if the *minifundium* is the historical result of the subdivision of the land, then the agricultural communities are the result of not being divided up. In that sense, I would suggest, that the semi-communal land ownership of the agricultural communities is a resource management solution, which acted as a brake to the process of '*minifundisation*', the fragmentation of the land in the Norte Chico. Therefore, to consider the agricultural communities as *minifundia*, misses this very important process leading to a management solution. Semi-communal land ownership represents, thus, historically, not only another pattern of development, but also another form of organising ownership and production, different both to the *latifundium* and *minifundium*.

Stavenhagen (1979:226-7) can help us to understand the question of the form. The difference between *latifundium* and *minifundium* is not a quantitative divergence between private properties of dissimilar extensions of land, but a qualitative difference between types of agriculture and between ways of life. The *latifundium* is not only a form of property but an economic system that constitutes a base of the ruling oligarchy. The *minifundium*, on its side, constitutes not only a property of reduced extension, but another socio-economic institution. Such is the case, I would suggest, with the agricultural communities. As an institution it is qualitatively different both from the *latifundium* and the *minifundium*.

Thus, without trying to be exhaustive, the form of semi-communal land ownership diverges from the *minifundium* in that it offers the advantages of the common land, which the *minifundium* lacks. This permits the advantage of the transhumance for the cattle, something that is not possible within the *minifundium* (Cañón, 1964). If the land of the agricultural communities were divided into *minifundia*, it would be almost impossible to productively use the hills of the common land for cattle raising. This may be one of the main reasons for the development of the semi-communal land ownership as a resource management solution, i.e., the material conditions.

Communal land also makes possible the temporary cultivation through the system of '*lluvias*' (land plots) on the hills, increasing the area available to exploit for every individual, while the *minifundium* is always compelled to use the same reduced soil. Common land also gives the *comuneros* a source of firewood, hunting, medicinal herbs and material for construction and fences. The advantage of soil rotation on the common lands could also be a disadvantage, inasmuch as the *comunero* has the possibility of obtaining new lands for dry cultivation through the petition of new '*lluvias*'. The *minifundium* peasant would take greater care of the only land he has, which results in a better conservation of the ecological system. However, dealing with the mentioned erosion, there are within the land belonging to the agricultural communities, 200,000 ha in extreme degree of desertification, which correspond to 20% of their total area (CIPRES, 1992:10). However, this does not imply that erosion will not also be common on small private properties (Cañón, 1964:112-113) and, as a rule, on agricultural land in Chile. The great property of the *hacienda* has, given its usually extensive economic management, generally a better conservation of its resources in comparison with the agricultural communities' intensive economic management.

It is also the successive formation of this third, 'alternative' property, which converts the agricultural communities both in contrast to the *latifundium* and *minifundium*, into communities in a deeper sense than the latter two. I will return to this in Chapter 3, and more systematically in Chapter 10. It is sufficient to point out here, that the co-ownership of the land in the agricultural communities is a material base for a permanent relationship between the *comuneros*, aggregating them into a cohesive group. As such, it is also fundamental for the potential organisation in defence of their interests, in spite of their geographical dispersion. In this, the agricultural communities differ from the *minifundium*, whose peasants also live in dispersion, but do not unite. So, if in terms of the potential organisation in defence of their interests, for the *inquilinos* and wage-labour the agglutination factor is joint labour, which potentially facilitates their organisation, and that can be opposed in collective form, to the landlord or patron, for the *comuneros* that is the co-ownership of the land. The *comuneros* lack the antithesis of the patron, or landlord, which presents itself historically for the *comuneros* in another context, the struggle for land. The geographical dispersion in which both the *comuneros* and the peasants of the *minifundium* live is, in itself, not necessarily a disadvantage. It may be, however, when the reason for the relationship between peasants is missing.

In the traditional *latifundium*, or in the post-agrarian reform modern estate, the relationship between the labour force and the proprietors is based on a commercial transaction, which furthermore is of a temporary nature. The *latifundium* is characterised by a notable social stratification between patron/owner and producers/not proprietors, *inquilinos* (tenants) in the case of the *hacienda* prior to the agrarian reform, and wage-labour in the case of the modern estate. These relationships are vertical. In the agricultural communities, owner and producer is the same person. As such, dealing with the organisation of the labour force, the *comuneros*, like other peasants can in fact, plan and control their process of production, administrate their resources and decide on the best form of using them (Pucciarelli, 1985:48). This will permit them to have the capacity of determining the destination of their surpluses, when obtaining them. So, not only is owner and producer one and the same, but also the Chayanovian producer and consumer (Chayanov, 1966). This is opposed to the estates that produce for profit and base their management on external labour, *inquilinos* (tenants) in the case of the traditional *hacienda*, and wage-labour in the case of the modern agricultural property. Conversely, the labour force of the agricultural communities, which consists of the family members including women, children and the elderly, produce primarily for subsistence and only secondly for the market.

Thus, the relationship between *comuneros* is horizontal. They are all equally owners, on one hand, of the agricultural community and, on the other, of the *hijuelas* or singular possessions. As such, they feel as proprietors, proprietors of the principal means of production that an agrarian producer can have: the land. The same cannot be said to be the case of the *inquilinos,* landless peasants, nor wage-labourers. In Marx's words (Vol. 1, 1983:713):

> private property based on the labour of its owner /---/ the labourer is the private owner of his own means of labour set in action by himself: the peasant of the land, which he cultivates.

Of course, within the agricultural communities there also exists a certain social stratification among *comuneros,* some have more land than others. The main channel for economic upward mobility is, nonetheless, according to my observations in the studied community, commerce and not land. In his situation as owner, the *comunero* does not enjoy the certainty of a salary and the protection of the social security laws. Conversely, the tenant of the traditional *hacienda* enjoyed the safety and certainty of a salary in kinds or money, and the paternalistic protection of the landowner. The worker of the modern estate enjoys both a salary and social security.

The social implication of the *comunero* as owner of his land is that he is not, as the *inquilinos* and the landless peasants, subjected to the *haciendas'* system of economic, social and political domination with all that that means of control over property, market, credit, coercion and paternalistic authority. This also has another important socio-cultural implication, which differentiates the *comuneros* from the *inquilinos*. I agree with the view of Bengoa (1988:83), that the *latifundium,* monopolising the land and its access, hindered the peasants becoming rooted in the land, and, accordingly, in developing a peasant culture. Their possessions were always uncertain. The *inquilino* culture, is not, according to Bengoa (1988) a peasant culture, but an agrarian culture of subordination that is very different. The *comuneros* are certainly not part of that culture.

I will now consider some differences and similarities regarding the question of the origin and emergence, between the *latifundium, minifundium* and agricultural communities.

Some of the historical processes that have taken place between the *latifundium* and the *minifundium* include; the natural subdivision by inheritance of the *latifundium,* resulting in the *minifundium,* the *latifundium's* land concentration at the expense of the *minifundium,* the secular relationship of interdependency between the *latifundium* and the *minifundium* and the political process of the agrarian reform that subdivides the *latifundium* that have, unintentionally, created the *minifundium*.

In contrast, the agricultural communities, with their semi-communal land ownership, having their origin mainly, as the *latifundium* or *hacienda*, in the colonial *mercedes*, do not properly fit into that scheme. They represent here, both historically and as a form of property, another pattern of agrarian development, which furthermore has the peculiarity of emerging from private property. This process is counter to the known historical tendency towards private property during the colonial period.

Semi-communal land ownership in Chile has become, more permanent than the *latifundium* as this disappeared due to the process of agrarian reform being substituted by smaller and more modernised productive units. Semi-communal land ownership is more constant, or at least, as constant as the *minifundium* which have resulted from the subdivision of the *latifundium*. Likewise, it is also much older than that *minifundium* created by the modern, political and urban phenomena that was the process of agrarian reform.

So far, some of the common and lesser common aspects of the agricultural communities' communal land ownership in respect to form and history have been illustrated specifically with the *latifundium* and the *minifundium*. Let me now refer to communal land ownership in two other Third World countries.

Examples from South Africa and Mexico

In spite of belonging to two continents, the Mexican and South African forms of communal land ownership have something in common in how they arose. Both forms are imposed and are result of political factors. They are neither residues of a pre-colonial or pre-capitalist period, or some type of 'original' Indian or African form of land ownership. Let me take first the case of the Mexican *ejido*, which is perhaps, one of the most well known and studied community structures in Latin America.

> The land expropriated through the Agrarian Reform and distributed among the peasants is called ejido and its beneficiaries are called ejidatarios. In most cases, the only difference between the ejido and the

Introduction

private lands is that the first cannot be mortgaged nor sold, nor distributed by inheritance (Krantz, no. 1, Vol. 4:95).

However, other communities also exist in Mexico. The difference between the Mexican *ejido* and other communities is not very clear legally in matters of form. Nonetheless, the difference has to do with the manner of obtaining the land, and the way it is administered.

> The ejido is obtained by 'donation', a donation on behalf of the State, of the lands expropriated from the latifundia and with surfaces greater than the maximum established by the agrarian laws, to attend the demands of groups of peasants that lack land (Warman, 1985:7; emphasis original).

The Mexican *ejido* is a legal figure for land tenure, established by the post revolution constitution of 1917. As Pucciarelli (1985:56) indicates, the '*ejidos*' *minifundium* is not a product of a social process of appropriation of natural resource (here we see how the *ejido* as a form of communal land ownership is reduced to the *minifundium*). The small peasant plots were born of the agrarian allotment of 1936 under the government of Cárdenas, the first president who tried to make land distribution effective. According to Stavenhagen (1979:214), in Mexico, the agrarian reform, by creating the *ejidos*, modified the nature of collective land ownership.

A Mexican community can, according to Warman, originate in two ways:

> ... the first is the 'confirmation', which is granted when the agrarian authorities recognise that the use of the land is communal. The other is the 'restitution' of a historical communal property that has been appropriated by particulars. To achieve the restitution it is necessary to accredit the property and its despoliation with documents - always of colonial origin - initiated during the Colony reaching its end in the XIX century (Warman, 1985:7; emphasis original).

In this way, these communities seem to be older than the *ejido* as an agrarian form. However, their precedents are not to be found precisely in the pre-Hispanic period, but rather in the republican or colonial period. Moreover, this seems to be valid also for a country like Guatemala and the neighbouring Chiapas region in Mexico, typical zones of peasant communities. There, very few communities with traditional communal land of pre-Hispanic precedents exist (Stavenhagen, 1979:219). For example, in the western zone of Guatemala, of 80 villages, only one had communal land. The community among these peoples, however, is given by ethnic affiliation, rather than by the common land.

However, the lands of the communities of Mexico are outside the market laws (Warman, 1985:7). In other words, the land cannot, or at least could not, be sold, rented, transferred or seized. The land is a property, but not a merchandise, a means of production, but not capital, a source of income, but not of revenue (Stavenhagen, 1979:219). See for instance, *Tepoztlán: Village in* México by Oscar Lewis, 1960 where he distinguishes between the *ejido*, communal land and private property.

The agricultural communities of Norte Chico, differ to some degree with the Mexican ones because the *comuneros* can now, according to the law, sell, in individual form, at least the lands in their personal possession, within the same community, or to a third party, provided that they are private individuals.

The agricultural communities of the Norte Chico have in common with the Mexican communities and *ejidos* the fact that once the right to become a member of the community has been established, the said right is transmitted only to a single person. This means that the individual possessions cannot be divided by inheritance. I can also add here that compared with private property, communal land ownership is more static, as several limitations hang on it regarding mortgage, sale and inheritance. This will be covered in more detail Chapters 3 and 9.

Let me now take the example from South Africa. Since, until at least the last days of the Apartheid, about half of the African population was compelled to live in the reserves. Thus, it seems that the communal system of the South African reserves was more extensive than the Mexican case.

However, communal land ownership in South Africa is disguised within the Apartheid system in the reserves. The organisation is based on the division of the land into residential, arable, forestry and grazing areas. Dealing with the individual possessions, the form expresses a kind of duality between the formal-legal and the factual practice. Communal land ownership in the reserves is based on the principle of one man, one lot. Formal-legally, under the system of quitrent, the Africans in the reserves are virtual tenants on state owned land, paying their annual quitrent, or local tax (Hendricks, 1990:2). In that sense, since the peasants have to pay for the land, which is individually registered in the name of the family head, the land is revertible to the State, and the peasants are tenants of the

State. The *de facto*, communal tenure is, according to Hendricks (1990:65), a facade, being 'a form of individual tenure under the commonage system', since the registered plots are heritable, which means that descendent groups are able to hold the original plots in perpetuity.

Regarding the precedents of the South African system, the situation seems to be not very different from the Mexican one, in the sense that they are definitely not to be found in the African pre-colonial period.

According to Hendricks, the communal land tenure in the reserves corresponds to a distorted version of the previous system:

> ... it is vaguely reminiscent of the pre-colonial system of land allocation.

'Colonial' capitalism constrained communal access to land and created reserves, replacing communal land tenure with a regimented form of land tenancy.

> By imposing a pseudo-egalitarianism on Africans, denying them the possibility of reaping sustenance from the soil but, simultaneously conjuring upon their minds the myths of home and homelands, this segregationist system of land tenure has shaped African proletarianisation in the reserves (Hendricks, 1990: Abstract).

One of the important local variations that the South African process of 'proletarianisation' presents is the policy of territorial segregation of demarcated rural area reserves for African residents. The distinctive character of this captive 'proletariat', created by state reserves policy through the relocation of millions of black workers into concentrated villages on the reserve, is that:

> they have been displaced from the urban and rural white claimed areas and [on the other] they retain a semblance of access to means of production in the reserves (Hendricks, 1990:4).

This short examination points at an important difference between the Norte Chico's communities and the Mexican and the South African ones, dealing with their divergent origins. The Norte Chico's agricultural communities are not properties especially granted to a certain type of social group. Their constitution into agricultural communities is *de facto*, resulting from private colonial property. Consequently, they are neither collectives created by legal decrees, nor a product of mainly urban, political decisions. They existed in spite of a hostile environment, where Chilean law did not recognise any other form of ownership than the private, except those created by the State itself, as we shall see below. Thus, different to the Mexican and South African cases, the Norte Chico's agricultural communities constituted already a long time ago a form, recognised by the State only post-fact.

As suggested, there is a difference between getting access to a form of property through up-and-down political decision and to obtain legal recognition for an already existing form. Certainly, it can be argued that from the moment any legal recognition becomes law, it also becomes imposed from above. This does not mean, however, that this law is not, as well, a result of down-up political struggle searching for legitimisation, as is for example, the case with the Norte Chico's communities. There is obviously also a difference between the Mexican and South African cases. In the former, the communities get access to the land through a political reform that intends to be progressive. In the latter, this form is imposed by and answers to, first of all, other social interests than those of the group submitted to live in the reserves - the apartheid system. So, if from the point of view of the involved actors, the former corresponds to a type of non-repressive imposition, the latter corresponds to a repressive, racist imposition.

The above suggests that the Mexican *ejidos* and the South African reserves, in terms of their creation, have more resemblance with the Mapuche indigenous communities of southern Chile, than with the agricultural communities of the Norte Chico. As the case of the reserves of South Africa, the Mapuche communities and its communal land system are also a political creation, product of the republican laws that confined the Mapuches to live in reserves. The semi-communal property of the agricultural communities of the Norte Chico, born out of private property also originated in the colonial period. It appears first, as a result of a spontaneous process, a combination of specific, ecological, economic, social and historical factors, and second, not as a system imposed from above, rather from below. Third, from the perspective of the territory occupied by the South African reserves, its tenants do not originally come from them, but have been displaced from other areas to the reserves. This can not be said to be the case of the inhabitants of the agricultural communities of the Norte Chico since they were not located there by force.

Introduction

However, this does not mean that there may not be cases where the *comuneros* may have their origin among indigenous people from different areas who mainly through the *encomienda* system were moved by force from their original places.

The national context

Communal land ownership in Chile is, thus, composed of the indigenous agricultural communities of the Norte Grande (Aymara), of the south (Mapuches), and of the semi-communal property of the Norte Chico's agricultural communities. The ethnic composition as a criterion to distinguish between different communities when dealing specifically with land ownership forms neither add or take anything relevant here. Obviously, when dealing with the anthropological aspects of ethnicity, this is certainly important. Ethnicity may be also of importance as in the case of South Africa, where the 'racial' distinction of apartheid between those living in the reserves (the blacks) and those who have imposed the segregationist system of the reserves upon them (the whites) is, due to power detention, very clear.

Table 1.1 Agricultural communities in Chile

CIDA	Baraona *et al*
Indigenous (or reserves)	Norte Grande Araucanian (Mapuche) of the south
Agricultural (also successorial)	Residual Norte Chico
Contractual (or successorial)	Pseudo-communities

Source: The author, based on CIDA (1966) and the criteria of Baraona *et al* (1961)

However, CIDA (1966:128) and Baraona *et al* (1961:125) describe for Chile several communities. With the help of these authors and other scholars, I will try to highlight the historical peculiarity of the Norte Chico's communities within the national context. Tables 1.1 and 1.2 tries to contextualise the Chilean agricultural communities within a bigger national context, that of different agricultural properties, independent of their form, using the same criteria as before, i.e., form and origin of property. I have even added the criteria of ethnicity whose adequacy, in this context, I have questioned above. This way, also the other land ownership forms, with which I, given my purpose, inevitably deal with in this publication, become contextualised.

Discarding the third group, the contractual or successorial (CIDA, 1966), or pseudo-communities (Baraona *et al*, 1961), which does not properly constitute communal land ownership, we have just two groups; the indigenous and agricultural communities. The pseudo-communities (contractual or successorial) are possible to find almost everywhere in Chile and, unless the fact of sharing with the Norte Chico's agricultural communities, the fact of being also undivided successorial land, they do not constitute agricultural communities, fittingly. This type of community would be:

> A form of structure recognised by the current legislation: undivided estates of properties belonging to the heirs of an individual or a family and that appear under community name /---/ They do not actually have the character of collective possession of the land and their undivided state is only temporary (Baraona *et al*, 1961:125).

Table 1.2 Agricultural properties in Chile, according to origin, land ownership form and 'ethnic' composition

Distinguishing criteria	Agricultural properties

1. *Land ownership form:*
   Communal
   Semi-communal
   Private
	Aymara and Mapuche communities
	 Agricultural communities (Norte Chico)
	 Latifundium, minifundium

2. *Historic origin:*
   Pre-Hispanic precedents
   Colonial private property
 	
   Post-Colonial antecedents
	Aymara communities (North)
	 Latifundium, minifundium (all over Chile) and agricultural communities (Norte Chico)
	 Mapuche communities (South)

Source: The author, based on CIDA (1966) and the criteria of Baraona *et al* (1961)

Introduction

The successions, specified by these authors:

> are units in undivided state in which there are portions that have not been distributed /.../ Often, this undivided state that should be temporary, is maintained during a considerable time, during which it presents a great variety of tenure forms (Baraona *et al*, 1961:124).

According to CIDA, these contractual communities are:

> ... undivided successions of properties or agricultural companies with co-owners that have not formed society (CIDA, 1966:128).

It generally deals with *fundos* or reserves of *fundos*, whose heirs usually live in other places, mainly in the capital or other large cities. Given their temporary undivided character, these homesteads can well be inactive from the agricultural point of view. Here, they would be not more than inactive rural properties, temporarily undivided, waiting for their effective division. If active they are generally given in share-cropping and/or leased for pasturage to the peasants or agricultural entrepreneurs of the surroundings. A clear example of this type of communities is the reserve Puerto Oscuro which stays undivided among a numerous group of descendants (see Chapter 6).

Let me now take the second group. The fact that the second agricultural group monopolises the appellate of agricultural communities can be misleading inasmuch as the indigenous communities are also agricultural communities.

Baraona *et al* (1961) say little about the communities of the Norte Grande and Norte Chico, perhaps because of the lack of information in the 1960s. However, within the group of indigenous communities, those of the south and of the north would be considered, but not those of the Norte Chico. According to the authors, these communities would have indigenous origins. However, the communities of the Norte Chico would be a colonial product in analogous form to the indigenous Mapuche communities. It would deal with:

> ... establishments derived from pueblos de indios [Indian villages] or from efforts to concentrate the scattered indigenous, or from attempts to establishing them outside of watered lands that came to belong to the haciendas (Baraona *et al*, 1961:125).

From this, Baraona *et al* (1961) indicate that the indigenous origins of these communities do not date from the pre-colonial period. Although, this argument does not exclude that pre-Hispanic elements could exist in them. I will return to this issue in Chapter 4 when dealing more properly with the origin of the *minifundia* and agricultural communities in Chile. In respect to their forms of land tenure, it deals apparently with communal land, since Baraona *et al*, underline that the *comuneros* are proprietors of their lands, for which they pay contributions. These *comuneros* can receive *'lluvias'* (usually, land plots on the hills) and possessions to build their houses. There seems to be no doubt that these communities should be included in the group that Baraona *et al* designate residual (or agricultural communities of the CIDA), unless by being composed originally of indigenous population. In my opinion, the indigenous traits are in any event difficult to find presently, after centuries of mixing between different people. The agricultural communities of the Norte Chico are even known under the name of historical agrarian communities (IREN, 1978, Vol. 1:17). With the exception of the presently known indigenous areas, the population of the Norte Chico is, as in the rest of the country, predominantly *mestizo*.

I now come to the communities of the North. In contrast to the Mapuches, Baraona *et al* (1961:124) indicate that in the communities of the Norte Grande:

> is maintained greater quantity of indigenous features in the forms of land tenure.

Indigenous features, I think should be understood here as pre-Hispanic precedents. The authors indicate that on their arrival, the Spaniards would have found the indigenous population in the north concentrated in the oasis of the desert, and therefore it was not necessary to gather them artificially in order to exploit their labour force, as in other parts of Chile. Although the knowledge about these communities is slightly better today, it is still rudimentary. In any event, with respect to their quantity, the Aymaras would amount, according to the Census of 1992 from INE, to a total of 48,447 people, i.e., around 10 thousand households.

Like the Mapuche communities, those of the Norte Grande are social entities with their own culture and language that separates them, not only from the other communities, but as a rule from the rest of the country as well.

Introduction

Regarding the form, the agrarian economy of the Aymara Indian communities of the plateau (3,000-4,000 metres above sea level), in northern Chile is based on the grazing of alpacas, llamas and sheep for which they communally own the pasturage, land and water resources. Note, however, that I am referring here to the communities of the plateau, and not to the one that may exist in the oasis of the desert, to which, for example, Baraona *et al*, seem to refer. According to CIDA (1966:123) in the Norte Grande exist approximately 11,000 ha under cultivation, disseminated in valleys and oasis with access to irrigation. In contrast, the seasonal steppe of the pre-mountain Andes, that provides forage resources, is estimated in 750,000 ha. According to Solis de Ovando (1989:128):

> The need to use the land communally is explained by the fundamental fact that the basis of the economy rests on traditional livestock and agriculture, which demands the coexistence in the use and possession of the land: communal for cattle and family based for agriculture.

The Aymaras are organised according to lineage or family-group and there is, according to this author, a coincidence between the possession of land for pasturage and the family group. In comparison with the Mapuche communities, those of the Norte Grande have less contact with the rest of the country, due to the geographical isolation of the high plateau in which they live.

Historically, I would say that, similar to the Aymara communities of the Norte Grande, in the Norte Chico, there is also a coincidence between the territoriality of the present communities with the colonial owners' land occupation and, in this way, a coincidence between communities and particular lineage or family groups. However, this is not to say that they, as in the case of the Aymara communities, were or are, organised according to lineage or family groups.

Let me now take the case of the Mapuche communities, located in the south. Communal land property in the Mapuche communities encompasses both cultivation land as well as land for shepherding, the usufruct being individual (CIDA, 1966:128). According to CIDA (1966:181), in the five Provinces (from Arauco to Llanquihue) where 98.9% of the Mapuches were concentrated in the 1960s, there were a total of 3,048 reserves with a total of 322,916 persons. The total area was of 565,931 ha giving a media of 1.8 ha per capita and 0.4 ha of cultivated land.

Apart from their form of communal property, the most outstanding feature of these communities is their ethnic identity, with a language and a culture of their own. Different to the agricultural communities of the Norte Grande, their contacts with the rest of Chile are greater since they are sharing their geographical area with the whites and mestizos. In their long struggle for land, they have been the losers. In comparison with other communities, the Mapuche are:

> the only peasant group that presents a certain degree of organisation, based on interest derived from their ethnic specificity (Campaña, 1985:38-39).

Peasants of Mapuche origin constitute approximately 20% of all peasants in Chile (Rivera, 1988a:41), approximately 70,000 households (Rivera, 1988a:166), or some 350,000 persons (assuming 5 persons to a household) The total indigenous Mapuche population in Chile is estimated at almost a million (INE, 1992).

On the origin of the Mapuche communities, all authors agree that their community organisation does not constitute a conservation of pre-Hispanic traits, but that their origin, or to be more exact, their creation:

> constitutes a republican interpretation of what was believed was the collective land tenure of the Araucanian [Mapuche], a product, on one side, of the incomprehension of the effective forms of the Araucanian land tenancy and of their social and public organisation and, on the other, of the intention of confining them to determined areas, much more scanty that those they were originally possessing (Baraona *et al*, 1961:126).

In this sense, they would not be 'more than a creation of our [Chilean] laws' (Baraona *et al*, 1961:124). This is, as well, the implicit sense in CIDA's specification of these communities, inasmuch as CIDA states that they are reserves or confining, i.e., an artificial creation by the centres of the economic and political power, and not an original organisation of the Mapuche people. According to Rivera (1988a), the Mapuche peasant community:

> was thoroughly transformed in its economy and social organisation because of its confining and compulsory settlement (between 1890-1910); from being collectors and extensive cattlemen into farmers of subsistence minifundium.

Dieterich confirms the same for the rest of Latin America, indicating, that indigenous collective property:

> was constituted through the adjustment and pragmatic-legislative modification of the structures of possession and pre-Columbian property to the needs of the Spanish Crown (Dieterich, 1978:198).

Originally the Crown's Indian legislation established three forms of land tenure in the indigenous communities; an individual possession for each family, a collective possession for all the community destined for shepherding and, finally a possession, also common, cultivated by all the members of the community according to an unpaid labour system and an obligatory rotation. These lands could also be leased to Indians or Spaniards. The income originated from their leasing was destined to pay the census, or taxes, to the exchequer and other social expenses of the community (Dieterich, 1978:200). The recognition and partial conservation of the indigenous, collective property was fundamentally compatible of private property, for which the indigenous communities constituted, mainly, a labour reservoir. Though the right to the land of the communities was, in theory, inalienable, their lands were subject to the voracity of the landowners, and these, with the passing of time and until today, are being reduced to a minimum.

Consequently, in Latin America, most of the present examples of communal land ownership, including its indigenous agricultural communities, are to a great extent an artificial creation. In this sense, their community formulas, whether colonial or post-colonial, does not have many pre-Hispanic antecedents.

Taking into consideration the impact of colonialism in Sub-Saharan Africa, the situation there does not seem to be very different. In his recent review about the land question, regarding the 'purity' of some customary African tenure systems, Havnevik suggested that we have to accept that:

> colonialism created a new conception of tradition that did not reflect past historical relations and further that colonial authorities did not freeze African societies in a timeless world of tradition and custom /---/ Colonial policy rather did shape the way in which rights of access to land and labour were defined (Havnevik, 1997:7).

The Norte Chico's agricultural communities may be summarised as being peculiarly historical in comparison to the other named communities. They are a product of a more spontaneous development process resulting from a colonial, Spanish land institution, mainly the *mercedes de tierras* (land grants), once owned by Spanish conquerors and colonialists. Against a widespread idea among academicians and laymen, including many *comuneros*, I will show that these people were not of low social rank in the colonial hierarchy. Quite the opposite, they were of relatively high position. It involves, therefore, a contradiction, to postulate on one hand, that the agricultural communities arose from *mercedes de tierras* and, on the other, that these lands, supposedly marginal, were given to low rank soldiers, since the *mercedes* were given to the most outstanding conquerors and colonialists.

What in this argument seems also to be taken for granted is that what today is marginal or poor land was also so in the past. Several studies do exist however, which show that the Norte Chico was until the middle of the 1800s covered with vegetation (Bengoa, 1988:215-217).

Significance of the study

The case of Norte Chico of Coquimbo, Chile is, according to the earlier exposed arguments, interesting within a national, Latin-American and even a world context, not only because of firstly its form, e.g. its present land tenure structure, but secondly, also historically. In other words, we have here two sociologically relevant, empirical issues:

- historically, the development of semi-communal land ownership form out of private property; and
- presently, the reproduction of this form of semi-communal land ownership.

Let me now more systematically develop the former significance, reviewing at the same time the contributions and shortcomings of the literature on the subject, as well as what I consider will be my particular contribution.

The Norte Chico of Chile is peculiar both within a national and a Latin-American context because the semi-communally owned property

Introduction

arose out of private property. Not only did the *latifundium* and *minifundium* arise from the colonial institution of land grants, but alongside them as a peculiar form in between; as did the semi-communal land ownership of the agricultural communities.

Though not originally intended by the Spanish Crown, the *mercedes de tierra* evolved into private ownership soon after they were distributed, first in the form of *estancias* and then, with the introduction of agriculture, in *latifundium* or *haciendas*. If both the *latifundium* and the agricultural communities in the Norte Chico have a common origin in the *mercedes de tierra*, only the gradual *de facto* conversion of certain landed private properties into agricultural communities, with time, changed the 1600s land tenure structure from private property into a mixed system. During the 1700s, this started to combine both private and semi-communal land ownership.

The major question concerning land stemming from the *mercedes de tierra* is the reason why only certain properties, or portions of them, evolved into agricultural communities, while others remained private. Why did some properties continue as private? With the exception of the agronomist Cañón (1964:46), this issue has not been explicitly contemplated from the perspective of a process giving rise to two paths of agrarian development: the *latifundium* or *haciendas*, on the one hand, and the agricultural communities, on the other.

The historical process of land formation in the Norte Chico is paradoxical because being the general tendency of the *mercedes*, and of *encomiendas*, towards private property, here the semi-communally owned land developed out of private property. Having the same origin, and neighbouring each other, the *haciendas* and the agricultural communities have been struggling for the same land. This struggle is interesting because it refutes several common conceptions about the peasantry to which I will return below.

Studies on land tenure in Chile (Borde and Góngora, 1956; Baraona *et al*, 1961; CIDA, 1966), and more specifically on the communities of Norte Chico, indicate that the communities have their origin mainly in the colonial *mercedes de tierras* (Cañón, 1964; CIDA, 1966, Albala *et al*, 1967; IREN, 1977/78; Castro and Bahamondes, 1986, Santander, *s.a.*; Bengoa, 1988). Unlike Cañón (1964:46), they do not, however, conceive their development from the perspective of a conversion of private property to semi-communal land ownership. At least, none of them seem to see anything special in this particular conversion.

Reviewing the literature on the origin of the communities, the few references are to other regions of the country, especially the Valle Central (Borde and Góngora, 1956), or the Valle Transversal (Baraona *et al*, 1961). The work of Borde and Góngora (1956), a geographer and a historian, is distinguished in that it constitutes the first specific study resuming the history of land ownership and the agrarian geography of the Puangue Valley (Province of Melipilla, Metropolitan Region). This work, produced within the framework of the Department of Sociology at Universidad de Chile in Santiago, is still considered one of the most valuable social science contributions in the country. Baraona *et al* (1961), historians and geographers, in another valuable contribution, follow the line of work of Borde and Góngora, but in the Valley of Putaendo (Province of San Felipe de Aconcagua, Region V).

Studies of the agricultural communities of the Norte Chico, generally written by agronomists (Cañón, 1964), geographers (Aranda, 1971), official institutions (IREN, 1977/78; CONAF, 1981), international organisations (CIDA, 1966), or other organisations, mainly concern problems of natural resources, poverty, marginalisation and land tenure structure. The work of CIDA embraces the land tenure in different parts of Chile. It also includes other Latin-American countries (CIDA, 1966).

Cañón (1964), as an agronomist, participated in CIDA's investigation, and made use of the data to write her graduation thesis using the agricultural communities in the commune of Mincha (today commune of Canela) as a case study at the time of Frei's (1964-1969) agrarian reform. Unfortunately, her work contains various errors dealing with the case study, an issue that I comment on in Chapters 5 and 7. This does not, however, take away the merit of it having been my main source of inspiration and the principal guiding source dealing specifically with Canela's history and agriculture.

Due to increasing poverty, periodic drought and ecological problems, from the late 1980s and 1990s, the interest in the agricultural communities has been renewed in agronomy, forestry, geography, veterinary science, ecology, etc., inside and outside the academic world. These areas have gained interest also among different kinds of organisations (governmental and non-governmental), many of which, in one form, or another, are working with them. These include the

Introduction

Universidad de La Serena, Universidad de Chile-Coquimbo and Universidad de Chile-Santiago; INIA, INFOR, GIA, INPROA, IER, INDAP, CONAF, AGRARIA, FAO/PAF-CHILE, SHALOM, CIDERE, JUNDEP, etc. The number of papers about the agricultural communities has increased considerably. To name just some of them; JUNDEP, CEDECOM, *s.a.*; FIDA, 1992; CIPRES consultores, 1992; INIA, 1992, etc.. Most papers, however, deal with diagnostics over the present situation, its problems - mostly through pilot studies - and proposals to solve them.

The interest of sociologists has been rather weak. Albala *et al* (1967), or Pascal (1968) - probably one of the first sociology works on agricultural communities - concentrates more on power relations between, on the one side, the *latifundium*, and on the other, the *minifundium* and the communities. In the work of Pascal, published by ICIRA (1968), only Pascal appears as author, who thanks Albala and Ruíz for their participation in the investigation. In the monographic thesis (1967), written for the Universidad de Chile, to obtain the title Licentiate in Sociology all the three before mentioned persons appear as authors. The versions are a bit different. Because of that I sometimes base myself in the latter (it was the first paper I had access to), and sometimes in the former.

Later, Castro and Bahamondes (1983) also approached the agricultural communities writing about mechanisms of subsistence, and peasant differentiation (*s.a.*). Their 1986 paper deals with the main issue in this dissertation, the rise and transformation of the agricultural communities' communal system (see Chapter 4).

Despite this increasing interest there is, however, no systematic attempt as to the question of their origin and development. Therefore, the knowledge about this issue still is fragmentary. An exception here is Santander (*s.a*). In a proposal made for CEDECOM (Centro de Desarrollo Comunitario Económico y Social - Communitarian Centre of Economic and Social Development) (*s.a.*), he makes a short, but interesting attempt to systematise what he calls the explanatory hypotheses about the origin of the agricultural communities. At the same time, he is not an exception; his work is also an example of those proposals aimed at solving poverty. Santander does not really develop the issue of the origin, limiting himself to presenting them in an appendix. Indeed, Santander rightly points out that the question of the origin of the agricultural communities is a historical problem, still without satisfactory solution. According to my review, the few references come from studies of other regions of the country; if they deal with the agricultural communities of Norte Chico, they have often not been written by social scientists.

This work attempts a contribution in the field of historical and agrarian sociology to the question of the origin and emergence of the form of the semi-communal land ownership of the Norte Chico's agricultural communities through the study of one specific case. The specific case, once forming one property, gave way to two different property forms: one private and one semi-communal.

From being one property in the middle of the 1600s, the *estancia* La Canela became two properties in the 1700s: the *estancia* La Canela and the *hacienda* El Totoral. Whereas El Totoral kept its character of private property, the *estancia* La Canela became several agricultural communities, among others the agricultural community Canela Baja. Together with the agricultural community Canela Alta, they are the main inheritors of the *estancia* La Canela from the 1600s. Therefore, I have an empirical case, which due to historic circumstances became two different forms of properties. While the semi-communal agricultural community Canela Baja constitutes both the main empirical case, and the point of departure for my theoretical concerns, the private property of the *hacienda* El Totoral, becomes an object of comparison.

Nonetheless, my contribution to local history goes beyond having El Totoral as an object of comparison. If there was something written about the agricultural community Canela Baja and, therefore, about its predecessor, the *estancia* La Canela, which embraced the lands of El Totoral, a specific history about El Totoral, as *hacienda*, and its *fundos*, then it does not exist.

The history about the struggle for Espíritu Santo, about which some few, scarce references exist here and there, it is also to a great extent, an unwritten history. Towards the end of the nineteenth century, the community became involved in a land dispute with a private person who claimed rights over Espíritu Santo, one of the eight sub-areas of the community (see Table 1.4 and Figure 1.2). The dispute resulted in a minor, armed conflict, which serves me to show that even on marginal lands one cannot disregard the attraction of land ownership. The conflict lasted a hundred years, and was not legally solved until the 1970s.

Thus, since the *estancia* La Canela, constituting almost the entire geographical area of the commune of Canela, became many distinctive

Introduction

landed properties, in reconstructing its historic development, my contribution to the local history goes beyond that of the agricultural community Canela Baja specifically.

Dealing with the agricultural communities of the Norte Chico, we know two facts; the result, the agricultural communities and their late legal recognition, and on the other hand, their origin, the *mercedes de tierras*. There, in between, however, we have a socio-historical process of over three hundred years, which needs to be covered in the best way archival material and the sociological imagination permits.

Accordingly, trying to relate the specificity of the case with the bigger colonial context, following Cañón (1964:47), I suggest that the agricultural communities of the Norte Chico have been strongly conditioned by the ecological environment. This factor, in combination with others will contribute in the formation of two different forms: semi-communal and private, each with its own socio-economic development. These factors relate to the type of colonial economy and its crisis, colonial social pattern of settlement, and its relation with the social status of land proprietors within the colonial society, demographic increase of population and hereditary subdivision of land. I shall return to this in Chapter 4.

One social condition is not taken into sufficient consideration for the question of the emergence of the agricultural communities' semi-communal land ownership, on one hand, and the continuation of private property of the *haciendas*, on the other. This is the importance of the settlement or non-settlement of the owners on their land during the 1600s and 1700s and its relationship with the proprietors' colonial social position within the bureaucratic and/or military hierarchy. Cañón (1964:46) is the exception to this. Why did the agricultural communities take shape along the *haciendas?* In contrast, most studies on the agricultural communities of the Norte Chico mainly concern the present and status quo. As a whole, it is my hope to show how the form evolved.

When I have pointed out what, in my view, is the first significance of this study - the developing of the form of semi-communal land ownership from private property, I will continue to its second significance, the reproducing of this form of semi-communal land ownership.

Why is the Norte Chico peculiar within a national context? With the exception of Los Vilos' commune, agricultural communities with their semi-communal land ownership are to be found in fourteen of the fifteen communes of the Norte Chico (see Table 1.3 and Figure 1.2), side by side with large *latifundium*. In 1992 the total number of agricultural communities of the Norte Chico were 200. Of these, 169 communities had in 1992 a number of 14,884 registered *comuneros* (CIPRES, 1992:15-16), and a probable population of 100,000 people, covering approximately 1 million hectares (see Chapter 9). In 1970, the 162 communities to be found in the Norte Chico supported around 75,000 people. This corresponded then to 21% of the region's total population and to 53% of the rural population (IREN, 1978).

Characteristic to the agricultural communities is their poverty, this region being one of the poorest in the country. Six communes whose rural population is in the majority composed by *comuneros* were between the 25 poorest of the country in 1983 (of a total of 238 studied communes). Punitaqui occupied the first place by poverty, Rio Hurtado, the third, and Canela the fourth place (CIPRES, 1992). At first sight, given the rudimentary means of production, limited use of money and social conditions in which the *comunero* peasants live, the agricultural communities of the Norte Chico stand out as a kind of social unit of their own, that seemingly have very little to do with the rest of the society.

The present agricultural communities are even more surprising, against the background of the changes that the agrarian structure have experienced during the last decades in Chile, marked by two opposed agrarian policies. First, the agrarian reforms of Alessandri (1958-1964), Frei (1964-1970) and Allende (1970-1973), and second, the "counter"-reform of Pinochet (1973-1989). So intense were these social changes that they led some authors to postulate that they even exceeded those that occurred in the four centuries after the colonisation (Gómez, 1990). As a result of the agrarian reforms, the *latifundium* or *hacienda*, for centuries the economic base of the ruling oligarchy in Latin America disappeared as a traditional institution based on peonage (*inquilinaje*). Up to 50% of Chile's agricultural land was expropriated between 1962 and 1973 (Rivera, 1988a:66).

During the same period, paradoxically, the process of legal recognition of the agricultural communities, until then without defined legal status, started to take form. Based on usage and custom, transmitted from generation to generation, the norms that had regulated the behaviour of the community members for a long time were central. In the absence of written laws, these rights and practices made possible the persistence of

Introduction

the institution of the semi-communal land ownership of the agricultural communities.

In other words, of these two institutions, the *latifundium:*

> the institution of the largest permanency in Chile's history, or the phenomenon of largest duration (Bengoa, 1988, Vol. 1:7,85)

and the agricultural communities, both rooted in the colonial period (approximately 1550-1810) - the form that, at the end of the twentieth century, still exists is that of the agricultural communities.

What is more, their legal recognition appears to have secured their semi-communal form of land ownership, at the same time as capitalist relations of production in agriculture experienced, and continues undeniably, to do so, a strong push forward, becoming more and more widespread. Relations of production are used here in its classical sense. It deals with the relations that are established between people in the production process, whose character is defined firstly by the producers' relationship to the means of production. In other words, it comprises, the means of production and the producers, and thereby, the relationship between them.

In spite of the long endurance of the institution of the agricultural communities and in spite of its legal recognition, which ratifies the long reproduction of the form of semi-communal land ownership, it still lacks a conceptual framework. Perhaps the absence of an appropriate approach depends on the fact that the form has, implicitly or explicitly, been reduced to the *minifundium*.

Baked, so to speak, into the *minifundium* or small peasantry, the 'survival' of these communities, is by extension, explained in terms of the lack of interest by (big) landlords of the marginal land occupied by the small peasantry. This view is to be found in the Latin-American discussion from the 1950s onwards (Borde and Góngora, 1956; Baraona *et al*, 1961; García, 1973, Rivera, 1988a; Kay, 1980; Astorga, 1985). However, as we saw in the previous section Borde and Góngora and Baraona *et al*, have also pointed out that the *minifundia* suffers, in its struggle for land and water, the hostility of the *latifundia* and modern agricultural enterprises (see also Chapter 4).

The agricultural communities and, in general, the *minifundia* or small peasantry in Latin-America, are said to be found in 'zones of refuge' (i.e. marginal land) (García, 1973:99). It is argued that these types of marginal, ecological zones and its peasantry do no longer suffer the pressure of the *latifundia*'s hunger for their land. If this were so, then I will suggest that the struggle for land would not exist in these areas. As my case study will show, however marginal the land, the struggle for its ownership - between landowners and/or capitalists and the peasants - is not as, for example, García (1973:99) believes, uncommon (I can here remind that the dominant terrestrial ecological system of the Norte Chico is arid or semi-arid. Only 0.4% of the total area of Canela's Commune is irrigated (CONAF, 1981:41, see Chapter 3)).

Table 1.3 Distribution of the agricultural communities by communes in the Norte Chico

Province	Communes	Number of Communities		Percentage
Elqui			15	
	La Serena	2		1.3
	La Higuera	2		1.2
	Vicuña	4		2.5
	Paihuano	4		2.5
	Coquimbo	1		0.6
	Andacollo	2		1.2
Limarí			119	
	Ovalle	12		7.4
	Samo Alto	17		10.5
	Monte Patria	42		25.9
	Punitaqui	24		14.8
	Combarbalá	24		14.8
Choapa			28*	
	Illapel	1		0.6
	Salamanca	1		0.6
	Los Vilos	-		-
	Canela	26		16.0
Total		162	162	99.9

Source: IREN (1978), Vol. 1:36-37
* According to this source, the agricultural communities in the Canela commune are 26, but there are only 24. This means that in the Choapa province there are a total of 26 and not 28 agricultural communities.

Introduction

If examined further, this argument about marginal land falls apart. If *latifundia* and agricultural communities have a common origin, they share the same or similar type of land and natural environment. Facts are relevant here. According to CIDA (1966:126), the *latifundium* and the agricultural communities share the dry land of the Norte Chico in equal proportions, even though the estates have more irrigated areas. In which case, the land of the *haciendas* is not necessarily better than that of the agricultural communities or the *minifundia*. If landlords and small peasants share the same natural environment, marginal or not, the struggle for land between these two large groups is given. If we accept this view, the peasantry cannot be seen as passive recipients of a mode of production; but as actors, who defend their land, as we shall see in Chapter 8 about Espíritu Santo. There I will also develop, following Feder (1977/78), another argument against this view about marginal land.

The explanations of the survival of the peasantry in societies 'in transition' to capitalism in terms of the lack of interest from the big landlords, has partially its parallel in the discussion about the survival of the peasantry in the advanced economies. Their non-disappearance is also explained here, implicitly or explicitly, almost exclusively in relation to capitalism's needs and dynamics (Alanen, 1991:325). If the dynamics is recognised, it is not the peasants' own, but:

> a matter of external constraints shaped by highly abstract capitalist forces (Jonsson and Pettersson, 1989:543).

It is certainly difficult to see the peasant struggle at all, seen politically as conservative, as petty bourgeois (Alanen, 1991:325).

Peripheral, but not because of that less global as a phenomenon, communal land ownership is not only a form which is not usually associated with modern capitalist societies. Furthermore, the development of the semi-communal land ownership of the Chilean Norte Chico's communities from private property does not agree either with the general tendency towards private property during colonial or post-colonial time.

To conceive, however, within the context of the present modern society, communal land ownership as pre-capitalist relations of production, 'remnants', 'anomalies', 'paradoxes' or 'incongruities', though convenient, does not say very much about the peasant societies themselves, except by reducing them to a one sided view of the small peasantry. Missing there is

Communal Land Ownership in Chile

the specificity of the communal form itself, its constitution and the historical process of this particular form of agricultural social institution.

Figure 1.1 Agricultural communities of Region IV

Introduction

Within a new framework, these communities will appear, not as a remnant of the past but, as a result, of a socio-economic process which parallels the consolidation of private property.

Not only, as suggested, is communal land ownership different from the *minifundium*, but what is more, it is also a way of avoiding it. Therefore, with the present legal recognition on behalf of the state, the history of the agricultural communities, initiated some 300 hundred years ago, comes to an end. This recognition is not merely a legal matter. It stabilises the form against its fragmenting in the scattered *minifundium*, or small peasantry, reaffirming it as an economic management solution. It also means the legalisation of the form and its conditions of reproduction. Obviously, the struggle for survival is therefore not finished; what is finished is the struggle for the recognition of the form, which creates a fundamental security, that of the law sanctioned by the state.

However, how to conceive the existence of this kind of semi-communal land ownership? Basing myself on Stevenson's (1991) book, *Common Property Economics: A General Theory and Land Use Applications*, I finally intend to give a concept to the studied phenomena. This will neither be as archaic, pre-capitalist or irrational, nor inferior to the other today predominant land ownership, the private, but just another, traditional, though not less valid, form of appropriating the resource of land.

The choice of case study

> *The past and the future do not exist in themselves, but are the past and the future of a particular present (Tillman, 1970, in Charon, 1998).*

I have chosen as a case study the agricultural community Canela Baja. It has its starting point in the colonial *estancia* La Canela, as the old neighbouring ex-*hacienda*, or *latifundium* El Totoral, which I use as a comparative case study. This partially includes the three rural landed properties (*fundos*) that resulted from its subdivision at the end of the nineteenth century (El Totoral, Las Palmas and Puerto Oscuro). Of these three, I have chosen to follow the post-Allende fate of the *fundo* Puerto Oscuro, or Society Pereira, Cortés, Brito and Co. Ltd., as it is also called today. The inclusion of El Totoral, which as a private property, represents the other predominant form of land property in the commune, will help us both to follow, and to compare the two historical processes, as well as the development of the agrarian structure in the commune as a whole.

The choice of Canela Baja among almost two hundred agricultural communities in the Norte Chico depends on several factors. It was this particular community that first made me reflect about communal land ownership and its history, my theoretical question being how to conceive this form of ownership and production organisation. Then followed the scientific curiosity about the origin of the form itself. Not until long after the work was begun, did I realise that I was writing the history of my own village, which slowly appeared also to be the history of the structuration of landed property of the commune as a whole.

Both the agricultural community Canela Baja and the former *hacienda* El Totoral are relatively unknown. From the point of view of history, these places have not propitiated events of national relevance, nor have they given birth to personalities granted a place in the list of the 'notables' in the national chronicle. The references to these places, in colonial and modern history, are scarce, except for the last two decades within the disciplines mentioned above. In agronomy, however, the interest started earlier.

The commune of Canela shares certain things with the Mexican Municipality of San José de Gracia, about which Gonzáles (1972:2) writes:

> It seems to be the historical insignificance in all its purity, the absolutely unworthy of attention /.../ meagre land, slow life and population without brilliance. The pettiness, but the typical pettiness.

Even though my case study represents a 'typical' example inside the historical development of the structure of land property of Chile's Norte Chico, as any type of social collective, they have their own identity. As Warman points out, the peculiar is not but '... the way between many that exist to adapt to general conditions' (Warman, 1976:13), or to say it with Baraona *et al* (1961:13) the specific and original are not but '... the local combinations of modes...'.

As social and spatial units, the choice of the agricultural community Canela Baja and the *hacienda* El Totoral is justifiable, because they once formed a single territorial unit, the extension of which almost conforms to the commune of Canela today. The area of the commune is 2,213 km² (IGM, 1981:50), which corresponds more or less to the present State of

Luxembourg (2,586 km²). Since I am dealing with the reconstruction of land tenure structure over time, a detailed estimation of the size of the involved properties, and the specification of their borders, is in this work done along their subdivision, heritage, sales, etc., from colonial time until today.

The geographical space of my case study contrasts with its chronological amplitude. To use the words of Gonzáles' (1995:162), I study a long time in a reduced space. The trajectory of my case study starts in the 1600s and 1700s. It ignores the pre-Hispanic life because it is not of interest for my purpose, since the agricultural communities of the Norte Chico do not have their origin in pre-Hispanic forms of land tenancy. The first two colonial centuries give us a general historical background to the period that follows, which is principally the formation of the semi-communal property of land from the middle or later part of the 1700s in the commune.

Since the empirical part deals both with the conversion from private property to the semi-communal, and with the continuance of private property, it is necessary to make clear that, when I speak of history, this principally takes the form of history of property rights. In this sense, it is a limited history different for La Canela compared to El Totoral. While in the case of the former, it very much takes the form of family history, in the latter it is very much a history about legal transactions. This is so because they came to constitute two different forms of land ownership.

The history of the agricultural community Canela Baja has its starting point in the colonial *estancia* La Canela. We know two facts, the result and the beginning, a socio-historical process that embraces over three hundred years. The mechanisms that brought this about are unknown, except for the fragmentary information that diverse archival sources can provide for my inquiries. It is only from a detailed reconstruction of the existing archival material that some traits can be drawn.

Consequently, the elaborate reconstruction of the archive material, which very much takes the form of family histories, is recourse to draw some threads from the historical process represented by the conversion from private property to the semi-communal. I mean *some* threads because it would be naive to think that any reconstruction would grasp a socio-historical process in its totality. Since also the archive documents are fragmentary, the reconstruction of this process is necessarily incomplete, presenting some lacunae. However, this is not to say that if the archival sources had been richer, the researcher would be able to successfully reconstruct this long, social process.

What the historical actors have left behind is, firstly, the land and its descendants. Special aspects of their lives have been written down only in testaments, sales, subdivisions and property litigations, and not systematically. Unfortunately, the documentation about La Canela remained more silent to my inquiries than that of El Totoral.

The history of El Totoral and the rural properties, which sprung from it, from the second half of the 1800s and onwards, is the history of property transactions (sale and purchase agreements, expropriations, devolutions and auction sales, etc.). This concentration on the legal material of the *fundos* depends on one of my thesis: that the agricultural communities, as opposed to the *haciendas* and *fundos*, are characterised by hereditary maintenance of the property between the descendants of the original proprietors since colonial times. My purpose is consequently, to show how the property of the *fundos*, in contrast to the agricultural communities, was constantly transferred through the years.

This legal history concerns the owners of the *fundos* rather than their peasants. Therefore, I do not pay much attention to the system of *inquilinaje* on which the *latifundia* based its exploitation (these issues are otherwise developed in Chapter 4. For further information about the *inquilinaje* in Chile, see Góngora M., *Origen de los inquilinos de Chile Central*, 1960, Santiago, Editorial Universitaria; Góngora and Borde, *Evolución de la propiedad rural en el valle del Puangue*, 2 vols., Santiago 1956; Bauer, A., *Chilean rural society from the Spanish Conquest to 1930*, Cambridge University Press, 1975; CIDA, *Tenencia de la tierra en Chile*, Santiago, 1966; Baraona et al, *Valle de Putaendo*, Santiago, 1966; Bengoa José, *Historia Social de la Agricultura Chilena*, Santiago,1988).

A major part of this transaction history is based on legal documents, among which the most important were the Real Estate Registers (RP or Registro de Propiedad) of the archives of the Conservatory of Real Estates (CBR) from Illapel (concerning the content of the Property Registers, see Archival sources in this chapter). To cover, panoramically, the history of these transactions, I made a chronological graph of the transfers for each rural property.

Looking at the present situation of the twenty-four agricultural communities within the commune of Canela, the chosen one, Canela Baja, presents the following characteristics:

Introduction

- it is the largest with respect to the number of *comuneros*, representing 27.4% of the total within the commune (668 of 2,431). It also represents 35% of the total commune population (4,000 of 11,338 inhabitants) (CBR of Illapel, 1986);
- within its boundaries is the village Canela Baja, the main centre of commerce in the commune. Being the central part of the commune, the village plays an important role within the system of socio-economic interchange between *comuneros* and merchants;
- the community Canela Baja is also the scene of the mentioned land dispute over Espíritu Santo, one of the eight sub-areas of the community (see Table 1.4), which implied the death of several people.

Table 1.4 Sub-areas of the agricultural community Canela Baja

Sub areas of the community Canela Baja	Total number of comuneros per sub-area
Canela Baja	161
Canela Alta*	72
El Chircal	57
Fasico	84
Poza Honda	73
Jabonería	71
Las Palmas	25
Espíritu Santo	125
Total	**668**

Source: The author.
* This is a sub-area of the agricultural community Canela Baja and should not be confused with the agricultural community Canela Alta.

The *hacienda* El Totoral, on the other hand, presents the following characteristics:

- together with the community Canela Baja it formed one single landed property during the second half of the 1600s;

43

- adjoining the agricultural community, the *hacienda* El Totoral shares a similar topography and soil composition, which means that I am comparing two units which, although they differ somewhat in their natural endowments today, did not do so originally. This is important since the development process of La Canela and El Totoral is to be traced back through the colonial period;
- historically, the evolution of El Totoral shows several facets of the changes that have commonly affected private land ownership, not least during the past two decades. More generally, this is especially true in the case of the *fundo* Puerto Oscuro, where the changes arising from the agrarian reforms of the early 1970s and Pinochet's policies after 1973, have led to the acquisition of Puerto Oscuro by a group of people, many of whom also are *comuneros* from the Canela Baja agricultural community.

The new owners of the *fundo* differ from those previous to the *fundo's* expropriation, both regarding class background and the organisation and exploitation of the property. This is interesting because it resulted in the formation of new agricultural societies as a result of the series of changes that had their beginning in the agrarian reform. As an unintended consequence, through the application of Friedman's economics, the *comuneros* could buy former *fundo* land.

In short, since the middle and later part of the 1700s, the agricultural community Canela Baja represents semi-communal ownership and the *hacienda* and the *fundos* that resulted from its subdivision, represent private land ownership. While the *hacienda* institution in Chile was the economic and social pillar of the oligarchic class, the *comuneros* of the agricultural communities came to belong to the poorest in the country.

Some methodological considerations are necessary here regarding the connection between history and sociology. The frontier between them should be open, and as Bourdieu expresses it, many times the division between sciences, 'justifies not so much the science as the researcher' (Bourdieu, *et al*, 1976:103). If the sociologist has to do with a social process where the roots are to be traced in the past, the study inevitably includes history. Historical sociology works with past events and persons, offering particular and 'unique' cases, but is convinced that diverse epochs are not just a handful of facts, persons and dispersed ideas without connection with each other. The researcher also deals with a chain of events for which he tries to find historical coherence (Paz, 1983:38). The social scientist interested in historical events does not understand his investigation as the art of recuperation of the real past, but as a reconstruction of it. All historical investigation thus has its start in the present (Anrup, 1990:13). The selection of problems to be investigated, is partly a matter of subjective preferences. Being a part of the scientific community, the selection is also made according to contemporary considerations of current paradigms, where the selectivity also changes with the preoccupation of the scientific society (Anrup, 1985:8). Therefore, facts make sense and have relevance only in a theoretical context (Bunge, 1975:VII/I). For Bourdieu *et al*, (1976:50), reality never has an initiative of its own, and the facts do not speak by themselves; they only respond to the degree and way the scientist 'asks them'. For Gramsci, (1980:143), the material cannot be considered as a 'thing in itself', but a historical category. Since I am concerned with the configuration, from colonial times, of semi-communally and even privately owned land property, this is a sociological study of an agrarian process that needs to be seen in a historical perspective. It belongs to the terrain of historical, agrarian sociology.

Data sources

The investigation embraces the use of diverse types of resources. My first step was the collection of qualitative data among the *comuneros*, through interviews carried out with qualified informers. For the collection of quantitative data, I conducted a survey in the community Canela Baja, the purpose of which was to get an idea of the socio-economic conditions of the *comuneros*. A description of part of the survey is given in Appendix Two.

I have spent many months of fieldwork in the village Canela Baja, especially between 1987-1990, while I was living in Chile. During this time, I also did participatory observation to some extent. The interviews with qualified informers were of great value, and they guided me in the beginning through to the search for written documentation, both primary and secondary (as most of the bibliography and other sources are in

Spanish, they have been translated to English by me, the responsibility rests with me).

Figure 1.2 Settlements in the Canela Commune

Introduction

A first run through the actual bibliography helped me in different ways: to gain knowledge about the history of the commune, to clarify ideas, for the formulation of my theses, and for the search of primary data in the historical archives.

The historical analysis includes archival data from several primary sources such as testaments, notaries, judicial and parish archives from the 1600s onwards, property registers, sales of land, private archives, etc., enabling me to develop principally the historical-empirical chapters. The secondary sources consist of biographies of selected historical personages (used principally for Chapters 5 and 7), as well as bibliography on different matters regarding the formation of land structure in Chile, an item belonging to Chapter 4.

Archival sources

The greater part of the historical material, as the notaries and judicial archives, is found in the National Archive in Santiago (ANCH). Both the Notaries archives (AN) and the Judicial ones (AJ) are of a great significance for the historical investigation.

The notaries' archives are not catalogued, which constitutes a serious difficulty in the search for material. According to a letter from the National Archives' chief, M. E. Barrientos H.:

> an archive or document collection is catalogued when each of its documents has been itemised through a register for each of them; registers that can be accessible in lists or cards alphabetically, onomastically, by items, etc.

The notarial archives have only been inventoried. This means:

> through the inventory an approximation about the global contents of a book or other type of unit (case, dossier) is given (Letter no. 058, Santiago, September, 5 of 1994. Signature: María Eugenia Barrientos H., Conservator of the National Archive, Chile. The letter is an answer to a request made by me to Mr. Jorge Hidalgo (today ex-conservator of the National Archive) August 2nd, 1994).

The judicial archives, however, are catalogued. Therefore, the order of importance of these documents is inverted, the latter becoming the most important. Had the notary's archives been catalogued, it would have been the other way around. This is because they contain deeds from purchase and sale agreements, census, dowry and wills, all of this of fundamental importance in order to restore the history of land ownership and "to get to know the economical and social situation of the owners" (Borde and Góngora, 1956:20). The notary's archives make it possible to correct and control the judicial archives, which deal with land litigations. Such litigations demand the showing of the title of domain, or at least its allegation and that makes it possible to see the succession of owners. The arguments and proofs in the disputes provide, apart from occasional maps, various kinds of information regarding the exploitation of the land and labour force (Borde and Góngora, 1956:19).

Since the Notaries Registers of Illapel start in 1751, I have tried to cover the period prior to that with the judicial registers, from Illapel as well as from La Serena and Ovalle. Those from La Serena have documents dated prior to 1660 (Góngora, 1970:233). The Notaries Registers of Illapel, also known as the Registers of the Conservatory, embrace 40 volumes, spanning from 1751 to 1873. After that date, the Notaries Registers are to be found at the Conservatory of Real Estate (CBR) of Illapel. This collection includes a chronological inventory and a catalogue of items: Public deeds: 1751-1872, Mortgage deeds 1848-1858, protocolised documents: 1840-1844, 1853-1868, 1870-1872. Real Estates Register: Mortgages and obligations: 1859-1871; Interdictions and Prohibitions: 1859-1871; Property: 1859-1871. Register of mines and denounces: 1857-1873, Grants: 1863-1867, Property: 1857-1873. The first volume, that contains public deeds for the period 1751-1814, is not available to the public, except with the permission of the National Archives' chief. The second volume is only available as microfilm.

From the Notaries Registers, and in respect to the 1800s, the Registers of Property and the Registers of Mortgages are of great importance, with whose help I partially develop the chapters about the *hacienda* El Totoral and Espíritu Santo. The obligation to register the

Introduction

property in the Conservatory of Real Estate was established in the country in 1857, after the dictation of the code of civil laws in 1847. The registration thus guaranteed the legal possession of the land (IREN, 1978, Vol. 1:22).

The Registers of Property allow us to see the transference of domains and mortgages on the property. Both registers, of domains and mortgages, contain an index with the name of the buyer, the seller or the mortgage debtor, depending on each case. Furthermore, name of the property, the number of the folio and the number it has been given in the Register of the Conservatory. The inscription of the property contains the information included in the public deeds, that is, identity of the participants in the purchase and sales agreement, property limits, price or amount of the mortgage, etc. The description of the property's boundaries contained in the different records through the years allows us to see whether there are differences in the boundaries.

The old (1698-1915) Parish archives (AP), important for Chapter 7 on the historical background of the agricultural community Canela Baja, reviewed in Chile in February of 1993, belong to the Parish San Vicente Ferrer of Mincha. These archives, like the ones in the rest of the country, and in many other countries like for example Mexico or Sweden, have been microfilmed by the Genealogical Society of Utah. Said archives exist in Salt Lake City, and also in the Iglesia de Jesucristo de los Santos de los Ultimos Días in Santiago, Chile. The mentioned archives also exist in the Seminario Mayor Library of the Catholic Church, Santiago. The parish archives of Mincha also include information from Illapel and a few other neighbouring villages. The archives include Marriage registers (from 1689), Baptisms (only of 1834 and onward), Confirmations (from 1894) and Deaths (from 1694). The Genealogical Society notes that years are missing. These old parochial archives are important as they concern some of my theses.

I also reviewed some old parish archives from other places for the following reasons: the ones concerning baptisms from Illapel (1698-1782), since those from the parish of Mincha start only in 1834. The archives of La Serena and Sotaquí were reviewed due to the fact that some of the historical personages investigated were born or lived part of their lives in these places. The archives here reviewed were the marriages index and marriages with deaths (1658-1701) as well as baptisms (1659-1743), from the Parish Church of La Merced in La Serena. Also reviewed were the baptism's index and baptisms (1648-1753) the marriages index and marriages (1648-1682) from the Parish Church of Sotaquí (Ovalle).

Contemporary sources

For the current state of land property, the lists of the Roll of Collection-Contributions of Real Estates (RCCBR of SII) were reviewed. They are organised by communes. The list includes; names of the proprietors, address or name of the property, roll number and valuation of the property. This data was combined and compared with the data from CIREN, which in its list also has the size of the property in hectares, as well as the land exploitation capacity (classification that includes whether the soil is irrigated or not, and type of soil according to scale from I to VIII). The list from CIREN, however, does not include the valuation of the properties. Part of these data constitutes the base of Chapters 2 and 3.

A necessary step during the recollection of current statistical data was the official census of INE (National Statistics Institute). However, the INE data, even though useful, can be misleading. An example of that is the categorisation of occupations within the commune, according to which in 1982, only 22.4% of the labour force of the commune is occupied in a category that covers agriculture, hunting, silviculture and fishing. As we shall see in Chapter 3, this figure is strange since in the commune the majority of the labour force, live on agro-pastoral activities (INE, 1982:4-5). However, INE performs its census during the first week of April, when many agricultural producers work in other activities, being thus registered as wage-labourers (Rivera, 1988a:271) or as unemployed. The question dealing with occupation refers to the occupation the person had during the period of reference or to the work he/she had last time, if unemployed. The period of reference corresponds to the week before the census (INE, 1982:XXXI). The periods of high and low occupation within agriculture are November-January and May-July, respectively.

As we shall also see, a lot of data regarding the area of the communities, number of *comuneros*, the area of the commune, of the *fundos*, etc. from different instances such as IREN, CBR and the agricultural communities themselves, are very inexact and frequently do not agree with each other. When necessary, I will confront them as they arise in different chapters. Otherwise, the data from IREN, the Municipality, the agricultural community itself and INE principally, constitute the basis for part of Chapter 3.

There was some information about the commune belonging to the Municipality that I would have liked to use, but which I was not given access to. An example of this was the CAS (Comisión Asistencia Social), 'because the Governor of Illapel did not give authorisation', as expressed by the social assistant there. CAS is the Government's own data (to be found in the Municipality) on poverty in the commune, and deals with social stratification and evaluation of the economic situation of families in the commune. This information would have helped me to make comparisons with the results of my own inquiry. It can be added here that the old Municipal archives are of little value, and deal with questions concerning decisions of the Municipal Council about taxes on the merchandise and other economical details of the commune.

Other information that I was unable to obtain, was the number of emigrants in the copper mine of Chuquicamata born in the commune of Canela. I tried to obtain this information from CODELCO (Copper Corporation) - Chuquicamata. Chuquicamata and most of the saltpetre mines are in Region II of Antofagasta, at a distance of more than 1,000 km from Canela Baja. Traditionally, from the end of the nineteenth century, the migration in the community has gone to these places (see also Chapter 8). I would have liked to use it to complement the information I collected on emigration. Both the latter and the former information I tried to obtain while Pinochet was in government.

As to secondary sources used for the description of the development of land tenure in Chile, of special importance were, among others, the already named works of Borde and Góngora, Baraona *et al* and CIDA, whose works pioneered the study of land structure in Chile, as well as the cadastre about the agricultural communities of the Norte Chico completed by IREN (1977/78), which comprises several volumes.

The qualitative analysis

Due to my initial ignorance about the history of the agricultural communities, the interviews with qualified informers were developed with many general questions, and without a previous systematic questionnaire. With this, I hoped firstly that the informers would guide me with their knowledge. Secondly, it seemed the best way to gather qualitative data among the *comuneros,* the kind of data not to be measured in quantitative terms. Thirdly, with the help of interviews carried out with qualified informers, I also wanted to give the *comuneros* themselves a voice in narrating how they remembered the events regarding the conflict of Espíritu Santo (Chapter 8).

The oral memory of the *comuneros* collected by me, through which I partially reconstructed the history of the conflict of Espíritu Santo, corresponds, because of its character, to the method of oral history (Thompson, 1980:9; Vansina, 1989). According to Vansina (1989:565):

> Oral traditions are accounts, which may or may not be historical in content, transmitted verbally from one generation to another.

They are usually transmitted by hearsay, not writing. Their principal characteristics are that they:

- refer both to the past and to the present as they are being retold;
- are made of a welter of testimonies which form a corpus;
- are expressed in all varieties of oral form (prayer, song, poetry, narrative, etc.).

As Vansina (1989:565) points out:

> Any oral tradition is a product in a process, a stream of orality that begins with the recollection of an incident or a situation either by an eyewitness or as a rumour. Thereupon human memory takes over and recreates the event or the situation, providing logical links between the items observed, and making the whole intelligible by the attribution of continuity and motivation. At this stage, testimony is oral history. It becomes tradition only after transmission from one generation to a following one.

Introduction

Since my intention was to give a voice to the *comuneros*, material collected with the help of qualified informers has been transcribed with maximum fidelity. However, it was often necessary to modernise the Spanish, reduce the text, insert some punctuation and take away repetitions, in order to make the translation and the understanding easier. Only three of the interviews with qualified informers were recorded. In the other cases, I took notes. The recording or none recording of the interview depended initially on whether the person gave their permission or not. In spite of the fact that the majority of the informers agreed to be recorded, I decided to abandon this alternative, as I very soon noticed that most of them felt uncomfortable in front of the tape recorder.

The greater part of the current information about the agricultural community Canela Baja and the present *fundo* Puerto Oscuro, comes principally from the interviews with qualified informers. By mid 1998, nine of the 21 had died due to their advanced age.

The information obtained from qualitative data from the *comuneros*, helped me to understand the community organisation and the way it functions. Of crucial importance here was the collaboration of Pedro Carvajal, who served several times as a qualified informer. From him I obtained the list of *comuneros* from the community Canela Baja (and even from other communities in the commune) that helped me to collect the population sample for the survey. The list also helped me to do a statistical study over the more common names of the *comuneros* (included in Appendix 1), in order to see whether the colonial names had been maintained over the time within the community. I also obtained part of the material and information about the community from the Junta of *Comuneros*.

As indicated, part of my information about the community comes from own observation made during my visits there. This information comes mainly from participatory observation. I was present at the annual meeting of the Junta of *Comuneros* (1st March 1988), where decisions were taken about the distribution of land and other matters concerning the organisation of the community. On this occasion I interviewed the lawyer from OBN (Office of National Estates) of Ovalle, Patricio Velázques, who at that time counselled the Junta of *Comuneros*.

As to the conflict of Espíritu Santo in its several phases, the testimonies of several *comuneros* were important, among them, the two elderly Joel Muñoz and Samuel Jorquera (deccased). Muñoz participated, as Mayor of the Municipality, in the recovering of the sub-area Espíritu Santo. From this sub-area I also interviewed Guillermo Castillo, and from the sub-area Canela Baja, Emiliano Cortés. They also participated in the recuperation of Espíritu Santo at the beginning of the 1970's. Emiliano Cortés was at that time (1988), President of Junta of *Comuneros* for the second time.

The information about the present *fundo* Puerto Oscuro (Chapter 9) was obtained, with the permission of the *fundo* directors, from Carlos Rocco, at that time the *fundo*'s manager, who also participated as a qualified informer. Information and documents related to the *fundo* before its expropriation was obtained from J. A. Echavarría E. (deceased), one of the ex-proprietors of Puerto Oscuro. As for the functioning of the property before its expropriation, I interviewed Desiderio Collao (deceased), a former *inquilino* during the time of the Echavarría's. For the collection of qualitative data, some private documentation dealing with letters and titles of property which I was given access to was also useful, especially from Oscar Ollarzú (deceased), who also served several times as qualified informer.

In the narrative of the historical course of the agricultural community Canela Baja, the *hacienda* El Totoral and the three *fundos* born out of it, I have conscientiously used the proper names. This was for three reasons. Firstly, due to the fact that I do not want this history to be anonymous. Secondly, the importance of proper names is related to part of one of my theses, i.e. that related to the hereditary maintenance of the land property between the descendants of the original proprietors of the land since colonial times. Thirdly, as every history is always incomplete, the use of proper names would also serve as guide to those studious who wish to go further in the investigation about the formation of the structure of land property in the commune of Canela. Fourthly, since I have a personal debt to propagate this study among the *comuneros* because some of them explicitly requested it, the importance of actual past individuals is justified for the case of the communities. This way, the *comuneros* would recognise themselves in their ancestors, and would probably gain a deeper awareness about their cultural inheritance.

As to the names of historical or past persons, I am of the opinion that they belong to the historical and cultural funds of the commune, as do all the deceased owners of the *hacienda* and the *fundos* and those from the communities. Dealing specifically with colonial personages, when the second family name is not given in the historical archives, as often happens, I have always added it in parenthesis. In order to realise what the second name was, I based myself on other data, like the year of birth or/and death when available, as well as the military title of the personages in question.

Dealing with qualified informers, the use of proper names, as I see it, does not represent any ethical problems, as long as these names do not concern the survey. In this case, every one of the interviewed *comuneros* was orally informed of their anonymity. However, little of what the qualified informers have told me is unknown to the community itself. It is because they are known that I recurred to them. Many are, or have been, public figures within the community. Since both their political preferences and their engagement in social questions concerning the community are known both by the *comuneros* and by the official instances, as some of the informers were arrested for a short time of period during the coup d'état of 1973, I am not discovering anything new when I refer to their leftist sympathies. Indeed, I never refer to their political party membership. Fortunately, the political situation of the country looks different today. As also indicated, many of my qualified informers, unfortunately, have died. However, there is no doubt that I was there just in time to rescue for the following generations a great deal of the community's valuable cultural inheritance from the now deceased qualified informers. This has given me a great deal of satisfaction; permitting me to feel that at least I was making a contribution to the people this work is about.

Disposition of the investigation

The dissertation is divided into three parts: the General Introduction, Historical Past and Contemporary History. The General Introduction includes this chapter as well as Chapters 2 and 3. Chapter 2 is divided into two sub-chapters. To contextualise the investigation, I present in the first sub-chapter, the present-day land structure in Chile and its changes during the last decades as a result of the agrarian reforms, including the agrarian structure in a short historical retrospective. I also discuss some problems regarding the statistical estimation of the small peasantry, and some current trends within agriculture. The second part of this chapter also contextualises the investigation, corresponding to the socio-economic setting of the study object. It situates my study within the greater social structure of the commune, including its present land tenure structure and general data dealing with its population, which to a very large extent, is the population of its agricultural communities.

Chapter 3 comprises the physical description of the Canela commune where the agricultural community Canela Baja and the former *hacienda* El Totoral are located, contextualising them here within a greater geographical framework than that of the commune. Particular attention is paid to the physical environment, whose description permits us to understand the life conditions for a predominantly agricultural population, composed mainly by the *comuneros* and their families. Then it becomes easier to present a more detailed characterisation of the agricultural communities and their property rights. This will help to explain the phenomenon of agricultural community itself as a social institution.

Taking us up to the colonial period, Part 2 (Chapters 4 to 7) embrace both the development of land tenure in Chile, as well as my historical case. In order to put the development of land structure of the Norte Chico within a national framework, Chapter 4 starts with an overview of the formation of land tenure in Chile since colonial times. Terms related to the Chilean and Latin-American agrarian structure are specified as *mercedes de tierra, encomienda, estancia, hacienda and fundo*, among others. In this connection, the historical precedents and endurance of the small property in Chile are also discussed. There, I also discuss the problem of the origin of the semi-communally owned land property in the Norte Chico. To analyse this particular process, I discuss and contrast different authors who have tried to explain the formation of the agricultural communities or, in my view, the conversion of certain private properties into semi-communal, and the mechanism that would explain the continuity of other properties in private ownership. This part serves as a base for the development of my own theses in respect to the origin and formation of the agricultural communities, constituting the last item of Chapter 4.

In Chapter 5, I start properly with my empirical case. Through a common introduction for both El Totoral and Canela Baja, I try to elucidate the scarce, but intricate and contradictory information that exists about the origins of these properties. Since, in my view, both the *latifundium* and the agricultural communities of the Norte Chico mainly share their origin in the *mercedes de tierras*, this chapter tries to empirically support this argument.

Introduction

In the two subsequent chapters, I try to follow and contrast the two properties. As specified, the historical process of land tenure formation in the commune of Canela is interesting because the *hacienda* El Totoral and the agricultural community Canela Baja, in spite of sharing a common origin, developed into two different forms of land ownership. Around each of them, two different types of economic and social development began to form. Chapter 6 deals with the case of the *hacienda* El Totoral, and the *fundos* into which it was divided at the end of the nineteenth century. My purpose here is to illustrate how the property of the *haciendas* and *fundos*, in contrast to the agricultural communities, is constantly transferred through the years.

Chapter 7 continues with the *estancia* La Canela, which later on became at least fourteen agricultural communities. In this chapter, I also briefly take the case of the *estancias* Mincha and Conchalí and Chigualoco, parts of which belong to the commune of Canela. Here, ten agricultural communities developed from one *merced de tierra*, later on the Mincha *Estancia*. This case further supports the agricultural communities having their origin in the colonial *mercedes de tierra*. The case of Conchalí and Chigualoco, different to the *estancia* Mincha, but similar to El Totoral, illustrates the other developmental variant, the continuation of these properties as private, still being *haciendas*.

Hopefully, Part 2 will as a whole show how two land ownership forms in fact developed from one, and how thereafter different types of socio-economic development resulted from it. The analysis and summary of this historical process will be developed in the last chapter of this dissertation.

However, the scope and detail of Part 2 follows several reasons. This is due to the long historical period it embraces, and to the hitherto existing lack of systematic knowledge about the origin and development of the agricultural communities. The detailed information is also aimed to serve in the reconstruction of land tenure structure over time, but also to illustrate my theses. Last, but not least, because this work has been written as a contribution to the local history of the people it deals with, the *comuneros*, which supposedly is the real aim of the scientific work, i.e., the people outside the limitations of the academic's walls.

Taking us back to the present, Part 3 embraces Chapters 8 to 10. Chapter 8 describes the struggle for the land of the ex-*fundo* Espíritu Santo, the part of the agricultural community Canela Baja that was seized in the 1800s. Here I try to focus on the dynamics of rural societies this particular example helping to refute the theoretical positions above mentioned, among them, 'marginal land'.

Chapter 9 is divided into two sub-chapters; one is specifically about the *fundo* Puerto Oscuro, and the other, more general, about the legal recognition of the agricultural communities. Both sub-chapters deal with two different processes, both being the indirect product of the changes initiated by the agrarian reform in the Chilean agrarian structure. Here both processes come to an end and so does the history about the former *hacienda* El Totoral and that of the communities.

As a result of the changes introduced by Pinochet's agrarian policy in the 1970s, the contemporary *fundo* Puerto Oscuro comes to represent, once again, under a new form of ownership, a private property; but a private property owned by *comuneros*, and organised in a way that parallels, in some aspects, the one which is today proper to the agricultural communities. The second sub-chapter describes the coming into legal recognition of the agricultural communities as from the 1960s onwards, as well as the modification of their law until the last one of 1993. The legalisation is relevant in several aspects. It helps me first to illustrate an apparently paradoxical process, that of the legal recognition of the agricultural communities, occurring within a bigger one: the expansion of the capitalist relations of production within agriculture in the rural areas of the country. The latter will be partially taken in Chapter 2. In the recognition process, we see how the state through its different institutions, plays a central role in securing the semi-communal form of land ownership of the agricultural communities, at the same time as its intervention destroys the social institution of the *latifundium*, as the agricultural communities have their roots in the colonial period.

In Chapter 10, the final chapter, I first present an analysis and a summary of the empirical chapters in order to gather the principal issues about the origin and emergence of the semi-communal land ownership in the case study and its contrast with the *hacienda* system. Then, the hitherto postponed Swiss and English cases are described to make a comparison with the Norte Chico's agricultural communities. With the help of Stevenson (1991), I finally come to a formal definition of communal land ownership, distinguishing this form both from open access and private property. This way, the semi-communal property of the agricultural communities will, in a conceptualisation of its own, appear as just another form of ownership, and of organising resources and production, no less rational or inferior to the private.

2 Overview of the Chilean Land Tenure Structure and the Socio-Economic Setting of the Study Object

Overview of land tenure structure in Chile

This contextualising chapter is divided into two sub-chapters. Here will be developed some lines dealing with the Chilean land tenure structure and the changes that the agrarian reform process caused in it as from the 1960s. These changes are of special interest when dealing with Chapter 9, where two minor social and legal processes are presented that are the indirect result of the agrarian reform.

The structural changes suffered during the last decades by the agrarian structure in Chile has made some authors, such as Gómez (1990:i), point out that they are:

> equal, or perhaps surpass, the ones experienced in the almost five centuries after the Spanish colonisation.

One of the sectors that experienced large changes during the government of Pinochet was fruit and forest production. Its part in the export sector increased from 3% in 1975 to 20% in 1985, registering within the economy the highest productive expansion rate. In spite of the fact that fruit growing encompasses only a 3% of the total of 4.5 millions of hectares of the arable surface, it leads agricultural development. It gives:

> direct employment to some 200,000 workers and another 200,000 more indirectly; in technical assistance, transportation, trading and diverse services (Rivera, 1988b:94-95).

The agrarian reform initiated in 1962 did, in spite of three subsequent, different state policies implemented according to government ideology, doubtless change the panorama of Chilean agriculture. The most important achievement is perhaps having finished with the domination of the system of *latifundium*, as well as the system of *inquilinaje* on which it was based. However, the elimination of the *latifundium* in itself, conceived as an obstacle for the modernisation of the agriculture, was not the objective of the agrarian reform, but rather the distribution of its land. In agreement with the article 30 of the Law 15.020 of the 1962 agrarian reform, this was issued in order to:

> ... carry out an agrarian reform, that permits access to the property of the land to those who work it, improves the standard of living of the peasant population, increases the agricultural production and the productivity of the soil (CIDA, 1966:253).

According to CIDA's recommendations, the agrarian reform in Chile had to improve the living and working conditions for a population of between 200,000 and 300,000 rural families, consisting of workers without land, sub-family producers and *comuneros*. They represented approximately 66% of the agricultural population, and an even greater percentage of the economically active agricultural population. The agrarian reform had furthermore to increase the productivity and the revenue of another 60,000 families with family size properties (CIDA, 1966:274).

The agrarian reform did expand the number of small and middle landowners, but the objective of the agrarian reform was not either to create the *minifundium* or small peasantry. On the contrary, both in Chile and Latin America as a whole, the *minifundium* is the not anticipated result of these processes (Stavenhagen, 1979:267-268). The agrarian reforms have been concerned more with limiting the great property than with extending the small one. Nonetheless, if the agrarian reforms redistributed a great part of the land, Pinochet interrupted this process in 1973.

Examining the structure of land tenancy in the country today, one would have to state that land distribution is far from being equitable. Until the beginning of the 1960s in Chile, the great property, consisting of approximately 5,000 *haciendas*, held about 56% of Chile's agricultural land (7% of Chile's land is arable, 16% meadows and pastures, 21% forest and woodland, and the remaining 56% belongs to other categories). It is within this context that the changes began during the rightist, liberal president Jorge Alessandri (1958-1964) with the 1962 law of agrarian reform, which intended to eliminate the *hacienda's* inefficient system.

The agrarian reform deepened during the government of the Christian Democrat Eduardo Frei (1964-1970), but it is with the socialistic government of Salvador Allende's *Unidad Popular* (1970-1973) that it became even more intensified (Rivera, 1988a:13-14). From 1965 until 1973, out of a total of 21 million hectares, half of the agricultural land of the country was expropriated. In this process all the *haciendas* were affected, in one way or another (Rivera, 1988a:66; Rivera, 1988b:86).

The arrival of Pinochet's government with his neo-liberal project based on the concept of a social market economy changed the trends of the preceding governments, reversing part of the previous process. Of approximately 10 millions hectares of land expropriated during the agrarian reforms were, after 1973, affected by the government of Pinochet by giving 2,991,174 ha back to the ex-owners, transferring through the process of auctions 4,019,188 ha to third persons and public institutions, whilst 2,887,006 ha were assigned to peasants (Rivera, 1988a:66-67, 228).

According to Rivera, the last part was parcelled out into some 40,000 properties of approximately 6 equivalent irrigation hectares (basic irrigated hectares - HRB). This parcelling out provided land to two thirds of the former legatees of the *asentamientos* (settlements), or co-operatives created during the agrarian reforms by CORA. For CORA (the Agrarian Reform Corporation), the *asentamiento* corresponded to a transitional stage in which the state gave initial support to the peasants with the aim of getting them to start working for themselves (Gómez, 1981:74). The Agrarian Reform Law 16.640 stipulated that the *asentamientos* would last only three years, at the utmost five (Gómez *et al*, 1981:461).

As of the promulgation of the Agrarian Reform Law 15.020 of 1962, the CORA is created from the *Caja de Colonización*. According to this law CORA:

> is the commissioned organisation in charge of carrying out the agrarian reform and its principal functions are to divide the agricultural properties, to regroup the minifundium, to colonise new lands, to form small agricultural villages and peasant villages, to create special centres of agricultural production and to provide credit and technical assistance to the colonists and their co-operatives (CIDA, 1966:353,372).

With this distribution, the number of small proprietors in the strata of 5 to 10 HRB was tripled. In the decade of the 1980s, however, more than 50% of these legatees had sold their land (Rivera, 1988a:66-67). It is important to indicate, however, that it has not been a reconstruction of the *latifundium*, the medium sized property prevailing with between 40 and 200 hectares equivalent of irrigation (HRB) (Rivera, 1988b:95).

However, there also seems to be no doubt that in Chile, the small agrarian producers are numerically a more important social sector than 30-40 years ago (Rivera, 1988a:15). Their statistical estimation is nonetheless uncertain, due principally to the low reliability and contradictory existing data, and that in spite of that the empirical investigation of the peasantry has increased. The problems we find in Chile are probably valid for other countries as well. Therefore, before I continue with Chile's agrarian structure, I will briefly take into account some considerations regarding the numerical estimation of the peasantry, relevant even for the agricultural communities of the Norte Chico.

Statistical estimation of the small peasantry: some problems

The agrarian sector in Latin America shows today a rich complexity that varies from country to country, and even within different regions in the same country. The percentage of the *minifundistas* or small peasantry in Latin America varies considerably. Depending on the country, it makes up between 50% and 95% of the agrarian producers (Astorga, 1985:99). In Mexico, the estates of the *minifundistas* (*ejidatarios, comuneros*, private) constitute 72% of the total, while the impresario estates only make up 28% (Astorga, 1985:100).

Reforms and counter-reforms in the agrarian sector, and in the Latin American societies as a whole, have had different effects in different countries. Redistributing part of the land, the agrarian reforms did increase the number of peasants. After the refrain of the agrarian reforms in the 1970s and the following economic liberalisation, new processes of land concentration started to take place. Even new ownership forms in the shape of limited societies, also called dry land peasant societies (*sociedades campesinas de secano*) have emerged in Chile. An example of that is the actual *fundo* Puerto Oscuro or Society Pereira, Cortés, Brito and Co. Ltd.

Within Chilean agriculture, the uncertainty regarding the real number of landholders is valid for all forms of land tenure, whether it deals with private property, communal or semi-communal. From this follows that the figures in respect to the number of properties and peasant households are estimations. The figures that different authors and official sources present on the topic vary considerably. With respect to the total of peasants, the figures vary between 200,000 and 300,000 (Rivera, 1988a:269). The differences in the estimations depend, according to Rivera, on two measurement problems.

The first is that there is no correspondence between the number of properties delivered by the Internal Taxes Service (SII) and the number of peasant households delivered by the National Statistics Institute (INE), institutions that possess official data for the study of the social agrarian structure. The list of the Roll of Collection-Contributions of Real Estates (RCCBR) includes the names of the proprietors, the address or name of the property, the roll number and valuation of the property, but lacks an important data, which is the size of the property (see also Chapter 1). If there were the above-mentioned correspondence, it would then be sufficient to take the number of the records of properties from SII to have the total. However, it is not the case, because there are, on the one hand, properties individually registered, but that form part of a greater unit, and on the other, properties registered as one, but which include several small producers (Rivera, 1988a:269).

Examples of what is described exist within my own case study. An example of properties registered as one, but which include several owners, is that of the present-day *fundo* Puerto Oscuro or Society Cortés, Brito and Co. Ltd. This *fundo* is registered as one property, but 86 shareholders own it. A good example of the second case that is to say, of properties individually registered but that form part of a greater unit is the agricultural community Canela Baja. This is registered as a single unit in the CBR (Conservator of Real Estate) of Illapel, but whose *comuneros* have, for the most part, registered their *hijuelas* in an individual form in the properties record of the SII. These *hijuelas* also enter within the whole entity that comprises the agricultural community. To add to the complexity of this picture is also the fact that most of the shareholders of the mentioned *fundo* are, at the same time, *comuneros* of the agricultural community Canela Baja (see Chapter 9).

The second measurement problem originates in the fact that there are a great number of small producers who form part of the total number of peasant households, who do not own land, but have access to it under various forms; rental, share-cropping (*mediería*), or simply in charge. It is estimated that there are approximately 30% more peasant households than number of properties. In 1977, about 60% of the *minifundium* peasants were living in their own individual properties, while 40% had access to land under other forms (Rivera, 1988a:270). In any event, the total number of peasant households, including all the other social categories (large, middle, *minifundium*, precarious producers, salaried, etc.) would amount to some 400,000 households. However, of this total some 200,000 would correspond, according to Rivera, to exploitation with a certain level of agricultural production, whilst the remaining 200,000 live basically on properties of a residential type.

As is pointed out by Rivera (1988a:270), if we multiply the 400,000 households at a rate of five persons per household, it would turn out that the result is equal to the total rural population. This is factor would indicate that the appraisals on the number of peasant households are overvalued. While on one hand, the censuses of the INE overvalue the number of peasant households; on the other they also undervalue them, when counting many *minifundium* peasant conglomerations within the category of urban localities. To this must be added the fact that the censuses are made during the first week of April, when many agricultural producers are engaged in other activities, being thus consigned as wage-labour (Rivera, 1988a:271), or unemployed (see also Chapter 1).

The lack of reliable data dealing with the statistical estimation of the peasantry is not unique for Chile or Latin America. Even though the reasons may be other than that of Chile, Djurfeldt (2-1990:iii-iv) declares that in Sweden the situation is not very different.

> We are lacking /.../ precise and systematic knowledge about basic social conditions within Swedish agriculture.

This is partially due to the fact that rural sociology in Sweden has a marginal place, in comparison with the sociology, in general. Of 201 doctoral theses written in Sweden between 1969-1986, only 6% can be counted as rural sociology and, of them, only 2.5% deals with Sweden (Djurfeldt, 2-1990:2-4;8).

According to Seyler's estimation of the agrarian class structure in Sweden in the beginning/middle of the 1970s, the small peasants constituted 40% (58,000) of the total population (142,000) working in agriculture and had land. The size of the other categories was capitalist 1,000; big-peasants 5,000; middle-peasants 23,000; and semi-proletarian 55,000. Of the small peasants, 87.1% had between 0.3 and 30 hectares of land (Seyler, 1983:272).

More recent appraisals indicate that there are approximately 105,000 farms larger than two hectares that are private property including the 8,500 larger farms that depend on wage-labour (Djurfeldt, 1994:124). However, the total of 105,000 farms does not include the 190,000 farms of less than two hectares that, according to the traditional approach of Swedish statistics, are not taken into account. Neither does it include the 10,000 farms that are the property of juridical persons. According to Djurfeldt's categorisation, of the 105,000 farms larger than two hectares and that are private property (i.e., belonging also to private and not juridical persons), 57,000 (54%) correspond to farms with extensive production and 48,000 (45%) to farms with intensive production (Djurfeldt, 2-1990:26, 30; see also Djurfeldt, 1994:116-126). It should be emphasised that Djurfeldt's and Seyler's estimates are not altogether comparable, since they use a different criterion. Central to Djurfeldt's estimates is, for example, the number of working hours per man required to make the farm produce.

It is interesting to note here that if we add together all Djurfeldt's previously mentioned categories, taking into account the farms of less than two hectares, as it is done in Chile, we would have a total of 305,000 'farms' in Sweden. As we shall see, this total falls somewhere in between the figures that is estimates for the Chilean agrarian structure, the country having an estimated population of 13,528,945 million people in 1997.

Development in land tenure structure and the current state

Having made these observations, there are present below some tables related to the development of land tenure and its current state in Chile. The two tables that follow correspond, according to Rivera, to calculations based on previous trends. The said trends suppose, on one hand, that there exists an increase of the *minifundium*, and on the other, a moderate level of land concentration in the hands of the commercial property. Rivera indicates that this hypothesis is different from that of Gómez and Echeñique (1988), who estimate that it has been rather a pronounced trend toward concentration (Rivera, 1988a:86).

In Table 2.1 it can be observed, firstly, that from 1924 until 1985, the total number of properties increased by more than 200%. Secondly, the large properties (>80 ha) is significantly reduced concentration in the total land tenure, at the same time as the number of owners within this category is reduced.

Toward 1985, the strata of owners with up to until 5 ha increased its participation in land tenure by 14.6% whilst at the same time their numbers also increased in 5.7%. In absolute terms, the small peasants increased from approximately 100,000 in 1924 to 330,000 in 1985.

Overview of the Chilean Land Tenure Structure and the Socio-Economic Setting

In the range of 5-10 and 10-20 ha, a decrease (smaller in the first case and somewhat greater in the second) in the number of owners may be observed, whilst an increase of 9.9% and 10.3% is observed in their participation in the total land tenure, respectively.

In the range of 20-80 ha a slight increase can be observed in the percentage of owners, followed also of a considerable increase by 18.2% in their participation of the total tenure. It is this range (20-80 ha), together with the *minifundium,* that most benefited with the redistribution of land.

Table 2.1 Development of land tenure in Chile (1924-1985)
(in percentage, size: basic irrigation hectares (HRB))

	<5	5-10	10-20	20-80	>80	CORA	Total of properties
1924							
% Owners	71.4	14.0	9.0	2.0	3.6	-	140,000
% Tenure	1.4	2.1	5.7	11.8	79.0		
1965							
% Owners	80.8	8.6*	5.0	3.4	2.2	-	232,955
% Tenure	9.7	5.0	7.7	20.3	55.9	6.1	
1976							
% Owners	68.2	20.4	4.7	3.6	2.1	-	317,955
% Tenure	12.7	23.7	10.5	22.3	25.7		
1980							
% Owners	74.3	15.4	5.2	3.3	1.8	-	342,702
% Tenure	14.7	7.4	12.6	28.2	27.1		
1985							
% Owners	77.1	12.8	5.8	2.8	1.4	-	428,000
% Tenure	16.0	12.0	16.0	30.0	26.0		
Difference in tenure 1924-1985	+14.6	+9.9	+10.3	+18.2	-53.0		

* The original figure in Rivera's table is 80.8%, just as that which precedes it in the left column. I deduced that it must be a mistake and that the correct figure is 8.6%.
Source: Rivera (1988a)

Thus, until 1985 the percentage of participation of the large landowners in the land tenure had decreased, increasing the participation of all the other strata. From this can be concluded that the land tenure structure, with the changes resulting both from the agrarian reforms and from the subsequent period shows, in comparison with the year 1924, a distribution of the land somewhat more balanced among the various social strata within agriculture (to compare 1985 with 1965 is not altogether appropriate, inasmuch as the agrarian reform had already begun. 1924 is, in the presented series, the only pre-agrarian reform year). Even so, it is still far from equitable, as only 1.4% of the owners (6,000) possess 26% of the land, while the *minifundium* strata, constituting 77.1% of the owners (330,000), only possesses 16% of the country's agricultural lands.

This inequality is made even more obvious if we add the two superior strata (20-80 and >80 ha), resulting in 4.2% of the owners (18,000) possessing 56% of the agricultural land. It is important to underline once again that in any event, it has not been a reconstitution of the *latifundium*.

Table 2.2 The structure of land tenure in Chile (1985)

Social category	Size	No. of proprietors	% of Tenure	% of Total	Average ha HRB
1. *Minifundium* Peasant	<5	330,000	16	77.1	1.4
2. Middle size and rich peasants	5-10	55,000	12	12.8	6.5
3. Commercial proprietors	10-20	25,000	16	5.8	16.1
4. Commercial middle size properties	20-80	12,000	30	2.8	65.
5. Large estates proprietors	80>	6,000	26	1.4	110.
Total		428,000	100	100	

Source: Rivera (1988a)

I continue now to examine in more detail the estimations about the *minifundium* where, as specified in Chapter 1, the agricultural communities of Region IV are normally integrated. In the Tables 2.2 and 2.3, the figures concerning the *minifundium* differ considerably from each other. Table 2.2

shows the land tenure structure in 1985 by social categories or type of enterprises according to Rivera. Table 2.3 presents the figures according to Gómez, who has estimated the *minifundistas* to 140,000 by the end of the 1980s (Gómez, 1989:4).

Table 2.3 Types of agricultural enterprise, number, percentage and total area in Chile, 1989

Type of enterprise	No. of enterprises	% of Total	% of Tenure
1. Modernised entrepreneurs	5,000	2.1	15
2. Traditional entrepreneurs	25,000	10.6	55
3. Peasant of family exploitation	66,000	27.9	16
4. *Minifundium*	140,000	59.4	14
Total	236,000	100	100

Source: Gómez (1989)

Though Gómez' and Rivera's tables deal with different years (1989 and 1985, respectively) and different criteria of the social strata, which does not make them totally comparable, it is still possible to draw some conclusions that reveal the considerable differences that exist on this matter. If for example, in the table of Gómez we add, on one hand, the categories 1 and 2, we would have a total of 30,000 enterprises. They would correspond to 12.7% of the total, occupying 70% of the agricultural area. Conversely, if we add the categories 3 and 4, we would have a total of 206,000 enterprises. They would represent 87.3% of the total, occupying only 30% of the total agricultural area. I believe that this regrouping is correct, inasmuch as for Gómez, the peasants are those who directly work the land. The modern and traditional entrepreneur would correspond to the categories of owners who run their enterprises on the basis of wage-labour.

If we do the same thing to Rivera's table adding the categories 3, 4 and 5, they would add up to 43,000 proprietors. This would represent 10% of the total, occupying some 72% of the total agricultural area. If we then add the categories 1 and 2, they would amount to 385,000 proprietors, corresponding to 89.9% of the total occupying 28% of the land.

The first major difference in comparing the tables of Rivera and Gómez, has to do with the total number of properties: 428,000 in Rivera and only 236,000 in Gómez. According to what is observed, the greater difference is in the figure of the *minifundium*, since if we add the rest of the agricultural, social categories in both authors' tables the figures are similar: 98,000 in Rivera and 97,000 in Gómez. In the following table, Gómez also separates the peasant or family exploitation and the *minifundium* according to some other criteria.

Though it is not clear in Table 2.4, the category of communities that Gómez calls 'of the North' (1.b), it probably refers to the agricultural communities of the Norte Chico, since the ones of the Norte Grande should enter into the category 1.a (Indigenous). Thus, according to this table, the agricultural communities of the Norte Chico would represent 9.3% of the *minifundium* and 6.3% of the total of the peasant exploitation (*minifundium* and family exploitation) and 5.5% of the country's agricultural properties. Though it is not totally comparable with the data of Table 2.4, according to Rivera (1988a) in 1976, 59.4% of the land was in individual owner hands, while the remaining 40.6% were found within other forms of tenure: family successions 10.2%; the communal property regime 16.5%; occupants 6.7; tenant 3.7; share-croppers 1.8%; and other forms of tenure 1.7%.

Table 2.4 Categories of peasant exploitation in Chile, 1989

Categories	No. of proprietors	% of Total
1. *Minifunium* (poor peasants):	140,000	68
a. Indigenous	40,000	
b. North Communities	13,000	
c. Traditional	87,000	
2. *Family Exploitation* (middle size peasants)	66,000	32
a. Traditional	30,000	
b. Colonisation	6,000	
c. Agrarian Reform	30,000	
Total	**206,000**	**100**

Source: Gómez (1989)

Current trends. It is interesting to verify that, as Rivera indicates, despite the fact that various Latin America countries may or may not have had agrarian reforms, agriculture shows (excepting Cuba and Nicaragua) similar trends. One can observe an increase of the seasonal wage-labour, extreme rural poverty, an increase of subsistence peasants, urban marginalisation and food crisis. In addition we see a virtual disappearance of the landowner oligarchy, an increase of the wealth among the rural elite, a wider transnationalisation of agriculture and a technological distancing of the exportable top items, with respect to those aimed for the internal market (Rivera, 1988b:96).

In the Chilean agriculture of the 1980s it was possible to distinguish four processes; the deepening of the changes in tenure structure; changes in employment; the new place for agriculture on the world market; and pauperising peasantisation (Rivera, 1988b:96-97). The consequences of peasants pauperising are, on one hand, the land concentration through purchases by commercial enterprises, a process that marginalises the peasantry to ecologically marginal areas. On the other, it increases the technological difference between commercial enterprises and the peasantry, something which threatens the peasantry's position on the market, due to the difference in the productivity of for example, wheat, corn, potatoes, rice, etc., in both types of economy (Rivera, 1988b:95).

According to Rivera, it is difficult to make a global estimate regarding the peasants' contribution to the national food market. It is, however, possible to observe; on one hand, an expansion of the production on large and middle size properties, yet on the other, that subsistence agriculture continues to prevail among the peasants. He deduces that in total value, the peasants produce less basic foods than they consume, supplying the difference with incomes of various types, such as subsidies and wage-labour (Rivera, 1988a:92-93). According to this author, of a total of 300,000 peasants, only some 100,000 are represented on the market. Gómez (1989:8), however, indicates that the peasant sector's participation of the agricultural production compared to the national total was 24.7%. In the vegetable production this percentage amounts to 53%.

In respect to the marginalising of the peasantry to the ecologically poor areas, Rivera (1988a:171) specifically supports, that in the case of the *minifundium*, this tends to be concentrated in zones with marginal lands, on the edges of the central valley and in the far reaches of the country (Norte Chico and IX and X regions). According to his figures, the irrigated land of the *minifundium* only corresponds to 11.6% of the total while, of the total arable the *minifundium* would occupy approximately 20%.

Once again, though the categories of Rivera and Gómez, are not totally comparable (Rivera refers to the *minifundium*, Gómez includes in his estimate also the peasants' group or family exploitation, see Table 2.4), the data that Gómez presents give a somewhat different picture. According to Gómez, 28.1% (58,000) of the total number (206,000) of peasants and *minifundistas* are found located in the irrigated land within the Central valley, where it is possible to find the better lands, and this participation would be a product of the agrarian reform (Gómez, 1989:6).

Socio-economic setting of the study object

Introduction

In this section I will contextualise my study within the greater social structure in which it is immersed: the Canela commune. *Comuneros* and their families compose the majority of the commune's population, and although it is possible to say that in dealing with the *comuneros* we are very much dealing with the commune, they do not, however, constitute the whole population. Thus, the present section treats general socio-economic aspects of the population in the commune, but also its agricultural communities. That is why I will be oscillating principally between the commune and its agricultural communities. The commune's general land structure, including private property, will also be briefly described here.

More than in other chapters, it would be true to say that data on the same topic varies according to the sources that it comes from. When necessary, I will emphasise the differences. Since some sources deliver information on certain topics that others do not, I have to alternate between them. This means that often when discussing and comparing some topics, depending on the source I use, the data on the same item will vary. While the specific information on the agricultural communities originates mainly from IREN (or current CIREN), CBR, RCCBR of SII, and CONAF, the general data for the population of the commune (gender, age, occupation, etc.) originates mainly from INE.

Sometimes, in developing these items, I will also confront them with the data of my survey. Finally, taking into consideration the approximate character of all existing data on the commune and its communities, the need to make my own survey among the *comuneros* in order to get more detailed data on their life conditions will hopefully appear clearly.

Overview of the Chilean Land Tenure Structure and the Socio-Economic Setting

Population and land tenure structure in the commune

The strong emigration that characterises the zone explains perhaps, in part, the variations in the calculations for the population of the agricultural communities and the commune. Another reason may be the difficult accessibility and geographical dispersion of the houses in this predominantly rural commune. According to my own survey made during 1987, of the total of 185 *comuneros* interviewed with their spouses, a minimum of 50% had emigrated at least once. Of these, 40.9% had emigrated between one and two times, 30.1% between three and four times, 19.4% between five and six times, and 9.7% more than seven times. Even though the survey did not require information about the emigration among *comuneros*' children, 77.3% of the *comuneros* gave this information spontaneously. Of this total, 42% had children who had emigrated.

According to IREN (1977 (11):42-43), in 1977 the population of the agricultural communities was 16,029 inhabitants (see Table 2.5, column E). On the other hand, according to INE's 1982 census, the total population of the commune amounted to 10,703 persons (INE, 1982:2). In agreement to the CBR of Illapel, in 1986 it was 11,338 inhabitants (see Table 2.5, column A).

As seen in Table 2.5, IREN's figures are significantly greater, not only from CBR's figures, but also from those of INE. I think that such a difference cannot be explained only by the year. If we examine Table 2.5, we can see that, according to IREN, the total number of *comuneros* with rights in 1977 was 2,021 and that the number of families of non-*comuneros* was 123. Taking the regional average of 5.31 persons per household, given by IREN, we could then estimate that the total of *comuneros* (independently of whether they reside in their communities or not) with their families would total some 10,731 persons. Correspondingly, the 123 families of non-*comuneros* would total some 653 persons. All this makes a figure of 11,384 persons. This is very much less than the 16,029 persons indicated as the total population living in the communities by IREN. If we now take the regional average of 5.31 persons per household only for the *comuneros* that live in the communities, added to the families of non-*comuneros*, the total would be yet smaller (9,515 inhabitants). Apparently, there is an overestimation, especially with respect to the population for both Canela Baja and Canela Alta villages. CBR's figures on population seem to be more appropriate, which does not mean that IREN's other data is not.

Table 2.5 Total population in the agricultural communities, number of *comuneros* with rights, of resident *comuneros*, and of families of non *comuneros*, according to CBR of Illapel (1986), IREN (1977) and number of *comuneros* according to the communities (1979) in the Canela commune

Agricultural communities by areas	A	B	C	D	E	F	G	H	I
CHOAPA									
1. Huentelauquén	1,050	347	200	10	1,272	300	160	10	343
2. Huinchigallego	60	26	12	-	60	24	18	1	37
3. Mincha Sur	740	148	148	-	940	148	148	-	131
4. Mincha Norte	325	65	62	-	450	65	65	9	75
5. Las Barrancas	80	10	3	3	10	10	2	1	18
6. Las Paredes	30	10	3	3	10	10	2	1	18
ATELCURA									
7. Atelcura	200	43	33	7	270	43	33	7	71
8. La Capilla	60	200	10	2	68	20	10	2	32
9. La Leona	30	7	5	1	40	7	7	1	-
10. Cabra Corral	115	28	20	3	100	28	20	3	40
AGUA FRIA									
11. El Pangue	55	25	11	-	64	25	11	-	21
12. Agua Fria Alta	172	70	35	11	262	40	30	15	70
13. Agua Fria Baja	408	181	118	81	560	120	75	-	70
14. Las Tazas	125	32	24	1	150	32	24	1	38
15. El Potrero	115	12	12	11	100	12	12	11	28
16. El Chiñe	25	5	2	3	30	5	-	-	10

Overview of the Chilean Land Tenure Structure and the Socio-Economic Setting

Agricultural communities by areas	A	B	C	D	E	F	G	H	I
THE CANELA RIVERSIDE AREA									
17. Carquindaño	167	30	28	10	182	42	37	-	40
18. Yerba Loco	166	55	30	7	250	55	30	-	55
19. Los Tomes	95	19	19	-	95	19	19	-	19
20. El Almendro	50	10	8	2	50	10	10	-	10
CANELA									
21. Canela Alta	2,800	520	480	80	4,800	246	200	50	-
22. Canela Baja	4,000	668	500	300	5,680	660	660	-	668
23. Canelilla	330	70	60	6	350	70	60	6	83
24. Angostura de Gálvez	140	30	28	-	114	30	28	-	27
Total	11,338	2,431	1,858	544	16,029	2,021	1,669	123	1,886

Source: The author, based on CBR of Illapel (1986); IREN (1977) (2): 26-27; (11): 42-43, Annex no. 2, List no. 1 of the agricultural communities in the commune of Canela (1979)

A: CBR Total population;
D: No. of non *comunero* families;
G: Live in the communities;

B: CBR number of *comuneros* with rights;
E: IREN Total population;
H: No. of non *comunero* families;

C: Live in the communities;
F: IREN no. of *comuneros* with rights;
I : No. of *comuneros* in the communities.

Since, according to CBR, the 1,858 *comuneros* that lived in the communities in 1986, together with the 554 families of non-*comuneros*, total 2,402 families. Thus the average number of persons per family was 4.72.

While the resident *comuneros* with their families would be some 8,769 persons, the 554 non-*comuneros* family groups would add about some 2,567 persons. This means that 22.6% of the population who lives in the communities, and consequently in the commune, was not directly *comunero* families. A large part of this population should correspond to the adult children of *comuneros* who are left without land. According to my survey of 1987, the average number of persons per family among the interviewed *comuneros* was 5.29.

Comparing the total of the columns B and C of CBR, we can also see that 23.6% (573) of the total of the *comuneros* were absent. With their families those absent would add some 2,704 persons, taking CBR's average to 4.72 persons per family. The absenteeism of *comuneros* by areas, and from community to community, can be deduced following the mentioned columns. For example, for the Choapa area, the absenteeism of *comuneros* would be 28.2%, 30.6% for the Atelcura area, 37.8% for the Agua Fría area, 25.4% for the riverside area of the Canela *estero* (small river), and 17.8% for the Canela area. Taking Table 2.5, it is possible to look at the agricultural communities area, which varies from source to source.

The area of the communities is the land the *comuneros* own in a common form, their property. The larger the land in relation to the number of inscribed *comuneros*, the bigger the common land for goat rearing. The amount of hectares per *comunero* varies from community to community. The said relation for all the communities is of 69.5 ha *per capita*, taking as base the data from CBR.

As may be seen in Table 2.6, the agricultural communities of Canela Alta and Canela Baja are the largest in the commune (see in this case IREN's column). They make up about 60% of the total area of the communities (162,772 ha), and 44.2% of the commune, which according to IGM is 221,300 ha. According to the CBR, the agricultural community Canela Baja possesses 37,000 ha. According to the *comuneros*, the community has 30,700 ha, and according to IREN 30,770. In my estimations, I have taken the total of 169,002 ha, of the CBR's figure, minus the 6,230 ha that the agricultural community Canela Baja does not possess.

Table 2.6 The total area of the agricultural communities

Areas	CBR	IREN	Communities
CHOAPA			
1. Huentelauquén	7,426	6,750	7,426
2. Huinchigallego	900	875	930
3. Mincha Sur	3,438	3,437	3,393
4. Mincha Norte	625	625	643
5. Las Barrancas	1,563	1,562	1,465
6. Las Paredes	375	375	470
ATELCURA			
7. Atelcura	2,813	2,812	2,675
8. La Capilla	500	500	455
9. La Leona	125	125	300
10. Cabra Corral	1,250	1,250	1,200
AGUA FRIA			
11. El Pangue	1,077	1,062	1,077
12. Agua Fría Alta	2,645	2,562	2,645
13. Agua Fría Baja	4,832	4,687	4,800
14. Las Tazas	2,375	2,375	2,037
15. El Potrero	2,250	2,250	1,200
16. El Chiñe	2,000	2,000	2,061
THE CANELA RIVERSIDE AREA			
17. Carquindaño	2,813	2,813	2,830
18. Yerba Loca	3,686	3,750	3,686
19. Los Tomes	3,000	3,000	2,700
20. El Almendro	563	562	596
CANELA			
21. Canela Alta	67,000	67,000	67,000
22. Canela Baja	37,000	30,770	30,700
23. Canelilla	4,000	4,000	3,859
24. Angostura de Gálvez	1,438	1,437	1,503
Total	**169,002**	**146,579**	**145,651**

Source: The author, based on CBR of Illapel (1986) IREN (1977); List no. 1 of the Agricultural Communities of the Commune (1979)

The data recorded by IREN, agrees more closely with that of the community itself. Thus, in agreement with these calculations, the total surface of the communities would be of 162,772 ha taking also for granted the other data of the CBR.

Of a total of 162 agricultural communities registered in 1977 by the IREN for the Region IV, only the communities of the Choros and Olla de la Caldera, were larger than Canela Alta. These had an area of 69,250 and 102,312 ha, respectively. At present there are 200 agricultural communities. Jiménez de Tapia, with an area of 40,812 ha was also larger than that of Canela Baja (IREN, 1977 (2):23-27).

The agricultural communities of Canela Alta and Canela Baja comprise as well, 60% of the commune's total population and 52.7% of the *comuneros* (see CBRs column A, Table 2.5). In them, as in the community Agua Fría Baja, is found a relatively large number of non-*comuneros* households; 80 in Canela Alta, 300 in Canela Baja and 81 in Agua Fría Baja. The agricultural community Canela Baja also contains 55.1% of the non-*comuneros* households. This is explained by the fact that the urban village of Canela Baja is located within this community where the administrative and most of the public services are concentrated. It constitutes the largest commercial centre of the commune and is the capital of the commune.

Together, the agricultural communities occupy 77.4% of the total territory of the commune (221,300 ha) providing we follow the IGM (1981:50) and CBR's data about the commune's and the agricultural communities' area, respectively. Thus, the remaining 22.6% is occupied predominantly by private property *fundos*, reserves of *fundos*, parcels and also by ecclesiastic and State properties.

However, if we look closely at the commune's general land structure, the relationship between private and semi-communal property will vary, depending on the year and the source I use. Reference should also be made to IREN's Map (Figure 3.4) in Chapter 3 where the white space denotes the private property of the *haciendas*.

In spite of the agrarian reforms of the 1960-70s, and the latter changes in land tenure structure that occurred in the commune during the Pinochet government, the part of the land that continues to be concentrated in the hands of a few *fundos* is still significant. Following RCCBR and CIREN's data, I have recorded 21 agricultural private properties of over 500 ha, but the number of private properties is higher.

It is necessary to point out, however, that several of the *fundos*, which in Table 2.7 appear as private properties in the examined lists, have become with the indemnification of the agricultural communities' property titles, part of the latter, or have formed independent communities.

Overview of the Chilean Land Tenure Structure and the Socio-Economic Setting

Table 2.7 Fundos and reserves of the Canela Commune, including only those properties of over 500 ha

Property	Owner	Area
1. Hacienda Huentelauquén #	Vial Espantoso C.	3,707.50
2. Reserv 1 PC Millahue #	Vial Espantoso C.	27,620.80
3. Hijuela Lo Gallardo #	Chuminatto R.J.	4,000.00
4. Santa Margarita	Chuminatto R.J.	1,500.00
5. Fundo Santa Amelia	Chuminatto R.J.	800.00
6. Talinay	Cortés Olivares C.	900.00
7. El Totoral #	Toro Robles J.A.	6,132.00
8. Reserv El Totoral #	Fuenzalida, González & Co. Ltd.	2,865.00
9. Reserv Puerto Oscuro #	Echavarría Tagle J.A. & others	2,700.00
10. Puerto Oscuro	Soc. Pereira, Cortés, Broto & Co. Ltd.	11,781.10
11. Las Pameras #	Soc. Dabed Poza Ltd.	3,500.00
12. Fundo La Alcaparra #	Soc. Las Palmas of Mincha Ltd.	4,569.00
13. Fundo Las Palmas #	Soc. Las Palmas of Mincha Ltd.	9,600.00
14. Fundo El Coligue	Sagrico Co. Ltd.	16,231.00
15. Fundo Espíritu Santo #	Cambise Fressero J.	10,000.00
16. El Durazno #	Contreas Contreras E.	15,155.00
17. El Retiro	Díaz Carvajal J.M. Bransch	600.00
18. Los Gallardo #	Villaroel Villaroel L.	3,000.00
19. Las Tazas #	Jorquera Gallardo Bransch	1,249.00
20. Fundo El Arrallán #	Arellano Izquierdo J.	17,786.00
21. Los Tomes #	Echeverría Lizama H.	2,778.00
Total		146,474.40

Source: The author, based on CIREN, List of properties in the commune of Canela (1983)
#: All of the properties marked with this sign correspond to properties valued at more than 1 million Chilean *pesos* in the RCCBR, June 1988. The value of the Chilean *peso* was, in March 1991, 355.38 per $1US. The two highest valuations of these properties correspond to the Huentelauquén *hacienda* at 21,308,719 *pesos* (US$59,960.377), and the Millahue reserve valued at 12,793,090 *pesos* (US$ 35,998.339), both having the same owner. The first is located on the margins of Choapa, which explains its high valuation in comparison to the number of hectares. The *hacienda* Huentelauquén was expropriated from Víal Espantosa during Frei's government (1964-1969), but was given back to him during Pinochet's government.

Communal Land Ownership in Chile

For this reason, the concentration of land in the hands of the *fundos* is less (102,310 ha) than it appears in Table 2.7.

For example, according to the *comunero* Pedro Carvajal, both the *fundos* El Coligue and El Durazno became part of the agricultural community of Canela Alta. The same is true for the *fundo* Espíritu Santo that appears with 10,000 hectares but that, as we will see later on, has become part of the agricultural community of Canela Baja. Los Tomes (2,778 ha) became an agricultural community in 1973.

Table 2.8 Distribution of all forms of agricultural estates by size in the Canela commune, 1983

Range in ha	No. of estates	% of total estates	Total ha	% of total ha	Average size in ha
0-5	784	85.6	1,100.6	0.4	1.4
> 5-10	34	3.7	210.5	0.1	6.2
> 10-20	36	3.9	496.5	0.2	13.8
> 20-40	8	0.9	180.1	0.1	22.5
> 40-50	2	0.2	83.3	0.0	41.7
> 50-70	4	0.4	230.7	0.2	57.7
> 70-100	1	0.1	99.5	0.0	99.5
>100-200	1	0.1	163	0.0	163
>200-500	4	0.4	1,242.7	0.5	310.7
>500	42	4.6	268,436.9	98.6	6,391.4
Total	916	100.0	272,243.8	100.0	297.2

Source: CIREN, based on the SII, REA, updated (1983)

Excluding the land of these four properties (approximately 44,164 ha) that do not make up *fundos* any longer, the remaining 17 *fundos* (102,310 ha) comprises 37.5% of the total of the 272,244 ha, corresponding to the 916 agricultural estates of the Canela commune, if we follow CIREN data from 1983. If, however, we follow IGM's data about the commune's area, that of the mentioned *fundos* will correspond to 46.2%. Accordingly, the total area of the agricultural communities (CBR's 169,000 ha), will be only 53.8%. Independently of the source we take to measure this relation, a great part of the land is still, as mentioned, concentrated in few hands.

The distribution of all the agricultural estates, i.e., private, semi-communal or other, is according to CIREN by size in the commune for the year 1983, listed in Table 2.8.

As can be seen from this table, there are 42 properties of 500 ha or more. Among these 42 properties should be included the 22 agricultural communities that have the above mentioned areas. The remaining 20 estates should then correspond to the *fundos*. The 17 *fundos* of Table 2.7 should in number here represent 1.9% of the 916 estates registered by CIREN.

It should be stressed, once again, that all these figures should be taken as highly provisional. For example, the figures from CIREN about the total area occupied by the 916 agricultural estates are higher than the total extension of the commune given by the IGM (1981:50). As mentioned, according to IGM, the commune had 221,300 ha in 1981, which gives us a difference of 50,943 ha less in comparison with the dates of CIREN. Another example, according to CONAF (1981:41), is that the total extension of the commune makes up 235,272 ha.

Even though the figures from CIREN correspond to 1983, it is possible that they still include the agricultural communities Tunga Norte and Tunga Sur that from 1979 belong to the commune of Illapel (INE, 1982). However, if so, their area does not explain the difference since the agricultural communities Tunga Norte and Sur together make up only 11,625 ha (5,250 and 6,375 ha, respectively) (IREN, 1977 (2):27).

As can be observed from the following figures, the dates from CIREN, according to which the agricultural estates make up 916, do not correspond either with the figures from the RCCBR (June 1988-89), according to which the agricultural estates rose to 951, which makes a difference of 35 more estates. This difference could, however, be explained by the different years.

Table 2.9 Total number of estates in the Canela commune, 1988-89

Urban estates	Agricultural estates	Total	Estates exempt from tax	Total that impose
1,511	951	2,452	2,338 (95.4%)	114 (4.6%)

Source: RCCBR (June, 1988-89)

Comparing the total of the estates in the commune with that of the year 1929 (Table 2.10), it would appear that there are 569 less agricultural estates in the commune. This decrease, however, is due to the fact that the commune included, up to 1979, the Tunga Norte and Tunga Sur communities, which now belong to the Illapel commune. This would explain the apparent decrease in the number of agricultural estates in the commune.

Table 2.10 Total number of estates in the Mincha commune (now Canela), 1929

Urban estates	Agricultural estates	Total	Estates exempt from tax	Total that impose
282	1,520	1,802	11 (0.6%)	1,791 (99.4%)

Source: RA, commune of Mincha (1929)

What is not clear, however, either from CIREN's (1983) or from the RCCBR's list (1988-89) is whether, in the inclusion of the agricultural communities as estates, the area of the *hijuelas* belonging to the *comuneros* is discounted. If not, certain properties should be counted twice. Anyway, if that were the case, its extension is not significant. The 784 estates that in the list of CIREN have 0-5 ha and that, if they correspond to the *hijuelas* of the *comuneros*, only makes up 1,100 ha, which correspond to 0.4% of the total area of the communes estates.

Considering indeed, that only the *comuneros* of the 24 agricultural communities make up 2,431 and that in theory, the majority of them have one *hijuela*, the total number of agricultural estates for the whole commune should be higher than the total number of *comuneros*. That the total number of agricultural estates in the commune only makes up 916 or 951 could be explained, on one side, by the fact that the *hijuelas* are considered within the communities. On the other hand, it could also be explained by the fact that there are many *comuneros* who have not registered their *hijuelas*. The reason for that is, as some *comuneros* manifested, the 'fear that the land will be taken'. That is the case, for example, of one of the surveyed *comunero* who has more than 40 ha distributed between several *hijuelas*, but only had one *hijuela* registered in the CBR.

To now breakdown the commune's population according to gender, age, occupation, etc., I will refer to INE's census from 1982. The figures of the total of the population will vary with respect to that indicated previously. Here, I will sometimes compare them with the data of my survey. However, based on the general statistical information obtained from the interviewed, it is possible to say that they, with the exception of the population of the urban areas of the commune, show the typical features of a majority rural population. There are high rates of illiteracy. Furthermore, the family structure is composed not only by the nuclear family but also by other relatives. There is a high percentage of people older than 50 years old and a high percentage of women who assume both the roll of *jefe de hogar* (household's breadwinner) and *dueña de casa*, (household's owners). The concept *jefe de hogar* stands normally for breadwinner, but within a patriarchal system this concept is much wider, representing authority and decisions making. However, when the man dies, if there are no adult sons, the woman assumes this role. So, a woman can thus be *jefe de hogar* and *dueña de casa* (household's owner). There is also a low standard of living and a lack of electricity supply. The same pattern that distinguishes rural from urban areas in a national context is also reproduced within its communes.

Urban and rural population

According to INE (1982:2), the commune's total population (10,703) represents 2.5% of Region IV and 15.3% of the Choapa province. Some 82.3% of the commune's population live in the rural area, with the remaining 17.7% living in small urban centres. The commune has four urban villages, none with more than 1,000 inhabitants. INE defines a village (*aldea*) as:

> an urban entity that poses an amount of population between 301 and 1,000 inhabitants (INE, 1982:XXXV).

Of the remaining 41 populated localities registered by INE in the commune, three are entered in the category of a small village (*villorios*) and 38 would be in the category of hamlets (*caseríos*). A small village or *villorio* corresponds to:

> a rural entity that has more than 20 grouped houses, as long as its population surpasses 100 inhabitants (INE, 1982: XXVI).

A hamlet is:

> a set of mutually nearby rural houses, located generally in connection with a road or roads confluence, and that in its site are independent of a specific

agricultural exploitation. It must have between 5 and 20 houses and its population should not be superior to 100 inhabitants (INE, 1982: XXVI).

For the Choapa province, the rural/urban distribution of the population is almost the same as in the Canela commune, or 80.1% and 19.9%, respectively. For the Region, however, this relationship is 50.7% and 49.3%, respectively (IGM, 1981: 50). Thus it follows that the Canela commune is eminently rural. Of the total of interviewed *comuneros* in 1987, 30.8% belonged to the urban villages Canela Alta and Baja, while the remaining 69.2% belonged to the rural areas.

As seen in Table 2.11, the male population in the commune in 1982 outnumbered the female by a factor of 1.04 man to every woman. However, as seen, the ratio of men to women in the four urban villages differs from that of the commune in general, showing in some cases a clear gender disproportion. There are 2.8% and 15.5% more women than men in Canela Alta and Canela Baja, respectively. In Huentelauquén and Mincha, on the other hand, there are 32.5% and 9.8% more men than women. This tendency would suggest that emigration among women is greater than among men. Contrary to men, most young women go south to the big cities were they sell their labour as domestic employees.

Of the total of 185 interviewed *comuneros*, 65.9% were men and 34.1% women. Of the former, 92.6% were so-call household breadwinners (*jefe de hogar*). Of the total of 63 interviewed women, 33.3% were exclusively so-called household owners (*dueñas de casa*) while the remainder 66.7% assumed both roles.

Table 2.11 Population by gender in the Canela commune and its main urban villages, 1982

Villages	Total	Men	Women	Distance from Canela Baja (km)
Canela Alta	357	176	181	8
Canela Baja	878	402	476	-
Huentelauquén	407	243	164	32
Mincha	253	133	120	43
(Total Commune	10,703	5,468	5,235)	

Source: The author, based on data from INE (1982)

Literacy

The illiteracy index rate for people over 15 years of age in the commune is 26.6% (1,742 of 4,800) (INE, 1982:3-4). The commune has the largest illiteracy index of the Choapa province (11.9%) and of Region IV (11.4%). As a definition of 'literate', INE considers:

> all the persons capable of reading and writing a simple paragraph (INE, 1982:XXX).

Although it is certain that a person who knows how to read and write a simple paragraph cannot be considered as thoroughly illiterate, many of these persons are in reality 'social illiterates'. In practice it would be very difficult for them, to give just one example, to fill in a bureaucratic form by themselves. Among the interviewed *comuneros*, almost 50% were illiterate, and 67% were over 51 years of age.

Housing

INE distinguishes between housing and household. Housing refers to the physical construction, which harbours the household(s). Thus a housing unit can harbour more than a household. According to INE, a particular household:

> embraces all the members of a particular housing units living under family regime, satisfying in common their nutritional needs. It is constituted, often, by the Family head, his relatives (the wife or cohabitant, children, grandsons, nephews, parents, father-in-law, daughters-in-law, etc.), the allied, the boarders in number not superior to five and the domestic service that the household lodge (INE, 1982: XXX).

The total of the commune's households (2,203) is slightly higher than the number of dwelling units (2,181). That is to say, more than one household inhabited by some house units. This relationship should not hide the fact that a household, as INE's definition itself emphasises, embraces an extended family structure. Without ignoring that kinship bonds in rural zones could be stronger than in the cities, the agglomeration in which parents, children, grandsons, sons-in-law, daughters-in-law, nephews and other familiar live, is mainly the product of the dominant socio-economic conditions in the zone. This compels several families to organise around one household/housing, instead of several. According to my survey, in 50% of the 179 households with more than a person, there also lived other persons not belonging to the nuclear family. Most of these were relatives, and of them, the majority were grandchildren.

The standard in both houses and households is generally low. Electricity is to be found only in the urban villages and even there it is not in every house. Electricity supply among the interviewed *comuneros* was 19% in 1987, being centred in Canela Baja and Canela Alta. The percentage of *comuneros* who use gas for food preparation was 44.3% and of this, 54.9% corresponded to Canela Alta and Baja.

Dealing with availability of water and where it comes from, according to INE, of all inhabited housing units (2,181), only 18.2% receive piped water, while the remainder 81.8% does not (to show the availability and origin of the water in the commune, INE relates it to the housing, while to show the availability of water closets and the disposal of waste waters, it relates it to households). The former units are to be found in the urban villages. Of this (397), 86.3% receive water from the public net, 10.3% from a well or noria (or chain pump) and 3.2% from other origin. Considering the housing units that do not receive piped water (1,784 or 81.79%), 70% receive it from wells or norias.

Thus to summarise, 57.3% of the commune's total housing units (1,250 of 2,181) have access to water only through the traditional wells or noria system. The same relationship for all Region IV is of 10% (INE, 1982:76).

Not very different is the situation dealing with the availability of water closets and disposal of wastewater. Of the total (2,203) of particular households with present persons, 84.4% (1,905) have the availability of a water closet. Indeed, of this total, 95.6% have privies and only 3.5% (67) water-closets have disposal of waste water through the sewer or septic pit system (INE, 1982:7). It is pertinent to stress, that most of the few particular households that have a septic pit, only a few, according to my observations, use it to dispose of waste water originating from the kitchen. This is poured away in the patios, outside of the house or in separate places, generally in the river, which contributes to its contamination. The availability of water closets for Region IV is 93.6%. Of this total 51.7% have a privy and the remaining 46.2% have water closets with disposal of wastewater through the sewer or septic pit system.

Age distribution

38.9% of the commune's population is under 15 years of age (4,161 persons). Most persons older than 15 years of age, who do not continue their studies in the secondary school, enter the category of the economically active population. The economically active population is according to INE, constituted:

> by persons of 15 years and more of age who were found to be employed or unemployed during the reference period (week before the census) (INE, 1982:XXX).

Table 2.12 Population by age groups in the Canela commune, 1982

Categories by age	Total by age	% of the total
0- 5	1,592	14.87
6-14	2,569	24.00
15-24	1,979	18.49
25-64	3,774	35.26
>65	789	7.37
Total	10,703	100.00

Source: Based on data from INE (1982)

INE's occupational situation

According to Table 2.13, the population of 15 years and older totals 6,542 persons, representing 61.2% of the commune's total population (10,703). Of them, only 49.6% (3,245) is, according to INE, within the economically active population, while the remaining 50.4% would correspond to the non-economically active population (house owners, students, retired, etc.) (INE, 1982:XXXI).

Of the economically active population, 88.6% were employed, while 11.3% were not. If we analyse the table from another perspective, we will get another picture about the occupational situation in the commune.

Let us consider as an economically active population all those between 15 and 64 years old. This is because a large part of the group that INE indicates, as non-economically active population, corresponding to the youths of 15 to 24 years of age, does not continue in the secondary school. We will find that the economically active population of the commune should be 5,753 persons, and would represent 53.8% of the total of the commune's population. Hopefully, I am not exaggerating when I include the youths of 15 to 24 years of age in the economically active population. According to the Municipality (Diagnóstico, MM, 1985:54), the theoretical demand of secondary school was in 1982, of 1,880 pupils. The vast majority of these pupils were not able to attend this level outside the commune, passing at that time, consequently to integrate in the economically active population. There is from the 1990s, an agricultural high school. However, according to the Chilean law, it is not obligatory to continue in secondary school.

Table 2.13 Population of 15 years of age and more, according to occupational situation (occupied-vacant) in the Canela commune, 1982

	Total	%
1. Population of 15 years and more	6,542	100.00
2. Outside economically active population	3,297	50.3 (2:1)
3. Economically active population	3,245	49.6 (3:1)
A. Occupied	2,877	88.6 (A:3)
B. Vacant	368	11.3 (B:3)

Source: The author, based on data from INE (1982)

If from these 5,753 persons, whom I have considered economically active, we subtract the 2,877 indicated as occupied by INE, the unemployment index would be 50% and not 11.3%. But this unemployment index of 50% is not the case, as we will see below. I opt for including within economically active population those people that INE locates outside it for two reasons. First, because many of these persons, which correspond in large part to *comuneros'* children, help these in their agricultural labours. Second, if there were other sources of salaried labour in the commune, a large part of this labour force would probably be occupied in those. Youths, who have never before had salaried work, have no right to any unemployment support, nor does any state social support system exist to help them to manage economically. But let us continue with the statistics of INE and see how the 2,877 occupied of the commune are distributed according to economic branches.

Overview of the Chilean Land Tenure Structure and the Socio-Economic Setting

Occupation by branches

INE's economic branch 1, which includes agriculture, hunting, forestry and fishing, gives the low figure of 645 persons. They would represent 22.4% of the commune's total employed labour force, which contrasts with 49.7% occupied within the economic branch corresponding to communal, social and personal services. Seen from that perspective, the principal labour source of the commune would be that of the services, while the primary activities - agriculture in this case - would only be secondary.

Table 2.14 Occupied by economic branch in the Canela commune, 1982

Economic branches	Total by economic branch	% in each branch in respect of total of occupied
1. Agriculture, hunting, silviculture and Fishing	645	22.41
2. Mines and quarries	160	5.56
3. Industry and manufacture	70	2.43
4. Electricity and gas	2	0.06
5. Construction	385	13.68
6. Trade, restaurants and hotels	106	3.68
7. Transportation, storage and Communications	46	1.54
8. Financial establishments, real estate Goods, insurance, services to the Companies	1	0.03
9. Communal, social and personal services	1,430	49.70
10. Unspecified activities	32	1.11
Total occupied	**2,877**	**100.00**

Source: Based on data from INE (1982)

According to my estimates, the labour force occupied within the economic branch 1 (Table 2.14) is considerably higher. If we recapture the data of the CBR, the *comuneros* living in the commune in 1986 were 1,858. As *comuneros* their principal occupation is agriculture, and the occupied in branch 1 should be at least 1,858, without recording those within the agricultural private property sector, or those who are occupied with fishing (categories that also would have to enter INE's branch 1). It is difficult to specify the number of those employed in the *fundos*, reserves of *fundos*, plots and other minor agricultural properties of the commune. Part of the labour in these properties can be constituted by *comuneros* that sell their labour force in these temporarily; part of these private owners are also *comuneros* of the agricultural communities.

As specified before, based on RCCBR, I have recorded 21 agricultural private properties, taking only those over 500 ha, which means that their number is higher. The labour force in fishing should be, according to my calculations, between 30 and 50 persons during summer. The 1,858 *comuneros* who live in the communities and who consequently are occupied within agriculture would correspond to 57.3% of the commune's economically active population estimated by INE (3,245) and to 30.6% of that estimated by me (5,753). Basing itself on INE's 1970 census, CONAF (1981:41), indicates that in that year, agriculture occupied 52.8% of the commune's economically active population. This figure differs radically from that of INE for 1982, which estimated the percentage of those occupied within agriculture to be 22.4%.

Even the above mentioned figure of 30.6% can be considered as being too low, given the predominance of agricultural labour. If we add to each *comunero,* minimally, one person who helps him in his labour, the proportion of those occupied in agriculture would rise to 3,516, representing then 61.1% of the population that I considered economically active. This figure would be more accurate considering the agricultural and rural character of the zone.

How can the big difference existing between the 645 occupied within INE's economic branch 1 and the 1,858 *comuneros* that would have to enter within the same branch be explained? As I have already indicated, the low figure of occupied in this branch registered by INE's census, may partially have its explanation in the fact that the period in which the censuses are realised, the first week of April. This coincides with a period of low agricultural activity and, therefore, the corresponding labour force within this branch was thus unemployed or occupied within other activities.

Let me now analyse the economic branch 9, corresponding to services. This branch, that according to INE occupies 1,430 persons, is very wide, encompassing a series of labours that often hide unemployment or underemployment. This category mixes equally, the salaried social and municipal services with those that are not. For example: 9.1. Public administration and defence, 9.2. Sanitation services and similar, 9.3. Social

Services, 9.4. Diverse services, 9.5 Personal and housing services (9.5.3. domestic employees, laundresses, baby-sitters, shoe repairs, electric, cars, watches, leather repair shops or service stations, etc.), 9.6. International and other extraterritorial organisms. The assorted range of occupations that enter branch 9 would explain the high figure of occupied in the commune within the services.

On my part, I have recorded a number not greater than 200 occupied within the municipal services and other services, such as health, post office, civil register, etc., which constitute the salaried occupations in the commune. From this can be deduced that the remaining 1,230 occupied within the economic branch 9 would be mainly within the sub item 9.5 of personal and housing services. This is to say domestic employees, laundresses, so-called baby-sitters, etc.

Taking this theoretically approach as being correct, to the total of 1,430 occupied within the economic branch 9 given by INE, we would add a further 1,858 *comuneros*. To the remaining of 802 occupied within the other economic branches (1-8 and 10) of INE would give a total of 4,082 occupied for the commune. This total agrees better with the total of 5,753 of the commune's economically active population. The comparison of these figures would show that the unemployment in the commune was about 30% in 1982, the year of the census.

Economic activities: a closer view

The principal economic activities of the commune are based upon agriculture. The commune lacks stable sources of employment apart from those related to the social and municipal services, which constitute the salaried occupations in the commune. Thus, the strongest link of men and women in the commune is with the land, not because irrigated land is abundant and of good quality, but because it is the main resource of which they have possession, and on which they depend for their survival. Their forebears were also tied to the land.

The minerals are of secondary importance, a source of subsidiary labour, though for those devoted to mining it can mean an important source of cash income, compared with those originated from agricultural activities. The sea and its resources have yet smaller importance for the commune. To specify the principal activities of the commune I will begin with those of smaller importance.

Fishing. Although the commune has approximately 60 km of coast, some suitable coves for fishing and a rich variety of edible marine species, fishing lacks importance for the commune's inhabitants. It seems rather that they are inclined towards the Provenzal proverb, "Praises the sea and stays in the land" (Braudel, 1981, Vol. 1:13). The explanation of this phenomenon lies in the tradition that the *comuneros* have inherited, and with the fact that, except for Angostura de Gálvez and Huentelauquén, situated on the coast, all the communities are located in the interior of the commune. Until quite recently, many peasants did not know the sea, in spite of living in one of the narrowest passages between the mountain and the sea (approximately 90 km) in the country.

In two main coves of the commune, commercial but rudimentary fishing is practised: Puerto Oscuro and Puerto Manso. The number of fishermen varies, and increases when restrictions to fish the *loco* are lifted, *Loco* being an edible shellfish of the Pacific Ocean. Fishermen amount to between 30 and 50, according to my own observations. According to CONAF (1981:44), they amount to about 80. With few exceptions, these fishermen are not native of the commune, and often originate in the fishing localities Los Vilos and Tongoy nearby.

The product of fishing is either bought directly in the coves by merchants and taken to the markets of the central zone, or sold by the same fishermen in Los Vilos, from where it is also sent to the central zone. The fishermen own their boats, artisan but motorised, and the other implements for fishing. Each boat generally requires a fisherman and two auxiliaries.

The conditions of the fishermen in these coves, especially in Puerto Manso, are extremely poor with respect to housing. They live in huts, without electricity, running water, and with minimal utensils and implements. The alcohol consumption among these fishermen in their free time is high, in part due to the low temperature they have to endure during the winter, though they also drink in summer, absence of family, the lack of other activities and isolation in general. Their women and children only join them during the summer, when the children are on vacation.

Though I do not know the income of these fishermen, there is no doubt that if I take in consideration the time in which the restrictions are lifted to fish *loco*, their income is higher than that an average *comunero* could dream of earning from his land. According to what some fishermen expressed, when they can fish *loco*, their monthly revenue can rise to 150,000-200,000 Chilean *pesos* or more (approximately 375 to 500 US dollars). The commercial exploitation of *loco* has considerably diminished the number of this appreciated shellfish, not only in the commune, but countrywide. In 1988 for example, *loco* extraction was only permitted during four days. Even so, several fishermen working in Chiloé, south of Chile, to give an example, indicated that they had earned almost three million Chilean *pesos* in the four days that the restrictions were lifted (Informe Especial, Televisión Nacional, 25 de Agosto de 1988).

The economic marginality of fishing in the Canela commune is common throughout Region IV in spite of 440 km of coastline. The artisan fishermen (3,133) represent only 2.8% of the labour force of Region IV (CONAF, 1981:44).

Industry. If this is defined as modern industry, it is different from fishing, inasmuch as it is totally non-existent. The oldest artisan industry, however, is represented by a small amount of butter and cheese production from cow's milk in Huentelauquén. The same processes, also in artisan form, involve local papayas. This small factory belongs to a proprietor who has the most highly valued private landed properties of the commune. In Huentelauquén Norte, as in other agricultural communities, small, artisan goat cheese factories have begun. There are, however, certain prospects of growth, thanks to the improvement of cattle food that it is being made to the shrub plantations forage (Atriplex repanda and Atriplex nummularia), implemented by projects subsidised by CONAF or some ONGs. These artisan cheese factories depend on rainfall and consequently they stay inactive during the dry years. According to INE, the number occupied within branch 3 (industry and manufacture) corresponds to some 70 persons.

Mining. During the nineteenth century the major Chilean mining fortunes arose (silver and copper) in Region IV, giving rise to capitalism in the country. At present, mining, in spite of important iron, copper, gold and silver mines, does not constitute a major labour demand in the region. It does not occupy more than 2.6% of the economically active population (INE, 1982:4-5).

Mining has no great relevance as a labour source in the Canela commune either. With the exception of two mines of certain importance, there are no mines of industrial character. One of these is Planta de Hornillos, located in the Northeast of the commune, with 300 monthly tons of elaboration capacity. From the 1990s there exists also a mine of calcareous stone of greater capacity belonging to Mining Co. Quelón Ltd. who extract some 17,000 tons monthly (Mahan and González, 1994:13), and employ some 60 persons. Artisan mining does have a certain economic importance as a complementary income source for those *comuneros* who wash gold in their free time. Gold panning is done locally and bought up mainly by ambulant, local merchants in the commune, or others through the traditional barter system (*trueque*) in which the peasants are normally the losers.

In 1981 there were six mills in the commune, devoted to the processing of gold minerals employing some 24 persons (CONAF, 1981:44). According to INE, 160 people were occupied in mines and quarries in 1982. The existence of 63 mining grants (SNGM, 1986:365-367) in the commune shows, at least in theory, the importance of the commune's mining resources. These 63 grants, however, do not necessarily mean that they are being exploited. The number of exploited grants is much smaller. Of 63 mining grants, only 19.3% are in hands of people residing in the commune. The remaining concessionaires have their residences outside the commune; 32.2% in Santiago, 38.8% in Illapel and the remaining 9.7% in other places. From this we can conclude that in terms of mining grants, the relevance of mining for the commune's inhabitants is limited, as it is in terms of sources of labour.

Trade. Trade is composed of small stores that are found mainly in the four urban villages. They supply the population of the hamlets and small villages as well as the population of the urban villages. The transient trade in the rural zones is composed mainly of the same established merchants as in the villages. The rest of the trade is composed of small restaurants and lodgings in the villages. According to INE, occupation within branch 6 (trade, restaurants and hotels) amounts to some 106 persons.

The number of commercial licenses (excluding those of restaurants and alcohol) amounts to 105 (Lista Pat. Com., MM, 1987). Of those, 40 are concentrated in Canela Baja, 21 in Canela Alta, 18 in Huentelauquén, while the remaining 26 are distributed throughout the rest of the commune. There are 53 restaurants and alcohol licenses, of which 16 are concentrated in Canela Baja, 6 in Canela Alta and 6 in Huentelauquén. The remaining 25 are distributed in the rest of the commune. 13 licenses are for restaurants and pensions or housing.

The number of ambulant merchants amounts to 50, that is, approximately 48% of the merchants who possess licenses of established trade and practise also, in parallel form, ambulant trade. The total of 158 licenses (105 commercial and 53 of restaurants and alcohol) correspond to 120 persons. From this we can deduce that 38 licenses are from proprietors who have more than one license and therefore, more than one business.

Restaurants and alcohol licenses relative to the total of commercial licenses make up 33.5% in the commune. For the Canela Baja village this relationship is 40%. Of 12 restaurants registered in the Licenses' list of the Municipality, eight are located in localities close to the North Pan-American, their service directed mainly to the traffic that use this route.

Communal and other services. The labour force within the communal services account for some 140 persons. Of these, 20 persons work in the Municipality, seven in the kindergarten and 104 in 37 educational establishments. The municipalisation, both of the educational and health services accomplished by law in 1981, has considerably increased the municipal personnel. Until 1973 the functions of the Municipality were restricted, and its personnel was composed of the mayor, secretary and treasurer. Its principal occupations were limited to the issuing of licenses of various types, whence came the main income of the Municipality. The increase of services related to the administration of the Municipality did not mean a greater increase of occupation for the commune's labour force, given the relatively specialised character of the occupational categories that the Municipality requires. Thus, of the total of 20 personnel in 1988, 11 were from other communes, occupying the most important and better-paid jobs. The other existing services in the commune employed about 60 persons. The total of the labour force of the commune, occupied in permanent and salaried services of various classes does not surpass some 200. Further information about other services in the commune is to be found in Appendix 3.

Agriculture and cattle-raising. In this section, I will only give some basic data referring to these two items since they will be partially developed in the next chapter.

Within agriculture, goat and sheep rearing show the greater development prospects. Cultivation, dry and irrigated, occupies a secondary position to cattle-raising. This is so because (see Table 3.2), only 4.5% of the commune's total area corresponds to the category of arable land, while the remaining 95.4% is unsuitable for cultivation. Furthermore, the irrigated area corresponds to 0.4% of the total. Accordingly, and as Table 2.15 shows, in the 24 agricultural communities of the Canela commune, goat and sheep rearing prevails. In second and third place would be the equine and bovine cattle, respectively. The two largest agricultural communities of Canela Alta and Canela Baja have 62% (34,300) of all the goats and sheep, 49.7% (2,640) of the total of equine and 41.3% (1,500) of the bovines.

Table 2.15 Cattle existence in the agricultural communities of the Canela commune, 1986

Areas	No. of sheep and goats	No. of Equine	No. of Bovine
CHOAPA			
1. Huentelauquén	3,200	600	400
2. Huinchigallego	100	30	25
3. Mincha Sur	1,500	444	420
4. Mincha Norte	600	186	200
5. Las Barrancas	200	30	30
6. Las Paredes	105	10	15
ATELCURA			
7. Atelcura	1,155	99	110
8. La Capilla	350	30	20
9. La Leona	175	15	13
10. Cabra Corral	700	60	50
AGUA FRIA			
11. El Pangue	385	33	40
12. Agua Fría Alta	1,225	105	100
13. Agua Fría Baja	2,400	354	300
14. Las Tazas	840	72	60
15. El Potrero	805	69	40
16. El Chiñe	175	15	5
THE CANELA RIVERSIDE AREA			
17. Carquindaño	2,000	84	50
18. Yerba Loco	1,050	90	46
19. Los Tomes	665	57	45
20. El Almendro	350	20	8
CANELA			
21. Canala Alta	16,800	1,140	600
22. Canela Baja	17,500	1,500	900
23. Canelilla	2,100	180	100
24. Angostura de Gálvez	980	84	35
Total	55,360	5,307	3,632

Source: The author, based on data from CBR of Illapel (1986)

Overview of the Chilean Land Tenure Structure and the Socio-Economic Setting

The average ownership of goat and sheep per resident *comunero* is 29.8, of equine 2.8 and of bovines 1.9. 58.3% (14) of the communities have an average of 35 goats and sheep per resident *comunero*. The communities of El Potrero, El Chiñe and Carquindaño have an average greater than this with 67, 87.5 and 71.4 goats and sheep per *comunero*, respectively. The highest average of bovines owned by a *comunero* is to be found in the communities of El Pangue (3.2), Atelcura (3.3), El Potrero (3.3) and Mincha Norte (3.2).

It is necessary to underline that the cattle presented in Table 2.15, only relates to the agricultural communities. Therefore, the commune's total cattle stock would be greater if we include the number of cattle of the private property. According to INE the number of bovines for the province was 9,130 (INE, 1986/87:10).

Consequently, the bovine cattle of the 24 agricultural communities of the commune of Canela represent 39.7% of the total number of bovines existing in the province. In other words, the biggest number of bovine cattle is raised on private property.

Goat exploitation is destined mainly for cheese production, jerked meat (*charqui*) and leather. Of these, cheese production is the most important. According to the president of the Regional Council of the Medical-veterinary Association of Region IV, goat cheese and meat was exported to Santiago in clandestine form due to the legal prohibitions that until the beginning of the 1990s forbid the sale of cheese outside the region. This is because of the low sanitary conditions in which it was produced. This situation meant that for a long time there was considerable wastage:

> quantities of protein resources (milk, cheese, meat, jerked-meat) which should arrive to a large bulk of consumers in optimum sanitary conditions, through normal marketing channels, in order not to under-utilise 600,000 kilos of cheese and meat that are produced annually in the region, so that the peasants may improve their scarce income (Revista Cauce, semana 21 al 27 de Sept. 1987:34).

3 On Agricultural Communities and their Geographical Setting

Introduction

The focus of the present chapter is on both the geographical setting and organisation of the agricultural communities covered by this study. First in order to contextualise the study within a greater geographical framework, I will give the general physical description of the commune of Canela where the agricultural community Canela Baja and the former *hacienda* El Totoral are situated. After I have discussed the geographical setting of the studied commune, it seems appropriate in this chapter to include a factual characterisation of the form, i.e., how the semi-communal land ownership of the agricultural communities is organised. Hopefully, this will help to better understand the institution that these agrarian collectives conform to.

The description of the physical environment begins with Norte Chico since what is valid here, is mainly true for the remainder of the area. However, some differences exist from commune to commune, or even within the same commune. The purpose of such a description is to give an understanding of the living conditions of a population that bases its sustenance mainly on agricultural labour. In the life of the agricultural communities of Norte Chico, the influence of the physical environment is not insignificant.

Two axes define the position of this region. From north to south, the region lays between the Atacama Desert of the Norte Grande, and the Central Valley of Chile. Thus, the ecological balance of the region is important also for the Central Valley. From west to east, Norte Chico lays between the Pacific Ocean and the Los Andes mountain chain. It belongs to the region of Transverse Valleys, which is defined:

> for the presence of river valleys that cross it from east to west and that have water the whole year, giving origin to extensive fertile land /.../ The coast band is more vast and does not crash with the mountainous /.../ raising

slowly up to the pre-mountainous and high mountainous region (Mostny, 1985:51).

The valleys of Elqui, Limarí and Choapa also constitute the three provinces of Region IV. The topography of the region is very accentuated and presents four morphological units; the high mountains, the middle mountains, the coastal band and the transverse valleys. The Canela commune belongs to the morphological units of the low middle mountains in the interior, to the coastal band in the littoral region and to the transverse valleys in the sub-area Choapa. The middle mountains are divided into high, middle and low. The middle high mountains are not higher than 3,000 m, therefore the middle low mountain, to be found in the interior of the commune, would not be higher than 2,000 m.

The commune is located in the northeast of the province of Choapa, between the latitude 31°30' and 31°40' South and longitude 71°15' and 71°35' West (CONAF, 1981:6). The administration centre of the commune is Canela Baja, located some 16 km to the east of the North Pan-American highway and some 30 km from Illapel, capital of the province. Canela is one of 15 communes in Region IV, bordering with five others (see Figure 3.1). These are, to the north by the communes of Ovalle and Punitaqui, to the east by the communes of Combarbalá and Illapel, to the south by the commune of Los Vilos and to the West by the Pacific Ocean. The area of the commune is of 2,213 km^2, representing 5.5% of the Region (39,647 km^2) and 21.9% of the province of Choapa (10,079.8 km^2) (IGM, 1981:50).

The ecosystem

Characterised by the existence of rows of hills that run transversally from the Andean mountains to the coast in Region IV, the hills dominate the valleys. Most of the region lacks irrigation, with 75% of it consisting of hilly and non-irrigated land (*secano*). Its agricultural resources were estimated by CIDA (1966:125) to be 2.3 millions hectares, of which only 5% is irrigated. However, of the Canela commune's total are, only 0.4% (1,024 ha) has irrigation (CONAF, 1981:41). Due to these conditions agricultural output is low, and goat rearing is the predominant agricultural activity.

Figure 3.1 The communes of Region IV (Coquimbo)

The climate of the coast is characterised by its abundant clouds and fog and the interior by its transparent skies, great atmospheric dryness and strong contrasts in the temperature. However, there are several micro-climates within this region. These micro-climates are the result of a variety of factors:

> ... the relief, the exposition, the rocks, the water bodies and the vegetation itself, varying the quality and intensity of energy, light and heat, reducing the speed of the wind near to soil, sheltering the flower and micro-flora, the fauna and the micro-fauna, favouring the cycles: mineral, of the organic material, and of the humus and the evolution of the soil, especially the structure of this and its capacity to infiltrate and retain the water (IREN, 1977(10):41).

Of the three most basic elements for agriculture, sun, rain and land, the most abundant is the sun. Rain is scarce, however, and the soil is meagre. In this arid or semi-arid climate of the Mediterranean type, the principal problem for agriculture is the shortage of rain. In fact, the economic survival of the *comuneros*, and all farmers in general, depends largely on its 'caprices'. The rain is problematic not only because of its shortage, but also because of its torrential and variable qualities. During 25 years (1935-1960s) of observed rainfall in the commune, the most frequent percentages were distributed between the classes: dry (8 or 32%) normal (7 or 28%) and rainy (7 or 28%) (CONAF, 1981:10-11, Table 1). The rainfall may be very heavy for a limited number of hours or days whilst there may be long periods without rain. In 1987, for example, 54% of the total (286.5 mm of 530.8 mm) of the rain in the year fell in only eleven days in July, while in September in eight days only 4 mm fell (Direction of Waters from the Ministry of Public Works for Region IV, Province of Choapa, Station Illapel, 1985-1987. Courtesy of A. Castillo). The quantity of rainfall also varies considerably from year to year. While 1985 was very dry, 1986 was dry and 1987 extremely wet. In theory, the average rainfall (222 mm) in the zone during the years considered to be statistically normal, should be sufficient for cereal production. For the farmer, however, this does not necessarily correspond to a good year, since for agriculture what is of fundamental importance is a good distribution of rain.

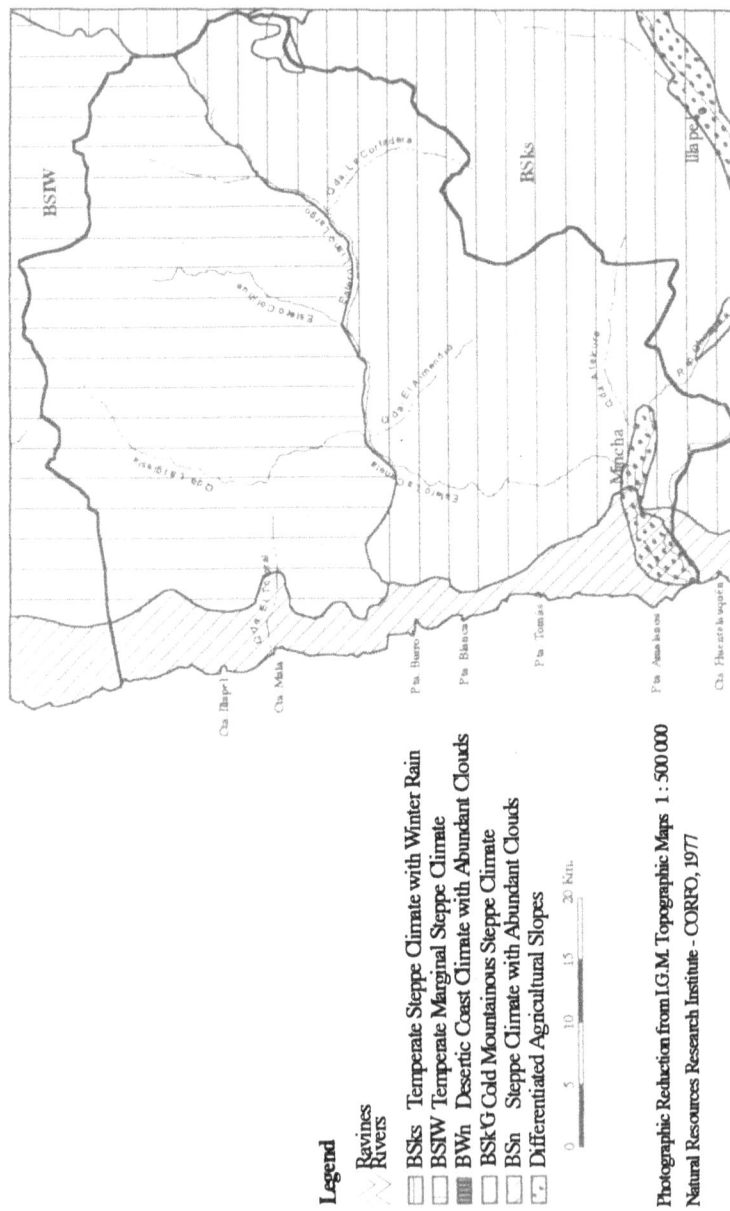

Figure 3.2 Types of climate in the Canela Commune

The very heavy (torrent-like) rainfall is another decisive element for the vegetation and the soils. If the rainfall is very heavy, the infiltration is insufficient, causing inundation, as happened in 1987 with disastrous consequences for the sowings and for the soils, aggravating the already existing erosion of the Norte Chico. To the drought and the general aridity of the climate must be added the effect of solar energy on the surface of bare soils which can be highly sterilising, since the temperatures reach during several hours a day in many days of the year, hinder all life, bar that of the most elemental organisms (IREN, 1977(10):38).

The hydrography

Taking the shortage and irregularity of the rains into consideration, the hydrographic resources, also of fundamental importance for agriculture, are not precisely examples of abundance in the commune of Canela. Of them, only the River Choapa belongs to the category of systems principally snow-pluvial with origin in the Andes Mountains (IREN, 1978, Vol. 1:53). The River Choapa is located in the southern part of the commune and crosses the agricultural communities of this sub-area, with exception of the community Las Paredes. The area of the watershed of the River Choapa is 8,239 km^2, and its middle volume is of 11.4 m^3/s (IREN, 1978, Vol. 1:51, 54).

The water resources of the northern part of the commune - where the agricultural communities Canela Baja and Alta are located - are the *esteros* (small rivers) and *quebradas* (ravines), all with irregular courses. Of the *esteros*, the Canela is the most important and belongs to the secondary system tributary, generally pluvial with pre-Andes or pre-mountain origin (IREN, 1978, Vol. 1:51-52). Its principal tributaries are the Espíritu Santo, Llano Largo and Colihue. The Canela provides seasonal irrigation to the scarce alluvial lands of the Canela Baja and Canela Alta villages. The basin surface area of La Canela is 1,363 km^2 (IREN, 1978, Vol. 1:54). It flows into the River Choapa, 3 km off the coast. The Espíritu Santo flows into the La Canela in the Northeast entry of the village Canela Baja. The remaining communities also receive seasonal irrigation from the small rivers and ravines in the margins of which they are located. Among the ravines are: Quelón, Carquindaño, El Almendro, Agua Fría, Atelcura, El Pangue, Yerba Loca.

It is worth noticing here the relationship between the toponomy and the names of the agricultural communities, most of them having the same name as the river and ravines where they are located. The ravines are of great depth and drain into rivers that are gently sloping. Given the irregular water volume of the ravines, these remain dry the major part of the year, or with low volume, which makes their utilisation very difficult. Cañón indicates that:

> due to the scarce and torrential rainfalls regime, and the reduced vegetable cover of soils, after rain the volume of these rivers and ravines increases in such form that the riverbeds become torrents or alluvions. This notably reduces the infiltration of the fallen water, which is drained pointlessly by the Choapa towards the sea. This loss is aggravated by the fact that the comuneros do not know measures that permit storage of water to be used in the periods of greater shortage (Cañón, 1964:11).

The situation is not very different today, and there is no long-lasting water storage systems or any other water supply for alternative irrigation for the commune. Any plan in this respect must come from the State, because of its large investment but there are, to date, no initiatives to solve this problem. All other kinds of improvements to production methods, such as those made in several co-operatives for local cheese production in the communities will be quite pointless until the fundamental problem of the water is solved. During the dry years, these cheese manufacturers remain inactive.

As the commune's water resources are poor, this makes the *comunero* more dependent on rainfall since the output of the cultivation on the hill's *lluvias* depends exclusively on the rain. The irrigated agriculture is to be found in the reduced land strips of the *hijuelas*. Their irrigation will be dependent on the amount of water in the rivulets and ravines. The lands located in the margins of the River Choapa are an exception, since they possess almost permanent irrigation. What is lacking here is according to Cañón (1964:65-66), land to irrigate.

Soil and morphology

The land, agriculture's basic element is not:

an elasticity model. In one of its aspects, its size or surface, there is nothing to do and it has to be taken as something fixed and invariable, perfectly located and limited. In other of its aspects, the land, as substratum for the growth of the plants, can be submitted to limited manipulation (Warman, 1976:295).

The soils of the agricultural communities are among of the most ancient in the country. Soils are divided, according to their contents of organic material, into: (1) granite material soils, (2) soils derived from sedimentary and volcanic materials and (3) soils of marine terraces. Within the first category, represented in the study zone, we have the: (a) soils of hills with pronounced pending, (b) soils of inter-mountain valleys of almost flat slope and (c) soils of alluvial terraces (CONAF, 198121-23). They are predominantly clay and the principal problem is the lack of water (IREN, 1977(8):7). The soils of the agricultural community of Canela Baja specifically belong to the category of soils derived from granite materials:

> with physiography of hills, hilly profile, gradient of 50 to 70%, superficial-abundant stony, moderate to deep; excessive superficial drainage, slow permeability /---/ very poor in organic matter. Brown colour in surface and brown yellowish dark in-depth, loose texture, slightly hard and compact, not plastic, not adhesive, without structure, without reaction to acid. It presents a strong to very strong mantle erosion, with abundant ditches in some places (CONAF, 1981:21).

Though reduced, the alluvial terrace between the urban villages of Canela Baja and Canela Alta, is significant since it represents the only irrigation soils, though temporary, for both communities. These soils are:

> terrace stratified soils, influenced strongly by the material of piedmont and by the sedimentary and volcanic materials /---/ they are moderate in-depth, with light texture, with abundant stones in part, soft slopes, brown colours to brown yellowish, good permeability... (CONAF, 1981:22).

Taking into consideration only the factors relating to soils, without yet considering those, which relate to the effect of mankind, the balance of the soils in the community is quite unfavourable. The slope that characterises these types of soils is negative, since it favours the superficial runoff, which is yet more aggravated by the loss of vegetation.

If we now add the human factors that have a destructive impact on these soils, we will get an even gloomier picture. The classic standard of agricultural, cattle and forest exploitation today and during preceding generations, is the most aggravating factor in the erosion process that characterises the Norte Chico. This includes the elimination of the species of vegetation when ploughing the land for the cultivation, or by the extensive exploitation of the goats. This pattern of exploitation within the agricultural communities does not exclude the hills where the *lluvias* are exploited in gradients of 70-90% (IREN, 1977(8):8), while what is recommended for this type of soil is of 20° to 35°. But the agricultural communities are not solely responsible for this situation since they only occupy 25% of the region's total area. Colonial and post-colonial mining exploitation is, historically, perhaps one of the main causes in the disappearance of vegetation.

However, as far as the agricultural communities are concerned, the soils around the human settlements, even the very small ones, are among those that show the most serious erosion (IREN, 1977(8):8). In all soils cultivated for more than 30 years, the disappearance of the indigenous vegetation is almost absolute. Nevertheless, this is not, according to IREN, necessarily a product of the erosion, but it can also be the effect of a loss in balance of the organic matter of the soil. Nonetheless, mankind has been and still is the principal active agent in a land degradation process that is known as the desertification process of the Norte Chico. The degradation caused by natural processes would be of an attenuated character. The desertification corresponds to:

> ... the notable disappearance of the scarce vegetation, it tends to be attributed to a cyclical decrease, or permanent, of the rains, due to fundamental causes as the change of the air currents bearing of dampness or to the influx of the disappearing of the vegetation, caused by the human felling of trees or by the abusive grazing of the cattle (IREN, 1977(10):7).

From the general ecosystem viewpoint, desertification is a serious problem not only because of the destruction of the Norte Chico's ecological balance in itself, but because this constitutes the frontier between the Atacama Desert and the Central Valley of Chile. Yet, with the aid of CONAF, programmes have been implemented for the forestation of the zone. Many agricultural communities have not without some reluctance, accepted the procedures established by D.L. 701 of 1974 on the bonus to afforestation.

Through the plantation of forage shrubs, imported originally from Australia (*Atriplex Repanda* and *Atriplex Nummularia*, species that manage to grow without much water and that serves as fodder for the animals) up to 1988 approximately 10,000 hectares had been afforested in the commune (CONAF, 1981:42-43). For the recovery of the ecological balance, many other measures should be implemented.

According to IREN (1977(10):37), the soil defects can be summarised as the loss of structure, loss of horizons by the pluvial erosion, loss of fine elements by the eolic erosion, high temperatures occurring in the surface and a lack of organic matter. Those defects are translated in:

> a reduced infiltration of the rain-water, greater superficial runoff and consequently, accelerated pluvial erosion, superficial stones, seeds and plants death by dehydration or high temperature and break of the own organic and mineral cycle of the association soil-plant (IREN, 1977(10):37).

To correct these defects and to recover the ecological balance, the reinstatement of the indigenous vegetation, among other measures, is necessary. The reinstatement of the recommendable indigenous species are those that possess the following qualities: good regeneration, protection of the soil with its foliage, contribution of organic material to the soil, enrichment of the soil (nitrogen), general wildness and resistance to the drought and to pests and plagues, available for the wildlife, available for the cattle, to produce fuel wood or wood (IREN, 1977(10):74). The following are the species that have most of, according to IREN, the mentioned qualities, also being the most threatened: Schinus molle (*pimiento molle*), Cordia decandra (*carbonillo*), Bálsamo cardon brevifolium (*algarrobilla*), Cassia spp Compounds (several kinds), Adesmia spp (*panza de burro*), Bridgesia incisaefolia (*rumpiato*), Chilean Porlieria (*guayacán*) (IREN, 1977(10)17-23, 74).

Classes of soils and need of vegetation improvement

Following the international soils classification, IREN have classified the soils into eight categories according to their exploitation capacity, as well as the degrees of improvement to which they should be submitted, taking as base the state in which they were found when IREN realised its investigation (see Table 3.1).

Table 3.1 The classes and soils and need for vegetation proposed by IREN in the agricultural communities of the Canela Commune, by area

Agricultural communities by area	Total surface area (ha)	Exploitation capacity of the soil (prevailing)	Proposed degree of vegetation improvement			
			0	1	2	3
CHOAPA						
1. Huentelauquén	6,750	IV-VII				X
2. Huinchigallego	875	VII		X		
3. Mincha Sur	3,437	VII-IV	X			X
4. Mincha Norte	625	VII-IV				X
5. Las Barrancas	1,563	III-VII				X
6. Las Paredes	375	VI				X
ATELCURA						
7. Atelcura	2,812	VII-VIII	X		X	
8. La Capilla	500	VII-III			X	
9. La Leona	125	-			X	
10. Cabra Corral	1,250	VII-III			X	
AGUA FRIA						
11. El Pangue	1,062	VII		X		
12. Agua Fría Alta	2,563	VII-VIII	X		X	
13. Ague Fría Baja	4,687	VII-III				X
14. Las Tazas	2,375	VII-VIII	X		X	
15. El Potrero	2,250	VII	X		X	
16. El Chiñe	2,000	VII-VIII	X		X	
THE CANELA RIVERSIDE AREA						
17. Carquindaño	2,813	VII-VIII	X		X	
18. Yerba Loca	3,750	VII-IX			X	
19. Los Tomes	3,000	VII-VI			X	
20. El Almendro	563	-			X	
CANELA						
21. Canela Alta	67,000	VII-VIII	X		X	
22. Canela Baja	30,770	VII	X		X	
23. Canelilla	4,000	VII			X	
24. Angostura de Gálvez	1,437	IV-VII			X	

Source: Based on IREN (1977)(10): 11-12; Table 1 and 72-73; Table 13

On Agricultural Communities and their Geographical Setting

116 - Canela Baja	131 - El Almendro	137 - Huentelauquen	143 - La Capilla
117 - Canela Alta	132 - Agua Fria Alta	138 - Huinchihualleo	144 - El Potrero
118 - Jimenez Y Tapia	133 - Carquindafio	139 - El Pangue	145 - Atelcura
128 - Canelilla	134 - Yerba Loca	140 - Las Paredes	149 - Cabra Corral
129 - El Chiñe	135 - Los Tomes	141 - Agua Fria Baja	150 - Barrancas E Higuerillas
130 - Las Tazas	136 - Angostura De Galvez	142 - La Leona	151 - Mincha Sur
			152 - Mincha Norte

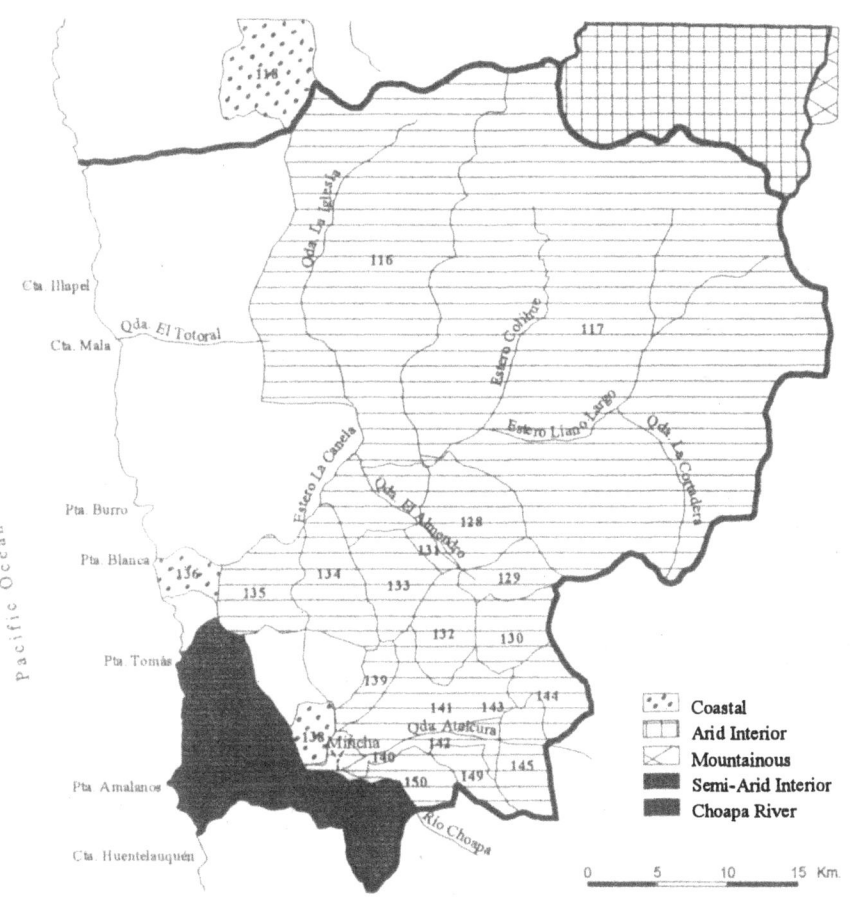

Photographic Reduction from I.G.M. Topographic Maps 1 : 500 000
Natural Resources Research Institute - CORFO, 1977

Figure 3.3 Land areas of the agricultural communities of Canela Commune

For that reason, such a classification is a technical guide aimed at determining the use that can be made of the soils:

> and the combinations of soil managing practices and water conservation for each one in particular (IREN, 1977(8):23).

The classes of soils were specified according to the possibilities of their exploitation, the erosion danger or other damages they can suffer as a product of mishandling.

Only those classes that are represented in the communities of the commune and in rising order, from class III and forward are described. The better lands, belonging to classes I and II exist neither in the communities nor in the commune. The soils belonging to class III are:

> of soft slopes or slightly inclined, thin, stony and with a moderate to low capacity of withholding available water (IREN, 1977(8):107).

The limitations of the prevailing soils, in general, are severe if they are destined for cultivation. Within the class IV are entered those soils that:

> present stronger gradient and need special practices if the erosion is to be controlled. In practice, they are considered soils for occasional cultivation or for special cultivation particularly adapted to a soil or to a climate or to both at the same time (IREN, 1977(8):107).

IREN does not specify class V. Class VI includes those soils that in their present state are uneconomic and should thus be devoted to:

> permanent meadows and require moderate practices of conservation or managing (IREN, 1977(8):107).

Within the soils of class VII comes the:

> strong slope soils, very thin soils and/or very stony and with scarce capacity of withholding available water (IREN, 1977(8):107).

These are soils with permanent meadows that need intense conservation practices and/or managing if its destruction is to be avoided. Finally, the soils of class VIII:

> includes all soils with severe limitations that produce scarce vegetation, which must be maintained because it belongs to the type of protection cover, or it deals with soils whose exploitation is absolutely uneconomic under current conditions (IREN, 1977(8):108).

These soils are destined fundamentally for the conservation of wildlife or recreation.

The vegetation improvement proposed by the IREN provides some compatible solutions within the complex problem the population-ecosystem-time (IREN, 1977(110):66). It includes four degrees going from 0 to 3, depending on the land's exploitation capacity and current state. While degree 0 means total exclusion of land exploitation, degree 1 and 2 means the need for mild and average improvement, respectively. Degree 3 is for land in better condition than that whose need of improvement is greatest. The requirement for the participation of the potential agents involved in the application (*comuneros*, technical advise and the state) of these measures vary according to the needed degree (IREN, 1977(10):75).

An analysis of Table 3.1 shows an unfavourable situation for the agricultural communities of the Canela commune, both regarding types of land and their current state. 87.5% of the communes have the worst classes of soils, i.e., from VII-VIII and to 37% of the communes (nine in total) has been recommended the degree 0, which means total exclusion of land exploitation. To all of them, with exception of Agua Fría Alta, some other degrees of improvement have been recommended.

I have to stress, however, that with regard to the land quality, the situation is not very different in the remaining 129 communities of Region IV as registered by IREN. Although IREN's study does not comprise the region's private property, the overall picture should not be completely different.

With so many communities in the Canela commune being within class VIII of soils, the whole situation will become a real dilemma if IREN's recommendations implemented. All the recommendations would, in theory, have to apply the degree 0 that would exclude the exploitation of goats, which is the pillar of the *comuneros* economy. In degree 0:

> the state of the vegetation, especially, and of some other resources, requires that the site is released from all immediate economic utilisation in order to let nature work freely in the preservation of the bio-mass and favour its regeneration, even though only in the long run. The exclusion, as any other degree, can affect all the community property or part of it (IREN, 1977(10):66).

The biomass comprises the total mass of all living beings, animals and vegetables in a given geographical space under relatively stable conditions. Degree 0 is a dilemma not only for the *comuneros* and their families, but also for the State, since it will have to face the cost of such a process. This may be the main reason for this measure not becoming effective, because the total exclusion of grazing would provide no revenue for the *comuneros*.

Table 3.2 Types of land in the Canela commune

Types of Land	Total ha	% of the total
A: Total Arable Land	**10,667.50**	**4.5**
Annual cultivation	4,599.00	1.95
Permanent cultivation	64.90	0.02
Artificial meadows	848.50	0.36
Fallow land	854.40	0.36
Rest of land	4,300.70	1.82
B: Other Land	**224,602.60**	**95.40**
Natural meadow	201,109.20	85.47
Improved meadow	8,575.30	3.64
Forest and mountain in forest exploitation and forest plantation	136.50	0.05
Non exploited forest and mountain	4,406.40	1.87
Arid and stony ground, etc.	8,642.80	3.67
Land occupied by construction, parks, lagoons, etc.	1,732.40	0.73
Total irrigated land	1,024.90	0.43
C: Commune's Total Area	**235,272.10**	**100.00**

Source: CONAF (1981): 41

As some consolation, it can be pointed out that the degree of improvement which corresponds to the total exclusion of goat farming and other type of economic utilisation, has not been recommended to all the communities in class VIII. However, this degree is recommended for some communities that have the class VII. The application of degree 2 of average improvement, recommended for the majority of the communities will require the participation of the *comuneros* in 45% of cases, 50% would require technical advice, while the interference of the state would be limited to only 5% (IREN, 1977(10):75).

Based upon the data derived from IREN, it is not possible to indicate the total amount of hectares for all the communities of the commune that corresponds to each class, beacause even in those communities that appear with only one class of soils, there may be other classes. This is because IREN have only specified the prevailing classes for each community. Therefore it is not possible either to indicate the total amount of hectares that correspond to each degree of improvement. Table 3.2 clearly shows the existing types of land in the commune (see also Figure 3.4). As I have already stressed, only 4.5% of the commune's total area corresponds to the category of arable land, while the remaining 95.4% is inappropriate for cultivation. The irrigated area corresponds to 0.4% of the total area.

In order to see how much land *per capita* every inhabitant of the commune has access to in this predominantly rural and agricultural commune, let us examine the density of the population with respect to the various types of land indicated in Table 3.2, by hectares *per capita*. This is based on the total population for 1986 of CBR (11,338 inhabitants). There are 20.75 ha of the total surface, 0.94 ha of the arable land and only 0.09 ha of the irrigated land per capita. While the area of annual and permanent cultivation represents 2% of the total, the artificial, natural and improved meadow represents 89.5%. All these relationships explain why cultivation occupies second place to cattle raising in the Canela commune.

Land ownership in the agricultural communities

> *Old institutions /---/ persist not only by the mere fact of survival, but also because there persists some trace of the needs to which they corresponded. Material proximity will always constitute a link between men. Consequently the political and social organisation based on territory will certainly subsist (Durkheim, 1984:lix; Preface to the Second Edition).*

The agricultural communities of Chile's Region IV conform to a complex land ownership form with an intricate organisation. Their legal situation has been, and still is complex, and so is the question of their definition. However, from the moment legal recognition started in the 1960s, their definition also began to change. To present the agricultural communities legal situation and their land ownership form, one would have to take into consideration at least two periods: the first period deals with the *de facto* existence of the agricultural communities, and goes as far as to the beginning of the 1960s. From there on, a second period begins, which would correspond also to the *de jure* existence of the agricultural communities. In presenting the characteristics of the land ownership form of the agricultural communities, I take some definitions from the period prior to the time of legal recognition, leaving the definitions of the latter period for Chapter 9. Table 3.3 (from

Communal Land Ownership in Chile

116 - Canela Baja	131 - El Almendro	137 - Huentelauquen	143 - La Capilla
117 - Canela Alta	132 - Agua Fria Alta	138 - Huinchihualleo	144 - El Potrero
118 - Jimenez Y Tapia	133 - Carquindaño	139 - El Pangue	145 - Atelcura
128 - Canelilla	134 - Yerba Loca	140 - Las Paredes	149 - Cabra Corral
129 - El Chiñe	135 - Los Tomes	141 - Agua Fria Baja	150 - Barrancas E Higuerillas
130 - Las Tazas	136 - Angostura De Galvez	142 - La Leona	151 - Mincha Sur
			152 - Mincha Norte

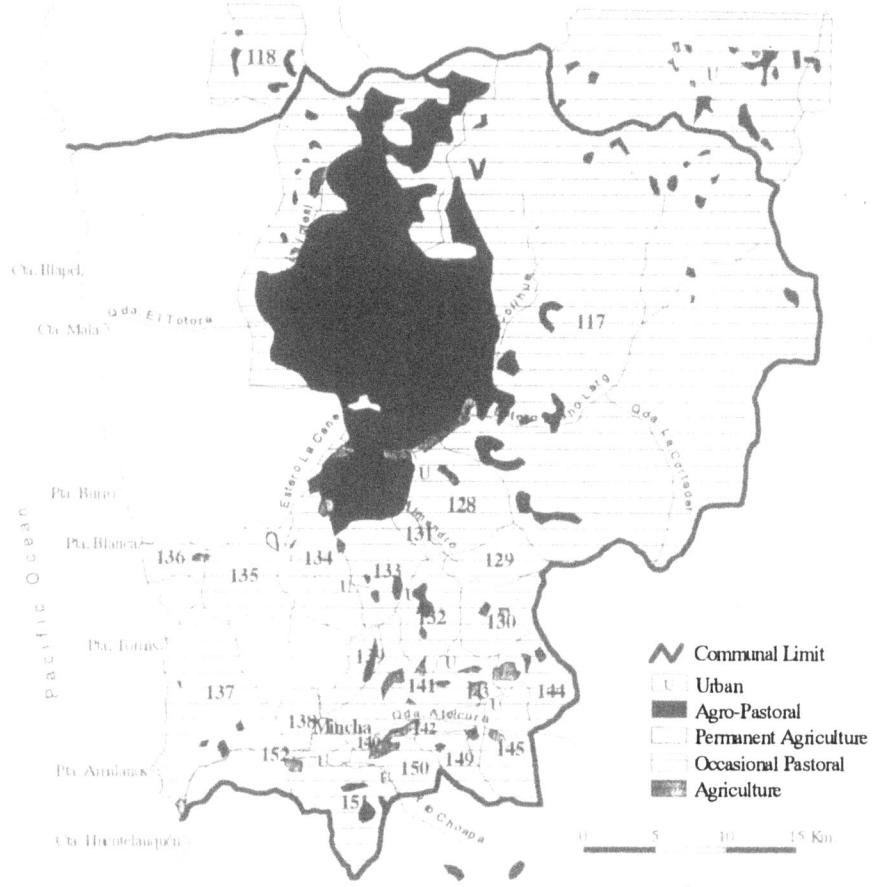

Photographic Reduction from I.G.M. Topographic Maps 1 : 500 000
Natural Resources Research Institute - CORFO, 1977

Figure 3.4   Land exploitation in the agricultural communities of Canela Commune

CIDA, 1966) corresponds to the period prior to the beginning of legal recognition of the agricultural communities. It can even be considered valid until 1993. A second scheme aimed at illustrating the situation from 1993 onwards is presented in Chapter 9, about the legal status of the agricultural communities.

The agricultural communities of Norte Chico were, before being legally recognised, described in the 1960s by CIDA (1966:128) as entities with both semi-communal and semi-individual features, characterised both by small irrigated plots for individual use (sometimes registered as individually owned property, so-called *hijuela*), and by common, non irrigated land. IREN described the agricultural communities as:

> ... a particular form of human settlements that is characterised by a group of people (comuneros), who are owners of an expanse of rural land, often of low productivity and within which different forms of land tenure coexist (IREN, 1977(2):17).

Table 3.3 Land ownership in an agricultural community of Norte Chico before 1993

Type of exploitation	Tenure*	Denomination
Individual exploitation	A. Private or considered private	*Hijuela, lluvia, posesión*
	B. Land granted by the community	*lluvia, posesión, piso*
Communal exploitation	A. Undivided property of all *comuneros*	Common land
	B. Undivided property belonging to several communities	Common enclosures

Source: CIDA (1966):131, Figure X-9 (* Tenure is the concept used by CIDA)

CIDA defines a *comunero* as:

> a natural person in order to simplify the picture, but in reality and frequently the strips of land, considered to be the property of individuals within the community, are in the hands of successors or descendants of *comuneros* from several generations back (CIDA, 1966:131).

The *comunero* Oscar Ollarzú gives one of the best descriptions of the agricultural communities before they became legalised. The Letter of Legal Consultation (*s.a.*) was written by Oscar Ollarzú. Ollarzú, who did not finish his law studies, but was also a merchant and mayor of the commune. He says that in the agricultural communities:

> the comuneros have registered the hijuelas, located on small parcels of land (10-20-50-100 metres across) in their own names, leaving the dry land on the hills and hillocks as COMMON GOODS, undivided for the community, on which the comuneros can sow, and graze their cattle, without the land ceasing to be common goods, even if small farm houses are put up where cattle are being raised (emphasis original).

That is:

> on the land belonging to any one of these communities /---/ the dry land on the hills and hillocks and on some plains that lack water, is *undivided property*, common goods or community, and the comuneros only have individual title deeds registered, either in their own name or that of their ascendants, for the small irrigated plot which constitutes their hijuela, and which gives him access to the common goods or *estancia*, giving him his status as comunero. The communities do not have a registered title deed for the common goods in the name of the community, nor in the name of the comuneros (emphasis added).

What characterises the agricultural communities is the coexistence of the communal and semi-private land property, within the limits of one territorial unit that in an undivided and permanent form belongs to all the *comuneros* of that community. The singular socio-economic organisation that conforms to the agricultural communities is created by the interweaving of these two forms of property into one unit. However, as I have been suggesting, the common land is the basic element of the organisation that conforms to the agricultural community, and its more distinguishing feature. Without the common land and its organisation, the agricultural communities would not be very different from the *minifundia* or small private peasantry.

Individual exploitation and semi-private property

The semi-private property of land is exercised by the *comunero* mainly on the *hijuelas*, but also on the *lluvias*. Apart from the *lluvias*, the agricultural communities also grant *posesiones* (possessions) and *pisos* (grounds), adding complexity to their land tenancy.

On Agricultural Communities and their Geographical Setting

The *hijuelas* - legally defined as *goces singulares* or *individuales* (singular or individual enjoyments or fruition) - are those strips of land that are considered by the *comunero* to be his own (CIDA, 1966:132). The term *hijuela* comes from son (*hijo*), and refers originally to the land part that the heirs of the proprietor of land receive as inheritance (Cañón, 1964; Diccionario Enciclopédico Planeta, 1984; Pequeño Larousse Ilustrado, 1989). In some cases the *hijuelas* are registered as individually owned property in the CBR (Conservatory of Real Estate). It happens that some *comuneros* who lack *hijuelas* may denote their *lluvias* as *hijuelas*, having them in some cases registered as individually owned property in the CBR. The same is valid for both *pisos* (grounds) and *posesiones* (possessions). Except for the land belonging to the *hijuelas* and *lluvias*, and also that of the *pisos* and *posesiones*, the rest of the land is communally owned.

The *hijuelas* or *goces singulares*, are commonly situated on the borders of a river or rivulet. They are flat and have access to irrigation, occasional or permanent, although there are even *hijuelas* without any irrigation.

Agricultural production carried out on the *hijuelas* is meant mainly for household consumption and consists of horticulture, involving the cultivation of corn, potato, onion, bean, tomato, carrot, pepper, green salad, cucumber, cabbage, chard, cauliflower, watermelon, melon, forage plants, etc.

It is the semi-private property made up of the *hijuelas* that gives the status of *comunero* to its owner. A *comunero* is then a person who, in being the owner of an *hijuela* within the geographical limits of the agricultural community, becomes a member and co-owner of that community. This implies that by selling his *hijuela*, he loses his status as *comunero*, that status being transferred to the new owner. The person who has the status of *comunero*, then has the right to use the rest of the communal property made up of the common land.

Hijuelas are semi-private and not altogether private, due to the fact that they are subject to some regulation, both traditionally and now legally, in respect to the rights to transfer the property (see also Chapter 9). The same is valid for the *lluvias*, in the sense that they are also considered as private or semi-private (more about these concepts, below). However, the *lluvia*, belongs to the community.

The *lluvias*, the semi-private property, is on the other hand also exercised by the *comunero* over the *lluvias*, which are the non-irrigated plots given by the community. The *lluvias* are commonly situated on the hills. The term *lluvia*, which literally means rain has probably, according to

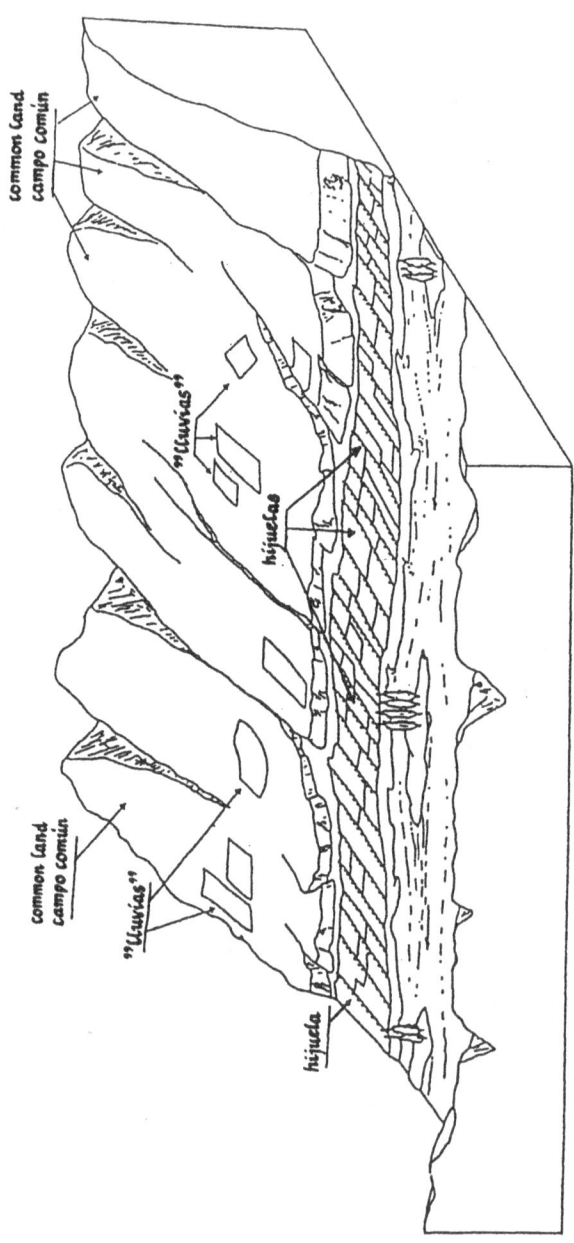

Figure 3.5 Land ownership in the agricultural communities

some *comuneros*, its origin in the fact that these plots of lands are dependent on the rain for their agricultural production. The right to obtain a *lluvia* can be implied, the *comunero* having the possibility to claim one whenever he considers it necessary. The size of the *lluvia* may vary depending on the size of the agricultural community. In some communities there are *comuneros* that have more than one *lluvia*. When the land of the *lluvia* is no longer suitable for cultivation, the *comunero* can apply for a new *lluvia*, having the responsibility to take the fences from the old one.

Agricultural production carried out on the *lluvias* is intended mainly for subsistence, and consists of cereals (wheat, barley) and spices (cumin, coriander). The yield of the *lluvias* depends on the rainfall. The yield of wheat for the province of Choapa - the lowest of all Region IV - is 14.7 qqm/ha, while for the country it is 23.7% qqm/ha (INE, 1985/86:2). The yield of barley is 6.9 qqm/ha for the province, while for the region and the country it is 11.7 qqm/ha and 30.0 qqm/ha, respectively (INE, 1985/86:2). Of importance for the agricultural production of the *lluvias* is also the humidity of the air and the constant fogs of the coast, characteristic of the Warm Steppe Zone. These climatic conditions permit the cultivation of potatoes and lentils on the *lluvias* nearest to the coast. These are products, which otherwise are cultivated in the south of Chile, e.g. on the island of Chiloé (Almeyda, 1948:13) where the average rainfall is 1,906 mm/year (Kaplan, 1948:616), whereas Region IV has an average rainfall of only 200 mm/year.

In spite of the fact that *lluvias*, 'grounds' and possessions belong in theory to the community, they can, as specified, also be considered as private. The fact that these are sometimes considered as private property, sometimes as belonging to the community, depending according to the *comuneros*, on whether or not they have been in the hands of the family for a long time (several generations). As for the *lluvias*, ground and possessions that have been given to the *comunero* more recently, they belong to the community.

Unlike the common land, both the *hijuelas* and the *lluvias* are fenced. The fact that the *lluvias* are fenced with line of cactaceous or drystones walls, which demands a substantial amount of labour from the *comunero*, is an indication of the permanent character that the *comunero* attaches to it.

The *posesiones* refer to a piece of land given by the community. These are meant for the construction of houses, corrals, but also for cultivation of vegetables and flowers in the orchards. The possessions are situated near to a stream or water well, by which the *comunero* and his family have access to water for the animals, irrigation for the orchard and domestic use (CIDA, 1966:133). In the orchards, fruit trees (apples, lemons, pears, medlars (*níspero*), oranges, quinces (*membrillo*), figs, grape, apricot and peach) can be found as well as walnut, almond and prickly pears or Indian figs (*tunas*). Many of these species are also to be found in the *hijuelas*, generally on their boundaries, acting as fencing.

On the *piso* or ground, the *comunero* builds his house, but the ground belongs to the community while the construction belongs to the *comunero*. The grounds are usually situated on the hill slopes and are of reduced extension. Many of these *pisos* have been given to people in the villages, where they construct their houses, by which these *pisos* enter into a grey zone. This is because incorporating them into the urban space, they practically cease to belong to the community and, on the other hand, when the person sells his house, he is in a way also selling the terrain.

All different productive spheres (*hijuelas, lluvias, posesiones*) may together consist of one united physical whole, but can also be distributed in different areas. That especially concerns the *lluvias*, which are to be found on the hills, often far away from the *comuneros* home. Following a traditional division of labour between men and women, the former answer for the predial sphere, thus, taking care of everything related to the cultivation of the *hijuelas, lluvias* and other activities, mostly those more physically demanding. Women take care of the domestic sphere, which is the household and its surroundings, which means taking care of the orchard, the small animals (chickens and pigs), milking the goats and cheese production. This does not mean that the members of the household do not help each other. The traditional division of labour between genders is in fact, with exception of some jobs, constantly transgressed, since there are jobs that just cannot wait. An example of this is the collection of fruit, like apples and pears, which have to be scalded, sliced and cut before it is put to dry in the sun.

Individual exploitation and common land

Within the communal ownership, we would have then the common land, which corresponds to the undivided property of all the *comuneros*, being the most defining feature of the agricultural communities and what converts them into such.

The common land, predominantly hills, is used primarily as pasture grounds for goats, as a source of firewood, hunting (hares), medicinal herbs, materials for construction and for fences (cactus and/or stones). Goat rearing is both for home consumption and the market. More than 90% of the domestic energy comes from the firewood extracted from the common land (CIPRES, 1992:14), a phenomenon that has had, and still has, profound consequences for the environment.

Referring to the *exploitation* of the common land, CIDA describes it (see Table 3.3) as communal, which could be interpreted as a kind of co-operative production (and even commercialisation of the products). But to call it communal exploitation is misleading, because the activities carried out by the *comuneros* - such as the pasturage of goats (which are privately owned) and the gathering of firewood - on the communal land are completely individual, as it is on the *hijuelas*, *lluvias* and *posesiones*. The *comuneros* are common pasture users who privately own and rear animals. So what is communal is not the exploitation but the property of the land resource. Indeed, viewing the community as a whole, I prefer to describe its form of land ownership as semi-communal and not communal, since it includes the *hijuelas* and *lluvias*, which are of semi-private character, something that in my opinion reduces the communal character of the agricultural communities.

Common enclosures are lands that belong to more than one neighbouring community and are used for temporary common grazing of the cattle once the cultivation season has passed. At the time of the new cultivation season the common enclosures are jointly fenced, in order to protect them from the cattle.

To summarise the above comments: when dealing with the productive sphere, wheat is cultivated on the non-irrigated land of the *lluvias*; goat rearing is concentrated on the common land, and horticulture is carried out on the irrigated *hijuelas*. The cultivation of wheat in the Choapa Province represents 71% of the total cultivation of cereals, and has an extremely low productivity of 14 and 15 qq/ha (Solis de Ovando, 1989), while the media for the country was in 1985/86 of 28.6 qq/ha (INE, 1985/86, Estadísticas Agropecuarias). A qq or quintal is a metric unit of weight, equal to 100 kilograms.

Out of the three named types of agricultural production in the Choapa Province, the most important for the subsistence of the majority of the agricultural communities is goat rearing. Crop production on non-irrigated land is uncertain due to the scarcity of rain, whilst the production on the *hijuelas* is not large enough to cover the families' basic needs.

The goats, grazing freely on the common land, do not require a major economic input to survive. That is, the *comunero* neither cultivates nor buys the necessary forage to feed them. Goat rearing is extensive, and their survival depends mainly on the resources provided by the hillside lands. Yet, the economic output from goat rearing that is the mainstay of the subsistence for the *comunero*. The artisan manufacturing of fresh cheese from goat's milk is both for sale and storage (dry cheese or *queso seco*); goat meat, which is not eaten fresh becomes jerk meat and the hides are tanned. The parts of these sub-products that are not consumed by the *comuneros* are destined for the market. The following data show the importance of goat rearing for the agricultural communities.

According to García *et al* (1986:78), Region IV accounted for about 50% of the country's total number of goats. Furthermore, in this region 85% of the goats are to be found in the agricultural communities. As we saw in Table 2.15, there were 55,360 goats in the 24 agricultural communities of the Canela commune in 1986, while for example there were only 3,632 head of cattle. The number of goats varies considerably from year to year, depending on whether the year has been 'good' or 'bad'. There is some old data that exists of the mortality among the animals in the Norte Chico due to the 'bad' years. For example, during the great drought of 1829-31, when a scarce 0, 11 and 0 mm of rain fell, a total of 77,375 animals died in Illapel during 1831 alone, with the major losses among goats and sheep: 10,600 bovine, 1,650 equines, 650 mules, 975 donkeys, 25,000 sheep and 38,500 goats (Almeyda, 1948:7).

Ownership or tenure?

Within the agricultural communities, even the concept of tenure could be used in the description of their form of land ownership, depending on whose the perspective from which it is examined. From the *comunero's* perspective, the *hijuela*, is considered to be his very own private property, inherited by him and his ancestors through generations, but at the same time, he is aware of the fact that his *hijuela* constitutes part of the agricultural community to which he belongs. He would accept the idea that his *hijuela* is not altogether private. Seen from the perspective of the community and its tradition, the concept of tenure may be more appropriate, as it does not necessarily involve property in the sense of 'totally' free disposal.

However, concepts are always relative and they should be analysed in their context. From the very moment that individuals, groups and institutions are involved in the social process, dealing with land ownership - even the most private property - is not totally private. Thus, different kinds of regulation, both traditionally and legally, which deal with both rights and obligations in respect to the use of the land, the usufructs of its products and its transfer, are attached to property.

Denoting, on one side, the agricultural communities' form of land ownership as semi-communal is appropriate because first of all there are the *hijuelas*, which reduce the communal character of these agrarian social entities. On the other side, within the agricultural communities, the *hijuelas* are semi-private because, compared to the private property, the *hijuelas* are less private. With regard to the use of the land, the usufructs of its products and its transfer, the field where most constraints on property are to be found is perhaps in the last, i.e., the rights to transfer the property, being therefore a fruitful field for contrasting different kinds of property.

Comparing the property of a *hijuelas* with the property of a *hacienda, fundo* and *minifundium*, it is quite clear that the former is less private than the latter three. If there are any constraints in relation to the transfer of the property of the *hacienda, fundo* and *minifundium*, these are less in comparison to those exercised by the agricultural communities, which have constraints on the matters of when to sell, and to whom. Therefore, the rights to freely dispose of land without permission are limited.

The concept of agricultural community

I would suggest that the concept 'agricultural community' is in its two components somehow inappropriate. Therefore, here I will briefly draw attention to this. However, since agricultural communities is the term traditionally used by the *comuneros*, the way they are known and the way they have been defined even by law, I shall continue to call them just agricultural communities.

The concept of 'agricultural'. Taking into consideration the description of the geographical region where the agricultural communities are located, the climate and physical conformation in general, I would say that due to the scarcity of arable land, as well as to the complementary importance of livestock production (predominantly goats) for the economy of the *comuneros*, the agricultural communities are rather agro-pastoral than agricultural. The difference between the terms 'pastoral' and 'agro-pastoral production systems' is defined in relation to the quantitative significance of either the agricultural (grain, vegetables, fodder, etc.) or pastoral products (meat, milk, cheese, hides, skins manure, etc.) in the household economy (Bovin, 1995:238). In trying to define the terms 'pastoralists', 'pastoral economies', and 'pastoral production system' - something she does in relation to West Africa - Bovin says that these terms are used to describe economic systems, where the dominant economic activity is the herding of domestic, ruminant animals on open bush land, 'range lands'.

I would not venture into the determination of the proportions of pastoral and agro-pastoral activities for the agricultural communities of Region IV, since in that respect they are not homogeneous. Some of them are more agricultural than pastoral and vice-versa, depending principally on the local natural environment and access to irrigation facilities. Nonetheless, considering the region as a whole, the term agro-pastoral could be more suitable. Bovin defines the pastoral production system as:

> one in which 50% or more of the household gross revenue, i.e., the value of marketed plus subsistence production, comes from animals or animal related activities /---/ or where more than 15% of the household food energy consumption consists of milk or milk products, produced within the household (Bovin, 1995:238-239).

The agro-pastoral production system is:

> a system in which more than 50% of the household income comes from farming, and 10-50% from pastoralism (Bovin, 1985:239).

The concept of 'community'. In the light of the predominance of the *comuneros'* individual exercise of production and reproduction, a legitimate question could be asked of whether the agricultural communities honour the appellate of 'comunidades'. My position is that they do. However, as to the term 'community', the situation is much more complex than with the concept 'agricultural', as it is of another character. There are at least 94 definitions of the concept 'community' (Schorne, 1967:90; IREN, 1978, Vol. 1:18). However, there is at least some general consensus about the elements required to talk about a community: the territory, the population, and the feeling of belonging to a particular group (IREN, 1978, Vol. 1:18); all of them being present in the agricultural communities of Region IV. Obviously, for symbolic communities, the territory is not a required element. However, when physical territory does constitute one of the basic elements of a community, it corresponds to a relatively specific and limited space, known by the community members who share it, whether it is for real or symbolic. The population consists of a group of people who are linked to each other by a network of relationships, sharing some common norms and values. The feeling of belonging to a particular group stems from the existence of linkages between people. These linkages can be such as kinship, ethnicity, friendship, common interests, etc.

In the case of the agricultural communities, I suggest that the territory and its co-ownership are the very fundament. It is the material base for their economic production and reproduction, and where the *comuneros* have as a group, their historical roots since colonial time. As such, the territory, which is their own land, is well defined and known by the *comuneros* who, together with their families, constitute the main population. Beside the *comuneros* and their own families, the communities are inhabited by the other relatives of the *comuneros* (their own children that are not *comuneros*, of which only one is going to inherit his father's or mother's rights), returned emigrants, children of former *comuneros* and immigrants of professional categories; medical staff and alike, policemen, the priest, nuns, some teachers and merchants.

In respect to the 'we-feeling' or sense of uniqueness, there are three important factors that can help us understand it. Firstly, as suggested, the co-ownership of the territory they live on is important. Secondly, they engage in the same type of agro-pastoral production for their subsistence, and thirdly, there is a kinship linkage. The *comuneros* know they have common ancestors in the old colonial owners who previously held the land they now live on. There exists, in many cases, a high degree of consanguinity. A contributing factor to the 'we-feeling' among the *comuneros* is that the zone is relatively isolated geographically. Due to this isolation, the language of the *comuneros* is, like in other parts of the

Chilean countryside, quite archaic with strong a resonance from ancient Spanish.

The members of the community share common values and attitudes, which differentiate them in the sense that they relate to people who belong to a higher socio-economic position on more equal terms, and with less feelings of inferiority and subordination than the rest of the Chilean peasants would probably do (IREN, 1978, Vol. 1:20). The reason for that lies in the fact that the *comuneros* are proud in being descendants of Spanish soldiers, many of whom distinguished themselves during the conquest and colonisation. No less important is the fact that they have their own land, which converts them into proprietors, being at the same time direct producers (see also the former discussion performed with the help of Bengoa, regarding the differences between the *comuneros* and the *inquilinos* in Chapter 1). Regarding this, it could be suggested that the *comuneros* are characterised by a dual, structural position. In theory, this dual, structural position could place them politically in different extremes. In spite of that, the left-wing and Christian democratic political tendencies predominate among the *comuneros* (for this, see also Chapter 8).

The agricultural communities satisfy, by far, the three minimal elements needed to consider them as communities. Now, on the one hand, it is certain that such characteristics are not exclusive for them since they are also common to other social collectives, agricultural or otherwise. On the other hand, the agricultural communities are somewhat more specific. Without ignoring that they possess these characteristics, their uniqueness is not based on them, but rather in the fact of constituting a common agricultural property, whose indivisibility is of permanent character and within which coexist the semi-private and the common property of the land. Precisely the coexistence of these two forms of property distinguishes the character of the agricultural communities and the institution, which is born in connection with them.

In other words, on one hand, we have the semi-private property, and bound to it the strong feeling of private property that the *comuneros* have on the *hijuelas* and the *lluvias*, and on the other, the communal property and the no less strong community feeling around it. In this dynamic, the first does not discard the second and neither does the second the first.

The *comuneros'* feeling for landed property, and as a rule, the peasantry's, is very strong, and opposite to other types of communities, where such feeling in respect to the land does not exist, as in the communities of Chan Kom in Yucatan, Mexico, where private ownership of land does not exist. Gómez (1989:21) summarises this feeling as the:

> ancestral aspiration of the peasant sector of achieving a safety by means of an individual tenure of land.

According to Gómez, this was not understood by the radical sectors that implemented the agrarian reform in Chile. It is, in my opinion, important to keep this in mind, since it is also a constitutive part of the *comuneros'* idiosyncrasy. In respect to this, and as Bobbio and Matteucci (1986, Vol. 2:1345) indicate, among the values connected to private property, there are the traditional ones that transform private property into a value of positive sign as a structure sanctioned by the economic and political system. Bobbio and Matteucci refer to private property in general, but this has relevant application with respect to the land. The individual is imbued with psychological need for security in order to survive. This has greater importance in those societies where the State does not assume the responsibility of guaranteeing the survival of the individual. As guarantor of the survival of man, private property acquires an almost metaphysical value that:

> is converted, as the divinity, into an entity with emotive contents, into something that does not betray in the moment of need.

As such, private property:

> is identified /---/ with the value of *freedom*; interpreted as independence of the realm of necessity and of the other men, but always in the sense of an exclusive good (Bobbio and Matteucci, 1986, Vol. 2:1345) (emphasis original).

To take a quite opposite example: the above mentioned communities of Chan Kom in Yucatan in Mexico, are, or were, characterised by a form of itinerary agriculture on communal land that cannot be the object of private property. Thus, the feeling for private property has not been developed. In these communities, land is not a resource susceptible to appropriation, but a means of production, something that does not have a value in itself. The ownership is exercised on what is the temporary result of labour, not on the land. Thus, in these communities, what is sold is a cleared patch, the cultivated plot or the crop. In this way, the manner in which the peasants organise the production does not enable the development of a strong feeling of private ownership in respect to the land (Archetti, 1978:10).

As opposed to the agricultural communities of the Norte Chico, where what defines the relations of production is just the fact of having possession of a *hijuela,* in the community of Chan Kom (Mexico), the relations of production depend on the social belongings, that is, community membership defines the right to access to land, on which private property can not be exercised (Archetti, 1978:10). In the agricultural communities of the Norte Chico, the concept of 'community' would be given in the first place by the common property of the land, and by the institution that emerges in connection with the co-existence of different forms of land ownership. While such a community only encompasses the land ownership - while the usufructs, so much of the common land as of the singular possessions, is strictly individual, as well as it is the sale of surplus products - it could be argued that the agricultural communities are communities only in a restricted sense of the term. Certainly it cannot be denied that the prevailing social dynamic is that each one of the *comuneros* individually takes care about his survival. The foregoing does not mean that the *comuneros* do not have the capacity to begin large-scale projects collectively. The fact that several of the existing initiatives of co-operative spirit have their origin outside the communities itself can be explained in large part by economic factors. The communities do not have the resources to initiate, for example, the forestation that was begun by CONAF or other NGO's projects or those, which depend on foreign aid as for example the production of goat cheese in certain communities. The results of such initiatives will depend in the last resort on the capacity of the *comuneros to* work jointly: in more lasting projects, associated with production and that go beyond those of restricted terms and goals, of the *comuneros'* capacity and will of assimilating new technology and knowledge, and also on the said projects' adjustment to the needs of the *comuneros* such as they perceive them.

Even though it is certain that the organisation of the agricultural communities neither embrace the common exploitation of the soils, nor the sale of surplus products, the common property of the land does require a definite organisation for the regulation of its usufruct. In their existence as communities, the agricultural communities have historically conformed and conform still to a specific social organisation with a certain level of formalisation (Rivera, 1988a:71), thus being able to operate both internally and externally, preserving their interest in respect to the surrounding social environment. The internal organisation must succeed in regulating:

> the use of large part of the land and water resources, thus creating the conditions for the emergence of the necessary co-ordination of the cultivation and of the distribution of the water (Rivera, 1988a:70).

This organisation is important in order to preserve the interests of the communities against those that threaten their territorial integrity from outside. For this purpose, and as Warman indicates about the Mexican communities, the efforts to agglutinate in greater organisations of national or regional type, serves the objective of establishing the communities as permanent collectives (Warman, 1985:18). In the communities:

> the primary unit /.../ is derived from a common link with the land, of the existence of a collective right to possess and administer its territory with freedom and autonomy in pursuant of its interest (Warman, 1985:10).

The community is for the *comuneros*:

> an organisation of people of the same social position, and who share the right to the same territorial space. Said in other words: it is an organisation of a specific class, the peasantry, through which are realised the collective negotiations with other forces of the society in order to obtain the conditions for the subsistence and reproduction (Warman, 1985:11).

It remains clear that within the indicated context prevails, on one side, product of the historically rooted feeling of private property, among the *comuneros*, the strictly individual exploitation. It is not only in relation to the land that it is object of semi-private property, but also toward those temporal *posesiones* that the *comunero* receives from the community, as well as the goat rearing. Now, historically this is totally congruent with the form of private property that the *comunero* has of the land, and whose explanation is found in the colonial origin of private property that the agricultural communities have. On the other side, in what has to do with the realm of the internal organisation of the community, a collective spirit prevails that serves as support in maintaining it as permanent collective toward the exterior, and that grants its members the feeling of being *comuneros*.

In spite of the individual usufruct of the land and selling of the surplus products prevailing in the agricultural communities, I am of the opinion that it is more than valid to view these agrarian collectives as communities. This, inasmuch as they historically constitute, first, collectives whose principal feature is the semi-communal land ownership, an infrastructure that permits their existence as such, and where the communal and the semi-private property of the *hijuelas* and *lluvias* coexist. Second, they fulfil the necessary formalisation - sanctioned or not - to operate internally as much as externally, besides all the other elements that characterises all types of social collectives, to have common interests and values. Strong ties of kinship, friendship, culture and common traditions mark their members, and it is possible to verify in them, efforts to solve common problems, which shows a collective spirit and tight bonds of solidarity. Third, and central to their values, a characteristic of the communities is also their high degree of attachment to the land, which in 1960 lead the agronomist Jorquera to define the agricultural communities as:

> a system integrated simultaneously by the land and the people who inhabit it, in which the land is undivided, belonging thus to all of them without the existence of established and recognised rights within the common land (Jorquera,G., in Cañón, 1964:4).

In relation to the land then, the norms that regulate the behaviour of the community members, based on usage and custom, transmitted from generation to generation have been, in absence of a written law, central, making possible their persistence and operation. The agricultural communities initiated their legal recognition at the beginning of the 1960s, but it was not until 1993 - a year in which modifications in the DFL (*Decreto con Fuerza Legal* or Decree with Legal Power or With Force of Law) 5 from 1967 were introduced - that their legal status can be considered to be in order, at least compared to the previous periods and private land ownership. In Chapter 9, I will extend this discussion on the legal status of the agricultural communities.

PART 2
THE HISTORICAL PAST

4 Land Tenure Formation in Colonial Chile

Introduction

Like in other regions of Chile, the origin of the land tenure structure in the Norte Chico is bound mainly to the *mercedes de tierra* (land grants), an institution created by the Spanish colonial regime. It should be noted that CIDA's and Stavenhagen's definitions of land structure and land tenure have been adopted (see Chapter 1). However, the development of the land grants in the Norte Chico, with time, not only resulted in *latifundium* (large landed property) and *minifundium* (small landed property), as in other regions of the country. However, alongside these, emerged the form of semi-communal property of the agricultural communities that is today so characteristic of this region. I need, therefore, to present an historical outline of this basic institution that was to shape the structure of land tenure in the then General Captaincy of Chile, as it was also from the *mercedes* that the agricultural communities will emerge.

Given the importance of the *encomienda* as a production system - mainly mining based on the exploitation of the indigenous labour force and its consequences for the formation of the land tenure structure - I will take up this institution together with the *mercedes*. I will for the most part, follow the pioneering works of both Borde and Góngora, 'Evolución de la propiedad rural en el Valle del Puangue' (1956) and Baraona *et al*, *'Valle de Putaendo: Estudio de Estructura Agraria'* (1961). Both valleys, the first in the Province of Melipilla, Metropolitan Region, and the second in the Province of San Felipe de Aconcagua, Region V, belonged, we should not forget, to the core of colonial Chile.

Mercedes and encomiendas

The *mercedes* and the *encomiendas* were at the beginning of the colonial period the principal pillars of the economy. Apart from the *mercedes* and *encomiendas*, other institutions existed that were created by the Spanish Crown for the administration and exploitation of the colonies such as the *mita*, the *yaconazgos*, *mitayos* of service and community Indians, salaried work and *obrajes* (For further reference see Dieterich, 1978). While the *mercedes* constituted the main legal mechanism for access to land, 'the only legally valid title for the occupation of the soil' (Borde and Góngora, 1956:30), the *encomiendas*, on the other hand, constituted the main mechanism for access to the available labour force of the local population. Taking into account that the Spaniards who arrived in America were soldiers or priests, and also their limited number, the running of the mines could be carried out only by exploiting the local labour force (Rivera, 1988b:26).

During the 1500s, the *encomienda* was, however, the principal institution of the State and the economy (Borde and Góngora, 1956:49). Athough the introduction of the *mercedes* from 1495 was connected with the Crown's interest in constituting a rich social class rooted on the land, it came to acquire importance as a source of wealth in Chile only around 1750, during the period that Mellafe designates as being of the traditional *latifundium*. Therefore, according to this author, it would be erroneous to think that the Spaniards at the beginning sought the possession of land because it conferred prestige and wealth. Those attributes, which in reality accompanied the usufructuaries of the *encomiendas*, first became characteristics of the *mercedes* almost two centuries after the conquest. To identify the owner of a *mercedes* during that period with a landlord would be wrong (Mellafe, 1981:88-91). As Dieterich (1978:131-132) indicates, during the period of discovery, we have the figure of the explorer-merchant who was active and financed by mercantile interests; in the period of the conquest there is the *segundón fijosdalgo*, i.e., the Spanish nobleman who was not the first-born son in his family and must because of the *mayorazgo* or right of primogeniture in Spain, among other things, seek wealth to accompany his social status in the colony. Finally, in the colonising period, we have the figure of the *encomendero*, the state official and the ecclesiastic.

For the land to acquire value as a source of wealth, the transition of a predominantly pastoral economy to a mixed agro-pastoral economy was necessary. Although it is true that the *mercedes* were obtained without payment, a certain amount of capital was required since their running required some degree of capital expenditure (Baraona *et al*, 1961:48).

Though the *encomiendas*, as opposed to the *mercedes*, did not give any right to own the land, in practice - in agreement with the common spirit of the colonial epoch among those who held power, according to which the real ordinances were respected but not fulfilled - the *encomenderos* used all available methods to pre-empt the lands of the local population that had been 'entrusted' to them (*encomendados*). That also happened with the *mercedarios* who continued to appropriate land in spite of the Royal orders, to the detriment of the weakest people whose interest the Crown, at least in theory, pretended to protect. While the *mercedes de tierra* constituted the legal mechanism of access to land ownership, the *encomiendas* came to be an analogous mechanism, but through practice:

> after a few generations the original purpose of the encomienda had been forgotten and it may be considered as another principal source of the hacienda [estate] system (Stavenhagen (ed.), 1970:7).

The *encomienda* that was nothing but the legal access to the appropriation and exploitation of the indigenous labour force, consisted, in theory, of:

> a right conceded by Royal mercy to the meritorious of Indies for their life, and that of an heir, according to the law of succession, to receive and collect for themselves the tributes from Indians, with the mission to take care of them, spiritually and temporarily, and of inhabiting and defending the provinces to them entrusted (Dieterich, 1978:138).

In other words, the *encomendero* or the beneficiary of an *encomienda*:

> had the right to exact tribute in kind, money and services from the native peasants, without however directly taking over their land (Stavenhagen (ed.), 1970:7).

Turning now to the *mercedes*: the obtaining of *mercedes* implied, at least in theory for its addressees, certain duties, limitations and conditions.

Among these, it was emphasised that they should be conceded without prejudices for both Indians and Spaniards:

> the fixing of the land and its boundaries; the prohibition of selling to the ecclesiastics /---/ the obligation of occupying the land within a certain period of time and the prohibition of selling it before; the condition of carrying royal consent (Borde and Góngora, 1956:30).

According to Dieterich (1978:185), an indispensable requirement for the dominion of the *mercedes* was to cultivate the land and live on it for a period that, depending on the colonial area could vary from four to eight years. While the objective of conceding the *mercedes de tierra* was to create a rich social group rooted on the land; that of the *encomiendas* was to assure the subordination of the labour force. As such, these rewards were reserved mainly for the highest colonial social strata, i.e., the highest rank of the military hierarchy.

For the lower social strata there were other legal mechanisms allowing access to land, among those the peonies (*peonías*) and cavalries (*caballerías*). The measure called peonies consisted of an area of land that was granted to the infantry soldiers. It consisted of field for wheat cultivation of 6.5 ha, and some additional plots for agriculture. The measure called cavalries, destined initially for the *caballeros* (gentile) of the conquest and colonisation period, could encompass a site double that of a peony, and additional agricultural land five times the size of a peony. The *mercedes*, on the other hand, could consist of several peonies or cavalries (Dieterich, 1978:187-188).

Differentiating between social strata with diverse degrees of loyalty and subordination to the Crown, this mechanism, through the concession of *mercedes* and *encomiendas,* establishes a given property administration of the land and of the local labour force in the colonies. According to Dieterich (1978:185), the *encomienda* is born as a product of the conflicts of interest between different social groups, the conquerors/colonisers and the Crown - followed by the Catholic Church - for the appropriation and exploitation of the indigenous labour force, which was necessary to extract precious metals, the principal wealth of the Indies. The *encomiendas* this way fulfilled four well-defined and particular social interests:

> the economic (utilisation of the indigenous population for the exploitation of the new territories), fiscal (income of the State), the political (whether or not

there should be the formation of a slave holding or feudal class) and, finally, the clerical interest ('*evangelisation*') (Dieterich, 1978:156; emphasis original).

For the *encomendados*, or entrusted ones, the *encomienda* meant entering into a non-voluntary relationship of subordination and dependency with the *encomendero*, who bound them through obligatory labour, disguised through a paternalist ideology, which transcended this institution.

The *encomienda* came to an end as an institution in some regions of the continent in the first decades of the 1600s, and in others around the end of that century. Several factors contributed to the end of the *encomienda*. Among these were; the demographic decrease of the indigenous population, the emergence of other labour systems (such as the *mita* and '*pueblos de indios*' (Indian villages), the increasing of the charges to the income of the *encomienda* on the part of the exchequer (the Crown) and, finally, the crisis within the mining activity. The *mita* was a recruitment form of the indigenous labour used in the mountain regions of Latin America, and the '*pueblos de indios*' were reserves for the indigenous population that were subordinated to the Crown (Dieterich, 1978:151).

The mining crisis manifested itself in a decreased demand for the local labour force and agricultural products, which diminished the exchange-value of the *encomiendas*' (Indians') tribute. This coincided with the crisis that was beginning to bring about a change in the colonial production structure, giving place to the consolidation of large *haciendas* or *latifundia*, which had originally operated as subsistence units (Dieterich, 1978:151-152).

I have, mainly with the aid of Borde and Góngora, and Dieterich, attempted to give the general outlines of how the *mercedes* and *encomiendas* evolved into the private properties of the *haciendas* or *latifundia*. I will now, in more detail, distinguish between different types of *mercedes* in order to see their relationship with the different forms of land property that developed from them. This is relevant because it will give us some keys to understanding how the agricultural communities developed.

Types of mercedes and their development

There were three types of *mercedes* (grants) that the Crown distributed:

[1] those referred to sites within the trace of the city [*chácaras*] located near this; [2] the cultivation grants [*mercedes de tierra*] and cattle ranches [*estancias*] [3] those of small sites, to build windmills [*trapiches*] for grinding precious metals in the contiguity of the mines (Borde and Góngora, 1956:30).

Of these three types of *mercedes*, the second two sub-types are the most important regarding land ownership, this inasmuch as they came to constitute the bases from which the dominant form of land ownership in Chile evolved. I will concentrate on the description of the *mercedes de tierra* (land grants), also called cultivation, labour or tillage grants and the *estancias de ganado* (cattle ranches), also called *estancias* or *mercedes* (grants) of grass or seats. In order to simplify, I will use the first terms: *mercedes de tierras* and *estancias de ganado* or just *mercedes* and *estancias*, respectively.

Of these two sub-types, only the *mercedes de tierra* conferred upon their holders, ownership of the land, while the *estancias de ganado* conferred a right to pasturage. On the latter, the Crown explicitly refused the right to property since they were of common type (CIDA, 1966:5). However, although the *estancias de ganado* did not imply property, in practice, according to the previously expressed idea that the royal decrees were respected, but not fulfilled, these were soon converted into private property. From this it is possible to conclude that, as with the *encomiendas*, through practice, the *estancias de ganado* also contributed to shape part of the structure of land tenure in Chile.

According to Borde and Góngora (1956) there appeared to be three meaningful dates connected with the development of the *estancias de ganado* in Chile. According to the decrees expressed by Pedro of Valdivia in 1549, it seemed that the *estancias de ganado* referred to their exclusive use, and the possibility of disposing of them freely (Pedro of Valdivia was the first governor and general captain of the Captaincy of Chile). In 1556, however, there is inserted, due to a trial and sentence with respect to some lands of Talagante (the current Province of Talagante, Metropolitan Region), a clause that establishes that such *estancias* neither grant possession nor property 'but only the right to graze and to build corrals...' (Borde and Góngora, 1956:34). This was valid for some decades, but in 1583 it began to disappear, giving place to the *estancias de ganado* to fuse with the right to property. Thus, a form of identification in the sense of

Land Tenure Formation in Colonial Chile

right to property, between the *estancias de ganado* and the *mercedes de tierra* is produced. It began as:

> a consolidation process of the property in a social framework where the value of the land had been increasing as a consequence of the growth in the value of the mercantile products originating from cattle-raising (Borde and Góngora, 1956:36).

The development of cattle economy:

> move the cattle raisers to build large compact territorial dominions, firmly set in the landscape, in order to have various places of grass for their cows, sheep and goats (Borde and Góngora, 1956:53).

Even the hills were gradually being occupied and delimited yet not fenced. Even though the *estancias de ganado* became private property, the common usufruct of grassland persisted after the Republic has been created in the beginning of the 1800s. Due to a mutual need, the payment for grazing among cattle-raisers remained excluded. The common use of grassland between different private properties would be conditioned by the seasonal transhumance of the cattle pasturing imposed by the environment. As a tradition it originates:

> from the medieval agrarian system, with its fields without fencing, and its communal lands within the manorial and near to the villages, and the utilisation of the already cultivated lands for the shepherding and to collect the stubble (Borde and Góngora, 1956:35).

This phenomenon known as transhumance, a characteristic of a Mediterranean valley-mountain region, thus uses 'the grass that buds at the bottom of the valleys and on the hillsides of the Andes chain during the summer' (Aranda, 1971:149) as a complement for the shepherding of the cattle.

Braudel (1981, Vol. 1:109) distinguishes between three types of transhumance. In the most typical and of interest here, that of the Mediterranean, so called normal or summer transhumance:

> ... proprietors and shepherds are /.../ people of flatness, living in it and who only leave it in summer, unfavourable season for the cattlemen in the low land.

In the Mediterranean, the transhumance:

> ... is a movement in *vertical direction*, of winter grass of the flatland, to the summer grass on the mountain. And, vice versa (Ibid, emphasis original).

According to Braudel, the topographic relief and the seasons are the two factors that usually determine the most essential of what happens in this respect. So defined, the transhumance is one of the forms, regulated and rationalised, of the Mediterranean pastoral life, product of a long development process.

This practice of using grassland between private properties that were not yet fenced without payment for the grazing ended during the 1800s, as a result of the hills being fenced. The fencing of the flat land would have begun however, at the end of the 1700s as a product of the combination of cattle raising and agriculture, or the beginning of the co-existence of them (Borde and Góngora, 1956:67). This new productive mode - a combination of cattle raising and agriculture, or the transition from a pastoral economy to a mixed cattle and cereal production - took place at the end of the 1600s, with the introduction of wheat cultivation. It coincided with the replacement of the *estancia* (cattle ranch) concept proper of the 1600s, by that of *hacienda* (estates). In spite of this, the cattle raising would prevail for a long time.

However, in a rigorous sense of the term, the *estancia* concept would make reference to those rural properties that maintained their lands in an uncultivated state, while the *hacienda* concept would make reference to those where agriculture was introduced next to cattle raising. In this sense, the *hacienda* of the 1900s would be the inheritor of the land grants of the 1600s and therefore its fundamental character would be based '... on a certain nobility originating from their antiquity' (Borde and Góngora, 1956:149). If one understood the concept of *hacienda* strictly as that which has its roots in the *mercedes* of the 1600s, very few of the large rural properties up until the agrarian reform, initiated in 1962, could have been catalogued as *haciendas*, given the subdivision that they have suffered through time, though it is not discarded that there may have been properties that could have been a fusion of more than one ancient *hacienda*.

It is emphasised, however, that the antiquity criterion in order to differentiate the *haciendas* from the *fundos*, does not influence the organisation of their running. Until the moment that the new concept *fundo* came to be imposed, during the first half of the 1800s:

> the appellate of hacienda was always applied to stable holdings, with precisely elaborated limits which were well adapted to the landscape (Borde and Góngora, 1956:146).

Later, the *fundos* would be 'between the *estancias* and the small familiar holdings' (Borde and Góngora, 1956:146). As we can see here, in spite of the fact that Borde and Góngora historically differentiate between the *estancia* and *hacienda* concepts, in the previous passage they use these concepts as synonyms, which is not strange since this is what they became (see also Bengoa (1988) who does the same). Two things should, however, remain clear: firstly, that the *fundos* became an intermediate kind of property between the *haciendas* and those properties with smaller territorial extension than a *fundo*; and secondly, that the *fundos* are a result of the division of the large *haciendas*. The *fundos* would neither be fittingly a *hacienda* nor a small familiar holding or *minifundium* and, as Borde and Góngora also indicate, in nine cases out of ten, the *fundos* would have their origin in the subdivision of the *haciendas*. Interestingly, Borde and Góngora verify that a *fundo* is defined according to what it is not, rather than to what it is:

> It never deals with a land whose borders are very ancient and it is without a doubt due to this aspect more than by its extension, that it is different, in a very uncertain way indeed, from the large landed properties of other times. It never deals /.../ with a small property either, and it is under this aspect that it is different, and in much more rigorous terms, not only from the traditional chacras [farms] but also from the plots born of the large rural land distributions (Borde and Góngora, 1956:165).

The *haciendas*, on the other hand, are characterised by:

> a certain occupation and utilisation level of the land, which continues to be extensive and incomplete at the same time /.../ Generally, the hacienda encompasses a sufficient extension so that their limits adapt themselves to the large lines of the relief or hydrography (Borde and Góngora, 1956:147).

Nevertheless, it is common to find, in the analysed sources, a warning on the limited validity of the size criterion to determine the differences, not only between the *haciendas* and *fundos* but, as a rule, for all types of agricultural property, above all because of different land qualities.

I consider it interesting to note here, however, that the substitution of the term *estancia* by that of *hacienda* and last by that of *fundo*, obeys different criteria and processes. While the first substitution would make reference to a production change - transition from a pastoral economy to a mixed pastoral-agricultural - the second would refer to a change in the structure of land property, product of the subdivision of the large *haciendas*.

It is also important to add that the concept of *fundo* did not altogether substitute that of *hacienda* or *latifundium*, which is another concept used as a synonym of *hacienda*. Thus, for example, Mellafe (1981) distinguishes three types of *latifundia* from the colonial period up to the mid-1850s: the ancient (1600-1750), the traditional (1700-1800) and the modern (1800-1850). Mellafe's chronological division does not necessarily correspond to the changes previously mentioned, based on those of Borde and Góngora. The difference between Mellafe's three types of *latifundia* is made in relationship to the criterion of strengthening the landowners as a dominant class within the Chilean social structure.

It is evident that the variety of denominations used to designate the different types of rural properties reflects the transformations in the agrarian structure and, as indicated by Borde and Góngora (with the exception of the properties of the urban periphery):

> it is the hacienda with its transformations from which all the current diversities of rural properties were born, independently of whether they are haciendas, fundos or hijuelas, plots or simple sites (Borde and Góngora, 1956:145).

Or, I would also add, agricultural communities.

Of fundamental importance for the economic development in the colonies was the specialisation in diverse products that interconnected different regional economies. In the case of Chile and Argentina the scarce importance of minerals contributed to the development of agriculture. This was strengthened by the weak, dependent and disarticulated agricultural economy of Peru that was not able to produce enough for its self-supply, since the principal destination of the labour force was mining.

In Peru, the Crown would have avoided the strengthening of the *hacienda* (Rivera, 1988b:29). In regions with a limited mineral exploitation, the rise of the system of cattle *estancias* and *haciendas* developed earlier than in those regions where the mining activity was the axis of the economy. In these, the *estancias* and *haciendas* only emerged after the decline of the mining activities in the mid-1600s, as was the case in Mexico and Peru (Rivera, 1988b:29).

The importance of the development of the agricultural activities in the colonial marginal areas, such as Chile and Argentina, is revealed in the early formation of a national 'bourgeoisie', which would come to establish itself as a dominant class against the Spanish Empire. Because colonial war never ceased altogether in Chile, due to the fierce resistance by the Mapuches, the army was closely bound to the configuration of the *estancias* (Rivera, 1988b:35-36).

That is how, during the 1600s, the expansion of the *estancia*, intended for the rearing of equine, bovine, sheep and goats, is related to the market of tallow, cordovan (crowding or Spanish leather) and other products necessary for the mining activity and the war front. Though the meat and wool supply to Santiago and the garrisons, from the Bío-Bío to Valdivia (the current Regions VIII and IX) - where the war continued - constituted an important market for the cattlemen, even more important was the tallow (*sebo*), destined for candle manufacture, the cordovan (fine leather of goatskin or *piel de cabra curtida*), the *charqui* (beef cut into strips and dried in the sun), the sole-leather (*cueros para suelas*) and basils or *badana* (dressed sheep-skin, or *piel curtida de ovino*). These constituted the principal trade items aimed both for the Peruvian foreign market and for the interior market. The elimination in Peru in 1594/95 of the rights payment (*almojarifazgos*) to the exchequer for the sales of tallow and cordovan meant a great boost for the *estancia* (Borde and Góngora, 1956), expanding the Chilean foreign trade.

However, in the 1600s, agricultural activities consisted mainly of vineyard cultivation together with cereal cultivation, but it is only from around 1687 that export of wheat rose substantially, becoming the main item of Chilean agricultural economy (Borde and Góngora, 1956:70).

Summarising, the principal economic activity during 1500s was mining, aimed principally at gold and silver extraction, the exploitation of which was based on the local labour, instrumentalised by the *encomienda* institution. In this first period, agriculture played a complementary role to mining. When mining declined, land property, distributed through the concession of *mercedes*, acquired importance as the pillar of the economy.

In this second stage, cattle raising, developed on the large uncultivated *estancias*, was transformed into the principal item of economic development, giving way, thereafter, to agriculture which had started to develop on the large *haciendas*. In this way, the *hacienda* was converted into the base institution of the colonial social order, hegemonised by the landlord class.

By the end of colonial period, landed property belonged mainly to four groups in the Ibero-American colonies: the Crown, the Spaniards and *Criollos* (children of Spaniards born in the colonies), the clergy and, finally, the indigenous population's common property. To these, I would also add, in the case of Chile, the non-indigenous agricultural communities that otherwise could be categorised as property belonging to the former group, Spaniards and *Criollo*s, but which took another pattern of development than the *latifundium-minifundium* complex.

In the following, I will refer briefly to the origin of the two major groups of peasants, the *inquilinos* (tenants) attached to the large *latifundia* or *hacienda* and the independent small peasantry of the *minifundia*. They are relevant for different parts of the text. The latter because it will lead us to the agricultural communities, the former because, I also have the *hacienda* El Totoral as a comparative case study. For this reason, a short introduction about the principal characteristics of the *hacienda* and its *inquilinos* will be given. This will relate, in particular, to the case of El Totoral and the *fundos* that arose from it, and I will not, with some limited exceptions, make any further reference to its *inquilinos*, but concentrate on the history of property transactions.

The hacienda and its inquilinos: basic characteristics

Much has been written about the *hacienda,* and its *inquilinos,* and the debate about its character (feudal, semi-feudal or other) has been long. I do not intend to go into this debate (for further references, see Chapter 1). I limit myself here to present some of the criteria used to characterise this institution where, depending on the author, emphasis is put on different aspects.

The origins of the *inquilino* system within the *hacienda* can, according to Borde and Góngora (1956:75-76), be traced back to the first half of the 1700s. It would keep a close relationship with what is designated as the *cerealización* (cerealisation or wheat cultivation) of the land, the consequent increase in land value and the growing need for labour in comparison with the pastoral economy, whose need of labour was less.

According to these authors, the *inquilino* system does not have its origins among Indians, at least in the Puangue Valley. On the contrary, due to the scarcity of the indigenous labour, the need for tying the white or *mestizo* to the land as producers grew. To these groups, the juridical statute of the indigenous labour could not be applied. As a solution, the *hacienda* would first have to give part of its lands in sharecropping (*mediería*) and in rental to the poor peasants who were paying revenue, in kind, or money for the land. The payment in kind and money was gradually substituted for the personal labour service, with which the *hacienda* assured the access to a constant labour force. Personal service for the *hacienda* on part of the labourer became the real form of payment for using the land of the landlord.

The substitution of sharecropping and rent for payment in labour would reflect the strengthening of the relations of production of the *hacienda* since the landless peasants, or those with insufficient land, was being subjected to the *hacienda*. By mid 1800s, the large *haciendas* of the Central region - which during that period had a great vogue in wheat production - continued to combine production based on the *inquilinos* with different forms of sharecropping, at the same time as some enterprises started to use wage-labour. These enterprises also had their activities enlarged through the exploitation of minerals and the saltpetre (Rivera, 1988b:50) in the north.

For Borde and Góngora (1956) the *hacienda* is characterised by an extensive production, generally accompanied by a sub-utilisation of the land, being in between the *estancia ganadera* (cattle ranch), with its lands in uncultivated state, and the most rationalised agricultural properties.

Baraona *et al* emphasise, the relations of production, whose core is the relationship *hacienda*/owner-direct producer within a traditional context of labour relations. The labour force is composed by *inquilinos* (tenants) and *peones* (day labourers). While the first sell their labour force for a payment in kind, the second do so for a salary. The *inquilino* system would represent the traditional semi-feudal element of the *hacienda* and the *fundos*. The *peonería* system, on the other hand, would represent the *hacienda*'s mercantile element. The *hacienda* makes use of the *peonería*'s advantages, still keeping the *inquilinos,* combining both systems (Baraona *et al*, 1961:226-228). From the *hacienda*, the *inquilinos* receive:

> a productive potential in land or in pasturage land, but the fulfilment of this potential depends on their work. They do not receive a harvested product but the opportunity to obtain it (Baraona *et al*, 1956:227).

As *inquilinos*, the Social Security Service understands:

> those agricultural workers for whom the hacienda-owner provides adequate room for them and their families, a piece of cultivation land, pasturage land for animals, etc., those which are empowered to send somebody else in their place [to work on the *hacienda*] (CIDA, 1966:6).

Mellafe emphasises the type of property. The *latifundia* is characterised as a form of:

> personal property, relatively vast, that constitutes a social and economic unit with some degree of rationalisation of the production that tends to be excluding with respect to the productive distribution and to the use of the agrarian resources /---/ it is unpersonal opposing this term to common usufruct, though many times, by testamental succession, its management is delivered to a hereditary community (Mellafe, 1981:92).

Gómez *et al* (1981, Vol. 5:771) stress the political aspect that the *hacienda* exercises, being the form of property that:

> was the central axis of the agrarian production and of the political domination in the countryside.

These authors indicate that the *haciendas* - studied by them during the 1960s - were in general terms divided between:

> those that undertake a modernisation process and those that maintain traditional relations of production and deteriorated.

While the first is characterised by the:

exploitation by their proprietors through administrators, efficiency in the use of the productive resources, modern technology and adequate life and work conditions for their peasants...

the second, on the other hand, is characterised by being:

> leased properties, with a low capitalisation level, inefficient use of the productive resources and insufficient life and work conditions for the peasants (Gómez *et al*, 1981, Vol. 5:781).

Like Baraona *et al*, Gómez *et al* (1981, Vol. 1:34), emphasise the double role that the *inquilino* has:

> on the one hand, is entrepreneur of its own productive royalties and by the other, receives a part of the salary in money and another in consumption royalties.

Within this context, the diffusion of the *inquilino* system on the *hacienda* is conceptualised as an index of traditionalism, while the inverse, a smaller quantity of *inquilinos* with respect to the wage-labourers, is considered as a modernisation index in the relations of production of the *hacienda*.

The proportion between these types of labour will, in any event, depend on the *hacienda's* endowment of land resources and capital. There is a clear relationship between the endowment of lands and capital on which the *hacienda* counts, in such a way that, the greater the endowment of lands in respect to the capital, the greater the lands delivery to the *inquilinos* will be, and the less widespread the wage-labour system. Now, I would suggest that it must not necessarily be that way. There may be the case of a landowner with either capital and land abundance, or more capital than land, but the land resource, whether in abundance or not, is normally less costly as a payment form than a wage in cash. More important, the land still belongs to the landlord. In other words, while the *hacienda* was not definitely converted into a 'fully-fledged' capitalist enterprise, through the exclusive use of wage-labour, the keeping of the *inquilino* system was always functional to the *hacienda*. This because the land delivered to the *inquilinos* constituted a resource that the *hacienda* had in abundance and that once it is in the possession of the landowner, it costs him nothing. This way the landowner can dispose freely of his capital for other purposes, not necessarily agricultural.

Gómez *et al* also refers to the system of domination on the *hacienda*, of which a central element is paternalism (existing between the *hacienda*-owner and the *inquilino*). As Mellafe (1981) and Gómez *et al* (1981), Albala *et al* (1967) also underline the element of domination that the *hacienda* exercises over the peasantry. The system of clientele through which the *hacienda* operates is based on the control that the landowner exercises:

> ... over the property of the land, the labour market, the exchange and the credit, the coercion and the authority... (Albala *et al*, 1967:36).

Thus:

> the peasants related with the landowner as a 'client', that is to say, he offered him his services and personal loyalty. In exchange for this, he could expect protection and paternal aid from the landowner (*Ibid*).

Patenalism deals with a form of social relationships characterised:

> by being asymmetrical, diffuse and shared. It is in first place a relationship of domination and subordination where the one who commands, expects to be obeyed and the subordinated expects to be commanded. This means that the expectations of the relationship are shared. The diffusion refers to the fact that this type of relationship covers all the aspects of the subordinated group, beyond all that is specifically labour related (Gómez *et al*, 1981, Vol. 2:134).

As a result of this, the *inquilino* is characterised by what Gómez *et al* - following Lehmann's typology of peasants' class conscience - designate a dependent class conscience, based more on a moral obligation than on a purchase-sale relationship. Archetti also emphasises that:

> ... the phenomenon of the bonds between patron-clients, appears in a certain structural situation in which the peasants depend on the land assignment and on work; basic resources controlled by a landlord. The landowners' class power /---/ is a mixture of legal privileges, the use of the coercion and the consensus of the clients. In regard to the peasants, it has been emphasised that in such situations esteem demonstrations, deference, loyalty and political passivity are the most common answers (Archetti, 1978:23).

Thus to summarise, the *hacienda* represents, from a class perspective, the private ownership of the land on behalf of a landowner and his family. This form of property, excluding others from the principal means of agricultural production (land), constituted the principal source of wealth and status, converting the *hacendados* or landlords into the economically and politically dominant class.

In its productive aspect, the *hacienda* is a traditional agricultural exploitation unit that produces - when it does - for the purpose of profit, either for an external or an internal market. This it does with an extensive production through the use of non wage-labourers that live within the limits of the property and are excluded from the ownership of the principal means of production. In exchange for their labour, the workers are compensated through payment in money and kind. Payment in kind is translated mainly into a temporary and conditioned access to an area of land, whose production will depend on the *inquilino's* own effort, the right to pasturage and other consumption royalties.

The labour force is subordinated to the patron through a paternalistic relationship that encompasses other economic and social aspects of the workers' life. For example, in domestic matters, making the landlord the godfather of his children, involving him in marriages, etc., or in political matters, at election time to vote for the landlord's candidate, in many cases the landlord himself. Accordingly, the dominance of the *hacienda* transcends the limits of the commercial transaction of purchase and sale of the labour force. It also constitutes a system of domination that reaches far beyond the limits of the property. Its domination circle is extended not only towards other economic fields as market, exchange and credit, but also towards the social arena of authority and coercion of its own labour as well as of the labour of the surroundings areas.

Until 1929 the landowner's class was indisputably the hegemonic class of the country, controlling 80% of the agricultural land of the central zone - the richest for agricultural use. With the 1929 crisis, the great properties in this zone began to lose their dominance in the Chilean agricultural system, and the division of an important number of *haciendas* into average size properties took place. In many cases, this division gave rise to an important expansion of the small property. Before the first agrarian reform process began, the great *haciendas* still controlled 56% of the country's agricultural land (Rivera, 1988a:66). With the agrarian reforms of the 1960s and onwards, the *inquilinos* disappear along with the vast properties of the *haciendas* (Rivera, 1988a:69).

Having discussed the *hacienda* and its *inquilinos* I will now turn to the origin and endurance of the small independent peasantry - the *minifundium*. Although, this term usually refers to a homogenous group, it is possible to differentiate at least three criteria. The one relevant here is its origin and endurance, because it will permit us to examine the origin of the agricultural communities of the Norte Chico (see Chapter 1).

The historical precedents of the *minifundium*

In the former section I attempted to give the general evolution of land structure formation in Chile, whose roots were to be found mainly in the colonial land grants distribution, which later gave rise to the *hacienda* institution. Here I will deal with the *minifundium* and its origin and preservation. As before, I will principally follow the pioneering works of both Borde and Góngora and Baraona *et al.* These authors give, in their description of the fragmentation and endurance of the agricultural property in the valleys Puangue and Putaendo, several keys towards an understanding of the development of the agricultural communities of Norte Chico. This is especially valid in the formation of the common mountainous or hilly land between the valleys.

There seems to be a general consensus in dealing with the origin of the *mininfundium* in Chile. Rivera suggests that in Hispanic America the peasantry originated basically through two processes. The first stems from the indigenous population incorporated into the mercantile economy, and the second from the *mestizo* population. The first is to be found in several Latin American countries, where the indigenous population was slowly incorporated into the colonial economy, but managing to preserve, on the whole, the specific features of their productive procedures (Rivera, 1988a:43-44). Chile would correspond to the second case, where the pre-Hispanic agriculture on the arrival of the Spaniards was incipient. Agriculture was only found in some irrigated valleys in the north-central regions of the country, under the dominance of the Inca Empire. Since the Inca Empire had only reached Chile some 50 years before the Spanish conquest, the indigenous population did not have the advanced type of agricultural economy that the Spaniards found in the heart of the Inca Empire (Rivera, 1988a:45).

Given the weak existence of pre-Hispanic agricultural productive forms and the sparse local population, which further decreased as a result of the conquest and colonisation processes, the peasantry originated fundamentally from the Spanish military *mestizo* population. This was achieved without managing to preserve any significant feature of the indigenous agrarian economy (Rivera, 1988a). In the Chilean case, the formation of the agricultural and peasant population as a rule:

> was originated largely by the processes of conquest and territorial occupation through colonisation. Because of this it is possible that the pre-capitalist forms of production that could be observed, originate rather from the European immigrant population themselves, representing adjustments to the concrete conditions of the occupation and colonisation zones (Rivera, 1988a:45).

Consequently, the Chilean peasantry would fundamentally originate from the colonial pattern of population settlements in the agricultural zones as a result of the concession of *mercedes* (and even *encomiendas*) and other forms of grants to the subjects of the Crown. This process was, according to Rivera, quite unusual in comparison with other Latin American countries.

Though in Hispanic America the major part of the indigenous population was confined in the so-called Indian villages, in Chile - where the indigenous population in comparison with other regions was not very numerous - most of these 'Indian villages' did not prosper as agricultural communities. The great *haciendas* mainly absorbed their population and land (Rivera, 1988a:70). These factors contributed to the consolidation of the *hacienda* system as the prevailing land tenure pattern, and to the settlement of the rural population during the colonial period.

From that time, and until the decade of the 1960s, two large categories of peasants existed in Chile; the *inquilinos* that emerged within the *hacienda* system and the small independent owners, peasants or *campesinos* of the *minifundium*. The *minifundium* originated during the colonial and the republican period, directly through donations of land to the soldiers of the conquest, or indirectly through the subdivision of the large *haciendas,* either due to inheritance or sale. This gave rise to a form of scattered rural settlements called *campesinado parcelario* (plot or parcelling peasantry). The prevailing social dynamic of this type of peasantry, with its distinguishing neighbourhood, is that each peasant lives on his own property and the relationships with neighbours is not very close. Therefore, it is not proper to consider them as peasant communities, inasmuch as they lack the specific social organisation and level of formalisation of those communities, which the 'Indian villages' gave rise to, and that were not absorbed by the *haciendas* (Rivera, 1988a:70-71). Accordingly, of three possible historical origins that I distinguish for agricultural property in Chile - pre-Hispanic, colonial private property and post-colonial (see Table 1.2) - the principal for the *minifundium* is certainly the different colonial land distributions, and within these, the great property of the *hacienda* emerged from the colonial *mercedes de tierras*. This inasmuch as the land grants became the principal land appropriation mechanism, constituting the dominant land ownership form within the Chilean agrarian structure, and from where the *minifundium* will predominantly emerge. This is the line supported by Borde and Góngora and by Baraona *et al*, and one that Rivera and I add to. Let me here examine with more detail, what these authors write about the development of the *minifundium*.

Borde and Góngora (1956:145) support the view that the origin of the small property in Chile is to be found - as the *fundos, hijuelas*, plots or simple sites - mainly in the institution of the *hacienda*, which emerged from the colonial *mercedes de tierras*. They exclude the communal property of the indigenous agricultural communities southern as well as northern parts from this origin, together with other types of property distributed by the Crown in the colonial period in the urban periphery such as *chacras, quintas* and *fincas*.

Baraona *et al* (1961:152) indicate that although there were many factors at play in the division of certain properties - and the maintenance or increase of others, the constitution of the small property would, as a rule, mainly be the result of the continuous paternal land partition of the properties originated by the land grants among all the heirs.

Excepting then colonial land distributions of the urban periphery and other indigenous sites, I would add other sources of origin of the small property, those of the distribution made by the Crown in rural areas. If we accept the line of Borde and Góngora, and also of Baraona *et al*, all rural land would have been distributed in the form of *mercedes de tierras*. But this was not the case. These authors are not unconscious of this fact, but

Land Tenure Formation in Colonial Chile

their thesis in its generalisation, obscures other possible origins of the small agricultural property.

It is therefore necessary to be reminded that the lower colonial social strata had access to the land in the form of peonies (*peonías*) and cavalries (*caballerías*). To these have to be added other types of resource and labour force distributions that gave, by various means, the property of the land. For example, the *encomiendas*, mining sites in the forms of *asientos* (mining settlements), and *placillas*, foundries and mills that gave rise to hamlets and villages (Cunill, 1975:69). Even without formal (colonial) support, the population of these mining sites probably appropriated the land in which they were seated, becoming *minifundia*. All types of previously mentioned settlements, alone or in combination with others, could in theory also be present in the origin of the agricultural communities of Region IV. This does not invalidate the thesis of the origin of the agricultural communities mainly in the *mercedes* and *encomiendas*. It does rather add complexity to the problem of the origin of these social agrarian institutions, pointing out the combination of several factors intervening in their development.

Endurance of the minifundium

In a social environment mastered by the predominance and power of the large *haciendas*, the conservation of the small private property in particular, according to Borde and Góngora, has depended mainly on the large *haciendas* (I will return to this observation in Chapter 8).

These authors distinguish between basic factors that have protected the small property, and subsequent conjunctural factors that, depending on their character, have been influential either in its preservation or its disappearance. Basic conservation factors are the same as those contributing to its appearance and are; the geographical isolation, the relative poverty which leads to an unavoidable continuation of its subdivision (a factor which placates the interest of the landowners of these extremely atomised and scattered lands), and the mountainous or hilly geographical environment that soon evolves into a semi-collective (read communal) state, permitting the cattle raising. Facing a land concentration process on the part of the large properties, in the small property 'an advanced enough subdivision will be more resistant than an elemental one' (Borde and Góngora, 1956:182).

Subsequent conjunctural factors could contribute to the conservation, or fragmentation, of the small property. An example of the first would be the labour demand from the large *haciendas* that allows the temporary wage-labour for the peasants, permitting them to preserve their properties instead of selling them. This point of view is interesting because is shows how wage-labour instead of meaning a definite proletarianisation, can rather represent a mechanism contributing in the conservation of the *minifundium*. An example of the second would be external factors such as the infrastructure development of highway construction with their following currents of traffic. This could lead to the emergence of towns in connection with the road construction. In a similar manner the installation of commercial or administrative entities into that zone could result in small property fragmentation.

Depending on all these factors, the fortune of these kernels or small property islands in the zone studied by Borde and Góngora (1956:182-194) differentiated between those that were in process of disappearance in the wake of their absorption into the great property of the *haciendas* and *fundos*, those which had been stabilised and not absorbed by the great property and, finally, those that showed progress and had left behind their character of hamlets and had developed into small towns.

Of these three groups, the one that is of greatest interesting here is the second since it corresponds to the *minifundium*. Borde and Góngora (1956:187) refer to it in the following manner, that there existed in the Puangue Valley, besides the *haciendas* and *fundos*, and in close relationship to them, old fractionated land that gave rise to:

> villages and diffuse hamlets, simple juxtaposition of tiny agricultural enterprises that live in symbiosis with the neighbouring fundos.

An example of this type of small property not absorbed by the great property, and thus becoming stabilised, would be according to these authors, the zone of Los Rulos in the Puangue Valley.

They indicate that these small property islands on the margin of the estates, remain in 'many aspects the minifundium of the Mediterranean and its small shepherds or farmers' (Borde and Góngora, 1956:184-185). In Los Rulos were gathered, '....all the conditions for a rapid subdivision and a long continuity of the small property...'. In this:

not lending themselves to quite rapid [physical] divisions, the hills stayed undivided, so that without having been ever *endowed* of real organisation they became a community of facto (Borde and Góngora, 1956:185; emphasis added).

However, these authors stress, that these are not communities in the strict sense. These *minifundia*, they categorically assert, are nothing other than ancient partition islands, inserted within the predominance of the *fundos* (Borde and Góngora, 1956:194). (If we examine IREN's Map, Figure 3.4, we will see that in the commune of Canela the properties that are inserted in the predominance of the agricultural communities are the *fundos*. See also Figure 1.1, showing the distribution of the agricultural communities in Region IV.)

These *minifundia* could be considered communities in the vague sense, because of the non-division or uncertainty of the boundaries, but not in the sense that is understood by sociologists and geographers; that is to say, a community organisation. Discarding the non-division and the usufruct of the hills, these small peasant agglomerations are devoid of all community content, representing, according to Borde and Góngora (1956:205), the antithesis of those communities of indigenous origin still in existence in the Norte Grande and in the Norte Chico. According to these authors, it seems that the existing regulation in the communities of the *Puangue* valley, would follow the desire of avoiding too much disorder, as nothing in them recalls the inheritance of community formulas. It deals rather with an experiment of co-operative documented by some 'illustrious' neighbours, sometimes, strangers to the place, in the case of Colliguay, where the inspiration of the reforms and administration came from an outsider.

I have to reject the last part of this argument by Borde and Góngora. The idea that the community organisation would represent a kind of experimental co-operative originating from some illustrious character is in my opinion simplistic, even if there were one or more cases studied by these authors. However, the presence of some illustrious individuals would hardly explain the emergence of so many communities in different regions. Would the current agricultural communities of Region IV, some two hundred in total, all have that origin? Or to express it with the help of Durkheim (1984:XXXVIII; Preface to the Second Edition):

so persistent an institution cannot depend upon special contingent and chance circumstances.

Such organisations emerge rather as an attempt to introduce order, where traditional formulas no longer fulfil their function. A new regulation must substitute the old one, or the absence of it, while population pressure on land grows. In this way, these communities were never 'endowed' with community organisation, as if they have stemmed from nothing. This was the case of the reserves of indigenous populations, endowed with land and a specific organisation to manage it by the Crown's decision, therefore implanted from above and mostly by force.

In the description by Baraona *et al* of the hill communities created in the Valley of Putaendo, these do not appear under the residual communities title (see also Table 1.1), as Baraona *et al* themselves, from the source of Borde and Góngora, call them. They write of 'small property islands', of '*minifundia*' or 'islands of peasantry', all under the generic title of 'common hills in villages and spontaneous hamlets in Central Chile' that Baraona *et al*, also take from Borde and Góngora.

Apparently, Baraona *et al*, consider this type of social collectives as communities in a deeper sense than Borde and Góngora inasmuch as they indicate that the community organisation in the Valley of Putaendo dates from the end of the 1800s. They indicate, however, that there is no evidence that their organisation will be prior to 1850 since they lack 'the traditional elements, which are present in the communities of the Norte Chico' (Baraona *et al*, 1961:130). However, it is not very clear from their text, which is the traditional elements of the communities in Norte Chico, but they probably refer to the land tenure (see Chapter 1).

In any event, with respect to the origin of the communities in the Valley of Putaendo, three instances can, according to Baraona *et al*, be singled out in their development:

> in the first place, the period of the non-division of the hilly land; in second place, the period in which the rights of the hilly land are recognised, but still not crystallised into the so called communities, and finally, the appearance of these (Baraona *et al*, 1961:129).

According to these authors, several factors contributed to the conversion of the hills into common property. Firstly, the gradual deterioration of the environment progressively decreased the value of the mountainous land. This makes it necessary for:

> the regulation of the shepherding, of the number of cattle heads, the quantity of fuelwood and wood that can be drawn from the hills; [2] a considerable increase of the population in the irrigated area; [3] the threat of litigation with neighbouring *fundos,* demanding the registration of the property; and, finally, [4] the need for registration and legalisation of the mountainous land, stemming from new legal requirements with respect to property (Baraona *et al*, 1961:130).

The primary antecedent in the distribution of the mountainous land in the communities of the Valley of Putaendo is to be found, according to Baraona *et al*, (1961:130) in the organisation of the water for irrigation.

With respect to their geographical location, they affirm that the agricultural communities are presented 'where the contrast is abrupt, in relief and in agricultural value'. They are not found, therefore:

> in those areas of ancient subdivision where the difference of the agricultural value between slopes and flat land is little or insignificant. In Navidad [Prov. of Santiago], for example, where the small hills are only the remains of a dissected plain and the flat land generally lacks irrigation, the hillsides are of individual appropriation when they can be used for dry cultivation (Baraona *et al*, 1961:127).

Due to the impossible task of subdividing the mountainous land in the same way the irrigated land was divided, the former evolved into common land. In this way, common land substituted:

> the physical subdivision of the mountainous land by a subdivision of rights: divided the flat land into so many properties, the hill is divided into so many rights (Baraona *et al*, 1961:129).

Hence, the organisation and regulation of the mountainous land was only realised according to Baraona *et al*, long after the mountains were already common, this contrasting with the early water regulation for irrigation. One thing is clear, these authors underline that 'what at present is community (read communal) property, was private property in the past inasmuch as the current communities' territoriality coincides with the ancient properties of land occupation'. In effect, the agricultural communities, were neither founded as collectives, nor had they been granted land of collective possession:

> It deals with common land – generally hills or shepherding hillsides without agricultural value – that are owned in common by owners of agricultural properties forming an adjacent kernel. The kernels can have the current character of villages or towns, but their development, is always spontaneous /.../ is a product of local factors or advantages due to their location /.../ Coinciding with kernels of ancient subdivision, the successive subdivisions' process of the flat land could not proceed parallel in the hills that were part of the original properties (Baraona *et al*, 1961:126).

It is in this sense, that the affirmation of Baraona *et al* (1961:127) of this type of agricultural communities, because of a spontaneous development, must be understood. This is, as a form of land ownership which though not necessarily original, does not cease to be 'perhaps the most spontaneous and the most autochthonous of /.../ [Chile's] communitarian structures'.

The communities described here would correspond to the small agricultural property that managed to stabilise itself in time (from this probably the name 'residual') and where the hills evolved into communal property. It is interesting to verify that recognising a singular type of organisation of agrarian property and production in these communities - in which Baraona *et al*, differ from Borde and Góngora, they continue in the line traced by these authors, in not including these communities under an own name: residual communities. However, these types of communities, residual or not, bring us to the origin of the agricultural communities of Region IV, because the described process is also the most plausible for their origin.

The residual communities, apart from the so-called Norte Chico, were of the types of communities that, according to Baraona *et al*, existed in the Norte Chico (Chapter 1). According to these authors, the residual communities differ from that of the Norte Chico, being the result of a spontaneous process originating in the division of the large property. The so-called communities of the Norte Chico would have originated from settlements of indigenous population. These, opposed to the residual, were land plots in the form of reserves endowed by the colonial regime, once colonisers had expropriated their own land.

To be able to distinguish between the origins of these two types of community in Region IV today, according to the last two criteria, it would be necessary to study many of the 200 existing agricultural communities in this region individually. One thing is clear that these two origins can hardly be the only ones, since there was a series of other colonial distributions besides *mercedes de tierras*. To differentiate, in any event, the residual communities from those of the Norte Chico as described by Baraona *et al*, in terms of their land tenure forms is apparently more difficult, since the same characteristics seem to be valid for both. With time, these two (or more) types of communities would be merged into one form.

The Norte Chico's agricultural communities: historical precedents

Santander ($s.a.$:1) indicates that the origin of the agricultural communities is a historical problem still without a satisfactory solution. Part of the problem lays in the posing of the problem itself. This is the singular form in which the question presupposes that all agricultural communities have one and the same historical origin.

I consider it important to distinguish between factors, which explain the origin of the agricultural communities, from those that explain their emergence or formation, even though these are not easy to separate. Origin and emergence are certainly related. When examined them in the light of the development of the agrarian structure in the Norte Chico, one feature is particularly outstanding. Providing the hypothesis of the various origins of the agricultural communities is accepted, the most outstanding feature of this process must be that, in spite of having different origins, various properties evolved in only one form of land ownership: the semi-communal. This process would point towards other factors as being important in this historical development. This is not to deny the problem of the historical origin of the agricultural communities. To the contrary, the problem of the origin is important, because it is from this knowledge that the question emerges, of why, in spite of the diversity of origins, the semi-communal land ownership form of the agricultural communities started to take shape.

There are no systematic attempts to the question of the origin and development of the agricultural communities of Region IV, their knowledge being fragmentary and not always empirically documented. The information about the communities that has emerged in the last decades has rarely been derived from social sciences. On the few instances when it has, it does not deal with the socio-historical problems that are the main subject of this text, but rather with reports and improvement proposals about their actual situation and future.

Given this status quo, is not strange that Borde and Góngora and Baraona *et al*, are still so central. Although CIDA (1966), Cañón (1964); Albala *et al* (1967); IREN (1977/78); Castro and Bahamondes (1986) are aware that the origin of the communities is to be traced mainly in the colonial *mercedes de tierras*, they do not, however, contemplate their development from the perspective of a conversion to semi-communal land ownership from private property. Why did only certain land properties or portions of them evolve into agricultural communities and others remain private? Why did the latter properties continue to be in private ownership? Neither of these issues have been contemplated from the historical perspective of one process - towards the privatisation of land - giving rise to two modalities or paths of social development: the *haciendas* and the communities.

Santander is in this sense an exception and he has tried to make a brief attempt to systematise the different origins of the agricultural communities. He does it within a proposal aimed to eradicate poverty within the communities, and does not develop the issue further, limiting himself to presenting the various representatives of what he calls explanatory hypothesis.

According to Santander (*s.a.*:1-9), the hypothesis advanced by various authors in respect to the origin of the agricultural communities, can be split into five groups; pre-Hispanic origin, as of *encomiendas* and *mercedes de tierra*, derived from the fragmentation of the agrarian property, derived from ancient mining *asientos* (settlements), *placillas,* derived from the re-gathering of indigenous population during the colonial period. To these five hypotheses, Santander adds two others; derived from the '*pueblos de indios*' (Indian villages) and, finally, derived from the influence of the Castilian community system. Yet, these origins do not always appear in a 'pure' form. An origin is often deduced from another, and one and the same author can give more than one origin as an explanatory hypothesis. Some of these origins make reference to what is the result of a development, for example, the natural fragmentation of the agrarian property.

The seven advanced explanatory hypotheses can, however, be reduced to six, because I consider the fifth and sixth be grouped together as a single entity. Furthermore, they can be split largely into two groups; one pre-Hispanic and five of Colonial origin. I will now consider the first and less probable proposal.

Pre-Hispanic origin

One representative of this hypothesis is Ramírez, a veterinary. He emphasises, without ignoring other causes, that the agricultural communities emerged as a social system in areas dominated by the Inca Empire. Santander himself, although inclining more towards the hypothesis encompassing the colonial period, is of the opinion that for the most part the agricultural communities are products of the mixing of pre-Hispanic with colonial institutions.

As a first critical point to this hypothesis of the pre-Hispanic origin, I would indicate, firstly, that when dealing with Chile, the tradition of the Inca Empire was relatively new at the beginning of the Spanish conquest (1536) in Chile (Rivera, 1988(a); Mostny, 1981). According to the historian Grete Mostny:

> the Inca invasion and occupation in Chile was relatively short. It did not last for more than some 70 years in the Norte Grande and perhaps only some 30 years in Central Chile /.../ In that moment was produced the invasion and occupation of the Spanish, putting an end to the Chilean pre-history (Mostny, 1981:165).

The relatively short duration of the Inca domination on the systems of pre-Inca agricultural organisation makes the hypothesis unlikely. This however, does not annul any pre-Hispanic indigenous origin, but this must rather be Diaguita - the Norte Chico culture that existed prior to the arrival of the Incas - or more probably a mixture of both cultures, added thereafter to the Spanish. Secondly, an argument that weakens the weight of this hypothesis, is the reduction of the indigenous population in the Norte Chico during the 1600s and 1700s, although this was at a lesser pace than in the Central zone (Carmagnani, 1963:24). Many Indians in this zone were not, as Carmagnani shows, native of it. The agricultural communities, based on previous local tradition, could hardly have been constituted on such a basis. This author finds that the free Indians in La Serena in 1699 come mostly from the Araucanía (Region IX) and Tucumán (current part of Argentina), and from one or another places bordering La Serena. In 1740, the indigenous population again originated fundamentally from the Araucanía and neighbouring areas (Carmagnani, 1963:22). That is to say, of the free Indians, the majority had migrated into the region and nothing makes it reasonable to suppose that the situation of other groups was different.

According to Carmagnani, by the end of the 1600s three indigenous people existed in the region, each with a different juridical status; the *encomendados*, those of deposit and the free. The deposit Indians emerged as a separate group due to the end of the slavery of the Araucanian Indians. However, they continued to be 'owned' in much the same manner by their ancient owners but were, in effect, 'free'. Due to the abuse of the deposit Indians, the deposits were eliminated in 1703, by which they acquired the status of free men. Thus, the group of free Indians was composed of ex-deposit Indians, Indians uprooted from their originating place, or Indians who had run away from the *encomiendas*.

Towards the end of the 1600s, the group of free Indians, in relation to the group of the *encomendados*, increased slowly. However, the number of *encomendados* declined, mainly due to the destruction of the '*pueblos de indios*' (reserves) and their transportation to the *haciendas*. This was a process that took place parallel to the constitution of the large property of the *hacienda*. With the transportation of the Indians to the *haciendas*, their land remained without cultivation, thus being prey of *mestizos* and poor whites. This shows, according to Carmagnani, that it was not mainly indigenous people's land, which was of interest to the landlords, but their labour. The transportation of indigenous people to the *haciendas* accentuated the mixing process between groups, increasing the free *mestizo* population (Carmagnani, 1963:21-24).

All these factors combined to make the existence of any greater pre-Hispanic precedents unlikely in the agricultural communities of the Norte Chico, without any mixture with colonial institutions. If, for no other reason, the hypothesis of the pre-Hispanic origin of some agricultural communities falls by itself, this would imply that there were indigenous population groups that were not affected by the colonisation process, something that is unlikely. However, the indigenous population did not disappear. The first census, realised in the beginnings of the Republic, dating from 1813, shows this. Unfortunately, the schedules corresponding to the Department that today would include the current Canela commune are missing. However, some data can be presented in Table 4.1 that will show the number of indigenous population of the other departments of the current Region IV, at the beginning of the Republic.

Table 4.1 The percentage indigenous population with respect to the Province of Coquimbo at the beginning of the 1800s

Population Department	Total indigenous population	% indigenous population of the total	Total
La Serena	870	12.4	7,050
Elqui	1,157	22.7	5,085
Coquimbo	179	11.2	1,592
Ovalle	1,927	12.5	15,393

Source: Keller (1956):15-49

Colonial origin

Origin of the encomiendas and mercedes de tierras. To support the hypothesis that the agricultural communities have their origin in the *encomiendas* and *mercedes de tierras*, Santander cites, among others, CIDA (1966), González (1970), Gómez (1973), IREN-CORFO (1977) and Cañón (1964). To this group, I would also include Borde and Góngora, Baraona *et al*, González (1970), and Gómez (1973) are not included in my publication.

Santander also specifies that in the dry land of the Norte Chico, the beneficiaries of the *encomiendas* and *mercedes de tierras* were largely low rank officers in the Spanish army. The way in which Santander develops this view gives the impression that it has been derived directly from Cañón, but this is not her opinion. It is also the opinion of CIPRES (1992:6), who indicates that the origin of the agricultural communities:

> goes back to the XVII century, and they refer to land grants conceded by the Spanish Governors *to soldiers of low rank* /.../ While the land given as grants to the officers, occupied the better land of the valleys, this land given to the troops, lacked the sufficient resources to secure a sustained

agricultural activity. They corresponded to dry extensions with small, irrigated areas (emphasis added).

Santander adds another element to the *encomiendas* and *mercedes de tierras* hypothesis, the low social status of the beneficiaries. To this view of the agricultural communities, arising from land given to low-rank soldiers, would, I suggest, a contra argument - that the *mercedes de tierras* and *encomiendas* were reserved for the most outstanding conquerors and colonisers within the colonial society. Hence, to affirm that the *mercedes* and *encomiendas* were given to low-rank soldiers involves a contradiction.

As an example of this, it is interesting to note here that from Chile's colonial founding families (1540-1600), 64.8% (46) received *encomiendas*, 49.3% (35) got *mercedes de tierras* and the rest 38% (27) - the most favoured group - received both *encomiendas* and *mercedes*. Most of them belonged to the *hidalguía* or nobility (Retamal *et al*, 1992:726). One exception was Pedro Cortés Monroy, of *pechero* or plebeian origin, and his descendants, associated to the origin of the agricultural community Canela Baja and others. In spite of their origin, they came to belong to the most favoured group, receiving both *encomiendas* and *mercedes*. Thus, the hypothesis that the dry land of the Norte Chico assigned as *mercedes* and *encomiendas* to low rank officers is inaccurate, especially for the case of the Canela commune. Furthermore, to be rewarded with *mercedes* and *encomiendas* was not easy, and its beneficiaries had spent decades on the battlefields against the Indian population, partly financing the war from their own resources (see Chapter 5).

Santander supports the hypothesis that the *mercedes de tierras* and *encomiendas* have been best documented by the agronomists Gastó *et al* who have written about the agricultural communities Yerba Loca and Carquindaño in the commune of Canela. The work of Gastó *et al*, is not, as Santander indicates, well documented, if by that he means on colonial historical sources, as is the case with Cañón, whose work apparently serves as a base for Gastó *et al* (1986) and also for Villaroel *et al* (1988), without necessarily including her work in their bibliographies. This hypothesis is indeed the best documented but not because of Santander's argument. Santander himself misrepresents some historical details of the work of Gastó *et al*, for the case of La Canela (see Chapter 7).

If the version that the agricultural communities emerged in dry land given to low-rank soldiers were true, it remains to be explained why just parts of this land became agricultural communities, and others conformed into *haciendas*. Or, to put it with Cañón's (1964:46) words:

> it draws the attention to the fact that some of these primitive estancias have evolved into haciendas and others into communities.

Nonetheless, the hypotheses that the agricultural communities have their origin in the *mercedes de tierra,* and also in the *encomiendas,* are still the most plausible, but not necessarily associated to the idea of dry land given to low rank soldiers. With respect to this, it is important to differentiate between dry and marginal land. What was then dry land still is, - with the exception of those places where irrigation has been artificially introduced - but marginal land today was not necessarily marginal then. Marginality of the land is a relative matter, very much depending on available technology.

Origin of the fragmentation of the agrarian property. Within this group Santander includes Pascal's work from 1968 (a book that in this work sometimes appears as Albala *et al*) (see Chapter 1), and Castro and Bahamondes (1984). This work corresponds, in this book, to Castro and Bahamondes, 1983.

Albala *et al* (1967:13), studying power relations in Hurtado Valley in Region IV, explain, supporting themselves on Cañón, the emergence of the agricultural communities with the successorial or hereditary subdivision of property. The most important explanation is based on the economic crisis of agricultural wheat activity in the zone. This crisis would have restructured the land tenure in the zone, leading to a greater subdivision of property, either through sale or settlement of owners on their land. According to these authors, there was a reduction in the Norte Chico of the agricultural export trade towards Peru around the end of 1600s, caused by the increased exports from landowners of the Central zone. As a result, only the strongest *haciendas* survived, while the weaker ones would either have sold their land or the owners settled in them, the last becoming agricultural communities (Albala *et al*, 1967:12-13).

Like previous authors, Castro *et al* (*s.a.*), indicate that the communities coexist with large estates, with which they dispute the territory. They would then be the product of the subdivision of the great property and its inability to face the sway of the international economy from 1500s to the 1700s (see also Castro and Bahamondes, 1983).

All these authors base themselves on Carmagnani and Keller. For Carmagnani, the economy of the Norte Chico (particularly in the zone that supplied the Peruvian region with wheat) was established already by the end of the 1600s and the beginning of the 1700s, before the decrease of cereal production in Peru and before the Chilean Central zone was converted into the main exporting zone towards Peru. Wheat cultivation on a large scale began in the area of La Serena (Region IV) to Quillota (Region V) in the first decades of the 1600s, thereafter to not only become an agricultural zone but a wheat exporting zone. This resulted in a change of direction in the economic activity from a cattle-mining economy towards an agricultural-mining economy.

Towards the 1720s, however, the export of wheat began to decrease as a result of a series of crises, mainly due to a decrease in the mining activity in Peru. The strengthening of agriculture would have displaced cattle raising to less fertile and poorer quality land, leading probably, as Carmagnani (1963:33-36) indicates, to the disappearance of the bovine cattle and their substitution by goat rearing, which were less demanding and better suited to the poor land.

This hypothesis of the origin of the agricultural communities could be reduced to as it was before, i.e., the *encomiendas* and *mercedes de tierra*, because it would deal with the subdivision and economic fortune of the *hacienda* institution, which had emerged from the *mercedes de tierra*. Therefore, the hypothesis of the fragmentation of the agrarian property has more to do with the formation of the agricultural communities than with their origin.

In this socio-economic process, the role of the commercial relationships with Peru would have played an important role economically and ecologically. Firstly, this occurred in the economic exploitation of displacing and substituting cattle rearing by goat rearing from the valleys to the mountainous land. Secondly, the contraction of this trade led to the disappearance or fragmentation of those estates that could not withstand the crisis. Within this hypothesis of the fragmentation can also be included Cañón, who asserts that the heirs of these lands that become agricultural communities left the property, in common form, as an inheritance to their children (i.e., Estancia La Canela). According to Santander, Cañón emphasises that this was what the beneficiaries of the *mercedes de tierra* and *encomiendas* did, but this is incorrect since Cañón refers mainly to the

1800s; not to the 1500s and 1600s, the period in which the *encomiendas* and *mercedes* and were awarded.

According to Cañón, a particular method of land division was practised by the heirs from about the 1855s onward in the agricultural communities in the current Commune of Canela. This involved firstly measuring the land along the river or ravine, which was thereafter divided into equal parts for each heir, corresponding to a *hijuela* in the form of perpendicular corridors departing to and from both sides of the rivers and ravines. It was only this land that was fenced in the first instance, showing according to Cañón, their importance for the sustenance of the peasant family. The dry land, on the other hand, given its low profitability and inferior quality, did not justify a highly expensive enclosure (Cañón, 1964: 41,49). This argument is very similar to the one presented by Borde and Góngora, but especially by Baraona *et al*, for the Valley of Putaendo. This will also be referred to below and in Chapter 10.

The origin of mining asientos (settlements) and placillas. In this category, Santander includes the work of Borde and Santana, as well as Castro and Bahamondes (1986). The book by Borde and Santana to which Santander refers is *Le Chile. La terre et les hommes*, Paris, Editions du CNRS, 1980. I will also include Cunill (1975:60). According to him, the mining settlements, called *asientos*, were:

> basic concentrations of mining populations close to the mines. These unifunctional establishments, with a male population, dedicated exclusively to extraction work in the mines, are temporary and improvised, formed spontaneously without any kind of legal formality.

Although Cunill considers that most of these mining settlements, as *asientos*, *placillas*, foundries and mills, were only temporary, the fact that even Mincha (commune of Canela), is mentioned as an *asiento*, shows rather the opposite (see Chapter 7). This opposing concept is even supported by himself since, according to him, the cities Illapel and Combarbalá (Choapa and Limarí provinces) - also former *asientos* - have arisen from mining settlements during the 1700s. Even a place called Canela is mentioned, but since Cunill situates it in the then Petorca *Diputación*, it must deal with another Canela than the one that is the subject of this book. There are in fact today three Canelas (Canela Alta,

Canela Baja and Canela Media) somewhere in the border region between the present Valparaíso and Petorca Provinces.

This origin of the agricultural communities in various colonial mining grants (as *asientos* and *placillas*) also corresponds to an economic explanation. As Santander indicates, quoting Castro and Bahamondes, these camps of ex-mining population resulted from the decrease of the mineral they exploited, thus evolving towards cattle raising and agricultural subsistence in those lands bordering to the mining sites originally granted by the colonial regime, land that they *de facto* appropriated.

The origin of the re-gathering of the indigenous population and of 'pueblos de indios'. Though Santander separates the origin of re-gathering of the indigenous population (hypothesis 5) from the origin of the *'pueblos de indios'* (Indian villages) (hypothesis 6), it is possible to combine them as long they are not differentiated by any specific criteria, something that Santander fails to do. As representative of the first group, Santander includes the work of Castro and Bahamondes (1986), as well as Borde and Santana. In the second group is Santander himself. He adds the hypothesis of origin in the *'pueblos de indios'*. I include here both Borde and Góngora (1956), but especially Baraona *et al* (1961).

Returning to Castro and Bahamondes (1986), Santander indicates that a possible origin of the communities can be found in the displacement of the indigenous population to marginal land on the part of the *encomenderos*, who kept the better land. With reference to Borde and Santana, Santander indicates that some communities would correspond to indigenous groupings expelled by the Spanish occupation.

Santander identifies the *'pueblos de indios'* as a possible origin of the agricultural communities. This corresponded to the need of supplying the mining economy with a labour force, as was the case in the Norte Chico. With time, the population would have appropriated the neighbouring dry land, turning it into agricultural communities.

The main difference between hypothesis 5 and hypothesis 6 is that the *'pueblos de indios'* were organised by the colonial regime, while the agricultural communities resulted from other types of re-gathering of the indigenous population. The latter would be rather spontaneous, that is to say, a result of the utilisation of the prevailing circumstances, the indigenous population appropriating the land without necessary legal sanction on the part of colonial regime. In this concept, I would also include the work of Borde and Góngora, and particularly that of Baraona *et al*. It is not necessary to repeat their ideas; they have developed these hypotheses of the origin of the communities of the Norte Chico more clearly than any others. Baraona *et al*, included under the re-gathering of the indigenous, without distinction, all the other variations, establishments derived from '*pueblos de indios*', originating in efforts to concentrate dispersed population, or from being dismissed to land of lesser value (see Chapter 1). This explanation is socio-economic: the struggle for land between different social groups, a struggle in which the indigenous population has historically been the loser, first faced by the invading group, then by their heirs and finally, by the *mestizos*, the result of the mixture of both groups.

The origin of the Castilian community system. According to Santander (*s.a.*:7), the origin of the agricultural communities can in probability, also be found in the influence of the Castilian community system. The newly arrived Spanish would have attempted to implant the tradition of the *Mesta* from the Iberian Peninsula. According to Santander, the introduction of communitarian property, municipal and also inter-municipal in Spain, would have begun in those territories that remained free in the Re-Conquest (718-1492) against the Arabs. This system then became dominant in the economic and agrarian structure.

The *Mesta* would correspond to the peak and decline of cattle rearing, but above all to the powerful influence that the *Real Mesta*, or cattlemen association (1273-1526) (Braudel, 1981, Vol. 1:117-120) had in the Spanish Court. To the *Mesta* belonged the northern transhumant sheep and cattle owners of León, Segovia, Soria and Cuenca, who utilised the southern fields in a communitarian or common system in La Mancha, Extremadura and Andalucía, embracing a transhumance of almost 800 km. The private property did not escape from this system, which was also forced to open their fields to any cattle after the sowings season. Borde and Góngora and Baraona *et al*, as a form of organisation introduced by the colonial regime, has also been developed by this origin thesis.

Stringing together some threads

The arguments of Borde and Góngora and Baraona *et al*, constitute here a thread that provides practically all the explanatory hypotheses of the origin of the agricultural communities. These, I would suggest, are still the most complete, in spite of the fact that these authors do not refer specifically to the Norte Chico, but to other zones.

The most satisfactory of all these concepts is that of the *mercedes de tierras* and *encomiendas*, from the very beginning one of the points of departure for my own investigation. Logically, it is easy to adhere to this line. If the agrarian structure in Chile were related primarily to the colonial institutions of the *mercedes de tierras* and *encomiendas*, then why would the agricultural communities be an exception? This is not to deny other origins. On the contrary, to empirically establish the origin of the agricultural communities of Region IV presents a fascinating investigation that is yet to be completed. Before continuing the discussion, some of the threads relating to the formation of the agricultural communities of various origins should be strung together.

The interesting question that the perspective of the multiple origins of the agricultural communities' poses is that independent of the diversity, all these properties evolved into one type of integrated land property form: the semi-communal. This points then, to factors that are not related to the origin itself, but that impacts decisively in that development and defines the two forms of land ownership (private and common) that coexists in one socio-economic institution, the semi-communal of the agricultural communities.

The arguments of Borde and Góngora and Baraona *et al* are summarised below together with the key factors that imply the formation of the agricultural communities. The authors employed no form of hierarchical approach in dealing with these factors and, therefore, the important element of this discussion will be to identify a constant. The importance of the geographical environment in the formation of the agricultural communities will be stressed since that geographical environment maintains a close relationship to the colonial, political economy, constituting the base of the colonial order.

Borde and Góngora discuss the following factors in the conservation of the small property and the emergence of the common hilly or mountainous land:

- geographical location in isolated sectors;
- extreme subdivision of the properties, acting as a brake to the greed of the landowners by pre-empting extremely atomised land;
- mountainous or semi-mountainous landscape;
- neighbourhood composed of larger agricultural properties and also of mining zones, where the small peasantry sell their labour, helping to complement their economy and to preserve their land.

The authors suggest that in the case of a small property, the mountainous land stayed undivided due to the fact that, in comparison with the flat land, it was not easy to divide it in the same form and thus it was passed spontaneously to constitute the common property. In addition, the common land for shepherding has its historical precedents in the colonial period, in the *estancias de ganado* (cattle ranches). This phenomenon would find its explanation, at the same time, in the need for complementation of resources in areas where the vegetable development has different seasonal paces (geographic explanation). Generally, by the end of November, when the vegetation reduces in the valleys, the cattle is moved from the low and coastal sectors to the summer grass of the Andes mountain chain or *veranadas*.

When the flat land was then fenced, a product of the combination of cattle rearing with agriculture (the economic explanation) permitted the grass community to persist in the hills due to the transhumance of the cattle. Even this usage in the mountains would have resulted with the fencing of the hills.

Seeing it within the context of the historical Spanish precedents, the subsistence of the grass community or *estancias de ganado* within certain properties after the successive divisions appears as a continuation of a former tradition. Due to the functionality that it presents, permitting these sectors with many owners - that gradually evolved into agricultural communities - to enjoy the practice of common fields, allowing them to subsist with the help of goat exploitation in the hills, although having very small cultivation plots in the flat land. These are not small properties, in general, but small properties of arable and irrigated land.

Baraona *et al*, refer to three stages in the development of mountainous land:

- the non-division of the mountainous land (to which Borde and Góngora also refer);
- recognition of the rights of the mountainous land; and
- the consolidation of this form of property.

They suggest that the hills are not physically suited to subdivision in the same form as the irrigation land and were, therefore, divided according to rights, becoming communal property. Indeed, they consider as a primary precedent in the organisation of the mountainous land, the organisation and administration of the irrigation waters in the flat land.

According to Baraona *et al*, among the factors that contributed to the conversion of the mountainous land into common property are:

- a socio-ecological factor since it is the deterioration of the environment that reduces its value. This deterioration makes it necessary the mountainous land to be administered in respect to the shepherding, number of animals, quantity of fuel wood and wood, etc.;
- the demographic factor as the population pressure increases in the irrigated areas;
- a social factor, since the struggle for land or potential and real litigations with neighbouring properties, which will result in a situation that requires the registration of property; and
- a legal factor such as the registration and legalisation of mountainous land, which is a result of the pressure of legal requirements with respect to property.

These types of communities would emerge in the steeply contoured areas, which determine the differences in agricultural value between flat and hilly land. Conversely, they would not emerge in places where these differences are unimportant. According to Baraona *et al*, the fact that hillsides could be utilised for dry cultivation, as the case of Navidad (province of Santiago), would be a reason for their individual appropriation. Thus, there would not emerge a mountainous land community. However, this is not exactly the case with the communities of the Norte Chico, where dry cultivation is practised in the *lluvias*. However, many of these *lluvias* are certainly considered the property of the *comunero* who cultivates them, although their usufruct is temporary and forms part of the communal property. Being in the hands of the *comunero*, their usufruct is individual.

However, I consider that the geographical explanation of the formation of the agricultural communities constitutes a constant in the arguments of both Borde and Góngora and Baraona *et al*, distinguishing it as one of the most important element besides the economics factors. Even though it is certain that the utilisation of common grassland within the agricultural communities of the Norte Chico originates historically in the geographical environment, which gives the tradition of the common grass established in the colonial *estancias de Ganado*, the need to introduce this tradition is given by the geographical environment. That is to say, the geographical environment conditions the transhumance of the cattle.

The development of cattle rearing satisfies the political economy of the colonial regime. Cattle rearing was necessary for the conquest and the continuation of the colonisation process, *manu militare* against the indigenous population, as well as for the mining. The mining depends on the cattle raising, in terms of food (meat, milk, cheese) grown for the labour force (leathers, basil and wool), for the manufacturing of tallow for the candles, transportation for the minerals, and of the wood for fuel, transportation of people and food, and the running of the mines themselves. The troops also depended on cattle raising in similar form to the mines, for transportation of soldiers, weapons and food, clothes and tallow for the candles, and for the agriculture that must feed the urban population.

The extraction of precious metals was the principal interest in the beginning of the conquest and colonisation, whilst agriculture played a complementary role to the mining activities. Mining development is also closely related to the geographical environment and minerals cannot be exploited where none exist. However, the factors that lead to the substitution of the greater and bovine cattle for goat rearing depends on the expansion of agriculture, as may be argued with the help of Carmagnani (1963); this being an economic factor. But the mountainous or semi-mountainous environment influences once again the substitution of the greater or bovine cattle with goat rearing, being better suited to predominantly hilly land. With the hereditary subdivision of the agricultural property within those properties that became agricultural communities, being a product of the increasing population and with the decrease of the area for shepherding, the division of the mountainous land would have been directly uneconomic.

Baraona *et al* and also Cañón's argument that predominantly hilly land was not subdivided because it was considered land of little agricultural value is, in this context, secondary to the interest of maintaining open fields for the cattle otherwise not able to subsist in reduced areas. Borde and Góngora's explanation that the mountainous land stayed undivided due to the fact that, in comparison with the flat land, it was not easily divided is also secondary.

Since the physical space constitutes the base on which the colonial local economy was created, this decisively influenced the formation of the land ownership of the agricultural communities. It is strange that both Borde and Góngora, as well as Baraona *et al*, that is reality studied valleys that belong to the central zone, were able to elaborate the most congruent explanations, because there the landscape was also mountainous or semi-mountainous, and as a result a similar type of agricultural communities emerged there as in Norte Chico.

The origin and formation of the agricultural communities: posing the questions

The institution of the colonial *mercedes de tierras* played a major part in the formation of the agrarian structure in Chile. In the Norte Chico, this institution evolved not only into the great property of the *latifundia* and the small property of the *minifundia*, but also towards the semi-communal land property of the agricultural communities. I deliberately set aside here the *minifundium*, as what interests me is the development variant of the agricultural communities and the *haciendas*. As a form of property the *minifundium* constitutes, like the *latifundium*, private property, but as a form of production and reproduction it has much more in common with the agricultural communities, an aspect that I have partially considered in Chapter 1.

Against the context that colonial land grants gave rise to private property (large and small), the first question is why did the semi-communal land ownership form of the agricultural communities start to emerge here from the mid to end of the 1700s?

Having both forms of land ownership or property and their origin mainly in the colonial land grants, it is clear that it is the gradual conversion, *de facto*, of certain private properties into agricultural communities which, with time, begins to change the outstanding form of land property from the 1600s. This new form of property consolidation starts to convert, what was until then principally one form of land ownership, into two forms. Both forms were not only different but also sometimes antagonistic, giving place to a new land property structure in the zone; a structure that remained more or less the same until the agrarian reform of the 1960s.

Hence an important question in the colonial and historical development of the land property in the zone, is the variant represented by the agricultural communities. A second question is to ask why only certain properties became agricultural communities, and others not? Taking into consideration this parallelism, the first three theses will deal with both the *haciendas* and the agricultural communities. The other three deal with only the agricultural communities. Whereas the first three will relate to Part 2: The Historical Past, the last three will relate to Part 3: Contemporary History.

Initially and importantly, three historical moments in the structuring of land property in the Canela commune and its development will be identified:

- a common origin of land property, marked by the distribution of the colonial land grants and the constitution of the great landed property, first of the *estancias* (cattle ranches) and then of the *haciendas* (estates), a period that would last approximately until the beginning of the 1700s;
- the profiling of a new form of land ownership in the outstanding land property structure, labelled by the gradual formation of certain private properties into agricultural communities, and in the continuity of others in their character of private properties, a period that would encompass the 1700s;
- the gradual consolidation of a new structure of land property which clearly combines two forms of land property, each of them with its own (and different) development processes. This period would encompass approximately the beginning or middle of the 1800s until the present, or more properly, until the beginning of the agrarian reform of the 1960s as thereafter important changes take place which will influence both the

latifundia and the agricultural communities, yet in different ways.

My theses, six in all, with respect to the origin and formation of the agricultural communities in the studied zone are centred on the following topics:

- formation of the dominant forms of land ownership existing in the commune (first and second theses);
- relationship between land ownership forms and socio-economic development (third thesis);
- relationship between the agricultural communities' type of socio-economic development and their character of subsistence economy (fourth thesis), and
- effects of the character of subsistence economy on the agricultural communities and the life of the *comuneros* and the community (fifth and sixth theses).

Formation of the dominant land ownership forms

With respect to the formation of the dominant land ownership forms in the commune, the theses concentrate mainly on the second period, i.e., the outlining of a new land property structure in the zone. The gradual conversion of certain private properties into agricultural communities and the continuity of others as private properties characterise this period. Since I was interested in the emergence of the agricultural communities, it seemed consistent to leave out, in the formation of the theses the first historical period dealing with the distribution of the colonial land grants and the constitution of the great land property. Later on, my own historical investigation gave me a different picture to the one I had first taken for granted based on Cañón (1964). From there, a confusing historical picture emerged regarding my case study. This made it necessary to describe the question of the distribution of the land grants in the commune, the reason why this issue is included in the historical empirical study and developed in Chapter 5. Thus the first historical period is excluded from the formulation of the theses, but not from the empirical study. The examined historical documentation came to show that even though the grants distribution seems to have come to an end in Chile at the beginning of the

1600s, the present Canela commune apparently starts to be populated only around the end of the 1600s, and the first decades of the 1700s. Post factotum, I can say that leaving out the first historical period in the formulation of my theses was indeed consistent with the history of the studied agricultural communities.

The first thesis, i.e. the gradual conversion of certain private properties into agricultural communities and the continuity of others as private property, is that the profiling of the new property structure in the 1700s maintains a relationship with the factor of settlement and non-settlement and/or absenteeism of the old owners of the land (and/or its descendants) in their properties in the following way:

- those properties where the owners did not settle, or were largely absentees, maintained their character as large properties - first as *estancias* and then as *haciendas*;
- in contrast, those properties where the owners did settle and stay became, with time, agricultural communities.

In short what primarily defines, though only partially, the semi-communal form of the agricultural communities is the settlement of the landowners in their respective properties. For the formation of the agricultural communities, however, two more factors are necessary:

- the demographic increase of the descendants of the old proprietors (on the same land and same quantity); and
- the conditions of the hilly and semi-arid physical environment.

Thus, on the one hand, the shortage of flat and irrigated land made it necessary to define what belonged to whom, passing to conform the semi-private or individual property, on the other hand, the dry and high hilly land - the vast part - due to economic rationality, remained open as common property.

Summarising, in the case of the *haciendas'* large private property, their fencing, total, partial, or none, is not necessarily related to the type of semi-arid and hilly environment, which is also characteristic of the communities, unless perhaps in the determination to exploitation. The fencing of the *haciendas* has rather more to do with such factors as:

- a clearer character of private property (that is to say, in contrast with a 'diffuse' character of the agricultural communities, belonging to several families);
- geographical proximity to this 'diffuse', or not 'well defined form of property', i.e., belonging to several families, and with which they historically dispute the territoriality, potentially converting into an adversary; object of exploitation and, finally, economic capacity of the landowner.

Thus the same factor - prevalence of the semi-arid and hilly land, valid for the region - does not by itself have weight in the formation of land ownership form, but becomes a decisive factor together with the demographic growth. The formation of one or other form of land property (private or semi-communal) does not have a necessary relationship with better (irrigation) or worse (dryness) land, but in the settlement of the ancient owners (and/or their heirs) in their respective properties.

Assuming the first thesis as certain, we would then have to ask the second question, i.e., why only certain owners settled in their properties and others not? Here the second thesis is that the non-settlement (or just absenteeism) and the settlement of the owners in their properties, had to do with the position these occupied in the bureaucratic-military hierarchy and/or their socio-economic status within the colonial society. This may be summarised with the more general concept of colonial social position. In other words:

- the higher the social position of the landowners within the colonial society, the less time was spent and interest developed in settling and/or staying in their properties and exploit them directly. Without settlement, no local demographic growth occurs, and therefore the properties remain undivided, or if they are subdivided, this subdivision is much less - at least in comparison with those that were settled - preserving their character as large private properties;
- the lower the position of the owners within the bureaucratic-military hierarchy, or the lower their socio-economic status, the stronger the interest in settling and exploiting the land they possessed.

The statements above are with reference to the 1700s, i.e., more than a century after the distribution of the *mercedes* had come to an end. Therefore, this is not to say, as Santander does, that in the dry land of the Norte Chico, the beneficiaries of the *encomiendas* and *mercedes de tierras* were largely low rank officials in the Spanish army.

Forms of land ownership and socio-economic development

The gradual consolidation in the 1800s (third historical moment) of a land property structure that combines private and semi-communal property, constitutes the central axis around which began to outline two different types of economic and social development.

The large private property of the *hacienda* seen through the light of its historical development during the last two centuries shows for each certain period of time, the transfer of the property among different owners. In spite of the transfers of the properties and their hereditary subdivision among the heirs, the *haciendas* manage to maintain the dominance on a considerable land portion that keeps its status of great property in the hands of one person or family.

In the formation of the agricultural communities, it is possible, on one hand, to perceive an opposite process to that of the *hacienda*, i.e., the maintenance of the whole property among the descendants of the ancient owners of the land. With the consequent subdivision of the flat and irrigated areas the point has gradually been reached when it hardly manages to satisfy the needs of the *comunero* and his family.

The transfer of the *hacienda's* property between diverse economic agents, and the maintenance of the community property between the descendants of the ancient landowners of the agricultural communities, can be explained by their own type of socio-economic development. The type of economic power that traditionally accompanies both property forms is different, the economic power of the *hacienda*, generally in the hands of one proprietor or family - the landowner, is strong. With the semi-communal property of the agricultural communities, in the hands of multiple owners - the *comuneros* - their economic power has gradually diminished as a result of the subdivision of the flat and irrigated land. Therefore, if there is a shift of property between different economic agents, it is usual for the great property of the *hacienda*, and not for the individual or semi-private property (*hijuelas*) of the *comuneros* within the agricultural communities, except by hereditary subdivision. To the landowner, the alienation of his property permits him to change property or activity. The *comunero*, on the other hand, will hardly want to alienate his *hijuela* - probably his only means of subsistence - and with it the right to the communal property, since what he would receive in exchange would scarcely permit him to improve his standard of living. This means that the land, as a means of production, can easily be converted for the landowners of the *haciendas* into merchandise, which confirms the character of rent source or enterprise that characterises the *hacienda* institution.

In contrast, for the *comunero* his *hijuela* is, first of all, a means of production on which his survival depends, and that can only eventually be converted into a form of merchandise, with restrictions on the part of the community. For the *comunero* the road to improve his economic situation, above all in difficult years, will be to migrate and sell his labour, mostly beyond the frontiers of the commune, or to complement his economy with work of varying nature, which does not remove him from his land. The transfer of the property of the *hacienda,* and the family maintenance of the property between the *comuneros*, are decisive factors in the development of these two land ownership forms. They were related to the type of economic exploitation as well as with the character the subdivision of the land takes.

In the *hacienda*, in spite of the transfer of the property between different owners, the potential exploitation of the soils in the hands of a single landowner during an extended period of time has resulted in a better utilisation and exploitation of those soils. In the agricultural communities, a combination of factors has resulted in a significant deterioration of the land. These include the simultaneous and individualised exploitation of the land by multiple proprietary and successive generations on the common fields, as well as the reiterated exploitation of the *hijuelas*, in charge of the generations that have inherited them. To these may be added the extreme subdivision of the *hijuelas*. Consequently, the *hacienda* has a more 'rational' and extensive land exploitation than that of the agricultural communities. I mark with quotations the terms irrational and rational in order to give a reminder about their relativity. What is rational or irrational in a production form will be given by the perspective in which it is analysed. The 'rational' exploitation of a *hacienda*, in comparison to the 'irrational' of the agricultural communities, is made here from the perspective of the natural resources and the environment. This should not obscure, however, the perspective of the economic agents involved in the social process of production. Seen from the landowner's perspective, the rationality in the use of the resources will be given by the interest of his economic enterprise. In the case of the *comunero* and his subsistence economy, his rationality will be given by the amount of mouths to feed, yet to the cost of threatening the environment of future generations. But in this, the agricultural communities are not alone. Seen from the state's perspective, and from the general interest, the socio-economic system of the *latifundium* or *hacienda*, eliminated by the agrarian reform, was conceived as the principal brake for the modernisation of agriculture and, therefore, a highly irrational and ineffective system.

The land subdivision is a phenomenon that has certainly affected the great property of the *hacienda* as well as that of the agricultural communities. In this sense, it can be confirmed that in both forms of property, a major land concentration process has been excluded from the moment they became two radically different forms of land ownership during their virtually four centuries of history. It deals, however, with two different processes of subdivision both in degree and consequences. In the case of the *hacienda,* it deals with a series of relative subdivisions that in spite of them maintain the character of great property. This can, at least in theory, assure the economic solvency to his owner, in the case of this being his only economic resource. The subdivision the *hacienda* does not affect its character of rent source or merchandise, or its character of generating a surplus of produce for the market, since it does not reduce the property into subsistence economy. The subdivision of the land has of course a natural limit, even for the *hacienda*. A continuously divided *hacienda* will end as a *minifundium.*

In the agricultural communities, the subdivision of the *hijuelas* has led to such an extreme fragmentation of the flat land that it starts to generate an absolute decrease, being unable to assure the economic survival of all the potential heirs, including the heir in charge. The two types of development speak of a close relationship between forms of land ownership and socio-economic development.

In summary (third thesis) the form of land ownership influences the development type in the following parallel ways:

- in the continuity or discontinuity of the owners in such a way that (a) the private property influences the transfer of property,

for each certain period of time, between different economic agents, while (b) the form of semi-communal property of the agricultural communities influences the maintenance of property between descendants of the ancient landowners;
- the land ownership form also influences the development of the type of economic exploitation of the properties while, (a) the great property is characterised by an extensive and 'rational' exploitation, and (b) the agricultural communities are characterised by an intensive and 'irrational' one;
- the form of land ownership also influences the development type in the character of the subdivisions of the properties while, (a) the private property of the *hacienda* is characterised by a relative subdivision of the land, and (b) in the agricultural communities it is characterised by a subdivision that, with time, has converted in absolute in the areas of flat land.

The current states of both forms of property are the combined results of these factors.

Development of the agricultural communities and subsistence economy

The outline of the two different types of socio-economic development in both forms of land ownership, decisively influences the character that these will take in time, especially in the agricultural communities. The type of development they have undergone has established their present subsistence economy. Given the social problems and the fact that the institution of the *hacienda* has been widely studied, at least in comparison with the agricultural communities, my theses described below will be limited to the latter only.

The process of land subdivision of the *hijuelas* - apparently the most visible feature of their socio-economic development - appears to maintain a close relationship with the character of subsistence economies. Even the legal definition of the agricultural communities up to 1993 emphasised this resource shortage as:

> those rural lands owned in common by different landowners, on which the number of comuneros is clearly greater than the productive capacity of the

property so that the respective familiar groups can provide for their essential subsistence needs (Decree Law 5, 1967).

The same law did not permit any increase in the number of *comuneros* in a community, regulating the transfer of the inheritance to only one heir. This simply legalised a practice that through necessity had been exercised for a long time, due to the impossibility of subdividing the *hijuelas* and to the progressive incapacity of the soils to produce crops to satisfy the basic needs.

The character of a subsistence economy is manifested mainly in the fragmentation of the flat land and it must remain clear that such subdivision is the result of factors concerned with both their origin and their physical environment. It therefore follows that (fourth thesis) the character of the subsistence economies in the agricultural communities is a consequence of a series of phenomena. These are related to their long development process, and are inherent to the geographical environment (compounded predominantly by semi-arid and hilly lands with little irrigation) and in the climatic conditions characterised by irregular rainfall. It is worth emphasising that both the geographical environment and the climatic conditions are common for the entire zone and to the private property.

These factors are vitally important in the strengthening of the character of the subsistence economy of the agricultural communities. If dry land predominates, it depends exclusively on the rain for its agricultural utilisation. If the rainfall is scarce or irregular, the development of any activities will be highly insecure, determining the search for alternative, local sources of economic sustenance among the *comuneros,* or to migration beyond the community as a last economic resort. Under such conditions, the sum and combination of the productive factors that the *comuneros* and their families develop in order to satisfy their basic needs will be - product of a series of limitations - negative, or almost insufficient to provide their basic needs, conforming their character of subsistence economy. Not in vain, IREN (1977(2):13) supports that such collectives constitute those of smaller income in the country, and that is how Region IV during the 1970s had the 'privilege' of occupying the first place in the poverty by province figures. In 1990, in FAO's celebration of the Day of Nourishment, carried out in Canela, this was declared Capital of Poverty (Iván Badilla, Revista Análisis, Año XIII, no. 357, 12 al 18 de Noviembre, 1990, p. 23). Due to successive droughts, in 1994 Region IV was included by the government in the Emergency Agricultural Zones (Mahan and González, 1994:3-4). See also Chapter 1.

Effects on the life of the comuneros and the community

The subsistence economy has repercussions for the life of the *comuneros* as well as for the communities as a whole, in at least two senses: by the answers or strategies that the *comuneros* develop to adapt to them, and by the later consequences for the community. The fifth thesis is that the character of subsistence economies, in which the agricultural communities are unfolded, is translated into various social phenomena emerging as palliative answers to the subsistence economy.

Among these to be emphasised are:

- the search, on the part of the *comuneros* for complementary employment in the same place or nearby, either because the property is insufficient, and/or because the climatic conditions are not favourable for agricultural activities. Facing frequent 'bad' years, the *comunero* would be obliged to migrate beyond the commune, abandoning the property for some years, or leaving it in charge of some relative or *compadre*; and
- an inability on the part of the agricultural communities to absorb their economic, active labour force, as a result of the extreme fragmentation of the *hijuelas* which does not permit further subdivision, both practically or legally. The owner of a *hijuela* can only be replaced by one heir, depriving the remainder of the heirs access to the land as a means of production.

The inability of the agricultural communities to absorb their active labour force results in the creation of an excessive labour force. The natural expulsion process of this labour force from the land becomes a migration process. The major unemployment or underemployment among the *comuneros* before the sequence of bad years in agriculture reinforces this. Migration then, occurs both among the *comuneros* and the reserve labour force both as the result of the fragmentation of the *hijuelas* and of irregular climatic conditions. Migration fulfils several functions. If migration occurs among the *comuneros*, this complements the economy of the familiar nucleus in charge of the property. The migration among the excessive labour force contributes to a more expedite and less painful transfer of the inheritance among the various petitioners who would otherwise compete for it if they did not migrate, alleviating the community of its landless labour force. Migration assures also the sustenance of the *comunero* heir with fewer mouths to feed.

Migration has a variety of effects. One effect deserves special attention: the political consequences produced by a certain part of the migration on the communities and in the commune as a rule. This refers specifically (sixth thesis) to the migration towards the mining centres of the north and to the subsequent return of the migratory labour force to their places of origin. It relates to the existence of a significant contingent of left-wing support within a peasant zone. This would be the consequence both of the former proletarian condition and of the union experiences obtained by the *comuneros* when incorporated in a strong and militant union organisation, supported by the economic importance of the national copper mining centres. The existence of a left-wing party representation in the agricultural communities constitutes a peculiar fact if seen from the perspective of the marginalisation of the zone. This is both from the mining and industrial centres of the country, but not from the point of view of the migration provoked by subsistence economies of the agricultural communities. This is peculiar because where landed property exists; this is not normally conceived as a fertile arena for a socialist utopia.

5 The Hacienda El Totoral and the Agricultural Community of Canela Baja: a Common Introduction

Introduction

Whilst the former chapter dealt with the formation land tenure structure in colonial Chile, the present introduces that specifically of the Canela commune, or at least with my efforts to reconstruct it in the form of a common introduction for both the *mercedes* El Totoral and Canela Baja.

Much of this chapter will deal with the document, 'Pedro Cortés with Diego Cortés' from 1696, which turned out to be one of the principal historical documents used by Cañón. Cañón actually refers to the Legajo as 115, when it is in fact no. 15 (ANCH, AJ La Serena, Legajo no. 15, 1696, pieza 18 'Pedro Cortés con Diego Cortés', folio 1 to 14 verso). Below the place where it is written that the case concerns Diego Cortés with Pedro Cortés, is some writing in a different handwriting, 'It contains some declarations about *estancia* La Canela'.

Unfortunately, when confronted with historical and biographical literature my examination of the document did not provide a completely clear picture as to the origin of the properties in question. In spite of all efforts, the question of El Totoral and La Canela being originally one or two *mercedes de tierra* still remains uncertain. Since Cañón's analysis in this respect is not altogether correct, and since her work contains various inaccuracies, it became necessary to write the present chapter in an attempt to explain the scarce, but intricate and contradictory information that exists about the origins of these properties, from which the structure of land tenure in the Canela commune was developed.

This chapter also deals with the issue of the origin and emergence of the agricultural communities. Here the problem is not only that this is a historical problem although still without a satisfactory solution, but also

The Hacienda El Totoral and the Agricultural Community of Canela Baja

that there are no systematic efforts based in empirical case studies in that direction.

In this chapter, my empirical case study will be developed to demonstrate two issues; that on one hand, both the *latifundium* and the agricultural communities of Region IV have their origin mainly in the *mercedes de tierra*, yet on the other, that the agricultural communities have not necessarily arisen from land given to low ranking soldiers. Firstly, this chapter will illustrate that what today constitutes agricultural communities in the commune of Canela, were in the past colonial *mercedes*. Secondly, the chapter will illustrate how the hypothesis of the Norte Chico's dry land assigned as *mercedes* and *encomiendas* to low rank officials, turns out in my empirical case, to be wrong as well, since Pedro Cortés Monroy, and his descendants, associated with the origin of the agricultural community Canela Baja among many others, belonged to the highest colonial strata, and as such received both *encomiendas* and *mercedes*.

Cañón's version of the origin of the estancia La Canela

According to Cañón's version (1964:33), La Canela and El Totoral, which today represent two different forms of land ownership, have their origin in a single *merced de tierra*. According to her, this *merced* was given to Francisco de Aguirre y Cortés in 1605 by the Governor Alonso García de Ramón (García de Ramón was governor of Chile twice: 1600-1601 and 1605-1610 (Fuentes *et al*, 1984)). Later the same year, García de Ramón granted another *merced de tierra,* the Mincha *estancia*, to Juan de Ahumada. Today the lands of El Totoral, La Canela, and Mincha constitute practically the entire geographical area of the commune of Canela. As pointed out before, the figures concerning the area of the Commune vary considerably depending on which organisation is consulted. For example, according to the IGM (1980), the Commune has an area of 2,213 square kilometres (221,300 ha). However, according to CIREN, the 916 agricultural estates of the Commune alone total 272,243.8 ha (CIREN, List of Properties in The Commune of Canela, 1983) (see Table 2.8).

The historical development process of these *mercedes* came to structure the land properties of the commune, constituting, on one side, the large private property of the *haciendas* and, on the other, the semi-communal land property of the agricultural communities.

Whereas El Totoral today has become seven *fundos* and reserves of *fundos*, La Canela and Mincha have become fourteen and ten agricultural communities respectively. Studying the principal historical document on which Cañón bases herself, it is possible to come to another conclusion regarding the information that El Totoral and La Canela arose from firstly, a single *merced de tierra* and, secondly, its original owner.

The document in question, 'Pedro Cortés with Diego Cortés', from 1696, is a petition for the title deeds to the land of La Canela and El Totoral. Diego Cortés (Pérez), who had inherited these lands in 1679, instigated the petition in 1696 and Pedro Cortés (Castillo), the son of the former, continued it in 1719. As will be seen, Diego Cortés (Pérez) brings to his aid ten witnesses in his favour, some of them making statements about El Totoral, others about La Canela. This is perhaps a good place to point out that where family names are concerned, the Spanish tradition is somewhat complicated. A person carries two family names. Unfortunately, the second family name, usually the mother's maiden name, of the people involved seldom appears in historical documents. This makes it difficult to know which Cortés Monroy they refer to. Basing myself on other data, like the year of birth and/or death when available, as well as the military title of the personages, I add, when it is not given, the second family name in parenthesis. Since there were no rules until the 1700s, the family names were used in different forms, the same being valid for writing, as there were no established grammatical rules (Retamal *et al*, 1992:62). For example, the children could have the mother's maiden name and then the father's second family name as in the following case: the father of the *conquistador* Pedro Cortés Monroy was Juan Regas de Monroy. The mother was Maria Cortés. According to the present tradition the name of the *conquistador* would be Pedro Regas Cortés (the descendants of the *conquistador* keep until this day the two family names of the *conquistador* (Cortés Monroy) as their first family name). After that the mother's maiden name should come. In most of the literature containing information on the *conquistador's* descendants, the mother's maiden name instead of the first, appears as second family name. For example: the first son of the *conquistador*, also called Pedro, should be Pedro Cortés Monroy del Tobar, but appears in most cases, as Pedro Cortés Monroy Cisternas (his mother was Elena del Tobar Cisternas).

Diego Cortés (Pérez), born out of wedlock, was a great-grandson of the Spanish *conquistador* Pedro Cortés Monroy (1533-1617). In order to

The Hacienda El Totoral and the Agricultural Community of Canela Baja

simplify, I have reserved the title *'conquistador'* for the first Pedro Cortés Monroy who arrived in Chile, although his sons born in Chile could also be considered as *conquistadores*. The historical origin of the agricultural community of Canela Baja is associated with the legendary life of the *conquistador* Pedro Cortés Monroy, his wealth and land ownership, and especially that of his descendants. As Amunátegui appropriately comments about the *conquistador*:

> if the life of the Extramadura born Cortés Monroy is the story of the conquest of Chile, then the story of his family offers a complete picture of colonial society (Amunátegui, 1898:25).

Of the 8 children (four boys and four girls) Pedro Cortés Monroy had with Elena del Tobar Cisternas, only the lineage of the first-born is of importance when considering the origins of the agricultural community Canela Baja. His genealogical tree is illustrated in Figure 5.1.

While the left side of the tree shows the lineage of the first-born across three generations, the right side shows the descendants born outside marriage. Thus, Pedro Cortés Riberos is situated on both sides of the tree; to the left with his wife and to the right with Clara Pérez Flores, with whom he had several children, one of them being the inheritor of La Canela.

The genealogical tree covers the period from 1573, the approximate date for Pedro Cortés Monroy's marriage, to the first decades of the 1700s, the approximate date for the birth of his great, great grandchildren. In the family tree, the original spelling for the names and surnames of various people have been used. In the remainder of the text, except for quotes, the modern spelling will be used.

According to Cañón, the lands of La Canela and El Totoral were given as one *merced de tierra* to Francisco de Aguirre y Cortés in 1605, and the limits of the *merced* were:

> from the Totoral place to the Choapa river with six leagues of length, *three and half leagues breadth* (Cañón, 1964:33; emphasis added). (One Spanish league equals 5,572 meters, or five and half kilometres.)

Communal Land Ownership in Chile

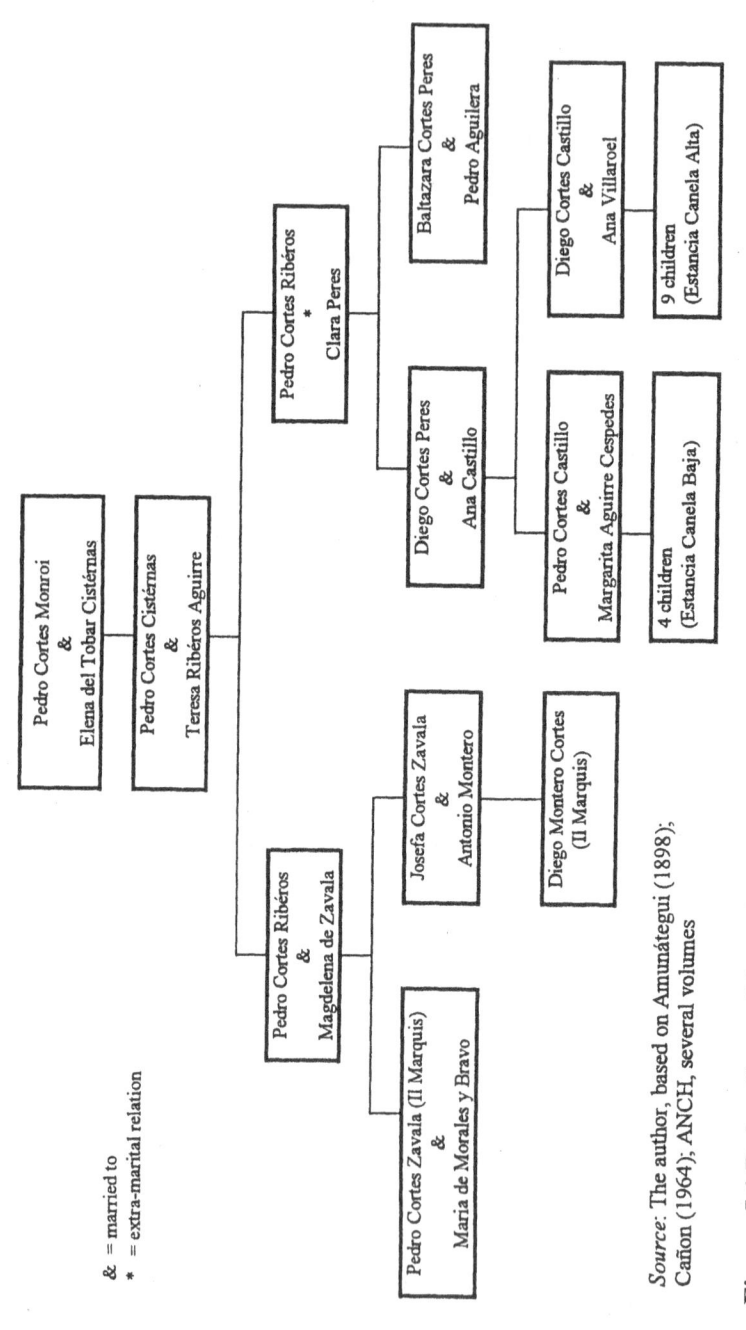

Source: The author, based on Amunátegui (1898); Cañon (1964); ANCH, several volumes

Figure 5.1 Pedro Cortes Monroi's descent

When Cañón in the paragraph prior to the quote refers to the breadth of the *merced*, she also writes that it stretches:

> from the sea to the hill Llampanguí, *estimated at a distance of six leagues from the sea* (Cañón, 1964:33; emphasis added; see Figure 5.2).

Obviously there is confusion here as far as the measures go of what Cañón believes to be the original *merced*. From the first quote it is understood that the *merced* measured six leagues in length (approximately 33.4 km) and three and half leagues across (approximately 19.5 km). This would imply from the Choapa River in the south, to El Totoral in the north, and from the sea towards the mountains as far as the Carquindaño hill. According to these measurements, the *merced* should have consisted of approximately 65,130 ha (i.e. 33.4 km x 19.5 km = 651.3 km^2). The Carquindaño hill, or Carquindañi as it was previously called, does not appear on modern maps, but it exists today as the agricultural community Carquindaño. I have taken it for granted that the community has its name after the mountain, using the location of this community as a reference point for my calculations. Following Cañón's handmade maps, I drew my own using the area of the present-day Canela commune as a base.

When she proceeds to write about the breadth of the *merced*, it turns out that it is also six leagues to Llampanguí Mountain and not three and half leagues as it is stated in the above quote. This confusion is understandable due to the complex nature of the archive's text. I believe Cañón confuses two different passages in the same document: the first one corresponds to the measures given by the witness who testifies specifically in relation to El Totoral. These measurements given by Cañón about the breadth of the *merced* corresponds to the limits of El Totoral, to be found in the declaration given by Diego Cortés Pérez at the beginning of the document, where he requests the title deeds. According to these new measurements, the *merced* should have consisted of approximately 111,556 ha (i.e. 33.4 km x 33.4 km = 1,115.56 km^2). Apparently, it is from here that Cañón draws the erroneous conclusion that the original *merced* measured six leagues lengthwise and six leagues across. As will be shown, these could not have been the dimensions of the original *merced* El Totoral, but the dimensions of the property that Diego Cortés Pérez received, which included El Totoral and La Canela.

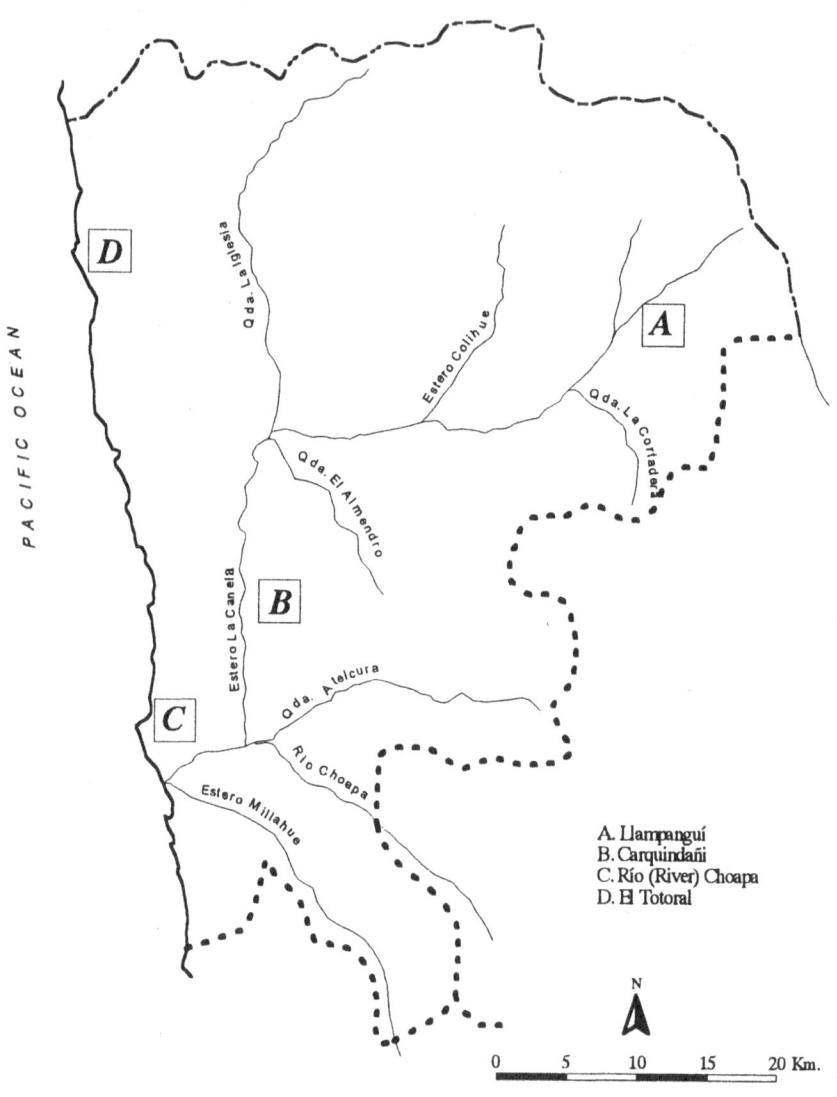

Figure 5.2 The boundaries of *Estancia* La Canela at 1679

There are, however, some simple facts that refute Cañón's thesis: firstly, that it was Francisco de Aguirre y Cortés who received the land of La Canela and El Totoral and, secondly, that they were a single *merced*.

The first fact that refutes Cañón's version, in respect to Francisco de Aguirre y Cortés receiving El Totoral as a *merced* in 1605, is his date of death. He died in 1695 (Retamal *et al*, 1992:129-130). There is no information available concerning the birth of Francisco de Aguirre y Cortés, but his parents married in 1619 and he was the second child. With that in mind, it does not seem very likely that Francisco de Aguirre y Cortés received the *merced* in 1605.

Cañón further claims, without giving the source of her information, that Francisco de Aguirre y Cortés, on an unspecified date near to 1605, and before 1626 as I understand it, exchanged part of his *merced* corresponding to La Canela for some land in La Serena. This land in La Serena would have belonged to Pedro Cortés Monroy (Cañón, 1964:34).

According to Cañón, both Francisco de Aguirre y Cortés and Pedro Cortés Monroy were *conquistadores*. From the date (around or before 1626) this Pedro Cortés Monroy should correspond to Pedro Cortés Cisternas, the son of the *conquistador* Pedro Cortés Monroy, but he died in 1621 (Cortés-Monroy, 1991/1992:186-187). (This author is a descendant of the family Cortés Monroy and should not be confused with the historical personages.)

Cañón must here be referring to Pedro Cortés Monroy Riveros, the son of Pedro Cortés Cisternas, since she indicates that he was married to Magdalena de Zavala. The problem is that Pedro Cortés Monroy (Riveros) - second generation in Chile and therefore grandson of the *conquistador* Pedro Cortés Monroy - in theory should have been born after 1618, since his parents married that year (Cortés-Monroy, 1991/1992:187). I can thus conclude that the possibility that Pedro Cortés Monroy Riberos could have carried out the exchange mentioned by Cañón is unlikely, since it must have taken place before he was born, or at least while he was still a child.

According to one of the witnesses (number eight) who gives testimony in the document, 'Diego Cortés with Pedro Cortés', which we will look at later, there existed an exchange carried out by Francisco de Aguirre y Cortés, but with Diego Cortés (Pérez). Francisco de Araya, testifies that he heard Francisco de Aguirre y Cortés, named as general, saying that the *estancia* La Canela belonged to him (something which I doubt):

before he exchanged haciendas with the Sergeant Mayor Diego Cortés (ANCH, AJ La Serena, Legajo no. 15, 1696, pieza 18 'Pedro Cortés con Diego Cortés', folio 12 to 12 verso).

The witness, Francisco de Araya, does not mention the date, but it is not likely that it was before 1626, as indicated by Cañón. The reason is that Francisco de Aguirre y Cortés was merely a child at this time and Diego Cortés Pérez was not born until 1645 (Cortés-Monroy, 1991/1992:190).

Given these dates, the exchange must have been carried out after 1679, the year in which Diego Cortés Pérez is granted these lands as a donation and probably also after 1696, the year in which he makes the petition of the title deeds of La Canela and El Totoral. Why would Diego Cortés Pérez be requesting the title over El Totoral if it were not his? A possible answer could be that this was necessary in order to legalise the exchange. One thing is quite sure, however, it must have been before 1709 because Diego Cortés Pérez died during this year.

If this is correct, it means that sometime during these dates (1679-1709) El Totoral becomes a separate estate from La Canela. It is probably at that time that Francisco de Aguire y Cortés became the owner of El Totoral. It is also conceivable that the exchange described by Cañón is the one mentioned in the witness, Francisco de Araya's, testimony.

One document could be taken as a confirmation that Francisco de Aguirre was the owner of El Totoral at the end of the 1600s. It deals with a litigation from 1691 about some land to the north of El Totoral. In the document, La Serena's Mayor, Don Juan Morales de Bravo says:

> I command that General Don Francisco de Aguirre be notified that he had been fined two hundred pesos /.../ and legal expenses by its Majesty to not upset or disturb Sergeant Mayor Don Jerónimo Pisarro Cajal in his [the latter] possession of the land between the [H]Ornillos and the Amolanas... (ANCH, AJ La Serena, Civil, Legajo no. 79 (1685-1726), 1691 'Pisarro Cajal, Jerónimo con Francisco de Aguirre. Derecho de tierras').

There is also another document, from the same period, where a certain Francisco Aguirre appears as having an *encomienda* in the zone, but it is unsure whether it deals with Francisco de Aguirre y Cortés, since this Francisco Aguirre is titled only as captain:

The Hacienda El Totoral and the Agricultural Community of Canela Baja

On the 20th of February 1694, I married and veiled Francisco Cortés, mulatto, [illegible] of the captain Don Diego Cortés [Pérez] with María Sanchi, Indian from the Captain Don Francisco Aguirre's encomienda... (AP Mincha, Matrimonios (Marriages) (1689-1796), folio 6).

The above Francisco Cortés would be the son born outside matrimony of Diego Cortés Pérez, and who is mentioned in his will. It is important for the archival searching here to note that the will of Diego Cortés Pérez appears in two documents, which deal with litigations over land. The first is 'Aguilera Santiago contra los herederos de Diego Cortés. Derecho de tierras' in ANCH, AJ La Serena, Civiles, Legajo no. 117 (1733-1765), 1733. The second is 'Francisco Cortés Espinoza y otros versus Lino Paez y otros sobre derechos de unos terrenos' in ANCH, AJ Illapel, Legajo no. 5, pieza 4, Caratulado 23 civil 1855, folio 3 verso. Given that the first document is incomplete due to its deteriorated state, I completed Diego Cortés Pérez's will with the one that appears in the second document.

In addition, Retamal et al, (1992:130) considers that Francisco de Aguirre y Cortés was at one point the owner of El Totoral. That is providing that these authors actually refer to the *hacienda* El Totoral in question here, since they do not mention in which commune it is located. Retamal et al, (1992:128) mention that El Totoral came into the hands of the family Aguirre via marriage, without specifying which marriage they were referring to. The families Cortés and Aguirre were related by various marriages, including the parents of Francisco de Aguirre y Cortés. Here, it can be added that Francisco de Aguirre y Cortés' parents were Fernando de Aguirre y Riberos (1569-1676) and Catalina Cortés y Rojas. While Fernando de Aguirre was the great-grandson of the *conquistador* Francisco de Aguirre (1508-1580) (Barrios B., 1949), Catalina Cortés y Rojas was the granddaughter of the *conquistador* Pedro Cortés Monroy. Being Francisco de Aguirre y Cortés the great, great grandson of the *conquistador* Francisco de Aguirre on the paternal side, and great-grandson of the *conquistador* Pedro Cortés Monroy on the maternal side, he belonged to one of the wealthiest families of La Serena's colonial society. Francisco de Aguirre y Cortés was married twice. The first marriage was with Catalina de Silva. After the death of his first wife, he married Micaela de Lisperguer y Andía. His first-born son with Catalina de Silva grew up to be the captain Francisco Antonio de Aguirre y Silva, who married his relative Francisca Gallardo y Riberos de Castilla. They never had children. The first son out of his second marriage was José Ignacio de Aguirre y

Lisperger, who in 1719 married Rosa Gallardo y Riberos de Castilla, sister of the above-mentioned Francisca. Rosa drew up her will in La Serena in 1765. The first-born son out of this marriage was José de Aguirre y Gallardo, who married Agustina de Fuica (Barrios B., 1949). It is uncertain whether the Gallardos that own El Totoral by the middle of the 1700s are related to the formers.

According to Cañón, in spite of the fact that the borders of the exchanged properties were never established with certainty, the Canela *Estero* (river) came to be the natural boundary (Figure 5.1). Today it also forms part of the boundary between the *fundo* Puerto Oscuro and the agricultural community Canela Baja. While Francisco de Aguirre y Cortés who, according to Cañón, kept the coast sector of the *merced*, Pedro Cortés Monroy (who should in fact be Diego Cortés Pérez) kept the major part. This was equivalent to the watershed of the Canela *Estero* and the strip of land in the northern part of the River Choapa, in the confluence of the Choapa with the River Canela and the sea (the latter corresponding today to the agricultural community of Huentelauquén).

Also according to Cañón, in 1626 Pedro Cortés Monroy (Riberos) sold Huentelauquén to Juan de Ahumada (Figure 7.1). Through this transaction Pedro Cortés (Riberos) limited his land to the watershed of the Canela *Estero*. This is another of Cañón's inaccuracies. Firstly, Pedro Cortés Riberos must have been approximately 7 years old in 1626, since he was born in 1619. Secondly, according to my own research, the sale to which Cañón refers seems to have taken place not in 1626, but 1726 (ANCH, AN Illapel, Vol. 4 (1775-1844), folio 42, 'Venta Pedro Cortez a Juan de Ahumada). Judging by the date, the vendor should have been, in that case, Pedro Cortés (Castillo), who together with his brother Diego had inherited La Canela from his father Diego Cortés Pérez in 1705.

The origin of the *estancia* La Canela

The document on which Cañón relies upon to affirm that La Canela and El Totoral consisted of a single *merced de tierra* comprises 14 folios. In the first folio, dated 1719, Captain Pedro Cortés (Castillo) makes a request to the judge of La Serena regarding the title deeds of the properties left by his father, Sergeant Diego Cortés (Pérez), when he died. Diego Cortés (Pérez) died in 1709 (Cortés-Monroy, 1991/1992:190). Pedro Cortés (Castillo) requests the documents on the basis of the testimonies given by witnesses who testified to the validity of his father's declaration.

In the following folio, dated 23 years earlier his father, Diego Cortés (Pérez), had declared in 1696 that the original documents, which certified that he and his ancestors had been the owners of La Canela and El Totoral, disappeared on two different occasions. According to him, the documents regarding La Canela got lost in a fire during the 'invasion by enemy pirates' in La Serena in 1680 (in 1680 La Serena was plundered and burned by the English pirate B. Sharp (Fuentes *et al*, 1984:298)). The documents regarding El Totoral became lost in 1695, when a brother of Diego Cortés (Pérez) crossed the river, which was very turbulent, and 'almost drowned'.

Diego Cortés (Pérez)'s declaration is followed by the testimonies, also given in 1696, of the ten witnesses who confirm the circumstances under which the documents disappeared. The total number of declarations was eleven, since witness number three testified twice (once about La Canela and the other about El Totoral). Apart from witness number three, the others who testify about the *estancia* La Canela are witnesses number one, two, six, seven and eight. The remainder testify about El Totoral.

In the document, Diego Cortés (Pérez) points out that El Totoral's land was given to his ancestors by the:

> Governor Alonso García Ramón who expedited above mentioned title and assigned six leagues length wise and across [,] from the bank of the Choapa river towards this city of La Serena until El Totoral and the breadth from the sea upwards (ANCH, AJ La Serena, Legajo no. 15, 1696, pieza 18, Pedro Cortés con Diego Cortés', folio 2). (My parenthesis.)

With the comma that I have inserted between parenthesis, the only coherent interpretation of the measures as described by Diego Cortés (Pérez) is that, as Cañón understood it, the (donated) property (not the *merced*) had six leagues long and six leagues wide. That is, as I have pointed out, from the River Choapa to the south, and to the north to the ravine called El Totoral.

Across, it stretches from the sea to the west, more or less to the Llampanguí Mountain (see Figure 5.1). I stress the fact that the border to the north should be the El Totoral ravine, for the reason that the distance from this location to the River Choapa is six leagues or approximately 33 km. The distance from the ocean to the Llampanguí Mountain is, however, more than 6 leagues (approximately 40 km).

In his request Diego Cortés (Pérez) does not give similar information about La Canela, although it did exist, and was, in fact, given by the witness who testified in his interest. I suggest that Diego Cortés (Pérez) refers only to El Totoral, due to the fact that the land corresponding to La Canela was included within its boundaries and that it was in such a way he received the donated property. It is also my opinion that he requested the title deeds in the same way. In other words, the aforementioned measures are correct only if the lands of these two *mercedes*, La Canela and El Totoral, had already become one property. The probability that they were originally two *mercedes* can be supported by the fact that, on one hand, he himself mentions that it was a matter of two original title deeds, lost on different occasions, and on the other, the witness constantly describes two *mercedes*.

The witnesses declarations concerning the merced La Canela

According to five of the six witnesses who attested about the *estancia* La Canela, the *merced* was given to Colonel Pedro Cortés Monroy by the Governor Alonso de la Rivera (Alonso de la Rivera was governor on two different occasions (1601-1605 and 1612-1617) (Fuentes *et al*, 1984:507)). The exception is witness number eight, Francisco de Araya, who declared that he heard Francisco de Aguirre y Cortés say that he was the owner of La Canela. This testimony does not contradict, as declared by other witnesses, that the Governor Alonso de la Rivera should have given the *merced* to the *conquistador* Pedro Cortés Monroy.

The military rank (colonel), as well as the year, makes it quite clear that the witnesses are referring to the *conquistador* Pedro Cortés Monroy. He received this rank, the highest within the military hierarchy, from the Governor Alonso de la Rivera in 1605 (Amunátegui, 1898:30-71; Cortés-Monroy, 1991/1992:177).

The year in which the *merced* was given is not specified, but two witnesses (number one and two) declare that it was given some hundred years earlier. That would mean around 1596. Even if this date were to be incorrect, it is very close to 1601 when the *conquistador* Pedro Cortés Monroy received his first *merced* from the Governor Alonso de la Rivera. The problem is, however, that the *merced* was located in Sotaquí (presently the commune of Ovalle, Province of Limarí, Region IV) and not in what today is the Canela commune. In addition, the *conquistador* Pedro Cortés Monroy was also the owner of the *estancia* Hornillos, which bordered El Totoral to the south, although Hornillos does not appear among the *mercedes* granted to the *conquistador* either. Nevertheless, when his daughter, Juana Cortés de Monroy y Tobar (Cisternas) married in 1612, the *conquistador* gave her the *estancia* in La Serena 'from Hornillos to El Totoral' as a gift (Cortés-Monroy, R., 1991/1992:184-185).

With reference to the boundaries of La Canela, the first three witnesses say that its borders are from the snowy Lampangui Mountain (it can also be read as Campangui, today known as Llampanguí) (to the Northeast) to the Carquindañi (today Carquindaño) hill (to the west) (see Figure 5.1). The witness number six just says 'from the snowy hill to the mountain'. Dealing with the measures of the property, these four witnesses declare that the *merced's* breadth was five and a half leagues (approximately 30.6 km). This would also mean from the Carquindaño hill to the Llampanguí Mountain. The witness number seven says 'from the mountains to the Carquindañi' and finally the eight witnesses simply names La Canela.

The witnesses only mention the breadth of the *merced*, not the length. Therefore, its size cannot be estimated. However, from the present agricultural community Carquindaño to the Llampanguí Mountain, the distance is approximately 30 km.

Of the six witnesses who testify about the *estancia* La Canela, only one, witness number eight: Francisco de Araya, supports something similar to Cañón's claims, namely that the *estancia* La Canela belonged to Francisco de Aguirre y Cortés before an exchange of properties. Apart from this, the witness Francisco de Araya does not specify, contrary to the other witnesses, the approximate date that the *merced* was handed over, or to whom it was originally granted. Neither does he specify which governor granted it, its location or measurements.

Thus it can be concluded that the quote presented by Cañón, that the *merced* stretched from El Totoral ravine to the River Choapa, with six leagues and three and half breadth, cannot be deduced from the declarations made by the only witness who claims that La Canela belonged to Francisco de Aguirre y Cortés. To stress it again, this witness says nothing about the boundaries or the location of the *merced*. Therefore, the quote has to originate from those witnesses who testify about El Totoral.

In other words, Cañón wrongly upholds that Francisco de Aguirre y Cortés received the *merced*, basing herself on the witness who in fact attested that what belonged to Francisco de Aguirre y Cortés was La Canela. Furthermore, she uses a quote where the measures provided by the witnesses concern El Totoral and not La Canela. We have also seen, that she wrongly believes that the original size of the *merced* to be six leagues long and six leagues wide.

Let me now momentarily leave the document 'Diego Cortés with Pedro Cortés' and Cañón, to examine the career of the *conquistador* Pedro Cortés Monroy, which earned him *mercedes* and *encomiendas* on behalf of the Crown. From this, his descendants came to belong to one of the most privileged groups in colonial society. This factor is important because it helps to reject the thesis that the dry land of the region (now considered marginal) was given to Spaniards of inferior rank within the military hierarchy. This thesis supported by Santander and CIPRES is not only incorrect but contradictory, since it is a well established fact that the *mercedes de tierras* were only granted to the most outstanding personages of the conquest. Some *comuneros* and journalists apparently also share this view today. A representative of the concept of the poor land is Julia Muñoz Estay, daughter of the *comunero* Joel Muñoz, who says that:

> this form of land tenancy exists since the time the Spaniards arrived to Chile, from the time of the encomiendas. Here, different to other parts, the private property was never established, due to the fact that the land was very bad and nobody was interested in it (Iván Badilla, Canela Baja, Capital de la Pobreza (Capital of Poverty) in Revista Análisis, año XIII, no. 357, 12-18 Noviembre, 1990).

The journalist Iván Badilla following Julia Muñoz and representing an example of the idea of low rank soldiers, writes:

> The origin of this always [sic] poor land /---/ goes back to the time of the encomiendas, in which was given to the encomenderos a patch of land to work it for the King. The beneficiaries were always soldiers and second lieutenants [alféreces], all the land of better productivity being reserved for the officers (*Ibid*).

The mercedes of the conquistador Pedro Cortés Monroy. A large part of what is known about the life of Pedro Cortés Monroy, as well as of the other *conquistadores*, comes from the *relaciones de méritos* (descriptions of merits or merits claim) that they send to the Crown. These *relaciones de méritos* exalted the *conquistadores* with the objective of obtaining a reward for their military services from the Crown. The number who received such rewards was, nevertheless, quite limited. The rewards meant the assignation of *mercedes* and *encomiendas*, institutions, which mainly came - each in its own way - to define the structure of land ownership in Chile.

During the 60 years of conquest that Pedro Cortés Monroy served under the Spanish Crown, he drew up four *relaciones de méritos*. In the first *relación de méritos* which Pedro Cortés Monroy made of his services, and which covered the period 1555-1571, he related how he arrived in Chile in 1557 at the port of Coquimbo (Region IV). He claimed that he served as a soldier for more than 14 years from 1557 in the interest of the Crown, without pay, participating in the reconstruction of Concepcion, which had been destroyed by the Araucanos or Mapuches, in the conquest of the island of Santa Maria (Bahía de Arauco), and in the defence of Cañete in February 1561. He claimed that:

> despite being on active service during the war in Chile and having spent a large sum of gold pesos, in weapons and horses, I have not received maintenance [entretenimiento] nor feud [feudo], as I received an encomienda at the end of the city of Castro, nine hundred Indians, but these happened to be uncertain. So, I find myself very poor and indebted... (Amunátegui, 1898:17).

It was, however, during the last years of his career, in which he was practically under the command of all the governors of Chile, that the *conquistador's* long years of service began to receive material recognition, but not before he had begun to rise slowly up through the military hierarchy. In 1597, with 40 years of service to the Crown in Chile, Pedro Cortés Monroy is named sergeant major by the Governor García de Loyola. In 1602, at the age of 69, he was promoted to grand master and sent to Peru to look for reinforcements in order to continue the Arauco War against the Mapuches. He returned in 1604. In 1603, while in Lima, Cortés Monroy used his stay to apply for his fourth *relación de méritos*. In 1604 he is once again promoted and named general grand master. In 1605, he was appointed colonel, thus reaching the highest post in the army except for the governor of Chile (Amunátegui, 1898:30-71). During his prolonged service under the Crown, he fought 119 battles. He also held several high posts in the colonial bureaucratic apparatus: town councillor in 1579 and 1586-7, mayor in 1580 and 1588 (Retamal *et al*, 1992:309).

As Amunátegui points out, Pedro Cortés Monroy was well qualified by his deeds to hold the post governor of Chile, but never came that far, probably because of his humble background (Amunátegui, 1898:87). His descendants were more fortunate and that was, more than anything else, due to the *conquistador's* persistent struggle for recognition of his services.

In respect of material rewards, Pedro Cortés Monroy managed to obtain both *mercedes* and *encomiendas* from the Crown. The *conquistador* was *encomendero* three times. The first time was before 1573 and it concerned 'Indians' banished from Coquimbo, reaching in 1579 up to twenty people (Vega, 1987:118). The second time was in 1602 in Atelcura (Atelcura is now one of the 24 agricultural communities in the Commune of Canela). This time there were sixty 'Indians' (Vega, 1987:120). The third time was in 1615, when he was appointed beneficiary of possible free *encomiendas* for two generations (Retamal *et al*, 1992:305).

In 1601, after spending 44 years fighting in Chile, the *conquistador* Pedro Cortés Monroy obtained from the Governor Alonso de la Rivera, a *merced* of 800 *cuadras* (approximately 1,333 ha) on the banks of the River Sotaquí, known as La Huana (Amunátegui, 1898:55-56; Retamal *et al*, 1992:309; Pinto, 1983:152; and Vega, 1987:120). According to Retamal *et al* (1992:309), Pinto (1983:152), and Vega (1987:120), this occurred in 1604. However, Amunátegui and Retamal *et al*, indicate that this land is called Huana, but according to Pinto it is called Sotaquí (Limarí Province, Region IV). Pedro Cortés Monroy transferred the *encomienda* of sixty 'Indians' from Atelcura, which he had received in 1602, to La Huana.

In 1608 Pedro Cortés Monroy, while still alive, left La Huana to Pedro Cortés Cisternas (also mentioned as Pedro Cortés y Tobar) (Retamal *et al*, 1992:309), his eldest son. It joined with the two *mercedes* that Pedro Cortés Cisternas had received from Alonso de García Ramón (Amunátegui, 1898:68). Before Rivera's mandate expired, the *conquistador* Pedro Cortés Monroy received a new concession of 2,000 *cuadras* of land (approximately 3,332 ha) along side the mine 'Madre de Dios', bordering the property of La Huana (Amunátegui, 1898:68). According to Retamal *et al* (1992:309), Pinto (1983:153) and Vega (1987:120), this occurred in 1612. Nonetheless, according to Amunátegui, Pedro Cortés Monroy died:

so poor that the custodian of San Francisco, Bartolomé Montero, buried him by charity (Amunátegui, 1898:97).

Cortés Monroy died in Panamá in 1617 while returning to Chile from his trip to Spain (Thayer Ojeda, 1939:261).

However, Pinto affirms that Pedro Cortés Monroy was one of the richest men in the region (Pinto, 1983:153). Yet, considering the size of *mercedes* Pedro Cortés Monroy received, according to the literature, it was not very large, but of good irrigated land. In spite of the fact that the *conquistadores* themselves paid for a large part the conquest enterprise, the *conquistador* Pedro Cortés Monroy commanded several different economical activities. For example, he had a copper mine, which demanded a large amount of food and livestock besides mules for transportation (Vega, 1987:120). Vega indicates that because of the resources demanded by this mine, the *conquistador* asked Governor Rivera for the second *merced* of 2,000 *cuadras*. The labour force, which consisted of the *encomiendas* of approximately 80 'Indians' he had received, must have been essential for the exploitation of his land and especially of his mine.

The *conquistador's* economic activities even covered the maritime sphere and by 1612 he had his own ship. This was employed in exporting his agricultural and mine products to El Callao in Perú (Vega, 1987:120-121). To this may be added his advantageous marriage in about 1573, when some 40 years of age, he married Elena de Tobar in La Serena, daughter of the Spanish captain, Pedro Cisternas and the Spanish citizen María de Tobar. As the daughter of Captain Cisternas, one of the first town councillors of La Serena and its feudatory neighbour, Elena del Tobar came from one of the most distinguished families of the time. She received as a dowry, twelve thousand *pesos* in gold (Vega, 1987:119).

Pedro Cortés Monroy died at the age of 84 (Thayer Ojeda, 1939:261) and although of humble origins, he was able to enter the so-called military aristocracy through his achievements during the conquest. Thanks to this, he died socially on a par with the nobility of the age. In his first *relación de méritos*, Pedro Cortés Monroy mentions his 'plebeian' condition:

> I am a soldier from Extremadura. I was born in the town of Zarza de Alanje /---/ My father was from Salamanca, belonged to the pechero class [which paid pecho or tribute, plebeian], and was called Juan Regas de Monroi. My mother, Maria Cortes, was born in Medellín, home of the conquistador of Mexico (Amunátegui, 1898:3-4).

From that described above, the two *mercedes* granted to the *conquistador* Pedro Cortés Monroy seem neither to correspond to the land on La Canela, which is mentioned by the previously examined witnesses. Nor do they seem to correspond to the land on El Totoral (or Hornillos, for that matter). Furthermore, neither of the two *mercedes* is situated in the Commune of Canela, but in the Limarí Province.

The witnesses declarations concerning the merced El Totoral

The second *merced* to be described by the witnesses was that of El Totoral. Of the five witnesses who made statements about El Totoral, four agreed in that this *merced* was given in 1606 to the captain Pedro Cortés Monroy (Cisternas) by the Governor Alonso García de Ramón. That is: witnesses number four, five, nine and ten. The witness number three, Francisco de Araya, does not mention to whom the *merced* was given (ANCH, AJ La Serena, Legajo no. 15, 1696, pieza 18 'Pedro Cortés con...', folio 5 verso to 14 verso).

Judging from the title of captain, the witnesses referred to the *conquistador's* first son, Pedro Cortés Monroy (Cisternas). This is confirmed by witness number five, Manuel del Castillo, who says 'Captain Pedro Cortés, the son of the Colonel Pedro Cortés' (ANCH, AJ La Serena, Legajo no. 15, 1696, pieza 18 'Pedro Cortés con...', folio 9).

The witnesses declare that the *merced's* breadth was three and half leagues with six leagues of length, from the Choapa River to El Totoral. This equates to approximately 65,130 ha (see Figure 5.1). As previously indicated, these are most certainly the limits used by Cañón in the quote where she first describes the size of the *merced*. The *mercedes* granted to Pedro Cortés Monroy Cisternas, the son of the *conquistador*, will be examined, as well as his military and bureaucratic career.

The mercedes of Pedro Cortés Monroy C., first son of Pedro Cortés Monroy. Pedro Cortés Monroy Cisternas was mayor of La Serena in 1613 and later magistrate (Cortés-Monroy, 1991/1992:186-187). He married Teresa de Riberos y Aguirre in 1618 (Silva Lezaeta, 1904:264). As a descendent of the conquistadores Francisco de Aguirre (1508-1580) and Francisco de Riberos (1512-1580) (Retamal *et al*, 1992:118-119), Teresa de Riberos y Aguirre belonged to one of the richest families in La Serena (Amunátegui, 1898:129). Teresa received a dowry from her parents of six thousand pesos, as well as the estancia Quilacán in the Elqui valley (Cortés-Monroy, 1991/1992:187).

In 1620, while he was ill, Pedro Cortés Cisternas drew up a will in La Serena (Amunátegui, 1898:145), and died later the same year (Silva Lezaeta, 1904:261) or in 1621 (Cortés-Monroy, 1991/1992:186-187), before reaching the age of 35. He seems to have been born around 1577 (Cortés-Monroy, 1991/1992:186-187). He was not able to enjoy the two life annuities, which the king had granted his father, Pedro Cortés Monroy (Amunátegui, 1898:145). Apart from the 800 *cuadras* of Huana inherited from his father, Pedro Cortés Cisternas received two *mercedes* from Alonso de García Ramón (Amunátegui, 1898:68). The first of the *mercedes*, given in 1606:

> consisted of one strip of two leagues and a half width from the Campangui range to the Colorado range [this distance is 14 kms], toward La Serena, in which district, as the merced scripture says, there are some 'white stones' (*Ibid.*).

The Campangui Mountain, also known as Lampangui, appears on current maps as Llampanguí, and is situated within what today is the agricultural community Canela Alta. The Llampanguí Mountain is well known, since gold and copper were extracted from it during the colonial period. Surrounding it there was also slag of quartz (silicone dioxide), also called rock crystal (Villaroel et al., 1988:78;85). It is likely that the existence of quartz can explain why white stones are mentioned in the handing over of the *merced*.

The present location of the Colorado hill, mentioned in the transfer of the *merced*, is problematic. There is a Colorado Mountain within the commune, situated southwest of the Llampanguí Mountain, at a distance of approximately 41 km. Due to its location and distance, it is clear that it is not the one mentioned in the delivering of the *merced*.

There is also a Loma Colorada (Red little hill), situated approximately 25 km northwest from the Llampanguí Mountain. At that location, it could be the Colorado hill mentioned in the transfer of the *merced*, but neither its name nor distance coincides. At more or less the same distance and direction is situated a place called Peñablanca (White Rock). This Peñablanca is currently within the limits of the neighbouring Combarbalá commune.

However, the *merced* granted to Pedro Cortés Cisternas, came to be known as Piedra Blanca or Piedras Blancas (White Stone or White Stones). This property, together with La Huana, granted Pedro Cortés Zavala, great-grandson of the *conquistador* Pedro Cortés Monroy, in 1697 the title of Marquis of Huana and Piedra Blanca. There are several variations of the title. According to Amunátegui, the title is not, as many authors have claimed, marquis of Huana and Huanilla, but marquis of Huana and Piedra Blanca (Amunátegui, 1896:50). Others like Pinto (1983:152) and Retamal *et al* (1992:193) call it marquis Piedra Blanca of Huana.

Apparently, at least part of the first *merced* granted to Pedro Cortés Cisternas would be situated within what is currently the Canela commune. According to other authors, the *estancia* Piedras Blancas was also situated in the Choapa valley (Cortés-Monroy, 1991/1992:193; Vega, 1987:170). If Peña Blanca and Piedras Blancas are the same property, at least part of it is today within the limits of the Combarbalá Commune.

The second *merced*, given in 1607 to Pedro Cortés Cisternas, consisted of:

> six hundred cuadras of land [approx. 1,000 ha] at the confluence of the rivers Huana and Combarbalá. The said lands border /---/ on one side the lands of Colonel Pedro Cortes, and on the other the mines of Nuestra Señora (known as Madre de Dios), and the head to the mountains (Amunátegui, 1898:68).

According to Cortés-Monroy (1991/1992:187), Pedro Cortés Cisternas received in 1617 a third *merced* of 1,000 *cuadras* (approximately 1,666 ha) between the Rivers Cogotí and Combarbalá from the Governor Fernando Talaverano Gallegos. According to Pinto (1983:153), Pedro Cortés Cisternas was one of the richest men in the region, owner of the land from Huana to Combarbalá, including the Quilacán *estancia*, which Teresa de Riberos y Aguirre had received as a dowry when she married him.

It can be observed that the description of the first *merced* granted to Pedro Cortés Cisternas in 1606, which due to its location at least partially coincides with the land of La Canela, does not correspond to the description provided by the witness, of a *merced* received that same year (El Totoral). As far as is known, Pedro Cortés Cisternas did not receive any other *merced* that year.

The mercedes of Pedro Cortés Monroy R., grandson of Pedro Cortés Monroy.

The *merced* given to Pedro Cortés Monroy Riberos, son of Pedro Cortés Monroy Cisternas, in 1651, does not correspond to La Canela's or El Totoral's land either. He received:

> a thousand cuadras of land [approximately 1,666 ha] in the neighbourhood of the village of Huana and Huanilla, and in that of Leiton and Porquéros (Amunátegui, 1898:147).

Pedro Cortés Riberos was baptised in 1621 (Cortés Monroy, 1991/1992:188). Like his father and grandfather, he was dedicated to a military career. He took part in the war in Arauco for more than 10 years, reaching the rank of infantry captain (Amunátegui, 1898:149) and of magistrate in Concepción (Pinto, 1983:153). In La Serena, he also held the posts of mayor, magistrate and lieutenant field marshal (Amunátegui, 1898:146).

Returning from the war in Arauco, Pedro Cortés Riberos dedicated himself to agricultural work in La Serena. He was *encomendero* of Huana between 1621 and 1659. In 1659, he obtained the *encomienda* for a third life in favour of his son, Pedro Cortés Monroy de Zavala (Cortés-Monroy, 1991/1992:188). In 1648, he married in Santiago Magdalena de Zavala y Amésquita, who was of high lineage and from whom he received a dowry of fourteen thousand *pesos*. Through this marriage, Pedro Cortés Riberos, like his father and grandfather, was able to improve the family's wealth. Notwithstanding this, in a merits claim that he sent (where he appears as Pedro Cortés Monroy) he claims that he does not have enough land for cultivation and animal rearing, asking thus for the mentioned *merced*.

By a decree of 20 July 1651 he received the *merced*, not as Amunátegui claims on his own merits, but by being a descendent of Pedro Cortés Monroy and Pedro Cortés Cisternas. Judging from the date of his will, he died in 1660, before reaching the age of 50. Pedro Cortés Riberos apparently had, before he married his wife Magdalena de Zavala, several children with Clara Pérez Flores. Diego Cortés Pérez was born out of this relationship. According to Cortés-Monroy (1991/1992:190), he was born in La Serena around 1645. Although neither Amunátegui nor Cortés Monroy mention it, a daughter called Baltazara was also born out of this relationship. She is mentioned in the testament of his brother, Diego Cortés Pérez (ANCH, AJ Illapel, Legajo no. 5, pieza 4 Caratulado 23 Civil, 1855,

'Francisco Cortez Espinosa y...', folio 1-2). According to Cortés Monroy (1991/1992:190), there is also another son, called Nicolás Cortés de Monroy.

In March 1660, Pedro Cortés Riberos gave power of attorney to his wife Magdalena de Zavala and to his uncle, Fernando de Aguirre y Riberos. Magdalena de Zavala, in her turn, drew up a will in La Serena during March 1680. She died in 1681 (Cortés Monroy, 1991/1992:188). Both Magdalena and her husband Pedro Cortés Riberos were buried in La Serena, in the Church of La Merced (Amunátegui, 1898:149). In her will, Magdalena de Zavala favoured her son Pedro Cortés de Zavala, the future Marquis of Huana and Piedra Blanca, with a third and a fifth of the wealth that she left (Amunátegui, 1898:148). From what I can deduce from the certificate of baptism quoted by Amunátegui, Pedro Cortés Zavala was born on 5th July 1651 (Amunátegui, 1898:155).

In 1679, one year before Magdalena de Zavala willed part of her wealth to his legitimate son, she donated two properties to Diego Cortés Pérez, her husband's son (Amunátegui, 1898:148). One of these properties corresponds to El Totoral's and La Canela's land.

Advancing some conclusions

Summing up what I have found, and judging from the mentioned historical document on which Cañón bases herself, I cannot affirm that La Canela and El Totoral originally made up one single *merced*, as Cañón indicates. According to the witnesses, it was a matter of two *mercedes*; La Canela, which was given to the *conquistador* Pedro Cortés Monroy and El Totoral, which was given to Pedro Cortés Cisternas, his oldest son.

When the *mercedes* are examined, which according to various authors were given to the *conquistador* and his son, it can only be affirmed that there is a similarity between the information regarding the *merced* that Pedro Cortés Cisternas received, within which is currently the Canela Commune. Needless to say, the current size of El Totoral and La Canela, which amounts to approximately 177,000 ha, has very little to do with the size of the *mercedes* which the *conquistador* and his descendants received.

One thing that seems certain though is that Diego Cortés (Pérez), through the mentioned donation in 1679, became the owner of the land from the River Choapa to El Totoral. In other words, he became the owner of this land 17 years before he requested the title deeds for La Canela and El Totoral in the aforementioned document 'Pedro Cortés with Diego Cortés'. However, that Pedro Cortés Pérez in 1679 became the owner of the mentioned land, can be read in a document which certifies that he received it from Magdalena de Zavala, his father's widow:

> at the same time she gives and donates some land that she has in this jurisdiction *that begins at the River Choapa in direction to this city [La Serena] joining the lands of El Totoral* and in the east borders the lands of Captain Pedro de Ahumada and by the other side with the sea of which such lands by the same reason of his services she donates (emphasis added) (ANCH, AJ Illapel, Legajo no. 5, pieza 4 Caratulado 23 Civil, 1855, Francisco Cortez Espinosa y...', folio 1-2).

From this endowment, it cannot be deduced, however, whether the land of Diego Cortés Pérez includes El Totoral, or if El Totoral constitutes its border to the north. However, on balance, I rather think it is the first alternative. Although Diego Cortés (Pérez) mentions six leagues, it would actually be more. If this is so, it means that the lands of El Totoral do not border to the north with the El Totoral ravine, a place six leagues from the Choapa river, but with the *haciendas* Hornillos and Guile. That this was the border of the property to the north can be read from the previously mentioned gift that the *conquistador's* daughter received in 1612. This border is also to be found in a much later document (1858) (ANCH, AN Illapel, Vol. 15, 1858, Doc. no. 279, folio 73 verso 72 - see sixth quote in Chapter 6 about El Totoral), which is some 14 km to the north from the El Totoral ravine.

Supporting this thesis, is the fact that Diego Cortés (Pérez) never claimed that the El Totoral ravine specifically constituted the northern limit of his property, only that the distance is six leagues. Neither did Magdalena de Zavala's endowment specify that the El Totoral ravine constituted the northern border of the property she gave to Diego Cortés (Pérez). The eastern border, or the land belonging to the Ahumada's, of which reference is made in Magdalena de Zavala's endowment, would correspond to the Mincha *estancia*. The Pedro de Ahumada mentioned in the endowment, was the son of Juan Alonso de Ahumada, who had received the aforementioned land as a *merced* from the Governor Alonso García de Ramón in 1605 (Cañón, 1964:42).

It may be clearly seen that the description of land, which appears in the quoted endowment, corresponded to the description given by Diego Cortés Pérez in 1696, when requesting the title deeds (that I reiterate here):

> above mentioned title [El Totoral] and assigned six leagues length wise and across [,] from the bank of the Choapa river towards this city of La Serena until El Totoral and the breadth from the sea upwards (ANCH, AJ La Serena, Legajo no. 15, 1696, pieza 18 'Pedro Cortés con...' folio 2).

Through the endowment it is understood, as I have maintained, that La Canela's land is located within the limits of El Totoral and that Diego Cortés Pérez received it as such. This means that by the second half of the 1600s the two properties had already become one, probably by heritage.

If it could be supposed that Pedro Cortés Monroy received La Canela and that his son Pedro Cortés Cisternas received El Totoral, then the latter would inherit La Canela on the death of his father in 1617. Therefore, these two adjoining properties would become one. Pedro Cortés Cisternas died (1620 or 1621) shortly after his father, at the approx. age of 35. His son, Pedro Cortés Riberos then inherited the property and in 1679, his son, Diego Cortés Pérez, in turn inherited the property.

If this version is correct, the family Cortés Monroy would have owned El Totoral and La Canela from the early 1600s. The lands of La Canela, through one of the out of wedlock lineage of Pedro Cortés Riberos, still remain with his descendants.

Nonetheless, if El Totoral and La Canela originally formed one single *merced*, as maintained by Cañón, or two, as maintained by the witnesses, it does not alter the fact that, as postulated here, both the *haciendas* and the agricultural communities share the same origin in the *mercedes*. As such, these two properties, together with Mincha and also partially Conchalí and Chigualoco, likewise *mercedes de tierras*, have come to represent the two dominant forms of land ownership in the Canela Commune. This gives rise, on one hand to the semi-communal land ownership form of the agricultural communities and, on the other, to the private property of the *haciendas*.

An estimate of the size and limits of Diego Cortés' received property

Due to the different versions presented here, it is difficult to determine the exact size of the property donated to Diego Cortés Pérez in 1679. There

The Hacienda El Totoral and the Agricultural Community of Canela Baja

are, however, at least three ways that could be used to estimate its size. The first is based on the testimonies of the witnesses, claiming that La Canela and El Totoral were two *mercedes* at the beginning of the 1600s, separate but adjoining.

If the dimensions indicated by the witnesses of the original *merced* El Totoral are accepted, three and half leagues across (approximately 19.5 km), it would indicate that the *merced* only stretched as far as the Carquindaño hill. This feature was also, according to the witness, the beginning of the *merced* La Canela, which measured five and half leagues in breadth. La Canela and El Totoral having been grouped into a single property would have resulted in a breadth extending to the Llampanguí Mountain. In summary, the combined breadth of both *mercedes*, from the mountain to the ocean, would have amounted to a total of nine leagues or some 50 km, which in any case goes beyond the Llampanguí Mountain, which is approximately 40 km from the coast.

When this dimension is adding to the length of the *merced* El Totoral, supposing that it stretched from the Choapa river to the El Totoral ravine, some six leagues or approximately 33 km, the area of the property endowed to Diego Cortés Pérez, would cover approximately 167,334 ha. This would be the first option.

The second option could be derived from the dimensions, as supported by Diego Cortés Pérez of some six leagues in breadth by six leagues in length, would give an area of some 111,556 ha.

The third option could be based on the supposition that the dimensions provided (in leagues) by Diego Cortés (Pérez) were incorrect. Thus the area could be based both on the limits indicated in his request for the title deeds, as well as in the endowment made to him by Magdalena de Zavala. This would result in the length of the property, from the River Choapa to the Hornillos *hacienda*, being approximately 47 km. The breadth, from the sea to the Llampanguí Mountain, would be approximately 40 km. This would give an area of some 188,000 ha (see Figure 5.2). These figures are much closer to those of the first option.

Of the different options used to estimate the size of the property, I am inclined to choose the third alternative. On one hand, because the 14 agricultural communities that had originated from the *estancia* La Canela today total approximately 129,000 ha (IREN, 1977(2):26-27), whilst on the other hand, the *fundos* and reserves of *fundos* arisen from the *hacienda* El Totoral total some 41,147 ha. This is El Totoral, Puerto Oscuro, Las

Palmeras, La Alcaparra, Las Palmas and, the reserves El Totoral and Puerto Oscuro (see Table 2.7: *Fundos* and Reserves of *Fundos* in the Commune of Canela). The total of approximately 129,000 ha does not include the approximately 17,623 ha of the ten agricultural communities in the Choapa, Atelcura and Agua Fría areas which, according to Cañón (1964), had arisen from the Mincha *estancia*. This means: from the Choapa area: Mincha Sur, Mincha Norte, Las Barrancas and Las Paredes. From the Atelcura area: Atelcura, La Capilla, La Leona, and Cabra Corral. From the Agua Fría area: Agua Fría Baja and El Potrero. These ten agricultural communities total approximately 17,623 ha (IREN, 1977(2):26-27). (See IREN's column in Table 2.6.)

Secondly, to these areas should be added five *fundos* that have also originated from the land endowed to Diego Cortés (Pérez), which have an approximate area of 10,000 ha (this is Hijuela Lo Gallardo, Santa Amelia, El Retiro, Los Gallardo and Talinay, see Table 2.7, *Fundos* and Reserves of *Fundos* in the Commune of Canela). This would give a combined total of approximately 180,147 ha, which is not far from the 167,334 ha calculated in the first option, nor from the 188,000 ha calculated in the third option.

Rounding off the common introduction

The historical roots of the agricultural community Canela Baja still remain linked today, through an out of wedlock lineage, to the descendants of Pedro Cortés Riberos, grandson of the Spanish *conquistador* Pedro Cortés Monroy. However, the roots of El Totoral partly lost, probably from the middle of 1700s, their connection with the descendants of the *conquistador* Pedro Cortés Monroy (see above).

El Totoral however, still maintains its character as a private property. From being a *hacienda* in the 1700s and 1800s, it became three different *fundos* towards the end of the nineteenth century; El Totoral, Puerto Oscuro and Las Palmas.

In contrast, the property of Diego Cortés (Pérez), evolved from a single *estancia* at the end of the 1600s, and began to fragment into several properties, both through hereditary subdivision and sales. Slowly they begin to lose their original character of a private property, to form the semi-communal land ownership of the agricultural communities of today.

Among them is the agricultural community Canela Baja. In the following chapters I will firstly deal with the *hacienda* El Totoral and then with the agricultural community Canela Baja. The implication of the historical processes of these two forms of properties will turn out to have a decisive influence upon their future socio-economic development.

6 The Hacienda El Totoral: the Development Path of Private Property

Introduction

The historical process of land formation in the commune of Canela is peculiar because the *hacienda* El Totoral and the agricultural community Canela Baja share a common origin and evolve to become two different forms of land ownership, private and semi-communal. The gradual consolidation during the 1800s of this form of agrarian structure that combines both private and semi-communal land ownership constitutes the central axis around which, two different types of economic and social development, sometimes becoming antagonistic, may be outlined. Since they both have the same origin and/or neighbouring each other, the *haciendas* and agricultural communities share borders and have often competed for the same land. The position that is often taken for granted, that the *haciendas'* neighbouring peasant societies, applied here to the agricultural communities, serve as labour reservoir for the estates, will be analysed.

This chapter deals with the subdivision of El Totoral and the rural properties that developed from it through inheritance, sales and shared ownership. As such, it deals very much with property transactions, but it also includes expropriations, transfers and auctions sales. My third thesis, that the agricultural communities - as opposed to the *haciendas* and *fundos* - are characterised by hereditary maintenance of the land between the descendants of the original proprietors of the land since colonial times, demands that the legal history of the *fundos* should be examined in detail. Thus, it will be shown how the property of the *haciendas* and *fundos*, in contrast to the semi-communal land ownership of the agricultural communities, is constantly transferred throughout the years.

In this chapter, dealing with the history of the *hacienda* El Totoral and the three *fundos* developed from it, as in the chapter concerning the agricultural community Canela Baja, I have conscientiously used the proper names. The most important reason for the case of El Totoral is that the relevance of proper names is related partly to my third thesis, the non-hereditary maintenance of the land property between the descendants of the original proprietors of the land since colonial times (see Chapter 4). All the detailed data given is aimed towards proving and supporting this thesis, including the detailed reconstruction of the many transactions of the *fundos*.

To cover the history of these transactions from a panoramic viewpoint I have developed a chronological table of the transfers for each rural property. The Registers of Property (RP), which contained the registers of domains and mortgages on the property, were of special importance for this task (see Chapter 1).

Both registers, of domains and mortgages, contain an index with the name of the buyer, the seller or the mortgage debtor, depending on each case; the name of the property, the number of the folio and the number it has been given in the Register of the Conservatory. The inscription of the property contains the information included in the public deeds, that is the identity of the participants in the purchase and sales agreement, property borders, price or amount of the mortgage, etc. The description of the property boundaries contained in the different inscriptions through the years, allow us to see whether there have been changes in this respect.

Before going into the specific cases, some of the general characteristics of the *hacienda* system and the consequences of some of its main features for the development of this institution will be described. This will put into context the history of the *fundos* that have been studied, whose development has evolved during two main historical periods. A clear watershed in the history of the *hacienda* El Totoral and the three *fundos* that resulted from its division in 1890 was the agrarian reform of Allende's administration. Therefore, this history can be divided into the periods before and after the agrarian reform. During the later period, the land structure in the commune went through its most radical change. This period can also be divided into two, the agrarian policy of Allende and the "counter" policy of Pinochet, which in its turn can also be subdivided.

Starting with the period before the agrarian reform and taking into consideration the evolution of El Totoral, Las Palmas and Puerto Oscuro *fundos*, as well as those created from them, they combine some of the characteristics indicated by some authors as being typical of the *latifundium* in Latin America. The *hacienda* or *latifundium* institution was more than a productive, economic enterprise. To express it with the help of García (1973:82), the *latifundium* was a multiform system of social domination, whose foundations traditionally consisted of three elements; the monopolisation of land, the paternalistic ideology and the hegemonic control of the mechanisms of exchange, transfer of resources and political representation.

The seigniorial monopoly of land that expresses a European man's ideology, based on a conception of land as an element of power, position and social domination, is, in this sense, opposed to the capitalist notion where the means of production are aimed to produce and valorise capital. The paternalistic ideology, inherited from the *encomienda*, which typifies the *hacienda*, is reflected in the dependency of the peasants to an authoritarian system characterised by top down decision making, non-existent or scarce contractual mechanisms of negotiation, and a tightly controlled social order.

The *hacienda* system's hegemonic control of the mechanisms of exchange, transfer of resources and political representation, forms an intricate network of relations between the *hacienda*, the market, the political organisation and the external influences of technological and cultural modernisation (García, 1973:79). The social effects of the monopolisation of land by the *hacienda*s can be seen in the concentration of the land, as well as in the disparity between the physical extension of the *hacienda* and the economic turnover of the enterprise. Such factors show the radical differences between the seigniorial monopolisation of land, and the capitalist concentration where the land is a means of production subjected to an intensive and rational exploitation in order to generate profits.

Although each of these elements has not been specifically examined, especially not the paternalistic ideology exercised by the landowner upon the peasantry, because it goes beyond the purpose of this study, I consider some of these elements characteristic of the *fundos* studied. In several of them, their owners were absentee landowners. This tradition of absenteeism, or as Bauer expresses it, the predominantly urban interests among the Chilean landowners, in comparison with a common feature for many centuries of the northern European landowners, was manifested, in architectural terms, in the absence of great manorial houses. The lack of a tradition of affection for an ancestral home among the Chilean landowners made it easier for them to sell or exchange, *haciendas* and *fundos* (Bauer, 1975:177). As Bauer indicates for Chile:

> It takes little imagination to see the relation between such owners [absentee] and their land. They lived most of the year in Santiago, rarely saw the hacienda whose rent paid the bills. At times the contract reserved part of the hacienda house 'to inhabit when suitable' or asked the renter to keep houses for the owners' periodic use (Bauer, 1975:139).

The predominant tradition of absentee land owners in this case study indicates that the estates were mainly a source of rent for its owners, in addition to a source of social standing and a place to spend the summer. The fact that the *fundos* were frequently sold shows that they were an easy object for commercial transactions.

It is also amazingly clear from the documents of sale, that when the *fundos* were transferred from one owner to another, they nearly always had a mortgage with the *Caja de Crédito Hipotecario* (CCH), or with another credit bank attached. From this can be deduced that borrowing money, by mortgaging the *fundos*, was fairly common among the landowners, perhaps not always with the objective of investing in the *fundo*. In many of those property changes examined, several owners kept the *fundos* for only short periods of time, which leads one to suspect that the purchase of the *fundos* and their later mortgage, was a way of obtaining capital that could be invested in other enterprises. In this way, the *fundos* represented a means of speculation rather than a means of production to their owners. This thesis validates Bauer's more general analysis for the whole of Central Chile (Central Chile comprises the Valparaíso Region V to the Maule (Region IX)). Bauer points out that for Chile, the credits based on mortgages at rural properties were of great importance. Probably 80% of the loans given by the CCH were secured by mortgages of this type (Bauer, 1975).

The CCH, legally created in 1885, became the first and most important mortgage bank in the country. Later on it became 'the most powerful lending institution of its kind in South America' (Bauer, 1975). The loans of this bank and others were limited to the owners of the greatest properties. According to Bauer:

> a list of Caja loan recipients in 1880 would be barely indistinguishable from a list of members of the Club de la Unión, the Club Hípico or Congress.

> From its foundation in 1885 down to 1930, the Caja was /.../ an easy instrument in the hands of the landowners (Bauer, 1975:91).

Club Hípico (founded in 1869) was along with the Club La Unión (founded in 1864), the principal social centre of Santiago's (landowner) elite (Bauer, 1975:206).

The 'landowners were not required to reinvest borrowings in the land or even mention the purpose of the loan' (Bauer, 1975:139). This is confirmed by CIDA:

> one can conclude that certain amounts passed to agricultural investment and another part to industry and mining (CIDA, 1966:9).

According to Bauer:

> To qualify for a loan from the Caja, the property to be mortgaged had to be worth at least $ 2000. The value was taken either from the tax rolls or based on special appraisal. No loan could be made for less than $ 500, nor in any case exceed one-half the value of the property. If approved /.../ the Caja did not lend directly but rather issued *letras de crédito* to the borrower in return for a mortgage on the property. Those *letras* /.../ bore fixed rates of interest. The borrower sold these *letras* on the open market and the receipts constituted his borrowing. The bank thus stood between the collective borrowers and lenders: it was the general debtor of those holding *letras* and the creditor of the persons who had pledged property in return for the *letras* (Bauer, 1975:90. Regarding the value of the Chilean *Peso* in respect to the £ sterling, see Table 6.4).

The *hacienda* El Totoral before its subdivision in 1890

This chapter deals specifically with El Totoral as from the second half of the 1800s. Because the historical records of this property for the period before this date are scarce, and sometimes contradictory, the information dealing with it is fragmentary (the 40 Volumes constituting the AN of Illapel that exist in the ANCH of Santiago starts only in the 1751). As an introduction, however, some items concerning El Totoral may be outlined to give a framework for the period prior to its subdivision.

The *hacienda* El Totoral apparently had its origin in another *merced de tierra* other than La Canela. According to my conjectures, El Totoral and La Canela soon after they were granted became one property. In 1679, it became the property of Diego Cortés Pérez through the endowment made to him by Magdalena de Zavala. According to the document 'Pedro Cortés with Diego Cortés', from 1696 this land again was divided into two properties, through an exchange between Diego Cortés Pérez and Francisco de Aguirre y Cortés. It is thought that this occurred sometime between 1679 and 1709. 1679 is the year when Diego Cortés Pérez inherited this land and 1709 the year when he died. These conjectures are based in the declarations of the witness Francisco de Araya to which I have referred in Chapter 5.

Francisco de Aguirre y Cortés took over the northern coastal sector, corresponding to the lands of El Totoral, whilst Diego Cortés Pérez kept the remainder, which corresponded to the lands of La Canela. It is estimated that the land of the former was some 40,000 ha, and the land of the latter, some 140,000 ha. Francisco de Aguirre is confirmed as the owner of El Totoral at the end of the 1600s in a document that deals with a litigation from 1691 about some land. In this document, Francisco de Aguirre is asked not to disturb his neighbour in the possession of his land between Hornillos and Amolanas, situated north to El Totoral (ANCH, AJ La Serena, Civiles, Legajo no. 79 (1685-1726), 1691, 'Pisarro Cajal Jerónimo con Francisco de Aguirre. Derecho de tierras', see Chapter 5). Besides this, the endowment of land carried out in 1679 by Magdalena de Zavala to Diego Cortés Pérez, and the document named 'Pedro Cortés with Diego Cortés' from 1696, the earliest indirect references that may be found about El Totoral dates from 1612. That year, the conqueror Pedro Cortés Monroy gave the *estancia* in La Serena to his daughter, Juana Cortés de Monroy y Tobar (Cisternas) as a gift 'from Hornillos to El Totoral' (Cortés-Monroy, 1991/1992:184-185). Here the property already appears with the name El Totoral, after the ravine within its territory.

From the middle of the 1700s to the first half of the 1800s, I found two (indirect) references. The first reference may be found in a document dated 1753, in which El Totoral is referred to in relation to the boundaries of the *estancia* La Canela. El Totoral now belongs to the Gallardo family (ANCH, AN Illapel, Vol. 3 (1826-1843), Testamento de Diego Cortés (Castillo), folio 354-355, see Chapter 7). It appears under the denomination of *fundo*. Concerning the surname Gallardo, it is interesting to note that the grandson of Francisco de Aguirre y Cortés was José de Aguirre y Gallardo (born during the second decade of the 1700s), but it is uncertain whether the former Gallardo family has to do with the latter. However, Francisco de Aguirre y Cortés' both sons (born from two different marriages) were married to two sisters with the surname Gallardo, but only the second of them had descendants (Barrios, 1949:11-13).

The second reference appears in a testament from 1844, where it is written that El Totoral belonged to Rafael Montes:

> ... I Pascuala Cortes, of 45 years, legitimate woman of my husband Alberto Contreras, original from the parish of this valley and resident in Mincha, *hacienda El Totoral of Don Rafael Montes*, believing as I do... (ANCH, AN Illapel, Vol. 1 (1751-1814), 1844, Testamento de Pascuala Cortés, folio 192-193, emphasis added).

It seems that from the middle of the 1700s to the middle of the 1800s, the *hacienda* was in the hands only of the Gallardo and Montes families. By the second half of the 1800s, El Totoral belonged to the Montt family. It is from here that, given the relative availability of documentation, I have been better able to reconstruct the fate of El Totoral and the three *fundos* created by its subdivision. On one hand, as it appears quite clearly in the testament from 1844, the name Montes should perhaps not be confused with Montt. It would also deal with two different families. On the other, the difference between 1844, the year when Rafael Montes appears as the owner of El Totoral and 1858, the year when Mariana Montt appears as the owner of El Totoral 'that correspond to her family *by inheritance*', according to a document from 1861, is not very significant. Therefore, in spite of the different surnames, it could be the same family. According to Oscar Ollarzú, former *comunero*, merchant and ex-mayor of Canela's commune, this Montt family were parents of both Chile's presidents by the name of Montt (Manuel Montt, 1851-1861 and Jorge Montt 1891-1896) (Reseña histórica y panorámica de Canela y Mincha (*s.a.*), O. Ollarzú, manuscrito). According to the document from 1858, Mariana Montt was also the owner of El Totoral. That year she mortgaged it, with the permission of her husband, Diego Infante, becoming a debtor for the sum of 16,000 *pesos* in *letras de crédito* (letters of credit) to the CCH (regarding the value of the Chilean *Peso* in respect to the £ sterling for this period, see Table 6.1). It is said that the *hacienda* consists of approximately 20,000 *cuadras* (approximately 35,000 ha). Three *cuadras* are equivalent to approximately five hectares (Baraona *et al*, 1961:207). As stated in the document, its borders were defined to the north by the *hacienda*:

The Hacienda El Totoral

... of [H]Ornillos and Guile, to the east by Espíritu Santo and the Estero [river] of La Canela and Guile, to the south by Angostura de Gálvez and to the west by the sea (ANCH, AN Illapel, Vol. 15, 1858, Doc. no. 279, folio 72 verso 73).

Table 6.1 Average annual value of the Chilean peso in terms of £ sterling, 1830-1925 (in pence of £, rounded to nearest penny)

1830-75	44	1897	18
1876	41	1898	16
1877	42	1899	15
1878	40	1900	17
1879	33	1901	16
1880	31	1909	11
1881	31	1910	11
1882	35	1911	11
1883	35	1912	10
1884	32	1913	10
1892	19	1914	9
1893	15	1915	8
1894	13	1916	9
1895	17	1917	13
1896	18	1918	15

Source: Frank W. Fetter, Monetary inflation in Chile (Princeton, 1931:13-14 in Bauer, 1975:239, Appendix IV)

In the document from 1861, it is mentioned (without giving the date) that Mariana Montt received from her brothers and sisters:

... Doña Rosario /.../ Don Manuel Montt, as curator of Don José Santiago Montt, Don Manuel Ramón Infante, for his wife Doña Ana Josefa Montt, was agreed to take /.../ the hacienda El Totoral /.../ and that corresponded to her family *by inheritance* for the sum of sixty thousand pesos... (ANCH, AN Illapel, Vol. 23, 1861. Doc. no. 14 Partición, verso folio 114 to verso 115; emphasis added).

Judging from the definitions of these boundaries, the northern limit of El Totoral is identical to that named in the document from 1612, which has been referred to before. The southern border is no longer the River Choapa, as in 1679, but Angostura de Gálvez's (Gálvez Strait) ravine, situated to the north of the mentioned river (1679 is the year when Diego Cortés Pérez received as donation the land of El Totoral and La Canela).

The southern border, given in the first mortgage from 1858 by Mariana Montt, would agree with what was suggested in Chapter 5. This referred to Pedro Cortés Castillo, the son of Diego Cortés Pérez, who in 1726 sold the Huentelauquén area, situated on the northern border of the Choapa River, to Juan de Ahumada, and not Pedro Cortés Monroy in 1626 as Cañón suggested. In the sale document of 1726 Talinay, situated to the north of the Huentelauquén area, appears as belonging to Lieutenant Juan de Céspedes. This makes it clear that Talinay, bordering the Angostura de Gálvez' ravine to the north, became another property before the Huentelauquén area was sold.

In 1865 (seven years after the first mortgage), Mariana Montt and her husband once again mortgaged the *hacienda* with the CCH, this time for the sum of 14,000 *pesos* (ANCH, AN Illapel, Vol. 23, 1865, Doc. no. 14, folio 41). In this document the *hacienda* appeared to have 24,000 *cuadras* (approximately 42,000 ha) an increase of 7,000 ha since 1858. The *hacienda* remained undivided until 1890, when Mariana Montt's three children divided it between themselves in equal shares (Illapel's RP, 1890, no. 63, folio 64). According to the document, the *hacienda* had, by then, an area of 26,508 *cuadras* (ca. 46,375 ha) some 4,375 ha larger than in 1865 and 11,375 ha larger than in 1858.

This document would suggest that each of the heirs would have been entitled to some 8,863 *cuadras* (15,507 ha) of land, although each of the *hijuelas* or *fundos* appear later on to have as much as 17,500 ha. In the partition document, Alejandro Infante Montt appropriates the third *hijuela*, to the north, which he called Las Palmas, for 40,905 *pesos* (Illapel's RP, 1890, no. 64, folio 65 verso). Juan Diego Infante Montt appropriated the second *hijuela* in the middle for 46,000 *pesos*, which kept the name El Totoral (Illapel's RP, 1890, no. 63, folio 64). Finally, Luís Alberto Infante Montt appropriated the first *hijuela*, which he called Puerto Oscuro, for 63,120 *pesos* (Illapel's RP, 1890, no. 62, folio 62 verso).

In a previous document, from 1889, Luís Alberto Infante Montt registered the *hacienda* El Totoral valued at 139,099 *pesos* with a mortgage debt:

> that was of 35,000 pesos in a 5% bill from the Caja de Crédito Hipotecario in favour of the Caja (Illapel's RP, 1889, no. 22, folio 32 verso).

Considering the size of this debt, it probably corresponded to the two mortgages that Mariana Montt took in 1858 and 1865, respectively.

In view of the boundaries of the El Totoral *hacienda*, it seems that once Diego Cortés Pérez had exchanged part of his land with Francisco de Aguirre y Cortés, it remained undivided for more than two and a half centuries. That is from between the years 1679 and 1709, assuming that the exchange took place sometime during this period, to 1890 when the children of Mariana Montt subdivided the *hacienda*. Judging from the varying sizes of the *hacienda* under the ownership of Mariana Montt, which gives a difference of 11,180 ha between 1858 and 1890, it is possible that first, the *hacienda* expanded through the acquisition of new land, although this cannot be confirmed. The breakdown of this is 35,000 ha in the first mortgage of 1858, 42,000 ha in the second of 1865 and 46,375 ha in the subdivision of the *hacienda* in 1890 between the Infante Montt brothers.

Secondly, it is also possible that the difference in size given for the *hacienda*, as well as for the *fundos* resulted from its subdivision, and can be related to the lack of information about the real size of the properties and/or inaccurate measurement. Thirdly, and most probably, the difference in the size of the properties may depend on the fact that land has been fraudulently added from the neighbouring properties, i.e., the communities.

This idea can be based on the fact that both the *fundo* El Totoral and Las Palmas returned part of their land to the agricultural community Canela Baja when it indemnified its property title during the 1970s. This third conjecture, however, does not invalidate the second. In the mortgage of 1858, the *hacienda* El Totoral is said to consist of 20,000 *cuadras* 'more or less'.

The *fundo* El Totoral from Juan Diego Infante Montt's time

From 1890, the year in which J. D. Infante Montt appropriated the *fundo* El Totoral, until 1972 when, due to agrarian reform the *fundo* was expropriated, the property passed through the hands of different owners, principally by sale.

As can be seen from Table 6.2, Juan Diego Infante Montt kept the *fundo* El Totoral in his possession for 23 years.

Table 6.2 The *fundo* El Totoral: 1890-1972

Owner	Place of residence	Occupation or profession	Area (ha)	Years of ownership
J. D. Infante Montt	-	-	15,507	1890-1913
G. Acchiardo Bertolotti	Santiago	Farmer	-	1913-1929
V. Blanco Lecaros	Santiago	Farmer	-	1929-1938
C. Charpentier Valim	-	-	17,500	1938-1941
Bros. Eguiguren Irarrázava	-	-	-	1941-1950
Family Cañas Errázuriz	-	-	-	1950-1972

Source: The author. Where dashes appear, the dates do not appear in the documents
In the case of transferred debts and Credits acquired, the empty space assumes that there were no debts transferred or credits acquired.

With this exception, of the five owners prior to the agrarian reform, only the Errázuriz family kept the *fundo* for more than two decades, a period that was interrupted by its expropriation in 1972. From 1913, when Juan Diego Infante Montt sold the *fundo*, until 1950, the last sale date before expropriation, the property changed hands six times in 37 years. From the sale documents it is possible to see that four out of the six owners acquired the *fundo* with one or two debts, normally to the CCH. The owner, from whom they purchased the property, had either mortgaged it or inherited a debt.

Although the residence of the buyers is not mentioned in all cases, they mostly come from Santiago, being absentee landowners.

Juan Diego Infante Montt, after keeping the *fundo* for 23 years, sold it in 1913 to G. Acchiardo B. (Illapel's RP, 1913, no. 15, folio 8 verso). The document of sale mentions neither the number of hectares nor the purchase price. Acchiardo, an Italian farmer living in Santiago, kept the *fundo* for 16 years.

Table 6.2 (Continued)

Purchase price Chilean $	Transferred debts at purchase time in Chilean $		Credits acquired in Chilean $		Sold to
	Entity	Entity	Entity	Entity	
HEREDITY 46,000	CCH 11,666				G. Acchiardo Bertolotti
-	-	-	-	-	V. Blanco Lecaros
340,000	Bco. Chile 40,000	Bco. Chile 40,000	-	-	C. Charpentier Valin
900,000	-	-	-	-	Bros. Eguiguren Irarrázaval
900,000	CCH 144,079	-	-	-	Family Cañas Errázuriz
5,000,000	CCH 144,079	-	-	-	1972 (*Expropriation*)

In 1929 he sold it to V. Blanco L. for the sum of 340,000 *pesos*. Blanco, also a farmer from Santiago, accepted the debt:

> ... that weighs upon the fundo, one of 40,000 pesos /---/ and another of 60,000 pesos in certificates, both to the Banco de Chile. Therefore Acchiardo receives 240,000 pesos ... (Illapel's RP, 1929, no. 15, folio 13).

Because of the debt transferred to Blanco, it can be assumed that Acchiardo, during his 16 years as owner of the *fundo*, mortgaged it twice with the *Banco de Chile*. The *fundo* remained with Blanco for 9 years. In 1938 he sold it to C. Charpentier V. for the sum of 900,000 *pesos*. The document specifies that the *fundo* had an area of 10,000 *cuadras* (approximately 17,500 ha) (Illapel's RP, 1938, no. 159, folio 148 verso). This suggests that the *fundo* had increased by some 2,000 ha since 1890.

Charpentier kept the *fundo* for only 3 years, selling it in 1941 to the Equigurren Irrarrázaval family (Elisa, Luís, Isabel and Alberto) for 900,000 *pesos*, the same amount as he paid for it. The buyers agreed to take over:

... a mortgage debt to the Caja de Crédito Hipotecario at a value of 144,079 pesos (Illapel's RP, 1941, no. 151, folio 87).

It can be assumed that Charpentier, during the three short years that he owned the *fundo*, mortgaged it above the amount of the debt he inherited from Blanco. The *fundo* then remained with the Eguigurren family for nine years. In 1950 they sold it to Alicia Cañas, widow of Errázuriz, and her children (Marcelo, Julían and Susana Errázuriz Cañas) for 5,000,000 *pesos*, two fifths going to Doña Alicia and remaining three fifths to her children.

The buyers agreed to take over:

....a debt of 101,882 pesos to the Caja de Crédito Hipotecario (Illapel's RP, 1950, no. 366, folio 215).

Judging from the amount of this debt it seems that the Eguigurren brothers transferred to Cañas the debt that they inherited from Charpentier. In the purchase agreement drawn up between Eguigurren and Cañas, it is also specified that the new road will connect Santiago with La Serena. The construction for which, the State treasury expropriated the corresponding land strips, which pass through the *fundo* from north to south, was also specified (*Ibid*).

Due to the fact that the size of the expropriated land area for the construction of the Pan-American Highway has not been mentioned, I have not been able to estimate the reduction in the area of the *fundo*. The last time the size of the *fundo* is mentioned before that was in 1938, when its 17,500 ha was purchased by Charpentier. The *fundo* remained with the Errázuriz Cañas family for 22 years until 1972 when, during Allende's government, it was all expropriated by CORA (*Corporación de Reforma Agraria*) (see Chapter 2). The *fundo* was expropriated because it was being run poorly, according to Clause No. 3 of the Law of Agrarian Reform (SAG, Rol no. 219-2, folio 3.616, Resolución del 25 de abril de 1972, Diario oficial del 15 de Mayo de 1972). (SAG took in transitory form in 1979, the regulation of the unsettled situations originated in the process of agrarian reform, taking over the functions and attributions of ODENA (Oficina de Normalización agraria) legal sucessor of CORA (Ministerio de Agricultura, Information via Internet, 07/22/97:http://www.minagri.gob.cl/minagri/sag/sag. html).)

In 1975, however, during the Pinochet government, a reserve of 2,300 ha was returned to Julían Errázuriz Cañas, one of the sons of the family who bought the *fundo* in 1950. The general purpose of giving the expropriated landowner the right to a reserve, which could be of 50, 80, 100 or 300 basic irrigated hectares (HRB) was the notion of transforming him into a modern agricultural entrepreneur (García, 1973:83).

Since the area of the *fundo* is not mentioned in the expropriation document, it is uncertain whether the expropriated part, which remained with CORA, consisted of 15,200 or 13,200 ha. According to the *comunero* P. Carvajal, El Totoral returned 2,000 ha, with three peasants, to the agricultural community Canela Baja during the 1970s (Pedro Carvajal, qualified informant, several interviews between 1988-1990). For this reason, the land area in the hands of CORA, and later on in the hands of CONAF, was probably of 13,200 ha, Miguel Astorga, a *comunero* and merchant of Canela Baja, and a shareholder of the actual *fundo* El Totoral, reports that in 1979, CONAF sold off the *fundo* to 14 members for 4 million *pesos* (Miguel Astorga, oral interview, June, the 27th, 1988). This was possible due to the agrarian policy introduced by Pinochet after the coup d'état in 1973.

Of an approximate total of 10 millions hectares of land expropriated by the agrarian reform in Chile, Pinochet returned something less than a third of the land to its former proprietors. Of the remaining land, more than a third was bidden to third parties and public institutions with the remaining third being parcelled into some 40,000 properties of approximately 6 equivalent irrigation hectares (Rivera, 1988:66-67,228). According to Rivera, the distribution of the last part was made through two modes; firstly 2,148,582 ha in the form of co-operatives and individual parcels and, secondly, 738,424 ha in form of societies for the peasants (*asentados*) (Rivera, 1988:228) of the ex-*asentamientos* (settlements) created by CORA and the ex-*inquilinos* of the expropriated *fundos*.

In the second mode, 326 estates were offered for purchase by the ex-*asentados*, but only 109 were bought in virtue of the Decree 2.247 of June 1978. This Decree made possible for the ex-*asentados* to get organised in Societies of limited responsibility in order to buy the estates. For this they needed 10% of the initial price. The remaining 217 estates were auctioned (Rivera, 1988). It is difficult to know if the actual *fundo* El Totoral was purchased through the mentioned alternative 3b or 2, since some of the actual owners, as is the case with some other actual *fundos* in the commune, were not only ex-*asentados* but also *comuneros* from the zone.

Even though the *fundo* appears in the name of one of the members, José A. Toro Robles in the CIREN list from 1983, the *fundo* constituted, according to Astorga, a limited society, as is the case of the other *fundos* I will examine later in this chapter. Of the 14 co-partners of the *fundo* El Totoral, all equal owners, 10 are former *inquilinos* from the *fundo* in question, or from adjacent ones, while the four remaining are from the village of Canela Baja. Three of them, the fourth being the mentioned Astorga, are brothers and monopoly bus owners in Canela Baja. The socio-economic position of all four co-partners is also, in comparison to the other *comuneros*, relatively high. At the moment of the purchase, the *fundo* had ca. 6,320 ha of land. In the 1983 list from CIREN, the *fundo* El Totoral appears, however, with a land area of 6,132 ha. In 1989 the *fundo* was paid off in total, at a final cost of 40 million *pesos*, on the basis of the UF (*Unidades de Fomento*) system. As additional information, it can be pointed out that the UF is an Economic instrument created during the government of Jorge Alessandri (1958-1964). The initial aim was for the recalculating of house credit mortgages using the value per square meter and the rise in wages rather than the IPC. Actually, the UF are adjusted daily in line with the Retail Price Index, which means that it rises constantly. The value of the UF in 1979, when the society bought the *fundo*, was around 640 *pesos,* while on 9 October 1990 it was 6,427,58 *pesos.*

Since the present *fundo* El Totoral consists of only 6,132 ha and considering that CONAF originally must have retained some 13,200 ha, it seems to be clear that CONAF sold off only a part of this property. It might well have sold the rest of the *fundo*, but, as far as I have been able to verify, reviewing CIREN's property list for the Commune of Canela, as well as the RCCBR list, no particular property corresponds to the missing 7,068 ha of the expropriated *fundo*. The Reserve El Totoral, equivalent to the expropriated part of the *fundo*, returned to J. Errázuriz C., appears in CIREN's list under the ownership of Fuenzalida, González and Co. Ltd. Its area is recorded as 2,865 ha, not the 2,300 ha returned to Errázuriz by CONAF. Judging by the change of ownership, I can only assume that Errázuriz sold it once it had been returned to him in 1975.

The history of the transfer of the *fundo* El Totoral shows how, in spite of successive sales, it remained one property until the agrarian reform era (1890-1972). By 1983 it had become at least two properties, the *fundo* and the reserve. Until at least 1996, both belonged to several owners, constituted in limited societies. This was a result firstly, of the agrarian policy followed by Allende and, secondly, by the Pinochet government which returned part of the expropriated *fundo* to the original owners, and sold the non returned part by auction, through CONAF. Unlike many of the previous owners of El Totoral, the present owners are natives of the zone, *comuneros* and former *inquilinos* of the *fundo* or other adjacent ones.

The *fundo* Las Palmas from Alejandro Infante Montt's time

In comparison to the *fundos* El Totoral and Puerto Oscuro, the *fundo* Las Palmas not only changed hands more frequently, but has also had several owners simultaneously during certain periods. This finally led to its early subdivision, many years before the agrarian reforms started to take place in the country (see Table 6.3). Alberto Infante Montt, who in 1890 kept that part of the *hacienda* El Totoral known as Las Palmas, leased the *fundo* in 1912 to T. Schuler, a farmer from Illapel. The contract was valid for a period of 5 years, obligatory on both parts. The rent was set at 9,000 *pesos* per annum (Illapel's RP, 1912, no. 12, folio 6). The contract also specified that the lease could be extended for a further two years. In the document, Alberto Infante Montt appears as *rentista*, living in Santiago (*rentista* means here that the landowner lives from the income coming from leasing his property). It is clear from the sale of the *fundo* by L. Puyó Medina, a physician living in Santiago, in 1929, that he bought Las Palmas in 1922.

The document does not specify who the vendor is, but it would have been Alberto Infante Montt since he leased the *fundo* to T. Schuler between 1912 and 1917. If this is the case, Alberto Infante Montt kept Las Palmas for 32 years (1890-1922). I can then deduce that at least from 1912 onwards, Alberto Infante Montt did not run the *fundo* himself but lived off its income in Santiago.

The *fundo* remained in L. Puyó Medina's possession for 7 years. In 1929 he sold it for 350,000 *pesos* to three Santiago buyers; G. Puyó León a farmer, E. Puyó León a lawyer, and G. Errázuriz L. also a farmer.

Table 6.3 The *fundo* Las Palmas: 1890-1939

Owner	Place of residence	Occupation or profession	Area (ha)	Years of ownership
Between 1912 and 1917, A. Infante Montt rents the fundo Las Palmas to				
A. Infante Montt	Santiago	*Rentista*	15,507	1890-1922
L. Puyó Medina	Santiago	Physician	-	1922-1929
G. Puyó León	Santiago	Farmer	½	
E. Puyó León	Santiago	Lawer	¼	
G. Errázuriz Larraín	Santiago	Farmer	¼	1929-1934
G. Puyó León	Santiago	Farmer	-	1929-1938
E. Puyó León	Santiago	Lawer	-	1929-1938
L. Puyó León	-	-	-	1934-1938
J. Parrisello Cuartrella A. Charles Tollin	-	-	17,005	1938-1939
E. Puyó León	-	-	16	1939-?
In 1939, Parrisello and Charles divide the fundo Las Palmas in two. Parrisello kept deniminated Las Palmas (7,605 ha)				

Source: The author. Where dashes appear, the dates do not appear in the documents
In the case of transferred debts and Credits acquired, the empty space assumes that there were no debts transferred or credits acquired.

G. Puyó León bought one half of the property and a quarter was sold to each one of the others. The transaction included an old debt to the CCH for 100,000 *pesos*, reduced to 96,627 *pesos,* and another debt to the *Banco de Chile* for 55,000 *pesos* (Illapel's RP, 1929, no. 127, folio 119 verso). Judging from these debts, L. Puyó M. took on two loans during the 7 years he kept the *fundo*. Five years later, in 1934, G. Errázuriz L., one of the three new owners, sold his part to Luís Puyó León for 60,000 *pesos*.

Table 6.3 (Continued)

Purchase price Chilean $	Transferred debts at purchase time in Chilean $		Credits acquired in Chilean $		Sold to
	Entity	Entity	Entity	Entity	
T. Schuler, a farmer from Illapel for $ 9,000 annually					
HEREDITY 40,905	CCH	11,666			L. Puyó Medina
-	-	-	-	-	G. Puyó León E. Puyó León G. Errázuriz Larraín
350,000	CCH	96,627	Bco. Chile	55,000	-
					L. Puyó León
60,000	- - CCH	- - 27,000	- - CCH	- - 12,500	J. Parrisello Cuartrella A. Charles Tollin -
900,000	-	-	-	-	E. Puyó León
1,000	-	-	-	-	*Subdivision of the fundo*

the part of the fundo denominated Las Palmas (8,400 ha) and Charles the part

Taking into account his family name, it seems likely that he was the brother of the two other owners of the *fundo*. The buyer also took over one quarter of the debt of the *fundo*:

> ... to the Caja de Crédito Hipotecario, a fourth part that amounts to 27,000 pesos, and another fourth part of a debt to the Caja de Crédito Agrario that amounts to 12,500 pesos (Illapel's RP, 1934, no. 114, folio 102).

From the size of Luís Puyó León's debt, it can be assumed that G. Errázuriz did not pay off, during the five years he owned the *fundo*, the part of the debt taken over by him when he bought it. Together, the first two of the Puyó León brothers kept the *fundo* for 9 years. The third one, who bought his part from Errázuriz, kept it for 5 years. In 1938 the three brothers sold the *fundo* for 900,000 *pesos* to J. Parricello C. and A. Charles T. (Illapel's RP, 1939, no. 14, folio 12). The *fundo* thus remained undivided up to this year. One year later, in 1939, Parricello and Charles sold a small part of the *fundo*, 10 *cuadras* (approximately 16 ha), in the southwest for 1,000 *pesos*, to Emilio Puyó León, one of the three brothers who had originally sold the *fundo* to them (Illapel's RP, 1940, no. 153, folio 119). Furthermore, the day after this sale, on 10 March 1939, Parricello and Charles divided the *fundo* between themselves. Parricello received 9,400 ha in the south and east, which kept the original name (Illapel's RP, 1940, no. 25, folio 31 verso). Charles kept 7,605 ha in the northern sector along the coast, which he named Las Palmeras (Illapel's RP, 1940, no. 26. folio 32 verso). Since the *fundo* Las Palmas was eventually divided into two, it was decided to follow the history of Las Palmeras and Las Palmas with Illapel's RP as source essentially only up to the 1940s.

Fundo Las Palmeras

Charles kept the Las Palmeras *fundo* for 3 years before selling it in 1942 to L. Margulis R. for 550,000 *pesos*:

> ... the buyer taking full responsibility for paying the debts to the Caja de Crédito Hipotecario, now reduced to 34,295 and 127,960 pesos (Illapel's RP, 1942, no. 178, folio 113 verso).

Judging by the amount of the second debt, Charles mortgaged Las Palmeras during the three years he owned it. The first debt would correspond to one of the old debts he had taken over when he bought the *fundo* in 1938 from the Puyó León brothers with Parrisello. The contract defined the area of the *fundo* as 7,590 ha, that is 15 ha less than in 1939.

Margulis, in his turn, kept Las Palmeras for only two years. In 1944 he sold it for one million *pesos* to L. Goycolea de la Cerda who agreed to take on:

> ... the obligations to the Caja de Crédito Hipotecario equivalent to 33,365 and 125,664 pesos (Illapel's RP, 1944, no. 40, folio 29 verso).

From the amount of these debts, one can infer that Margulis sold the *fundo* to Goycolea with the same debts that he took on when he purchased Las Palmeras two years earlier.

Since I have only followed the history of Las Palmeras up to 1944, I have not dealt with whether it was expropriated during the agrarian reform. However, judging from the fact that the Las Palmeras *fundo* had 7,590 ha in 1942 and that in the CIREN list of rural estates of 1983 it has only 3,500 ha, it is possible that this *fundo*, as well as the neighbouring one, Las Palmas, were expropriated and sold by CONAF to form two minor *fundos*. The missing hectares coincide with the area of a *fundo* with the name La Alcaparra, which in the CIREN real estate list appears as the property of the Soc. Las Palmas de Mincha Ltd. with 4,569 ha. This society also owns the present *fundo* Las Palmas. The *fundo* Las Palmeras appears in the same real estate list as the property of Soc. Dabed Poza Ltd. whose majority owner, Dabed Poza, are a miner and merchant from Illapel.

Fundo Las Palmas

Parricello, who kept the second *fundo* that arose from the division of the *fundo* Las Palmas, under the same name, kept it for only 3 years. In 1942 he sold it to L. Escala Coo. and M. Vidaurre Coo. for 900,000 *pesos*. The purchasers agreed to:

> take over the debt contracted with the mortgage guarantees to the Caja de Crédito Hipotecario amounting to 250,000 pesos (Illapel's RP, 1944, no. 40, folio 29 verso).

In the contract, it is specified that the *fundo* consisted of 9,400 ha. With regard to the size of the debt when Escala and Vidaurre purchased the property, it is clear that Parricello mortgaged the property at some time during his three years of ownership, in the same way as Charles did with Las Palmeras.

As I have only followed the history of this *fundo* until 1942, I have not determined how many owners it had until 1972, the year that the property was expropriated from its owner, L. Moya Ramírez. Through Agreement no. 1775 from the CORA Council, 9,600 ha of unirrigated non-arable land were expropriated from Moya R. (CORA, Consejo de, no. 1775, Artículo 4, 25 de April, 1972). Later, during the Pinochet government, the entire *fundo* was returned to L. Moya R. (CORA,

Resolución no. 1731 del 26 de April 1976, Oficina de cambios de tenencia de la tierra, no. 2843). On 30 January 1974, Moya R. requested CORA to review the expropriation agreement to which CORA replied:

> With regard to this matter, the Regional Office of the Zone II, has decided that, contrary to the ruling in Expropriation Agreement, the drought that has affected the area has made it impossible to determine if, before the expropriation, the relevant property was badly managed or not, and proposes the reversal of the expropriation as the said fundo is not suitable for the purposes of agrarian reform (SAG, Rol no. 221-5, folio 3.617).

Strangely enough, the *fundo* Las Palmas, which was expropriated at the same time as El Totoral and Puerto Oscuro, was given back to its former owner for reasons that were not arguable valid for the other two *fundos*, where only a reserve was returned. If the reason for returning the Las Palmas *fundo* was that it was not possible to tell if it was well or badly run, due to the drought, the same conditions obviously affected the neighbouring *fundos*.

According to the *comunero* P. Carvajal, Moya would have voluntarily given back approximately 200 ha with 25 peasants of the *fundo* Las Palmas to the agricultural community Canela Baja, when the latter indemnified its property title in 1970s. In the CIREN real estate list from 1983, the present *fundo* Las Palmas belongs to the Soc. Las Palmas de Mincha Ltd., of which Moya R. is a member, and covers 9,600 ha. This society is also the owner of the *fundo* La Alcaparra (4,569 ha), which I believe was formed from part of the *fundo* Las Palmeras.

In 1990, Moya R., over 80 years of age and living in Santiago, barely admitted to know the *fundo* or its size (telephone interview, 14th of October, 1990). He said that the *fundo* was in the hands of an administrator who lived in Valparaíso. This indicates that Moya had been an absentee landlord. The *fundo* is currently dedicated to cattle breeding.

To summarise, in comparison with the *fundos* El Totoral and Puerto Oscuro, the *fundo* Las Palmas of 1890 experienced the greatest problems during the period prior to the agrarian reform. After remaining undivided for 49 years, it became three different properties in 1939, including that formed by the sale of 10 *cuadras* to Puyó.

During the 17 years from 1922, when Alberto Infante Montt sold the *fundo* Las Palmas, to 1939 when it was divided, it changed hands three times, not including the transactions between G. Errázuriz and L. Puyó, and between Parricello, Charles and E. Puyó. Finally, if my conjecture is correct that the *fundo* La Alcaparra once formed part of the *fundo* Las Palmeras, the original *fundo* Las Palmas of 1890, had fragmented into at least three properties by 1983, not including the 10 *cuadras* that were sold off in 1939. The three properties now all belong to societies with multiple owners, the majority of whom, unlike the expropriated owners, come from the local area.

The *fundo* Puerto Oscuro from Luís Alberto Infante Montt's time

Luís Alberto Infante Montt, who appropriated in 1890 part of the original *fundo* El Totoral called Puerto Oscuro. The name of the *fundo* comes from the small natural harbour that was thriving during the second part of 1800s. Unlike his brothers, he kept and lived in the *fundo* until his death around 1912. In comparison with its neighbouring *fundos*, Las Palmas and El Totoral, the *fundo* Puerto Oscuro went through few changes of ownership. Its division takes place after the agrarian reform (see Table 6.4). When Alberto Infante Montt died, he left the *fundo* intestate. His six children (Rosa, Sara, Lucrecia, Luís, Samuel and Carlos Infante Fernández) applied for the inheritance to be registered in their name, but it was only completed in 1919 due to a sale compromise of the *fundo* (Illapel's RP, 1912, no. 155, folio 93). Alberto Infante Montt, not only kept and lived in the *fundo*, but participated in the political life of the newly created commune. According to a historical record of the Municipality in 1894, as a result of the 1891 Law of Autonomous Communes, Alberto Infante Montt was elected as President of the Preparatory Council.

In the Provisional Council of May 1st of the same year, Alberto Infante Montt appears as *edile* member and in the same month, after the mayoral election, which the Conservatives won, he was elected second Mayor. In the second election in 1897 he was once again elected second Mayor. From then on Alberto Infante Montt's name no longer appears on the list of municipal functionaries, possibly due to the fact that the Conservatives lost the elections of 1900.

Table 6.4 The *fundo* Puerto Oscuro: 1890-1972

Owner	Place of residence	Occupation or profession	Area (ha)	Years of ownership
L. A. Infante Montt	Puerto Oscuro	Politician farmer	15,507	1890-1912
Bros. Infante Fernández	Santiago	-	-	1912-1920
E. Lorenz	Santiago	rentista industrial	17,500	1920-1921
In 1921, E. Lorenz sets up an association with D. Ahumada,				
E. Lorenz	Santiago	rentista industrial	17,500	1921-1926
D. Ahumada	Puerto Oscuro	farmer		1921-1926
E. Lorenz	Santiago	rentista industrial	-	1926-1929
J. A. Echavarría Tagle	Puerto Oscuro	politician farmer	-	1929-1964
Bros. Echavarría Echavarría	Santiago	-	-	1964-1972

Source: The author. Where dashes appear, the dates do not appear in the documents
In the case of transferred debts and Credits acquired, the empty space assumes that there were no debts transferred or credits acquired.

The exact date of Infante Montt's death is not known, but since his children requested the inheritance in their name in 1912, he must have died in that year or slightly earlier. According to a *comunero* from Canela Baja, the now deceased Samuel Jorquera, the Infante Montt family had, before they sold the *fundo*, approxximately 800 cows, 70 mares and some 3,000 sheep in Puerto Oscuro (Samuel Jorquera, *comunero* of the Canela Baja sub-area, interview, May 1988).

Unlike their father, Infante Montt's children did not run the *fundo* personally, since they lived in Santiago.

Table 6.4 (Continued)

Purchase price Chilean $	Transferred debts at purchase time in Chilean $		Credits acquired in Chilean $		Sold to
	Entity	Entity	Entity	Entity	
HEREDITY 63,120	CCH 11,666				Bros. Infante Fernández (*Heredity*)
					E. Lorenz
260,000					
a farmer of the commune.					
					L. Lorenz
130,000					J. A. Echavarría Tagle
130,000					Bros. Echavarría Echavarría (*Heredity*)
					1972 (*Expropriated*)

In 1920 they sold the *fundo* to Ernesto Lorenz, originally from Germany, who also lived in Santiago, for the sum of 260,000 *pesos* (Laura Montenegro and Eugenia Ibacache, *comuneras* from Canela Baja, oral interview, March, 8th, 1988 and March 5th, 1988). The *fundo* consisted then of some 10,000 *cuadras* (approximately 17,500 ha) (Illapel's RP, 1920, 114, no. folio 60). The second sale clause stated that the *fundo* included:

> ... the water rights in the Estero La Canela and all rights that correspond to the fundo for its irrigation (AJ, Santiago de Chile, 2 de Enero de 1920 'Venta Infante Carlos...').

In the document of sale it is stated that the borders of the *fundo* are:

> ... to the north the middle hijuela of the fundo El Totoral, which belonged to Juan Diego Infante, and today belongs to Godofredo Acchiardo. To the south, from Los Tomes ravine, where it joins the Canela ravine to the dam called Los Tomes, and from where it climbs to the top of the hill that is to the south and continues along a small hill that surrounds Los Tomes' flat land until the last border line of Los Gálvez on the Talinay hill, and extending fully separated from the Cortéses' community. From the Talinay hill the border extends downwards towards the Gálvez's border line that is to be found at the beginning of the Angostura ravine, from which the border continues to the sea, separating the fundo from the Gálvez community. To the west from where the Angostura ravine flows into the sea, to the border of the middle hijuela of the El Totoral fundo. To the east, the Canela ravine, from where it joins the Espíritu Santo ravine, to the border of the middle hijuela of the El Totoral fundo (AJ, Santiago de Chile, 2 de Enero de 1920 'Venta Infante Carlos y otros a Lorenz Ernesto', no. 15, folio 14, B.P. 10c. C.18,813).

The third clause specifies that the sale included:

> ... the docks, warehouses, buildings and constructions of any kind existing in the harbour called 'Puerto Oscuro' and all rights in relation to the said harbour and the beach corresponding to any title of the vendors (*Ibid.*).

A year later, E. Lorenz formed a society with Donato Ahumada, who lived in Puerto Oscuro. The contract specified that they were equal co-owners (Illapel's RP, 1921, no. 84, folio 46 verso). Since Lorenz lived in Santiago, it was probably Ahumada who ran the *fundo*. In 1926, Lorenz and Ahumada dissolved the society. Ahumada sold his part to Lorenz for 130,000 *pesos*, i.e., half the price that Lorenz paid when he purchased the *fundo* in 1919. In the contract, Lorenz appears as *rentista* (Illapel's RP, 1926, no. 60, folio 25). In total, Lorenz kept the *fundo* for 9 years.

During this time Lorenz continued to live in Santiago and it is clear that after buying back the other half of the *fundo* from Ahumada, he continued to be an absentee landlord. According to distant relatives of Lorenz, he owned a coffee manufacturing business in Talagante, close to Santiago, and visited the *fundo* only occasionally (Ana Zavala, Lorenz's relative. Telephone interview through Edith Valencia Ollarzú, November 19th, 1990).

In 1929, Lorentz sold the *fundo* to José A. Echavarría T. for 350,000 *pesos*, but the *fundo* remained mortgaged to Lorenz (Illapel's RP, 1929, no. 70, folio 75). Echavarría T., was a native of the area and he both lived on and personally ran the *fundo*, except for periods when absent, being a deputy for the zone for two consecutive periods (1920-1924, 1924-1929).

Echavarría died still in possession of the *fundo*, which was inherited by his five children, Ramón J., José A., Edelmira A., Margarita C., María E., Echavarría Echavarría (Illapel's RP, 1964, no. 73, folio 67). The *fundo* was registered in their names in 1964.

Echavarría T.'s now deceased son, J. A. Echavarría E., informed me that when his father bought the *fundo* from Lorenz, he also bought approximately 10,000 sheep, which together with the 9,000 that his father already owned gave a flock of 19,000 sheep (José Antonio Echavarría E., (deceased) several oral interviews, between 1988-1990). Echavarría E. also told me that he had lived on the *fundo* between 1929 and 1958, managing it with his father. Between 1946 and 1955 he also produced gunpowder for use in the construction of the Pan-American Highway. On this he admitted to 'having made a good profit' that lately, due to a long period of illness and 'bad business' had vanished, forcing him to earn his living as a taxi driver in Santiago. In the hands of the Echavarría E., the *fundo* remained undivided until 1972. That year, under the Allende government, the *fundo* was expropriated, after having been in the family's possession for four decades, for the reason established in the 3rd Article of the Law 16,640 of the Agrarian Reform, which dealt with estates that were badly run. It also established that the compensation for the *fundo* would be paid with 5% cash and the rest in Agrarian Reform bonds, type 'C'. The amount of compensation was determined as E° (*Escudo*) 144,090 of which E° 119,486 corresponds to the value of the territorial tax of the *fundo* in respect of the SII, existing at the time of expropriation. The expropriation agreement was published in the Diario Oficial 15 de mayo de 1972 (CORA, Consejo de Secretaría, CHC/COW/amb. A/C no. 3,551, 12 de Julio de 1972. Courtesy of J. A. Echavarría E.). According to Cortázar and Downey (1977:700, footnote 27) 'The middle exchange in 1970 was E° 12 for a dollar. The dollars from 1975 are equivalent 1.39 times those from 1970'.

According to CORA's document, of the 14th November 1964, the date when the *fundo* was registered under the Echavarría E. succession on the Illapel's RP, at the time of the expropriation, the necessary improvements were not confirmed, and the general state of the property and its installations were considered poor. The *fundo* consisted in 1972 of:

- a 50 year old owner's house of 200 m^2 in fair condition with adobe walls, wooden floor and ceiling, and a roof of oak covered with zinc;
- a 20 year old administration building made of adobe of 120 m^2 in fair condition;
- ten 40 year old houses for the *inquilinos* of 32 m^2 in poor condition and made of adobe with earth floors;
- a 40 year old warehouse of 132 m^2 in poor condition;
- 5,300 metres of barbed wire fences in poor repair;
- 1,200 metres of dry-stone wall in fair condition;
- an installation for dipping sheep, in fair condition (CORA, Consejo de Secretaría...).

According to Echavarría E., at the time of the expropriation there were 40 *inquilinos* on the *fundo*. Desiderio Collao, a former *inquilino* (deceased) of the *fundo* claims that there were around 15, who with families made up more than 40 people. Considering that the previously mentioned document from CORA states that there were 10 *inquilinos*' houses on the *fundo*, it would appear that the information given by Collao is more precise. Desiderio Collao became a *comunero* of the agricultural community Canela Baja thanks to a donation of a *hijuela* that he received from a *comunera* from Canela after the end of the *asentamiento* that the ex-*inquilinos* of the Puerto Oscuro *fundo* had with CORA. Collao was also a partner of the society that presently owns the *fundo*. Collao worked on the *fundo* for 38 years while the Echavarría family was the owners, being its foreman for 28 years (recorded interview, 4th March 1988).

Collao informed me that the *inquilinos* received a piece of irrigated land from the *fundo* that they worked for themselves. They also received, if they wanted, *lluvias* on the hills. The patron paid them a small salary and their Social Security. They built their own houses for which they received timber from the patron. During January and February the *inquilinos* were occupied with the harvest and from May to August they sowed wheat, barley and cumin. During the remainder of the year, they tended and repaired the enclosures. In the middle of December some of the *inquilinos* transferred the sheep to the *veranadas* on the Argentine side of the mountain, 'where the grazing was better'. Two or three people stayed in the mountains to take care of the sheep, and to bring them back in the middle of March. Collao states that at the time of the expropriation, the *fundo's* stock was around 1,500 sheep, but at its peak the *fundo* had 7,000-8,000 sheep, 200 cattle and 100 horses. Collao also claims that during elections, the patron of the *fundo* instructed them to vote for him, but also adds that he and his sons were good people.

In 1974, during the Pinochet government, the Echavarría E. heirs of the Puerto Oscuro *fundo,* before its expropriation, requested CORA to review the expropriation and to exclude a part of the *fundo* from it. In the same year CORA approved the petition, and returned to the Echavarría's a reserve of approximately 2,700 ha, including 33 HRB (basic irrigated hectare) located along the coast, west of the Pan-American Highway. The borders of the reserve are:

> ... the El Totoral fundo to the north, the Angostura community to the south, the Pan-American Highway to the east, and the Pacific Ocean to the west (CORA, Consejo de Secretaría, CHC/COW/amb. A/C no. 1,773. Courtesy of J. A. Echavarría E.).

Now, the remaining sons of Echavarría T. and their children are trying, without success, to divide the 2,700 ha reserve into five parts. They all live in Santiago and only visit the reserve during vacations. Part of the reserve is leased to cattle breeders from the zone. One of these is the wealthiest merchant from Canela Baja, who is also a co-partner of the present *fundo* Puerto Oscuro, where he keeps some of his cattle. In turn he sub-lets part of the reserve, which he rents from the Echavarría's, to other farmers.

Once the reserve Puerto Oscuro was returned to the Echavarría's, the part of the *fundo* that remained under the CORA control was of some 10,800 ha in size with 146 HRB. The borders of the *fundo* are:

> ... to the north the fundo El Totoral and part of the community of La Canela; to the south the Angostura de Gálvez ravine and land belonging to the community of Angostura; to the east the Estero [river] of Canela and the community of Canela Baja as well as part of the community of Yerba Loca; and finally, the Pan-American Highway to the west (Fórmula Solicitud de Resciliación Parcial de Contrato, Piñeiro a CONAF, Ruíz-Tagle, Estudio Jurídico, Santiago, Courtesy of P. Carvajal).

According to Collao, the *fundo* functioned between 1972 and 1978 as an *asentamiento* (settlement), being both the property of CORA and of a society consisting of 19 former *inquilinos*. Of these, nine were former *inquilinos* of the *fundo* El Totoral (also expropriated in 1972) and the other from the *fundo* Puerto Oscuro.

Collao stated that CORA brought some 1,500 sheep to the *asentamiento* and that the economic situation of the co-partners, compared to when they were *inquilinos* on the *fundo*, had improved. The *asentamiento*, however, lasted only until 1978 when, under Pinochet, the *fundo* was transferred to CONAF. As a result, the livestock of the *asentamiento* was sold, and the money distributed among the former co-partners of the *asentamiento*.

CONAF took over the *fundo* Puerto Oscuro from CORA for a sum of 213,244 *pesos* equivalent to 442,90 UF. A year later, in 1979, CONAF sold the *fundo* by auction to a group of *comuneros*, mainly from the agrarian community Canela Baja, who organised themselves in order to purchase it. They acquired the *fundo* for 10,600,000 *pesos*, equivalent to 16,554,74 UF (*Ibid.*), a much higher price than that paid by CONAF.

In conclusion, the history of the Puerto Oscuro shows that between 1890 - when L. A. Infante M. appropriates it, and 1972, when it was expropriated - the *fundo* passed through the hands of only three owners: Infante, Lorenz and Echavarría. In comparison with the fate of the Las Palmas and El Totoral *fundos*, Puerto Oscuro changes owner only twice after the time of Infante M. Except for him, who appropriated the *fundo* with an existing debt, the other owners neither took over existing debt, nor took on new ones. As a result of the agrarian changes of the 1970s and 1980s, the *fundo*, which had remained undivided for 80 years, became two properties due to State intervention: the actual *fundo* Puerto Oscuro or Soc. Pereira, Cortés, Brito and Co. Ltd. and the reserve. The reserve is furthermore in a division process by the heirs of Echavarría E. into five smaller parts, and each one will probably be of ca. 540 ha.

Puerto Oscuro of 1890 was to be transformed 100 years later into six properties. While some of the Echavarría E. heirs are no longer alive and their heirs are numerous, the five parts into which the reserve is going to be divided, will continue to be divided into even smaller properties, most probably, to be used as at present, summer resorts for the owners.

The relationship between the *haciendas* and the surrounding agricultural communities in terms of labour force, will now be briefly examined in order to show, against the described empirical development some weak or unreflective points in a position that often is taken for granted, dealing with the relationship between *haciendas* and peasant societies.

The *hacienda* and the surrounding peasant societies

In Latin America, the relationship between the *haciendas* or *latifundia* and the neighbouring peasant communities, independently of its form, is usually described as symbiotic. This relationship is not equal, but asymmetric, the *latifundia* standing for the domination, and the small peasantry for the subordination. In terms of labour force, it means that the nearby peasant communities serve as a labour reservoir to the *latifundia* (Astorga, 1985; Borde and Góngora, 1956; Baraona *et al*, 1961; García, 1973; Rivera, 1988(a), Albala, *et al*, 1967). This is certainly the relationship in most cases, but in the *haciendas* and the agricultural communities in the studied zone, if deeply examined, this relationship, up until the agrarian reform does not appear obvious, and the same may be valid for Region IV. The explanation for this may lie in different factors, which will be examined here.

The principal reason for the *haciendas'* low labour demand from the nearby peasant communities is the *haciendas'* own traditional social system of *inquilinaje* on which it based its exploitation up to the agrarian reform. The family of the *inquilinos*, reproducing themselves within the *hacienda*, should have supplied these properties with the necessary labour force. In the case of the *fundo* Puerto Oscuro, there were 15 *inquilinos*, but up to 40 persons including their families, this being the principal labour reservoir. Due to the agrarian reform, the *inquilinaje* disappeared in Chile and the present *fundo* Puerto Oscuro today uses seasonal labour from the bordering agricultural community Canela Baja. However, it deals first of all with the landless sons of the *comuneros,* and not so much with the *comuneros* themselves.

Another factor that would explain the *haciendas'* low demand of labour in the area is the type of agro-pastoral economy, which characterises both the *haciendas* and the agricultural communities. Contrary to those *haciendas* that base their economy principally on agriculture, demanding bigger and different types (constant and seasonal) of labour supply, an agro-pastoral economy, generally of an extensive character, demands a smaller labour force. It is not always necessary to resort to the neighbouring peasant societies' labour force. It is reasonable to assume that the *haciendas'* extensive agriculture in the Norte Chico may have been reinforced by the competitive attraction pole of the mines in the north for the labour force.

Another element is the low interdependency in terms of labour between the small peasantry and the *hacienda*, is the coincidence of the time for sowing, harvest and livestock caring. Therefore, it is logical to think that the recruitment of labour mainly deals with landless labour.

The *comunero* being faced with the alternative of giving up his land because of recurrent bad years (droughts or floods), and the same valid for the *fundos*, not offering many possibilities to the *comuneros* interested in selling their labour there. The alternative and probably better choice for the *comuneros* would be to migrate. According to my interview, 50% of the *comuneros* and their sons used to migrate outside the commune. Customarily, they migrated to the copper and nitrate mines in the north of Chile. In the pre-agrarian reform period, if the need arose for an extra labour force in the neighbouring *fundos*, in addition to their own *inquilinos*, then the *comuneros*, confronted with the decision or necessity of selling their labour force, would opt for the mines.

This was so for several reasons. First, confronted with the alternative of giving up his land, the mines offer more stability than the neighbouring *fundos* with their seasonal agro-pastoral production. At the same time, the *comuneros* have for a hundred years commonly been migrating to the north, where they also have relatives and *compadres*, facilitating their insertion into the mining centres. Second, the high salaries paid in the mines contributed to its workers being considered the 'labour aristocracy' in Chile. Third, the working conditions in the mines subjected to regulations and negotiations by the traditionally strong presence of the trade unions, offered a major security to its labour force of a magnitude not offered by the landowners. The *hacienda*, on the other hand, is traditionally known by the seigniorial dependency of the peasants to an authoritarian system.

Fourth, but not least important, the characteristic resumed in the paternalistic ideology, which typifies the *hacienda* system in comparison to the working condition in the mines, does not appeal to the self esteem of the *comuneros*. The *comuneros* consider themselves as proprietors, and in this way, not inferior to the landowners. Therefore, opting for becoming a wage-labourer, at least for a time, the *comuneros* would probably rather be employed by a well-known, modern (up to its expropriation in the hands of North American companies), strong, international enterprise, than with a landowner who represents a less fair employer. This can be reinforced by the

The Hacienda El Totoral

traditional antagonism existing between the agricultural communities and the landowners in the struggle for the land.

Taking into consideration the constant transfer of the *fundos* between different owners in my case study, it seems clear that the productive process of these *fundos* could hardly have been the main interest of its owners. This would also explain the low demand for extra labour from the surrounding communities.

Concluding, I would say that analysing the relationship between the *haciendas* and the surrounding peasant societies (read agricultural communities) in terms of labour force, in the Canela commune and Region IV, the *hacienda* can be substituted by another counterpart, the mines in the north of Chile. I do not deny the fact that the *minifundia* or agricultural communities serve as a labour reservoir, but not automatically for the *haciendas*. The peasantry does not constitute an inert labour reservoir, since to some extent it can choose where to sell its labour.

Summarising the history of the *hacienda* El Totoral

Within the context of selling and re-selling of the *fundos*, the successive divisions that they experienced up to the agrarian reform of the 1970s, shows that no further process of land concentration was taking place, on top of what they had already monopolised to the end of the 1800s and the beginning of the twentieth century. The divisions that the *fundos* experienced, were not so much a product of hereditary partition between the owner's descendants, but mainly the product of the division that some of the owners made in order to create a separate property, and later sell. The absence of such a process of land concentration on part of the *haciendas* shows that a process of original accumulation of expenses of the agricultural communities has not taken place, not resulting in the divorce of the means of production from the direct producer. Or to express it with Marx (1983, Vol. 1:669):

> The expropriation of the agricultural producer, from the soil, is the basis of the whole process (of primitive accumulation).

After the agrarian reform, the divisions of the *fundos* were a product of the direct interference of the state. This was initially through the process of agrarian reform during the Allende government, and later during the Pinochet government. Pinochet's agrarian policy can be divided into two phases. The policy was firstly characterised by the return of part of the expropriated land, and secondly, the policy involving the sale, through auction, of land that was not returned. In this way and under radically different agrarian policies, the state, through its direct intervention, changed the structure of land ownership in the commune, which before was characterised mainly by two forms: the large private traditional *haciendas* and the semi-communal property of the agricultural communities.

Continuing with the agrarian reform of Frei, Allende's government, through its agrarian reform policy, fundamentally removed the institution of the great traditional *hacienda* and distributed the expropriated land among the ex-*inquilinos* of the *fundos*. The distribution was done through the creation of *asentamientos* that later, without the support of CORA, had to become independent through the distribution of land to the individual peasants, a process that was interrupted after the coup d'état of 1973.

With Pinochet, the state intervened again but this time with the opposite policy of giving back part and in some cases all, of the expropriated land known as reserves. In the second stage of Pinochet's government, the State, through auction, privatised the land that it did not give back to the expropriated landowners, and that CONAF had obtained from CORA, ending with the dissolution of the *asentamiento*s organised by CORA. In the second stage, with the auctions by CONAF, *comunero*s of some agricultural communities of the area were able to acquire land and get along with some of the ex-*inquilinos* of the expropriated *fundos*, access to land which the *comuneros,* in particular, had not had previously. The objective of this policy was not to benefit the *comunero*s in particular, but to reverse the previous policy of Allende's government through privatisation of the expropriated land. However, by putting the land on the market through auction for whoever wanted and was in a position to buy it, the *comunero*s had, for the first time, the possibility of acquiring it, be it on credit and mortgaged. This shows, however, that the defence of the interests of the former landowners was not the only interest of Pinochet, but rather primarily Friedman's market economy.

With the activation of a market in land, previously monopolised by the landowners and the acquisition of part of this land by the *comunero*s, some of the *fundos* expropriated during the agrarian reform represents private appropriation. This time, however, private appropriation is not concentrated in one or a few owners' hands, but in the hands of numerous people

The Hacienda El Totoral

organised into societies of limited responsibility, through the system of actions constituted primarily for a purchasing purpose. This way, state intervention, in spite of the opposing agrarian policies which were applied during the Allende and Pinochet governments, resulted in not only the redistribution of land, but also in the creation of a new type of property shared among numerous owners. These owners are different from the traditional landowner families, not only because of their class background, but also because of their organisation into a new, more modern and rational type of agricultural production enterprise, ready to share potential risks and profits. Interestingly, the land is held in common, as is the case within the agricultural communities. (This will be covered in more detail in Chapter 9.)

Even if all of these changes did not eliminate all large properties in the area (and in spite of Pinochet's agrarian policy), they did eliminate the *hacienda* as a social institution, at least as a seigniorial monopoly of land and its paternalistic ideology imposed on the peasants. The new *fundos* are, in any case, not only smaller than before, but their exploitation is not based on *inquilinaje*. The new societies function with a paid labour force, although only seasonal, who unlike the ex-*inquilino*s, do not live on the *fundos*.

Therefore, the *hacienda* El Totoral of 1890 has, over a century later, become seven different agricultural properties, or eleven if I take into consideration the partition of the Puerto Oscuro reserve, which is in the process of subdivision into five parts. It is arguable, however, whether the resulting parts of this division can be strictly considered as agricultural properties, given that the reserve constitutes, as it did before, mainly a place for summer vacations. Figure 6.1 (below) illustrates the subdivision of the *hacienda* El Totoral between 1890-1990.

Communal Land Ownership in Chile

Figure 6.1   The subdivision of *Hacienda* El Totoral: 1890-1990 (44,180 ha)

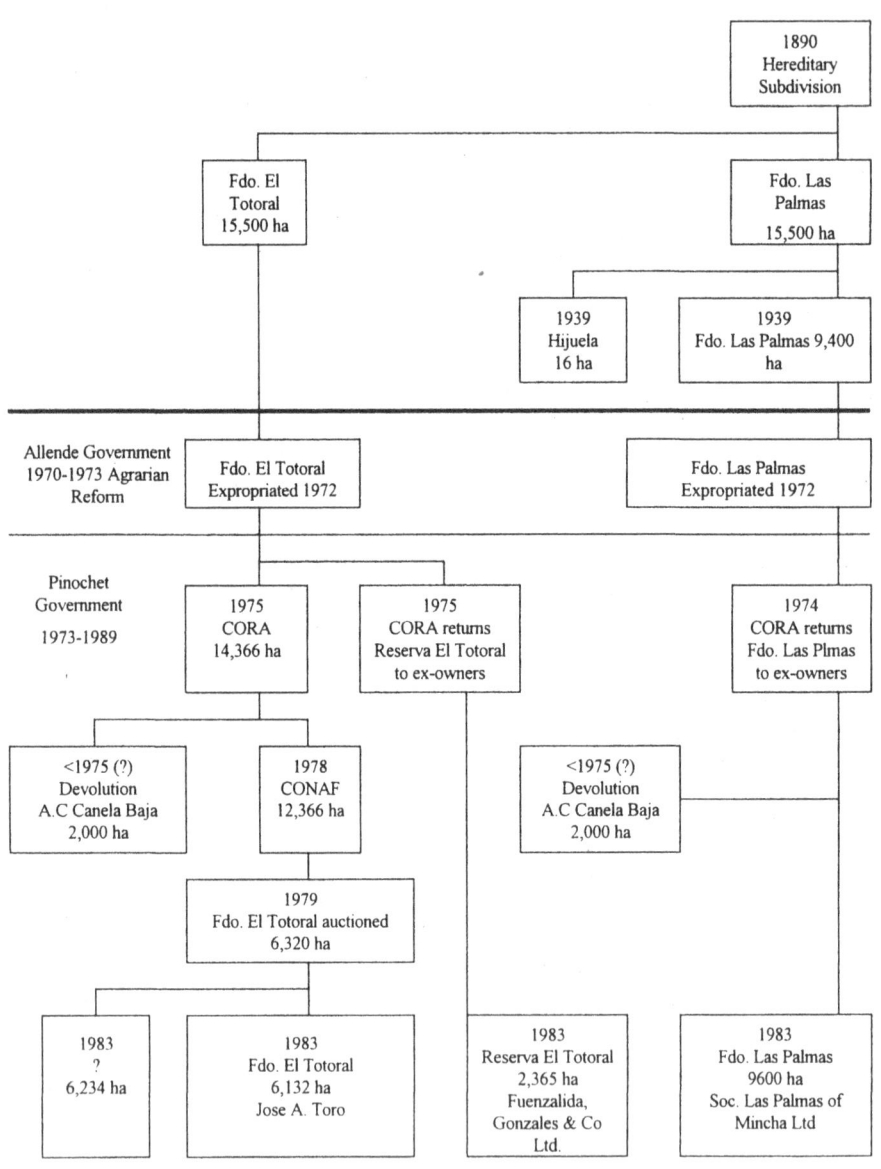

Source: The author. A.C. stands for Agricultural Community

The Hacienda El Totoral

Figure 6.1 (Continued)

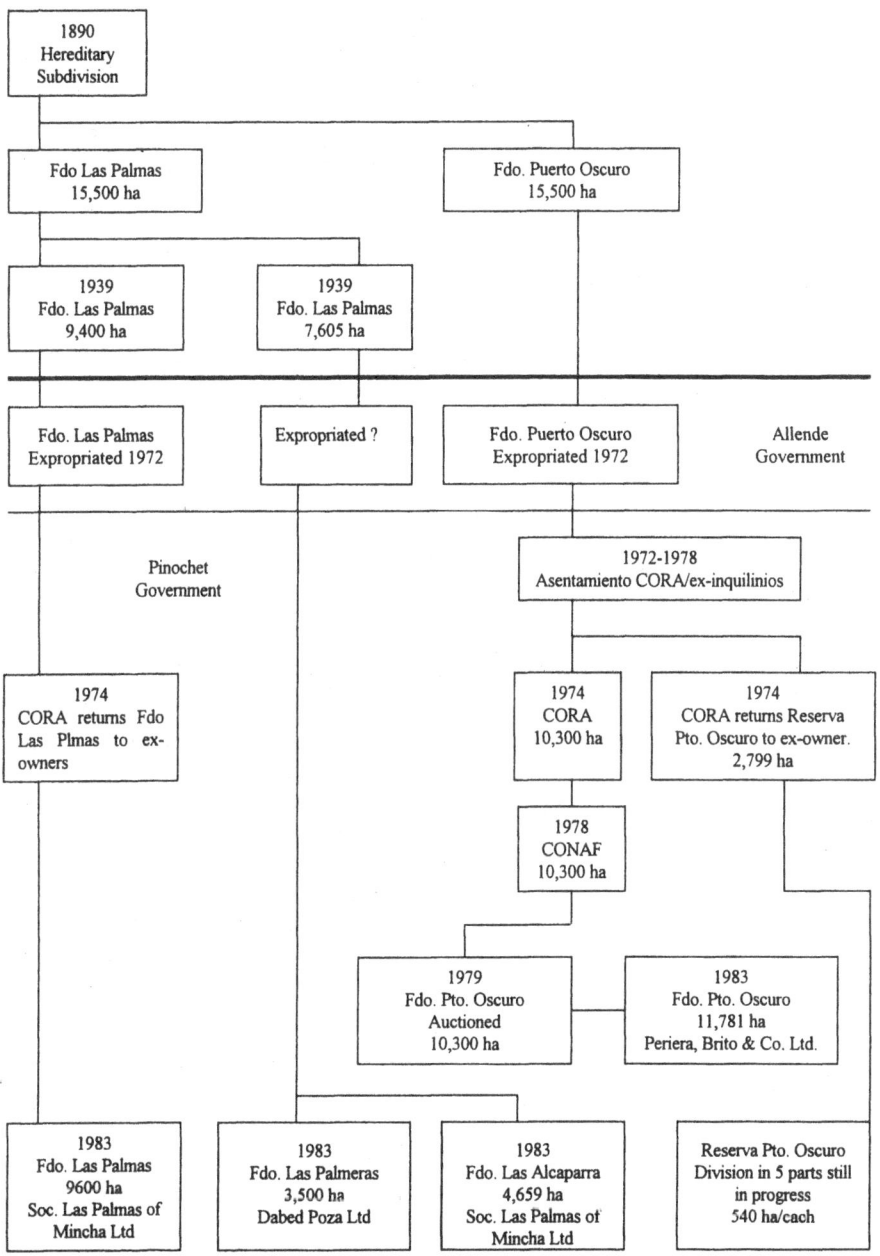

7 Historical Formation of the Agricultural Community Canela Baja: a Reconstruction

Introduction

The agricultural communities (of among others) Canela Baja, Canela Alta and Canelilla, as well as the *hacienda* El Totoral and the *fundos* that were formed from it, apparently have their origins in two *mercedes de tierra*, which later on became known as El Totoral and La Canela.

This part deals mainly with a reconstruction of the formation of the semi-communal land ownership of the agricultural community Canela Baja from the colonial *estancia* La Canela, principally with the help of the accessible historical documents. This chapter also deals briefly with the case of the *estancias* Mincha, Conchalí and Chiagualoco, parts of which belong to the commune of Canela, since here ten agricultural communities with semi-communal land ownership developed from one *merced de tierra:* the Mincha *estancia*. Conchalí and Chigualoco, on the other hand, being still *haciendas* are different from the *estancia* Mincha but similar to El Totoral and show the continuation of private property.

Let me take the *estancia* La Canela from 1679, the year when Diego Cortés Pérez obtains this land as the starting point and the resulting present-day agricultural community. In between there are over three hundred years during which a social process occurs that leads from the conversion of private land property to that of semi-communal land. The mechanisms, which in this particular case lead to this result, are not known except for the fragmentary information that diverse archival sources can reveal. It is only from a detailed reconstruction of the existing archival material that some guiding threads can be drawn.

The elaborated reconstruction of the archival material which results very much in a family history, although important as micro and local history, is also a way to grasp some lines of the historical process represented by the conversion from private properties to the semi-communal. It would be naïve, however, to consider that any reconstruction could encompass all the causes-and-effects of a socio-historical process of three hundred years so as to show a clear causal relationship between the studied phenomena. Several processes, circumstances, factors or whatever term we choose to use, have contributed to that conversion. These will be returned to at the end of this chapter, leaving their further analysis to the final chapter of the book.

The *mercedes* El Totoral and La Canela are probably through heritage, some decades after they had been granted combined into a single property of almost 180,000 ha (see Chapter 5). As such, they were passed on to Diego Cortés Pérez in 1679. Sometime between 1679 and 1709 (1679 being the year when Diego Cortés Pérez inherited this land and 1709 the year of his death) the *estancia* La Canela once again became two properties through an exchange that Diego Cortés Pérez made with Francisco de Aguirre y Cortés.

The former kept La Canela, which must have consisted of some 140,000 ha. Francisco de Aguirre y Cortés took over the northern coastal area of the *estancia* of approximately 40,000 ha, corresponding to El Totoral (Chapter 6). Whereas El Totoral and its resulting properties remain private property until the twentieth century, the part owned by Diego Cortés Pérez, through sales and hereditary subdivision, was split into several properties which slowly began to lose their character of private property, gradually taking the form of semi-communal land ownership.

As the historical origin of the agricultural community Canela Baja is associated not only with the legendary life, wealth and land ownership of the *conquistador* Pedro Cortés Monroy, but especially with that of his descendants, Pedro Cortés Zavala, marquis and half-brother of Diego Cortés Pérez, will, among others, be briefly introduced. Since Diego Cortés Pérez maintained a friendly relationship with the marquis - as well as with his father's widow, his half-sister and her husband - this will give an indication of the social position in which Diego Cortés Pérez lived, at least during part of his life, as well as why he inherited La Canela.

This will also serve to reject Aracena's suggestions that the residents of Canela had aristocratic ancestry (Aracena, 1941:160). This assumption is not correct, given that it was Pedro Cortés Zavala who received the title of marquis. For this reason, the 'aristocrats' would, if any, have been the offspring of the marquis, but he and his wife had no children.

The Marquis Pedro Cortés Zavala, half-brother of Diego Cortés

As the son born outside of matrimony of Pedro Cortés Riberos, Diego Cortés Pérez was half-brother of Pedro Cortés Zavala, who became the marquis of Huana and Piedra Blanca in 1697. During the time of Pedro Cortés Zavala, the heirs of the *conquistador* Pedro Cortés Monroy's experienced the height of their socio-economic splendour (Pinto, J., 1983:153). Pedro Cortés Zavala was granted the title Marquis of Huana and Piedra Blanca by Carlos II (1661-1700) for his services to the Crown (Amunátegui, 1898:162). Piedras Blancas, which corresponds to a different property than La Huana, is one of the *mercedes* that Pedro Cortés Cisternas, the marquis grandfather, received in 1606. This title was one of only nine, and the second of Castilla given in the General Captaincy of Chile (see Chapter 5). In his military career he reached the title of Grand Master. Among his bureaucratic positions he held the post of town councillor in 1692, the office of Mayor in 1684, 1695 and 1707, whilst in 1673, 1687 and 1708 he was the Town's General Representative (Amunátegui, 1898:163; Cortés-Monroy, R. 1991-1992:192).

Pedro Cortés Zavala married María de Morales y Bravo in 1683 (Silva Lezaeta, 1904:265), receiving a dowry of 26,000 *pesos* (Pinto, J., 1983:153). The wedding took place in La Serena:

> on the twenty-seventh day of February in the year sixteen hundred and eighty-three I married and veiled Grand Master Don Pedro Cortés, legitimate son of Grand Master Don Pedro Cortés and Doña Magdalena Savala, with Doña María Bravo de Morales, legitimate daughter of Grand Master Don Juan de Morales and Doña María de Riveros (AP La Serena, La Merced, Defunciones y Matrimonios (Deaths and Marriages) (1661-1733), folio 27 verso).

At the beginning of 1700s this marriage was one of the most prosperous, and Pedro Cortés Zavala one of the wealthiest men of the period. Apart from his military and bureaucratic career, Pedro Cortés Zavala also exploited copper mines, took part in commerce, cultivated wheat, raised livestock, and had vineyards on his *hacienda* Huanilla, as well as a dye-works (Amunátegui, 1898:164).

Magdalena de Zavala, mother of the marquis, managed to get the Indians from the village of La Huana, designated as *encomienda* to her son, an *encomienda* which allowed him to successfully exploit the family's copper mines (Amunátegui, 1898:156). The *encomienda* of Atelcura had been given to the *conquistador* Pedro Cortés Monroy in 1602.

The marquis owned the *haciendas* Huana, Piedra Blanca, Huanilla and Quilicán (Retamal *et al*, 1992:304). The *hacienda* of Huana, which gave rise to his title, was in the family until the beginning of the 1880s (Amunátegui 1898:145). The *hacienda* Huanilla belonged to the descendants of the Cortés Monroy family until the twentieth century when the La Paloma dam was built (Retamal, 1992:304). When Pedro Cortés Zavala died in 1716 (Pinto, J., 1983:154), the title was inherited by his nephew Diego Montero Cortés as there was no immediate heir. Diego Montero Cortés was the son of the marquis' sister, Josefa Cortés Zavala. She was married to the Grand Master Antonio Montero del Aguila, son of Diego Gonzáles Montero, twice governor of Chile and president of the colonial Royal High Court. Diego Montero Cortés, the second marquis of Huana and Piedra Blanca, held several important posts in the colonial administration (Cortés-Monroy, R., 1991-1992:188).

Magdalena de Zavala's donation to Sergeant Major Diego Cortés

Although Diego Cortés Pérez was born outside of matrimony, his father's widow, Magdalena de Zavala, gifted to him in 1679, the land of La Canela and El Totoral. This information, which I took originally from Cañón's work about La Canela, has served as a basis for several other authors (Gastó *et al*, 1986; Villaroel *et al*, 1988) without necessarily being included in their bibliographies. Confusing versions about La Canela have come from these works, which are not very rigorous in their character. Santander, to whom I have referred, itself misrepresents some historical details of the work of Gastó *et al*, for the case of La Canela. He indicates, for example, that Magdalena de Zavala, the owner of the e*stancia* La Canela, was a servant, and it is not clear whether it referred to Francisco of Aguirre or Pedro Cortés Monroy. She would have donated La Canela to Diego Cortés Pérez. This is not what Gastó *et al*, wrote, who correctly indicated that Magdalena of Zavala was the widow of Pedro Cortés Monroy, without indicating which one of the many Cortés Monroy this referred to (Gastó *et al*, 1986:74).

At the time that the property was gifted to Diego Cortés Pérez, he was 34 years old, having been born in La Serena around 1645 (Cortés-

Monroy, R., 199-92:190). In the will, Magdalena de Zavala says that as she found herself pleased with Captain Diego Cortés de Monroy, and she:

> bestows some land which she had and which she bought from Juan de Vélez de Alvares /.../ known as Las Porqueras which is bounded by María de Tapia's estancia to the south, the estancia Guanilla [Huanilla] that I own (sic) in the west and Miguel de Albassussa's estancia in the north. *At the same time she gives and donates some land that she has in this jurisdiction that begins at the Choapa river in direction to this city [La Serena] joining the lands of El Totoral and in the east borders Captain Pedro de Ahumada's land and by the other side with the sea of which such lands for the same reason of services she donates.* (ANCH, AJ Illapel, Legajo no. 5, pieza 4 Caratulado 23 Civil, 1835, "Francisco Cortez Espinosa y otros versus Lino Páez y otros sobre derechos de unos terrenos", folio 1-2, emphasis added).

The lands from which the agricultural community Canela Baja amongst others were developed, were not those called Las Porqueras (Ovalle), but those not given any specific name, mentioned only by their boundaries (from the River Choapa to El Totoral). Although it is very clear in this will that it was Las Porqueras that Magdalena de Zavala bought from Juan de Vélez, Ollarzú affirms that it was La Canela (Reseña histórica y panorámica de Canela y Mincha (*s.a.*), O. Ollarzú (deceased), Manuscrito. Ollarzú was also qualified informant, *comunero*, merchant and ex-Mayor of the Commune of Canela).

The versions in respect to the definite origins of the village Canela and its first residents vary to some extent. According to Cañón, the origins of La Canela stem from the time when Diego Cortés Pérez came to live on these lands after receiving them from his father's widow.

In Aracena's and Ollarzú's versions, with which I agree, those who came to live in Canela were the sons of Diego Cortés Pérez, Diego and Pedro Cortés Castillo, who came after the death of their father. Before this, Pedro Cortés Pérez had lived with his sons on the farm El Chañaral (Ovalle) (Aracena, 1941:160).

In 1705 when Diego Cortés Pérez wrote his will, his sons Diego and Pedro were 19 and 16 years old. Apparently, it was several decades later that the brothers decided to move to La Canela. They continued to live on El Chañaral off and on, and they still appeared to be living there in 1739. However, their mother, Ana del Castillo, probably settled in La Canela before her sons, since she was buried in Mincha in 1734 (AP Mincha, Defunciones (1694-1797), folio: illegible).

Aracena's and Ollarzú's version of Diego Cortés Pérez's place of residence is confirmed by his will, according to which he appears to be living on El Chañaral, and asks to be buried in La Serena, which he was (Cortés-Monroy, R., 1991-1992:190). He also says in his will that he was married to Ana del Castillo and, apart from the two named sons, he also had a son born outside marriage, called Francisco Cortés, and whose maternal name is not mentioned.

Oddly enough, the author Cortés-Monroy, R., who uses the same will as his source, sustains that Diego Cortés Pérez was a neighbour and resident of the La Canela valley, even though this is not what he himself says. However, Diego Cortés Pérez, who died on July 1709 at the age of 64, made his will some years before in 1705.

Sergeant Major Diego Cortés Pérez's testament

When Diego Cortés Pérez died, he left, with the exception of the piece of land called La Canelita, which later became the agricultural community La Canelilla, the complete *estancia* La Canela and some other goods to his two legitimate sons. The relevant parts of his testament are:

> I, Sergeant Diego Cortés Pérez, born out of wedlock, son of General Don Pedro Cortés Monroi and Doña Clara Pérez /.../ both originally from La Serena, ask /---/ to be buried in the convent of the Church of the Señor Santísimo Domingo /---/

> I declare that he is my debtor, my brother Mr. marquis Don Pedro Cortés of one hundred and sixty kids [young goats] /---/

> I declare that I have been married /---/ to Doña Ana del Castillo for a period of 20 years and that during this marriage we had two legitimate sons called Diego and Pedro, the elder being 19 years of age and the other 16 years of age and I appoint my wife as guardian, carer and good holder of my two sons Diego and Pedro, and as testamentary executor, my brother the marquis and my son Pedro Cortes. /---/

> I declare that Santiago Aguilera owes me one hundred pounds and more of wrought copper /---/

I declare as my goods the estancia named La Canela, in which I have three hundred and more breeding mares of mules with sixteen or twenty horses /.../ with the mules that could be found with my iron and signal.

I declare as my goods, *the farm called El Chañaral where I live,* of wheat and mill of grinding gold and in this farm I have eight fanegas and another seed-field of nine fanegas of white wheat seeding. (Fanega is a measurement of grain equivalent to 1.60 bu).

I declare that I have a gold mine in /.../ the Espíritu Santo, I declare it as my own and I order my inheritors to work them and share them fraternally. /---/

I declare that I have given my sister Baltazara Cortés, because of her kind services, a piece of land in the place called La Canelita, that is five hundred cuadras, I order my inheritors to give it to her after my death. /---/

I declare by my goods /---/ when I got married to Doña Ana del Castillo /---/ legally of her own five hundred sheep /---/

I declare that I have a son, born out of wedlock called Francisco Cortes to whom I have given nothing because he has spent too much money. /---/

I declare that it is my will to improve my son Pedro in the fifth of my goods because of him being obedient and I ask this son to protect my son Diego because he has a short discernment.... (ANCH, AJ La Serena, Civiles, Legajo no. 117 (1733-1765), 1733, "Aguilera Santiago contra los herederos de Diego Cortés. Derechos de tierras", folio 5-7 verso; and in AJ Illapel, Legajo no. 5, pieza 4, Caratulado 23 civil, 1855 "Francisco Cortez Espinosa y...", emphasis added).

His sister Baltazara, to whom Diego Cortés Pérez left La Canelita, was married to Pedro Aguilera. Pedro Aguilera, who was a native of Concepción, died in 1718 at the age of 80 and was buried in Mincha (AP Mincha, Defunciones (1694-1797), folio 9, verso). Santiago Aguilera, also named in the will, as a debtor of 'hundred pounds and more of wrought copper' was also nephew of Diego Cortés Pérez.

Historical Formation of the Agricultural Community Canela Baja

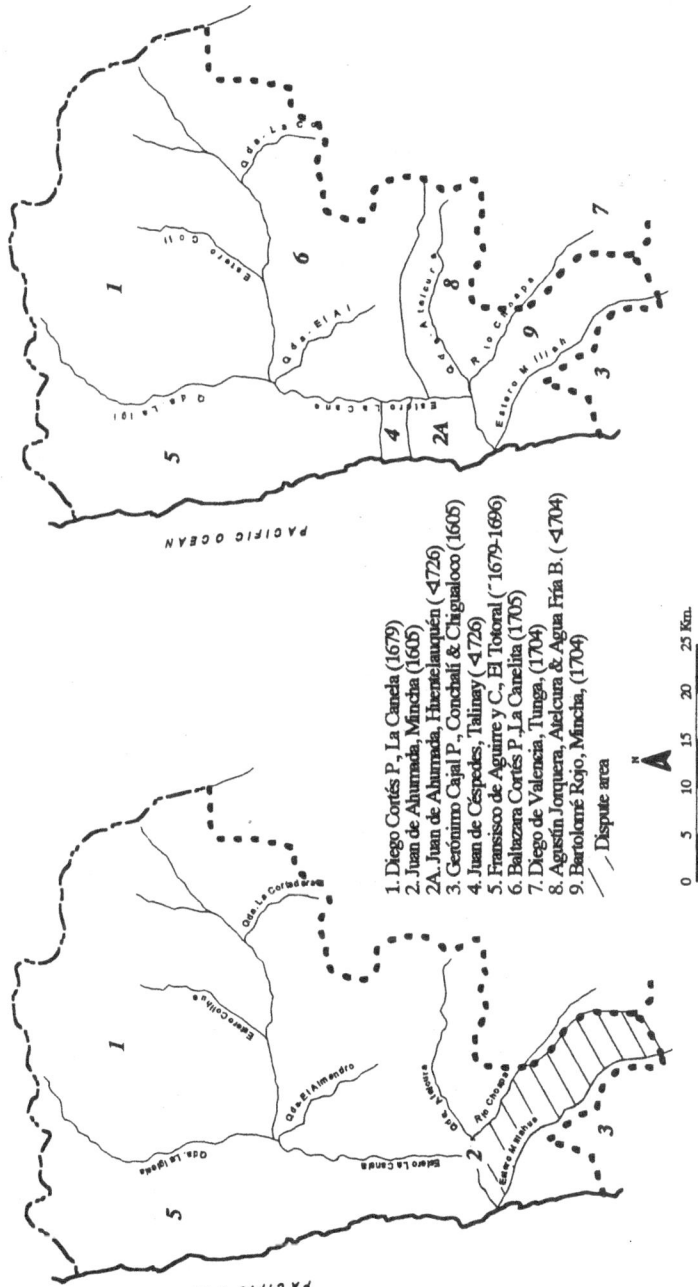

Figure 7.1 The *Estancias* La Canela and Mincha (~1605-1726)

1. Diego Cortés P., La Canela (1679)
2. Juan de Ahumada, Mincha (1605)
2A. Juan de Ahumada, Huentelauquén (<1726)
3. Gerónimo Cajal P., Conchalí & Chigualoco (1605)
4. Juan de Céspedes, Talinay (<1726)
5. Fransisco de Aguirre y C., El Totoral ("1679-1696)
6. Baltazara Cortés P. La Canelita (1705)
7. Diego de Valenzia, Tunga, (1704)
8. Agustín Jorquera, Atelcura & Agua Fría B. (<1704)
9. Bartolomé Rojo, Mincha, (1704)

Dispute area

The land La Canelita would, as we shall see some decades later, cause a litigation between the children of Baltazara and Diego Cortés Pérez, probably even leading the brothers Cortés Pérez to divide the *estancia* La Canela among them.

From the testament it is understood that even if Diego Cortés Pérez did not live on La Canela, he exploited it. He used this land for the rearing of equines according to the type of economy prevailing at that time in the area, on land not very appropriate for agriculture. The raising of mules must have been central to the exploitation of Espíritu Santo's gold mines, mentioned in his testament. These mines are mentioned as early as 1577, when the governor García Hurtado de Mendoza (1557-1561) appointed Diego Vásquez de Padilla:

> Mayor of the mining settlements [asientos] of Chuapa and Quillota and Curoamona and Alamillo; and other mining settlements that were to be discovered within the boundaries of the city of Santiago, and of *the mines Espíritu Santo* and the surrounding district within the boundaries of the city of La Serena, to supervise the work of the natives (Villaroel *et al*, 1988:59; my emphasis).

Referring to the serious consequences of the mining to the environment in Norte Grande and Chico during the 1700s, Cunill describes the mining settlements as:

> basic concentrations of miners population close to the mines. These unifunctional establishments, with a male population dedicated exclusively to extraction work in the mines, are temporary and improvised, formed spontaneously without any kind of legal formality (Cunill, 1975:60).

The fact that these settlements, just like any other kinds of mining sites such as *placillas*, foundries and mills, gave birth to many villages and cities shows that they were not that temporary. This is even confirmed by Cunill (1975:69) himself, when he points out that both Illapel and Combarbalá have arisen from these mining settlements. Mincha, which appears on the map of mining settlements provided by Cunill is, in my opinion, an example of a village that owes its origin through some connection to mining sites. However, according to Villaroel *et al* (1988:85), the Espíritu Santo gold mines were of great importance during the time of the conquest. According to Aracena (1941:160), a considerable part of the gold that was sent from Illapel to Spain, and which gave Illapel its coat of arms, came from La Canela.

Although, judging from his will, Diego Cortés Pérez possessed considerable wealth, one can imagine that he, notwithstanding the close relationship with his father's family, was of inferior social standing in the colonial society. Both when it came to his position as a son born outside matrimony and to his military rank, he was below his father and his half-brother. Indeed, the fact that Diego Cortés Pérez had a good relationship with his father's widow is shown by the gift of land she made to him, because 'she found herself pleased' with his 'many and good services'. That Diego Cortés Pérez furthermore had a good relationship with his half-brother the marquis, is something that can also be read from Diego Cortés Pérez's will. The marquis is not only appointed as his testamentary executor, but is even in debt to him of 'one hundred and sixty kids'.

Diego Cortés Pérez was also close to his half-sister and her husband Antonio Montero. Two of the witnesses, who in 1696 declared in favour of Diego Cortés (Pérez) concerning the original documents which certified that he was the owner of La Canela, documents which were burnt in the 'invasion by the pirate enemy' in La Serena in 1680, say that these documents were then in the Grand Master Antonio Montero's house, and they refer to him as Diego Cortés' (Pérez) brother-in-law (ANCH, AJ La Serena, Legajo no. 15, 1696, pieza 18, 'Pedro Cortés con...' folio 11 a 11, verso. Witness 8: Juan de Tapia, folio 12 to 12 verso. Witness 9: Francisco de Araya) (see Chapter 5).

In the military hierarchy Diego Cortés Pérez reached the rank of sergeant major (Amunátegui, 1898:149) and that is how he refers to himself in his will. In the gift that Magdalena de Zavala made to him, and which was prior to the will, he appears as a captain. The *estancia* La Canela (including the gold mine Espíritu Santo), besides the *estancia* Chañaral in Ovalle, apparently the principal landed property that Diego Cortés Pérez left at his death, consists, however, mainly of hilly and non-irrigated land in spite of its large land area. The best irrigated land and only a part of the property, corresponded to that situated on the northern banks of the Choapa River, which was sold to Juan de Ahumada in 1726.

Apparently, the father of Diego Cortés Pérez, Pedro Cortés Riberos, did not live on the lands belonging to La Canela either. This hypothesis is supported by his military career, the bureaucratic posts he held, his involvement in agricultural work on the land he owned in La Serena, and also by the fact that Pedro Cortés Riberos and his wife Magdalena de Zavala were buried in La Serena. Therefore, the lands belonging to La Canela, once El Totoral had become a separate property, most likely remained undivided and scarcely inhabited during the entire 1600s and started to become populated only at the beginning/middle of 1700s.

Table 7.1 List of marriages in Mincha Parish, 1689-1714

Year	Marriages		Other	Total	Year	Marriages		Other	Total
	M*	I*	**			M*	I*		
1689	1	1	0	2	1702	1	1	1	3
1690	1	2	1	4	1703	5	5	2	12
1691	4	1	3	8	1704	1	0	0	1
1692	0	0	5	5	1705	2	3	0	5
1693	1	1	0	2	1706	0	0	1	1
1694	0	0	3	3	1707	0	1	0	1
1695	1	1	0	2	1708	3	1	0	4
1696	3	1	0	4	1709	0	2	0	2
1697	5	4	2	11	1710	0	4	0	4
1698	3	1	1	5	1711	6	0	0	6
1699	1	3	1	5	1712	1	0	1	2
1700	4	1	0	5	1713	0	2	1	3
1701	2	0	0	2	1714	2	2	1	5
Total	26	16	16	58	Total	21	21	7	49

Source: The author based on AP Mincha, Matrimonios (1689-1796), folio 1-24
M* stands for Mincha;
I* stands for Illapel;
** stands for either: (1) the name of the place illegible, (2) corresponds to other places nearby or (3) the place was not specified.

This is furthermore supported by the first marriage register (1689-1796) of the Mincha Parish, wherein the low number of weddings per year gives a clear indication of the small population, which lived there during that period. The first marriage register of the Mincha Parish embraces the years 1689-1796. According to its register index, a total of 538 weddings took place during these 107 years, which gives an average of 5.3 marriages per year. However, it has to be pointed out that not all the above-mentioned weddings correspond to people who lived in what today is the commune of Canela, since the marriage register during this period also included couples from Illapel and other places nearby. Out of a total of 107 registered weddings that took place during the first quarter (1689-1714) of a century, 44% took place in the Mincha Parish and 34.5% in the Illapel Parish. The remaining 21.5% correspond to the category that I refer to as Other (Table 7.1). If I consider only the unions celebrated in the Mincha Parish during these first 25 years, only 47 weddings took place, which gives an average of only 1.88 marriages per year.

Also according to Aracena (1941:198), La Canela started to become populated during the 1700s and 1800s in connection with the exploitation of its gold mines.

How long the *estancia* La Canela remained an undivided property, once Diego Cortés Pérez's children had legally inherited it in 1705, is uncertain. Judging from the transaction in 1726, when Pedro Cortés Castillo (Diego Cortés Pérez's son) sold the Huentelauquén area (that is, the coastal area on the northern bank of the River Choapa) to Juan de Ahumada, it seems that prior to this date, the land to the north of the Huentelauquén area had also become separated from the *estancia* La Canela:

> Says I, Pedro Cortez, that I received two hundred and fifty pesos in counted silver from captain Juan de Ahumada for a parcel of land which I have sold to him in the area of Huentelauquen, whose borders we put in good conformity, the first *one parting from the Choapa river following the main road to Coquimbo* until it comes to a small stream that is called the salt water, division [illegible] and borders *with lands belonging to Lieutenant Juan de Sespedes...* (ANCH, AN Illapel, Vol. 4 (1775-1844), 'Venta Pedro Cortez a Juan de Ahumada', folio 42, emphasis added).

According to this sale, the land to the north of the rivulet Salt Water (*Agua Salada*), situated approximately 10 km from the River Choapa, already belonged to the Lieutenant Juan de Céspedes. This makes it clear that this part had become another property before 1726, the year when Huentelauquén area was sold.

While the part sold to Juan de Ahumada today constitutes the agricultural community Huentelauquén (approximately 7,426 ha), the part belonging to Juan de Céspedes corresponds to the present *fundo* Talinay (approximately 900 ha). (See Figure 3.4, where the white space between properties 136 and 137 is Talinay.) It is important to note that where the size of property is mentioned, it refers to the current size. As such, they are approximations that are not necessarily correct but extrapolating their present size might be a way of estimating the size they once were. Half a century later, in Diego Cortés Castillo's testament from 1753, the Céspedes family still appears as owners of Talinay. With these two separations, the *estancia* La Canela should have become restricted to the hydrographic bed of the river La Canela, which would mean that its area was approximately reduced from 140,000 to 132,000 ha.

The partition of the *estancia* La Canela

In 1739, Pedro Cortés Castillo divided, by mutual agreement, the *estancia* La Canela with his brother Diego Cortés Castillo. Diego kept Canela Alta and Pedro kept Canela Baja. It is interesting to observe the motive for the partition given by the brothers, who at the time were 50 and 53 years old. This was to avoid future disputes and the legal expenses that these might cause among their descendants. They come to this agreement only a few years after the litigation they had in 1733 with their cousin, Captain Santiago Aguilera, over the lands on the Canelita left by Diego Cortés Pérez to his sister Baltazara, and exactly two years before the death of Pedro Cortés Castillo. Santiago Aguilera Pérez was the nephew of Diego Cortés Pérez and the son of his sister Baltazara.

Santiago Aguilera won the case in January 1733 (ANCH, AJ La Serena, Civiles, Legajo no. 117 (1733-1765), 1733, "Aguilera Santiago contra..."). Although the land that Diego Cortés Pérez, according to his will, left to his sister comprised 500 *cuadras* (800 ha), the present-day agricultural community Canelilla is approximately 4,000 ha in size. Nevertheless, it seems that this litigation did not keep the cousins from at least conducting affairs since Santiago Aguilera appears later on in Diego Cortés Castillo's testament as his debtor.

It would seem that the Cortés Castillo brothers, influenced by the lawsuit, decide to divide the *estancia* La Canela in two, in order to establish exactly what will eventually correspond to their respective heirs:

> Let all who may see this letter know how I Pedro Cortés and Diego Cortés legitimate sons of the Sergeant Major Diego Cortés Monroy *neighbours in this valley of Limarí Alto* Jurisdiction of the city of La Serena of Chile the two of us together /.../ and we say it in name /.../ our own /.../ over the lands

that we inherited from our deceased father that we enjoy and own on the estancia the Chañaral and the estancia of La Canela jurisdiction of the city of La Serena and because of the disputes that could arise between our inheritors /.../ and keeping in mind /.../ and expenses and costs that from the disputes /.../ we have agreed and settled in the following manner to... (ANCH, AJ Ovalle, Legajo no. 1 pieza 4, 1739, Caratulado 'Sobre derecho de tierras en Tabalí', folio 166 to 167 verso, emphasis added).

According to this document, the brothers Pedro and Diego Cortés Castillo first divided the *estancia* El Chañaral among themselves, where they claimed to be staying. The statement confirms that they are not yet living permanently on La Canela. They subsequently proceeded to divide the *estancia* La Canela:

and for the same reason an estancia called La Canela, by the Choapa river jurisdiction of the city of La Serena of Chile, which we inherited from our deceased father and so (*Ibid.*).

The boundaries of present Canela Alta, which was kept by Diego Cortés Castillo, are:

from the hill that comes down from Cataguechún until it unites with the river, and on the side of Choapa Baja to a hillock until reaching the river, one in front of the other, and we separated between the two of us a boundary marker /[illegible]/ and it is the said boundary marker /[illegible]/ from a fig tree which we planted the /[illegible]/ two cuadras more or less upwards, and from this boundary marker a strip going upwards, was left to me, the said Diego Cortés, by inheritance like everything else, and these lands go /.../ from the said boundary marker until the top of the snow covered mountain Llampangui as it is stated in the bill of sale[!?] (*Ibid.*).

The boundaries of what today is Canela Baja, which was kept by Pedro Cortés Castillo, are:

from the said boundary marker towards the sea until the Choapa river mouth including the entire Talinay hill, the Espíritu Santo ravine with all Car quindañi which from the hillock that separates the Almendro ravine until the foothills of Castutos was left to me, the said Pedro Cortés, which was inherited from my father like everything else (*Ibid.*).

It is not easy to understand the boundaries of Diego's land, since it is not at all clear where they put the boundary marker between the *estancia* Canela Alta and the *estancia* Canela Baja. However, when Pedro specifies that his part stretches from the mentioned marker towards the sea 'until the River Choapa's mouth', a possible interpretation is that they drew the division between the two *estancias* at where the River Canela flows into the River Choapa (some 3 km to the west of the village Mincha). A curious detail to which I have no explanation is that Diego talks about a bill of sale. That is, supposing that my transcription is correct and that this really is the word that appears in the original text; *bentta*, today spelled *venta*.

Yet another curious detail is that Pedro says that his land stretches as far as to where the Choapa river flows into the sea, when he supposedly sold this land himself to Juan de Ahumada in 1726. The place, called Castutos, is not on the map. According to Villaroel *et al* (1988:85) there is, however, a place called Casuto close to Chigualoco, which today lies outside the limits of the commune. However, according to Cañón, the boundaries of the *estancia* Canela Baja, which remained with Pedro Cortés Castillo, were:

> to the north from the Catahueche hill to the top of the Guayacanes, the Raugel hill, from there to Paradero, and the Blanco hill, to the south from the Talinay hill to the foothills of Castuto or Casuto /.../ to the hillocks of Carquindañi, to the east, el Coligue to the hillock of the Almendro ravine, following the cordon of Talguén and from there to Catahueche and to the west the hacienda El Totoral (Cañón, 1964:37).

Strangely enough, the source that Cañón uses to present these limits for the *estancia* Canela Baja is a document from 1892 and not the document from 1739 concerning the division between the two brothers. The document used by Cañón, concerns a sale between Reinaldo Saavedra and Bernardo Silva, both *comuneros* from Espíritu Santo, today a sub-area of the agricultural community Canela Baja. In any case these limits, as presented by Cañón, are not the ones drawn up by the brothers at the time of the division, which does not mean that they are altogether incorrect.

In the document from 1892, it no longer says that the property stretches south and westwards to where the River Choapa joins the sea. In respect to the Castuto foothills the location remains unclear, since there is no place on the maps that correspond to the limits of the *estancia* Canela Baja.

Historical Formation of the Agricultural Community Canela Baja

In respect to the northern limit of his property, Pedro Cortés Castillo indicates, in the document from 1739, that it goes by the Espíritu Santo ravine, while in the document from 1892 several reference points slightly further to the north of Espíritu Santo are given. These reference points may only show a major precision of the *estancia's* northern limits. They do not contradict the limit as specified by Pedro Cortés Castillo (1739), whereas as we have seen in Chapter 5, the property donated to his father must have stretched approximately to Mantos de Hornillos and Guile (today, Limarí province). Three of the four specified reference points lie within or on the northern border of the present agricultural community Canela Baja (which coincides with the boundaries of the commune Canela). These are the Guayacán hill (or Guayacanes) which lies within the limit, and the Ranjel (o Raugel) and Paradero hills that lie on the border. The one point on the outside of the present boundary is the Blanco hill, situated some 7 km to the northeast from the Ranjel hill.

Apparently the *estancia* Canela Baja, which remained with Pedro Cortés Castillo, was smaller than that of his brother Diego, who kept Canela Alta. If my calculations are correct, the *estancia* Canela Baja must have included around 40,000 of the 132,000 ha that was left after the disjunction of Talinay and the Huentelauquén area (1726). The *estancia* Canela Alta must, therefore, have measured about 92,000 ha. It is probable that this difference is due to Pedro being favoured in his father's will with one fifth of his father's total wealth. According to Aracena (1941:160), Pedro also inherited the farm El Chañaral although it does not appear directly in the will left by Diego Cortés Peréz. However, this is not correct since it is written in the partition that the brothers made in 1739 that both inherited El Chañaral, dividing it up between themselves (ANCH, AJ Ovalle, Legajo no. 1 pieza 4, Caratulado 'Sobre derecho de tierras en Tabalí'). Located to the east, part of the landscape of the community Canela Alta is higher and hillier than that of the agricultural community Canela Baja.

However, as a result of the exchange, sales and hereditary subdivision, the *estancia* La Canela had in six decades, from 1679 to 1739, become six properties. These were, in chronological order: El Totoral, La Canelita, Talinay, the Huentelauquén area, Canela Baja and Canela Alta.

Communal Land Ownership in Chile

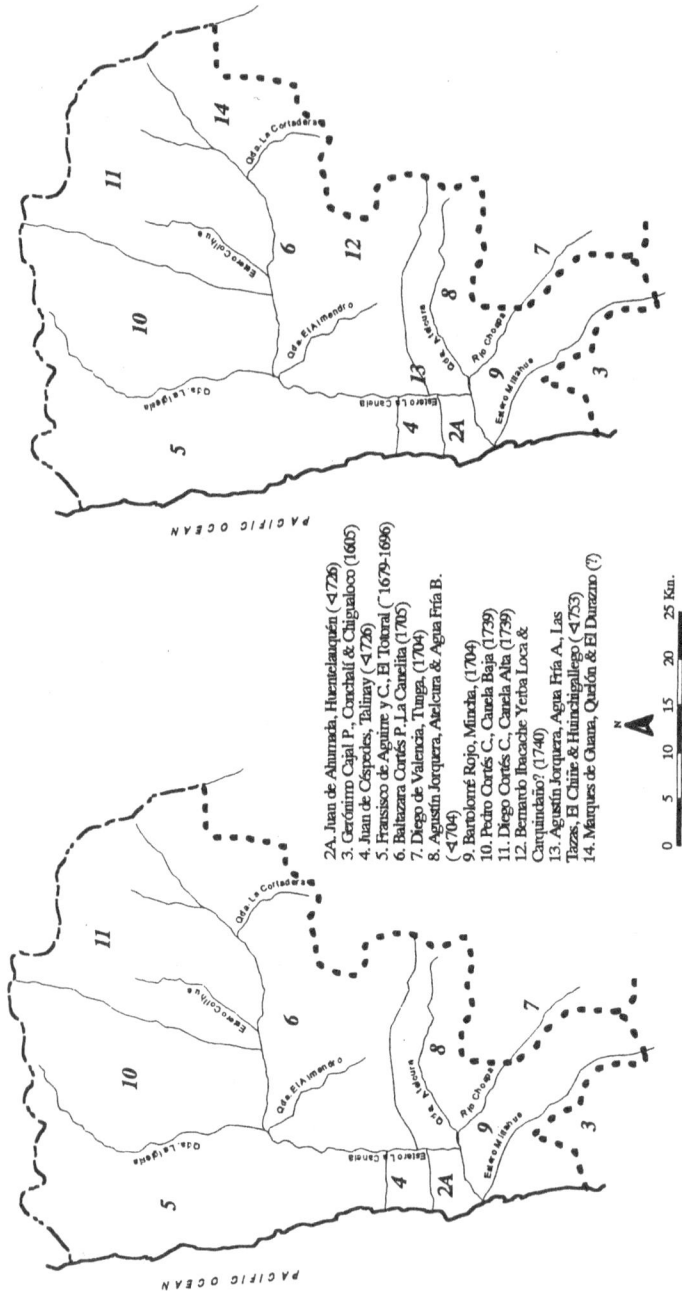

Figure 7.2 The *Estancias* La Canela and Mincha (~1739-1753)

Historical Formation of the Agricultural Community Canela Baja

The *estancia* Canela Baja under Captain Pedro Cortés Castillo

In 1740, one year after Pedro Cortés Castillo had kept the *estancia* Canela Baja for himself and two years before he died, the land belonging to Yerba Loca (present-day agricultural community with the same name covering 3,686 ha) was sold to Captain Bernardo Ibacache (Cañón, 1963:37). It is possible that this property included the land within the present-day agricultural community Carquindaño (2,813 ha). It is also feasible that the agricultural community Los Tomes (3,000 ha) and the neighbouring agricultural community Angostura de Gálvez (1,437 ha) have been separated from the Yerba Loca lands. If this is correct, I can calculate that with the sale of Yerba Loca, the *estancia* Canela Baja must have been reduced by approximately 10,936 ha, leaving 29,064 ha out of the 40,000 ha.

Although not mentioned in the agreement between the brothers it seems, according to their father's testament, that Los Tomes was also situated within the limits of Canela Baja. In that case, with the sale of Yerba Loca the *estancia* Canela Baja must have been reduced not by approximately 10,936 ha, but only by approximately 8,000 ha, leaving 32,000 ha.

However, with the exception of Yerba Loca, it is interesting to note that the present-day limits of the agricultural community Canela Baja is, more or less, the same as those established in the division that Pedro and Diego Cortés Castillo made of La Canela in 1739. These boundaries should include the sub-area of Espíritu Santo (10,000 ha), which for a period of some 100 years was a *fundo,* due to an illegal seizure, in the hands of different private owners (see Chapter 8). Therefore, and judging from the preceding discussion, the *estancia* Canela Baja must have consisted of 29,064 ha, after the sale of Yerba Loca (Los Tomes included), or 32,000 ha (Los Tomes excluded), an area which coincides quite well with the 30,700 ha of the present-day community Canela Baja.

Ollarzú agrees with Aracena's version, indicating that the sons of Diego Cortés Pérez, Pedro and Diego Cortés Castillo, performed their respective weddings in the Mincha parish, in whose archives they are registered. Their remains are also to be found in the said parish where the births of their children and their descendants are registered. Yet of the two weddings I only found in the parochial archive of Mincha, the register concerning that of Pedro Cortés Castillo's with Margarita Aguirre:

> In Mincha fifteenth day of November in the year seventeen hundred and twenty-six I veiled, by order of our Mother Church, the captain Pedro Cortés [Castillo], legitimate son of the captain Diego Cortés [Pérez] and Doña Ana del Castillo, originally from El Palqui /.../ from the city La Serena, with Margarita Aguirre, legitimate daughter of Don Pedro Aguirre and Juana Cespedes, both originally from this valley of Mincha (AP Mincha, Matrimonios (1689-1796) folio 38).

According to Cortés-Monroy, R. (1991-1992:190), Magarita became Pedro Cortés Castillo's goods holder, after he had passed away very suddenly and been buried in Sotaquí on the 18th of September 1741. According to Cañón's version, Pedro Cortés Castillo and Margarita Aguirre Céspedes had five children (Cañón, 1964:37), whose names I, like Cañón, was unable to find in the birth register because those prior to 1834 no longer exist. A fire destroyed some of the books from the Mincha Parish (Aracena, 1941:198). The Genealogical Society of Utah has microfilmed these archives especially that some of the documents concerning the baptisms are missing.

Another way of searching for information about the children is to check the marriage and death registers, as they may also include the names of the parents. The problem is that the alphabetic index of the marriage book is by the name of the man, making it possible only to find the male children. In the death book, married women appear with their husband's surname. Nevertheless, of the total of 538 marriages that appear in the index of the marriage book between 1689-1796, fourteen men have the surname Cortés, but only three deal with 'my' Corteses. However, not all of these fourteen weddings were performed in the Mincha Parish, and of those that were, not all the Cortéses involved come from Canela or Mincha. To take three examples: firstly, in 1716, at the Church of Mincha, Matías Cortés Godoy, a native from the Palqui, La Serena is married to Isabel Aguirre, a native from Mincha; secondly, in 1738, at the Church of Mincha, León Cortés, a native from Coquimbo is married to Josefa Rojo, also from Coquimbo; and thirdly, in 1740, at the Church of Illapel, Julían Cortés, a native from Guanilla is married to Dominga Manzano, a native from Illapel (AP Mincha, Matrimonios (1689-1796), folio 39; folio 69 and folio 76, respectively). The first relevant case is:

> On the twentieth of February, 1694, I married and veiled Francisco Cortés, mulatto /[illegible]/ of the captain Don Diego Cortés [Pérez], with María

Sanchi, Indian from the captain Don Francisco Aguirre's encomienda (AP Mincha, Matrimonios (1689-1796) folio 6).

As I understand it, this Francisco Cortés would be Diego Cortés Pérez's son, born out of wedlock, and named in his will:

> I declare that I have a son born out of wedlock called Francisco Cortes to whom I have given nothing because he has spent too much money (ANCH, AJ La Serena, Civiles, Legajo no. 117 (1733-1765), 1733, 'Aguilera Santiago contra...' and AJ Illapel, Legajo no. 5, pieza 4, Caratulado 23 civil, 1855, 'Francisco Cortez Espinosa y...', folio 3, verso).

The other two marriages registered concern Pedro Cortés Castillo's referred wedding with Margarita Aguirre and Pedro Cortés Villaroel's (son of Diego Cortés Castillo) wedding with Teresa Rojo.

Studying some of the marriage inscriptions in order to find some of La Canela's Cortés females, in those cases where the woman had the surname Cortés, I found, for example, that they are Indians or mulattos in 1714:

> Josefa Cortes, Indian from low Chuapa, legitimate daughter of Nicolas Cortes y Juana Pasten Indians married Bernabe Godoi, Indian from Mincha (AP Mincha, Matrimonios (1689-1796) folio 24).

Sometimes the names of the parents are not given. Such as, for example, at Illapel in 1732, in the wedding concerning '... Pascuala Cortés from Canela with Juan Bega from Guatulame and resident in Canela...' (AP Mincha, Matrimonios (1689-1796), folio 56). Another example is Pascuala Cortés who was married at Mincha in 1737 to Isidoro Tacas, not mentioning who the parents are (AP Mincha, Matrimonios (1689-1796), folio 67).

According to Cortés-Monroy, R.'s version (1991-92:190), Pedro Cortés Castillo and Margarita Aguirre had 3 children: Teodoro Cortés y Aguirre, born in 1727, died in his twenties and was buried in Mincha in 1746, single (AP Mincha, Defunciones (1694-1797), folio: illegible, but according to Cortés-Monroy, R., it is the folio 40, verso); Josefa Cortés y Aguirre from Canela, who was married in Mincha in 1747 to Juan Ignacio Bacho y Saso from Santiago; and Petrona Cortés y Aguirre from Canela, who was married in Mincha in 1744 to Juan Antonio Espinoza Bozo from Santiago.

Both the daughters' weddings and the son's death appear in the sources given by Cortés-Monroy, R. (AP Mincha, Matrimonios (1689-1796), folio 86 and 93, and Defunciones (1694-1797), illegible, but according to Cortés-Monroy, R., it is the folio 40, verso), but obviously there is at least one more son, called Pedro Cortés Aguirre. When Margarita de Aguirre died in 1772, it was written in her death register that she had made no testament, due to the fact that she had given her son Pedro the authority to do it (AP Mincha, Defunciones (1694-1797), folio: illegible). Pedro Cortés Aguirre's name does not appear in the registers of the first book of marriages. There is one Pedro Cortés who is really his first cousin from Canela Alta, married to Teresa Rojo. This is in spite of the fact that it has been written for posterity in different handwriting along the margin of the folio that he is the owner of Canela Baja. It is possible to deduce that it deals with Pedro Cortés (Villaroel) from Canela Alta since it specifies that he was the 'legitimate son of Diego Cortés [Castillo] and Ana Villaroel' (AP Mincha, Matrimonios (1689-1796), folio 86).

Due to the lack of information concerning Pedro Cortés Aguirre's actions once his mother Margarita de Aguirre had given him the authority to draw up her will in 1772, I have only been able to follow the history of the *estancia* Canela Baja to that date. At the end of 1700s and after the first brother's death, the inheritors of the *estancia* Canela Baja were, apart from Pedro, the two married sisters. Since Pedro Cortés Aguirre's sisters were both married, Josefa Cortés Aguirre to Juan Ignacio Bacho y Saso (1747) and Petrona Cortés Aguirre to Juan Antonio Espinoza Bozo (1744), their children, supposing they had any, should have had the surnames Bacho Cortés and Espinoza Cortés respectively, or alternatively: Cortés Bacho and Cortés Espinoza.

Dealing in the first place with the surname Espinoza, approximately one hundred years later (1855), the Illapel Judicial Archives register one Francisco Cortés Espinoza who asks for the lands of Yerba Loca. As it can be observed, the surname Espinoza appears in the second place, i.e. in theory as the maternal surname. He, also on behalf of Domingo Pinto and Anastasio Jorquera, enters in an action against Lino Páez, Pío Gonzáles y Santos Vicencio. He demands from the latter three:

> the estancia or land named La Yerba Loca, belonging to La Canela, which belongs to the undersigned as legitimate descendants of Pedro Cortés, its original owner (ANCH, AJ Illapel, Legajo no. 5, pieza 4, Caratulado 23 Civil, 1855, 'Francisco Cortez Espinosa y...', folio 1-9, verso).

Historical Formation of the Agricultural Community Canela Baja

They declared that the sale transaction of the land belonging to Yerba Loca, carried out by Pedro Cortés (Castillo) to the Ibacaches in 1740, is invalid since, according to them, for two reasons. Firstly there is no bill of sale to prove the transaction and secondly, the marquis Pedro Cortés Monroy, who was appointed first testamentary executor by Diego Cortés Pérez in his will 1705, did not consent to the sale. However, it seems strange that the plaintiffs claim the sale to be illegal since by 1740, Pedro Cortés Castillo was the actual owner of the *estancia* Canela Baja, after having divided the *estancia* La Canela in 1739 with his brother Diego Cortés Castillo. How Pedro Cortés Zavala de Monroy, the marquis, could have agreed to the above mentioned sale in 1740 is a mystery, considering that he died in 1716 (Pinto, J., 1983:154). It is also strange that the plaintiffs say that Diego Cortés (Pérez) died in 1734 when he actually died in 1709. This confusion is probably due to the fact that Diego Cortés Pérez testament, written in 1705, was not registered until 1734 in La Serena.

Secondly, dealing with the surname Bacho, the Illapel Notarial Archives registered two land sales in 1863 involving people with this surname. The first transaction was between Manuel Godoy, buyer, and Toribio Bacho and Gregorio Carvajal, vendors in Fasico, the present-day sub-area of the agricultural community Canela Baja (ANCH, AN Illapel, Vol. 23, RP, 1863, folio 59, Doc. no. 8. 'Transacción entre Manuel Godoy, como comprador y Toribio Bacho y Gregorio Carvajal, como vendedores'). The second is between Teodoro Chávez and Mariana Bacho, vendors, and Bartolo Paz, purchaser, in Yerba Loca (ANCH, AN Illapel, Vol. 23, RP, 1863, folio 53, Doc. no. 12. 'Transacción entre Teodoro Chávez y Mariana Bacho como vendedores y Bartolo Paz como comprador').

Judging by the lack of archival documents denoting other significant sales, it seems that there were no more large sales of the *estancia* La Canela Baja until the beginning of 1800s onwards. In contrast, the Notarial Archives of Illapel register since then, numerous small sales inside both Canela Baja and Canela Alta. I will return to these later. In several of the sales both the surnames Cortés and Ibacache are involved (see Table 7.1: Land Sale on *Estancias* Canela Baja and Alta, 1805-1868).

The *estancia* Canela Alta under Diego Cortés Castillo

Diego Cortés Castillo kept the *estancia* Canela Alta after the division of Canela in 1739, and lived there with his wife Ana Villaroel. Diego Cortés Castillo, weakened from an accident and in danger of dying, made his will, which is undated but probably in 1753, or slightly before that, since that was the year in which he died (ANCH, AN Illapel, Vol. 3 (1826-1843), Testamento de Diego Cortés, folio 345). In this folio is to be found the legalisation of Diego Cortés Castillo's testament, registered in Illapel in 1786. According to Cortés-Monroy R., (1991-1992:190), Diego Cortés Castillo died in 1793, but from the document and from the given year of legalisation of his testament, it is clear that he died in 1753. His wife died in 1762 and was buried in Mincha (AP Mincha, Matrimonios (1689-1796), folio 86 and 93, and Defunciones (1694-1797), folio: illegible).

In his will, Diego Cortés (Castillo) wrote that he was native from the valley of La Canela, 'neighbour and resident of the said valley…', and asked to be buried in the Santa Iglesia Parroquial of the Mincha parish 'with the shroud I have and make a minor burial as of a poor…' (ANCH, AN Illapel, Vol. 3 (1826-1843), Testamento de Diego Cortés, folio 354 to 355). According to his will, Diego Cortés Castillo left seven children (four males and three females) from his marriage with Ana Villaroel; Miguel, Pedro, José, Juan, Jaoquina, Teodora and María Cortés Villaroel, plus a daughter born out of wedlock, called Anita Cortés.

The marriage inscription concerning Diego Cortés Castillo and Ana Villaroel does not appear in Mincha's first marriage book, from which I deduce that this union took place somewhere else. However, I found the marriage inscriptions of some of their sons and daughters: firstly, in 1738 '… María Cortés, from Canela, legitimate daughter of Diego Cortés and Ana Villaroel…' was married to Francisco Collao, from Mincha; secondly, in 1740, '… Teodora Cortés, from La Canela, legitimate daughter of Diego Cortés and Ana Villaroel…' married Roque Collao, from Mincha; thirdly, in 1744 '… married Pedro Cortés from Canela, Spanish legitimate son of Diego Cortés and Ana Villaroel with Teresa Rojo…', the matrimony that I have already referred to (AP Mincha, Matrimonios (1689-1796), folio 70-71; folio 76 and folio 86, respectively).

Strangely enough, in a testament from the end of 1700s, another son called Justo appears who claims to be son of Diego Cortés (Castillo) and Ana Villaroel. To his seven children from the matrimony with María Rojo,

Justo leaves the land that he owns in Canela Alta, 'so they enjoy it in equal parts', i.e., in a common or indivisible form. The children are: Toribio, Lucas, Fernando, Joseph, P? (illegible), Teodora and Flora Cortés Rojo (Testamento de Justo Cortés, Canela, 28 de Abril, 17?? (illegible), ANCH, AN Illapel, Vol. 1 (1751-1814), folio 128 to 129 verso).

In his testament, Diego Cortés Castillo left the Canela Alta land to his seven legitimate children, without specifying how much would go to each one. An exception was made of his daughter, born outside of matrimony, Anita Cortés, to whom he gave one *cuadra* of land. I have only been able to follow the history of the *estancia* Canela Baja up to 1772, because neither Pedro Cortés Castillo nor his wife Margarita Aguirre made a testament. This is a major reason for presenting the testament of his brother Diego Cortés Castillo. While Margarita Aguirre, as wife, became Pedro Cortés Castillo's goods holder when he died in 1741, she in her turn, before dying, gave his son Pedro Cortés Aguirre authority to draw up her will in 1772. What Pedro Cortés Aguirre did after that is unknown to me.

In contrast to his father, Diego Cortés Pérez's will from 1705 who specifed clearly what would belong to whom, in the testament of his son Diego Cortés Castillo, some 50 years after, appears for the first time, in the examined documents, the formula 'enjoy and use the inherited goods in equal parts'. Thus, Diego Cortés Castillo left the property in common or undivided form to his inheritors. However, my reading of the testament differs in several points from the one given by Cañón:

> I declare that I leave to all my heirs so that they can fully enjoy it /.../ the upper estancia the Canela for being mine since I had to inherit it from my legitimate parents and I leave it with high and low hills all delimited that are all according to my rights and I say that the said estancia starts first of all from the hillock that is below the Barren hill, in front of the Sapo ravine which divides and limits the main ravine of the Canela from the place where Margarita Aguirre lived whose hillock marks the limit with the land belonging to the Corteses from down below, and following this hillock upwards it will pass by the top of the Barren hill upwards always in the following hillock it will come to Cataguechun still bordering on my /[illegible] / Margarita Aguirre's land and from Cataguechun it continues to the next hillock to /.../ where this estancia borders on the Teatinos monks' land and passing a low door continuing to the next hillock where this estancia divides with the Godoies' land and from there it goes down to the big ravine and will come to the small hillock /.../ and straighten up from the next hillock it will fall down into the Los Pozos ravine which /.../ for the east

side it will pass over to the other side bordering this said estancia on Mr. Marqués de Guara's [Huana] lands; and from there it will continue to the next hillock and will come to a low door; which divides the said estancia with Don Gaspar de Ahumada's land and continuing and always the next hillock, until the beginning of the Ataelgura corner; to the south this said estancia borders on land belonging to the Jorqueras and to finish the fulfillment of the said estancia one takes the hillock below which runs down towards the Canela, to its end /.../ it; which borders on the Aguileras [La Canelita]; until the said hillock reaches the rivulet of Canela's main ravine, where it concludes the whole circle of this estancia, which I leave all according to the law, in all conformity of right, without prejudice of third parties, nor any other with major right /---/.

... of all my children that I name as my universal and legitimate heirs of all my goods to enjoy and use them in conformity of brothers *in equal parts*.... (ANCH, AN Illapel, Vol. 3 (1826-1843), Testamento de Diego Cortés, folio 354 to 355, verso. The named Margarita Aguirre was his brother's widow; emphasis added).

From the testament we can deduce that after becoming the owner of the *estancia* Canela Alta, Diego Cortés Castillo, like his brother, sold part of his *estancia*. In his will, Diego Cortés Castillo declared that he had sold some land to Captain Agustín Jorquera, but without mentioning where it was:

I declare that from a sale of land which I sold to the captain Jorquera he ended up owing me the sum of 43 pesos 4 reales for a /.../ is left of what I have received directly from the said Agustín Jorquera I send my executors to collect 43 pesos 4 reales and I declare that they will be paid (*Ibid.*).

Cañón, however, indicates that this sale should correspond to the lands of the present-day agricultural communities Agua Fría Alta (2,562 ha), El Chiñe (2,000 ha) and Las Tazas (2,375 ha). According to the same author, Diego Cortés Castillo, had previously sold to the same Captain Jorquera, the land which now corresponds to the agricultural community Huinchigallego (875 ha) (Cañón, 1964:39). However, this does not come from the will, where Diego Cortés Castillo points out that Jorquera is 'pre-eminent' in buying such lands, which border the land he already had bought, something that could only be done once Jorquera had paid the debt of 43 *pesos* and 4 *reales*. It is uncertain when this debt was paid and the land of

Huinchigallego sold to Jorquera, but it seems as if it took some time to happen.

In Justo Cortés Villaroel's referred will, he asks his testamentary executor to collect the money still owed to his father, and that the land of Huinchigallego be sold as specified in his father's, Diego Cortés Castillo's, will. Unfortunately, the date on Justo's testament is illegible, but due to its place in the register, it should be posterior to the death of his father, which occurred in 1753 (Testamento Justo Cortés, Canela, 28 de Abril, 17?? (illegible), ANCH, AN Illapel, Vol. 1 (1751-1814), folio 128, verso). Since the land of the present agricultural communities Agua Fría Alta, El Chiñe, Las Tazas and Huinchigallego totals about 8,000 ha, I can deduce that after they passed on to Agustín Jorquera or to his children, the *estancia* Canela Alta must have been, in theory, reduced from 92,000 to 84,000 ha.

In his will Diego Cortés Castillo also declared that the land belonging to him, known as La Calderita, was marketable. According to Cañón, these lands had given rise to the communities of El Pangue (1,062 ha) and Lo Gallardo, both situated to the south of Yerba Loca. However, the latter has never, as I consider, constituted an agricultural community:

> I declare that on the fragment and estancia which is called La Calderita and the /.../ for being /---/ evaluated to one hundred thousand pesos is also up for sale; according to its borders which are and belong to /.../ that indicates the hillock of the rocky hill and following the hillock it borders on land belonging to the Jorqueras and still following the hillock it will arrive in front of the low doors Las Chilcas where the land with the Ahumadas' land and always looking towards the top of the big hill *until coming to the top of the Talinaicillo hill,* to the west this estancia borders on land belonging to the Céspedes [Talinay] and from there it continues down the next hillock below bordering the Llano de poya [probably Los Llanos], *to the north you will come to the Los Tomes' water where the said estancia borders on lands belonging to the Mr. Gallardo from the Totoral* and from there it continues from the mouth of the ravine to the said Tomes; still following the ravine downwards until coming to the big Canela ravine, still bordering on land belonging to the Totoral, now for the east part and from there always take the big Canela ravine, still bordering to the south until coming to the narrowness with which the whole circle of this fragment la Calderita and its value (ANCH, AN Illapel, Vol. 3 (1826-1843), Testamento de Diego Cortés, folio 354 to 355; emphasis added).

However, because of its northern limits, La Calderita apparently embraces not only the land south of Yerba Loca, as Cañón confirms, but I would say that since Diego Cortés Castillo also counted the area east of the Talinay hill as his, it is clear that the lands of La Calderita also embraced the land of Los Tomes. The problem is that by that time (1753), Los Tomes should belong to the *estancia* Canela Baja under Margarita Aguirre, Pedro Cortés Castillo's widow.

Comparing the boundaries of La Calderita with those established in 1739, during the division between the two brothers, it is difficult to make them coincide. However, apparently Diego Cortés Castillo, he who according to his father, had 'a short discernment', kept this part, although it is not mentioned in the agreement from 1739. An interesting detail concerning La Calderita is that, with the exception of the agricultural community Los Tomes, the properties originating from it are presently *fundos*. Los Tomes was also a *fundo* until 1973, when it became an agricultural community.

If we look at Lo Gallardo, there is today a property called Los Gallardo, but that is a *fundo* (3,000 ha) (CIREN, 1983:245). There is another property, which is also a *fundo* that in the RCCBR of 1988 and even in 1995 appears as *Hijuela* Lo Gallardo with an area of 4,000 ha. In this list the *hijuela* appears under the valuation roll no. 218-2 (RCCBR, 1988:20). In the list from 1987 it appears with the same valuation roll number under the name Santa Margarita (RCCBR, 1983:19), so that the owner, Chuminato, R. J., must have changed the name of the *fundo* that year since he has a second *fundo* with the name of Santa Margarita. It also belongs to Chuminato, R. J., and is located at the western border of the agricultural community El Pangue. To the west, it neighbours the *fundo* Santa Margarita (1,400 ha), also a property of Chuminato, R. J., who owns a third *fundo* in the commune called Santa Amelia (800 ha) (Table 7.3).

It is uncertain whether Chuminato's properties presently constitutes three separate *fundos* or two, due to the fact that it is impossible to distinguish on the maps which is the *fundo* Santa Amalia. However, this *fundo* does not appear in either the 1988 or 1995 lists from the RCCBR. The valuation number (218-18), which appears in the CIREN lists and which should be the same on the RCCBR lists, does not exist in the latter. In the commune's own list over the agricultural communities, the *fundo* Santa Amelia does not appear to be bordering on any other agricultural community, but it does border on the *fundos* Santa Margarita and Hijuela Lo Gallardo.

In any case, because of their location, it could be that these three or four properties; *Hijuela* Lo Gallardo, Santa Margarita, (Santa Amelia?) and Los Gallardo, all belonged to La Calderita. The *fundo* El Retiro (600 ha), located in the same area, could have been part of La Calderita. These properties altogether total approximately 9,800 ha. To that, one would have to add the size of the agricultural communities El Pangue (1,062 ha) and Los Tomes (3,000 ha), which would have been a part of La Calderita. In all, these properties add up to approximately 13,262 ha.

If we presume that the lands of La Calderita were all sold, as expressed in Diego Cortés Castillo's will, the *estancia* Canela Alta had probably been reduced from 84,000 ha, that was left after the sales to the Jorqueras, to approximately 71,000 ha. However, this is theory because obviously there was a juxtaposition of the borders between the northern part of La Calderita and the *estancia* Canela Baja. I am counting at least 3,000 ha twice, both for Canela Alta and Canela Baja. Looking at the eastern border of the *estancia* Canela Alta indicated in Diego Cortés Pérez's will, it no longer borders with the Llampanguí Mountain, as it did in 1605.

According to Cañón, the marquis of Huana, gained the 6 leagues from the west to the east that should have corresponded to the original *merced* measured in a trial, and finding that Llampanguí is not within those 6 leagues, he claims the part beyond the 6 leagues as his. According to Cañón, this land became the *haciendas* Quelón and Durazno (Cañón, 1964:41; see Figure 7.2). Cañón does not specify which of the marquises of Huana pursued the trial neither when it was, but it could not have been the first marquis, since he died in 1716. In a document from 1861, there is still a Cortés Monroy (Francisco) appearing as owner of Peña Blanca, Durazno and Quelón (ANCH, AN Illapel, Vol. 26, Doc. no. 37, 1861, folio verso 43-44). However, this means that at least the lands of Durazno and Quelón should be deducted from the calculated 71,000 ha. The former *hacienda* El Durazno, today returned to the agricultural community Canela Alta, had 15,155 ha (RCCBR, June 1988-89:1-43).

The *hacienda* Quelón neither figures in the former source or in a 1931 list of the properties in the commune, but it does figure in the list dated 1995. According to the informant Pedro Carvajal, part of this property is today a *hacienda*, which belongs to a person from Combarbalá, whilst the other belongs to the agricultural community Canela Alta. Judging from its evaluation number, it became a new property recently, but it is clear that it constitutes a private property inside the commune. The *hacienda* Quelón, a property of Tapia H. Amable Suc. (branch) with the evaluation no. 1,428-0001 differs clearly from the sequential numbers of the rest of the properties, the last one before the *hacienda* Quelón finishing with the no. 268-0033 (RCCBR, November 1995:21). Unfortunately, the number of hectares does not appears in this list, but its official value was in 1995 of 12,703,995 Chilean *pesos*, while the highest evaluated *hacienda* of the commune is of 62,878,867 *pesos* (RCCBR, November 1995:5 and 21). Regardless, if I deduce that 15,155 ha from El Durazno passed to the marquis de Huana and Piedra Blanca, the *estancia* Canela Alta would be left with approximately 56,000 ha, not very far from its present 67,000 ha.

The western boundary drawn up by Diego Cortés for the *estancia* Canela Alta towards Canela Baja constitutes, to this day, the boundary between both agricultural communities:

> from the hillock that is below the Barren hill, in front of the Sapo ravine which divides and limits the main ravine of the Canela from the place where Margarita Aguirre lived.

Judging from Diego Cortés Castillo's will, the brothers built their residence on this border, where the present urban villages Canela Baja and Alta began to be built, each one towards the opposite extreme. This is the area of the scarce alluvial land of the urban villages of Canela Baja and Canela Alta, which receives seasonal irrigation from the Canela river.

Today, both urban villages are among the biggest in the Canela commune. Canela Baja, also the capital of the commune, has a population of 857 whilst Canela Alta, occupying third place, has 357 inhabitants. The urban village Huentelauquén is the second largest, with 407 inhabitants (INE, 1982:XXXV). The last *hijuela* in the agricultural community Canela Baja, towards the urban village and agricultural community Canela Alta, still belongs, like many others, to a *comunero* with the surname Cortés. This *comunero* was until some years ago, together with his sisters, the owner of the *fundo* Talinay, which has now been sold to an outsider.

When Diego Cortés Castillo died, he left the *estancia* Canela Alta to his seven legitimate children without specifying how much would go to each one, i.e., in common form, but pointing out that his daughter, born outside of matrimony, Anita Cortés, was to be given one *cuadra* of land

(ANCH, AN Illapel, Vol. 3 (1826-1843), Testamento de Diego Cortés, folio 354-355). According to Cañón, Diego Cortés Castillo's seven children did not split up the *estancia* Canela Alta, but instead all occupied the irrigated terrain located beside the River La Canela. The hills were left for communal use, designated for pasture, firewood and rain-fed farming. This way the *estancia* Canela Alta, or the part of the *estancia* that was left after selling some areas, remained undivided for more than a century.

It was not until 1855 that the descendants of Diego Cortés Castillo's seven children divided the irrigated land among themselves, establishing among the inheritors, what became private property. The hills continued to be undivided as before (Cañón, 1964:41). It is exclusively the irrigated land or *hijuelas* that appear on diverse documents as objects of sale, always including and specifying the rights to the common hilly and dry land as evident. By the middle 1800s, the form of semi-communal land ownership among the users and owners of the land is already well established.

According to the partition that Diego Cortés Castillo descendants made of the *estancia* Canela Alta, the descendants of the daughter, born out of wedlock, Anita Cortés, were excluded from it, probably because in his will Diego Cortés Castillo leaves her a *cuadra* of land. Cañón does not specify the names or surnames of the seven hereditary branches of Diego Cortés Castillo's descendants.

In agreement to a sales document for one *hijuela* dated in October 1856, that is one year after the date when Cañón claims, the irrigated land on the *estancia* Canela Alta was divided. The eight people who declared themselves to be descendants of Diego Cortés Castillo together sold one *hijuela*. The eighth person probably corresponded, either to a representative of the branch of Anita Cortés, Diego Cortés' daughter born out of wedlock, or to the eighth son of the matrimony, Justo Cortés Villaroel. The sales document specifies that:

> In the town of San Rafael de Rozas [Illapel] on the 28th of October 1856 in front of me, the actuary /.../ turned up Felipa Pizarro, María Pinto, Juan Bugeño, Juan Montenegro, Cipriano Cortés, Juan Reyes Olivares, Mariano Galleguillos and Juan de la Rosa Cortés, the first two free administrators of their goods and all persons of legal age, neighbours of this department /.../ and they agree to sell in public sale and in an everlasting transfer of property to José Vicencio, one hijuela of wheat land inhcrited from /.../ don Diego Cortés, composed by two hundred and forty five yards frontage and the bottom is from the regal road to the main river of La Canela Alta where the

plots are located, and limits by the north with the regal road, by the south with the river, by the east with Maria Gallardo and by the west with the *hacienda* of the Corteses from below... (Courtesy of José Antonio Cortés, *comunero* of Canela Baja (AN Illapel, Vol. ?, 1856, no. 201, folio 285); emphasis added).

The variety of surnames among Diego Cortés Castillo's descendants shows, for example, how Cortés as a family name starts to become less common through marriages on the female side of the family. Nevertheless, during the 1800s Cortés is still the most common surname (Table 7.1). Of the 18 land sales registered there, between 1805 and 1868 in Canela Baja and Canela Alta involving a total of 30 vendors, 17 had the surname Cortés, while of the total of 18 purchasers, 5 had the surname Cortés. From these transactions, I can draw the conclusion that the descendants of Pedro and Diego Cortés Castillo who, considering the date, should correspond to somewhere between the fourth and sixth generation, often sold part of their land. At the same time, they sometimes purchased land either among themselves or from other residents of the area.

Some of them, such as Felipa Pizarro, Juan Bugeño and Cipriano Cortés (Table 7.2) must be the same people who, according to the sale quoted above, sold land to José Vicencio. For this reason, in spite of the fact that some of them do not have the surname Cortés, they should belong to some parts of the inheritance branches of Diego Cortés Castillo of Canela Alta. The variety of surnames also shows how, through successive sales of land inside the community, new families became integrated into it, and most probably became related via marriages. The children of the female Corteses marriages will not have Cortés as a first family name, but as a second.

When we examine the surnames, it becomes clear that the present-day *comuneros* of the agricultural community Canela Baja are descendants of the Corteses, who inherited La Canela during the colonial time. In Appendix 1, we can see that Cortés continues to be the most common surname in the community Canela Baja, even in the agricultural community Canela Alta.

Historical Formation of the Agricultural Community Canela Baja

The resultant properties from the *estancia* La Canela

Through sales, exchanges and hereditary subdivision, the original *estancia* La Canela, which Diego Cortés Pérez received in 1679, had by the middle of the 1700s become at least ten different properties (here I do not include the *haciendas* Quelón and El Durazno). The properties are, in chronological order:

- El Totoral: unknown data, but between 1679-1709, through the exchange of land between Diego Cortés Pérez with Francisco de Aguirre y Cortés;
- Talinay: unknown data, but before 1726 to Juan de Céspedes (today fundo Talinay);
- La Canelita: inherited in 1705 by Baltazara Cortés Pérez, the sister of Diego Cortés Pérez;
- The Huentelauquén area: sold to Juan de Ahumada in 1726 by Pedro Cortés Castillo before he divided the *estancia* with his brother;
- Canela Baja; and
- Canela Alta: in 1739 through the division between the brothers Pedro and Diego Cortés Castillo;
- Yerba Loca: sold in 1740 by Pedro Cortés Castillo from his *estancia* Canela Baja to Captain Bernardo Ibacache; and
- Agua Fría Alta, El Chiñe Las Tazas: unknown data but, before 1753 sold by Diego Cortés Castillo, or his sons from his/their *estancia* Canela Alta to Captain Agustín Jorquera, or to his sons, in two different sales;
- Huinchigallego: as above;
- La Calderita: unknown data, but after 1753.

Except for El Totoral, Talinay and part of La Calderita, the remaining eight properties (also including a part of La Calderita), evolved into the semi-communal land ownership, which is today characteristic of the agricultural communities. The agricultural communities El Pangue and Los Tomes, as well as several *fundos*, arose from La Calderita, but due to the lack of updated information, I can not determine how many, but seemingly the *fundos* Santa Margarita, Hijuela Lo Gallardo, Los Gallardo and El Retiro.

Communal Land Ownership in Chile

Table 7.2 Land sales in the *Estancias* Canela Baja and Alta, 1805-1868

Year	Vendor	Purchaser	Sold Land
1805	Pedro Cortés	José Valencia	some land in Canela (it is not specified whether it is Canela Alta or Baja) (1)
1832	J. M. & Vicente Ibacache	Pascual Gallardo	one site in the place of Canela (Baja) with the corresponding right to *estancia* (2)
1834	Ambrosio Ibacache	Nicolás Cortés	Three *hijuelas* of wheat land... in the place Canela Arriba, being one with the mentioned *hijuelas* with right to *estancia* of common goods (3)
1837	Pedro & Isabel Cortés	Pedro Zamorano	some land in Canela (it is not specified whether it is Canela Alta or Baja) (4)
1841	Francisco Cortés	Felipa Pizarro	'two sites in Canela Arriba(*)... whose borders are... to the north with the *estancia*'s common goods' (5)
1842	Cornelio Cortés	Felipa Pizarro	some land in Canela Arriba 'with the *estancia*'s rights or lands of common goods.' (6)
1843	Lorenzo Cortés & J. M. Beza & S. Bugeño representing his wife, Pascuala Cortés	Tomasa Bugeño	one *hijuela* in Canela Arriba: 'that borders... to the north with the land of common goods' (7)
1843	Tomás Ibacache	Francisco Cortés	'50 *varas* (**) of lands with *estancia* rights... in the Canela Abajo that borders in the east with the *estancia* of Carquindano... in the west with the *hacienda* El Totoral...' (8)
1845	José Antonio & Lorenzo Cortés	Miguel Bugeño	some land in Canela Alta with 'all the rights that correspond to the said hijuela in the *estancia* of common goods' (9)
1850	Prudencio & María del R. Ibacache	Cipriano Cortés	one *hijuela* in the Canela Arriba... and it borders... to the north with the exit to the land of common goods, with which right I also sell the mentioned land (10)

Table 7.2 (continued)

Year	Vender	Purchaser	Sold Land
1853	María del R. Ibacache	Cipriano Cortés	in Canela Alta... a land... that borders... to the north and south with the *estancia* that he has of common goods... (11)
1860	Fermín & Prudencio Gallardo	José Vicencio	a piece of land situated in the Canela Alta that has borders to... north with the *estancia* (12)
1866	Juan Cortés	Pedro Pablo Cortés	some land in Mantancilla (Canela Baja) which 'borders land of common goods to the north, south and east' (13)
1867	Isidoro Cortés	Vicente Tabilo	some land known as Marcelo 'with respective *estancia*'s rights and common goods that has limits to the north with common goods' (14)
1868	Cruz Cortés	Felipa Lemus	some land in El Chilcal (Canela Baja), 'whose extension and limits are not expressed because they are not divided, understanding that what is sold are all its rights and shares that correspond to this *estancia* by inheritance' (15)
1868	Juan & Bonifacio Cortés	Juan Bugeño	some land in Quillaicillo (Canela Baja), has 'limits to the north with the *estancia* of common goods' (16)
1868	Isidoro & Manuela Cortés	Juan Bugeño	some land in Quillaicillo (Canela Baja) that 'borders to the north with common goods' (17)
s.a.	Jorge Vicencio, Fermín Prudencio & Paulina & Francisco Gallardo	José del C. Vicencio	one *hijuela* in the subdelegation of the Canela (Baja)... with rights to *estancia* or common goods (18)

Sources for Table 7.2: ANCH, AN Illapel:

1. Vol. 6, folio 132;
2. Vol. 3, folio 288;
3. Vol. 6, folio 365;
4. Vol. 3, folio. 205;
5. Vol. 11, folio 9;
6. Vol. 12, folios 26-27;
7. Vol. 11, folio 197;
8. Vol. 11, folio 139;
9. Vol. 13, folios 236-237;
10. Vol. 16, folio 326, no. 253;
11. Vol. 17, folio 25;
12. Vol. 23, folio 28:20;
13. Vol. 33, folio 105, no. 103;
14. Vol. 34, folio 171, no. 182;
15. Vol. 35, folio 65 verso-66;
16. Vol. 35, folio 171, no. 159;
17. Vol. 35, folio 173, no. 161;
18. Vol. 36, folio 25, no. 2.

* Canela Arriba (Upp) refers to Canela Alta (High). (Alta or Baja): From the description of the borders, I have been able to deduce where it deals with Canela Alta or Baja respectively, putting it within parenthesis. All the cursives are added.

** *Vara* is a unit of length, about 2.8 ft

If correct, there will be seven *fundos*, thirteen adding those that resulted from El Totoral. Conchalí and Chigualoco became four *haciendas* (see below).

The final analysis of Part II will be taken in the last chapter of this book, where I will try to gather some of the most important factors leading to the two patterns of agrarian development examined in this Part; the *latifundium* and the agricultural communities. I will now advance some conclusions about the history of the *estancia* La Canela and how it becoming several agricultural communities.

Advancing some conclusions

If we analyse how these old properties, that became agricultural communities, have developed from the end of the 1600s to the second half of the 1700s, it is possible to distinguish two periods; one of sales and exchanges, and one of relative stability. It is interesting to note that the major sales and exchanges, which resulted in the above properties, were all carried out during the first half of the 1700s, from the end of the 1600s to the middle of the 1700s. Even the agricultural communities developed from the *estancia* Mincha become subdivided through sale during the first decade of 1700s, showing a similar process to the *estancia* La Canela.

From then on, the major sales apparently come to a halt. All the properties become more stable, and from the middle of 1700s until today, they increase from eight to fourteen agricultural communities in the case of the former *estancia* La Canela. In the case of Mincha, three properties resulted in ten, a total of 24 agricultural communities in the commune.

Viewing this process in the perspective of almost two and a half centuries and taking these communities as a whole, one cannot maintain that there has been any extreme fragmentation of the property, the average per capita in respect to the entire land within the agricultural communities being today 67 ha, per *comunero*. This is taking the figures from the Conservatory of Real Estates from Illapel, 1986, according to which the 24 agricultural communities have 2,431 *comuneros* and 162,772 ha. In fact, the Conservatory gives a total of 169,002 ha but since the agricultural community Canela Baja has 30,700 ha and not 37,000 ha, I have reduced the figures of the Conservatory to 162,772 ha (see Tables 2.5 and 2.6).

However, on the other hand, this land being mostly hills, the average per capita of arable land indicates that there exists an extreme fragmentation of the flat and irrigated land.

This further confirms my thesis that the agricultural communities organising themselves under the form of communal land ownership have avoided becoming a conglomerate of *minifundia*. It is, therefore, interesting to note that the *estancia* La Canela from around 1709, with approximately 140,000 ha had become 14 agricultural communities and some *fundos*. During the same period, El Totoral, with approximately 40,000 ha, has become 7 *fundos* (excluding the, as yet, non partition of the reserve Puerto Oscuro).

The *fundos* have not become fragmented to the same extent as the flat land of the communities because they usually belong to one proprietor or family. For example, the third biggest property in the commune, the *hacienda* Huentelaquén, measures 27,620 ha and belongs to one single proprietor who also owns the *fundo* Millahue, which is much smaller but of much greater value than the *hacienda* Huentelauquén.

The fact that the major sales cease from the middle of 1700s, stabilising the number of properties or *estancias*, does not prevent the existence of minor land sales within the properties during 1800s and 1900s. It is interesting to note that this does not result in new *estancias* or communities, which becomes apparent in the purchase and sales agreements registered in the Notarial Archives of Illapel from the middle of 1800s on, inside both Canela Baja and Canela Alta (Table 7.2).

Because of the names involved in the purchase-sale agreements, they suggest a form of family redistribution or subdivision of the landed property within its own limits due to the demographic increase of the population, and the consequent constitution of new families. Otherwise, the land continues to be transferred by succession in an indivisible form, in the same way as it have pointed out for other communities of Norte Chico, among others by Baraona *et al* (1961:125) and CIDA (1966:128) (see Chapter 2). From there the name successorial communities (*comunidades sucesoriales*), as they were also known.

After the period of some major land sales, the land of the *estancias* La Canela Baja and Canela Alta remains distributed among Pedro Cortés Pérez's descendants for more than a century. It is not until 1850 that the parcelling out of the irrigated land begins, defining what land is private and what is communal within the landed property. On the contrary, and as we have seen during the same period, the *hacienda* El Totoral not only managed to maintain its private status, but succeeded in remaining undivided for two centuries. That is from approximately 1679/1709, the date when it became the property of Francisco de Aguirre y Cortés, until 1890, when the heirs of Mariana Montt's split the *hacienda* into three different *fundos*.

The definition of what is private and communal land, within the properties that became agricultural communities through the separation of the irrigated land from the non-irrigated in this specific point of time (around middle of the 1800s), should be closely related to the new legal requirements (Baraona *et al*, 1961:130) (see also Chapter 4). This was the instruction of the code of civil laws of 1847 together with the Register of the Conservatory of Real Estate of 1857 (IREN, 1978, Vol. 1:22). These established the obligation to register properties, their constitutions and transfers in the Register of the Conservatory of Real Estate, as a legal means of guaranteeing the possession of the land.

The separation of the irrigated land from the non-irrigated is, to an even greater extent, related to the increased population pressure on the land, perhaps a significant factor for the regulation of the landed property in the relatively newly created republic.

As an example of the demographic increase of the population, the owner of the *estancia* Canela Baja, Pedro Cortés Castillo, left at least four heirs (including his son born outside matrimony) by the middle of the 1700s. His brother Diego, owner of the *estancia* Canela Alta, left nine heirs (including his daughter born outside matrimony). At the end of the 1700s, Justo Cortés Villaroel, one of Diego's sons who had married María Rojo, left seven children. As his father Diego Cortés Castillo had done with his own land nearly half a century earlier, Justo Cortés Villaroel, according to his testament, left the land he owned in Canela Alta in an indivisible form to his seven children. As another example of population increase, according to the will left by Marcela Valencia (daughter of Captain Diego Valencia and Agustín Jorquera's widow) they had 12 children, 6 boys and 6 girls. At the time of her death in 1753, only six were still alive (ANCH, AN Illapel, Vol. 1 (1751-1814), 1754, Testamento de Marcela Valencia, folio 51 to 51, verso).

Communal Land Ownership in Chile

Figure 7.3 The sub-division of *Estancia* Canela Baja: 1679-1974

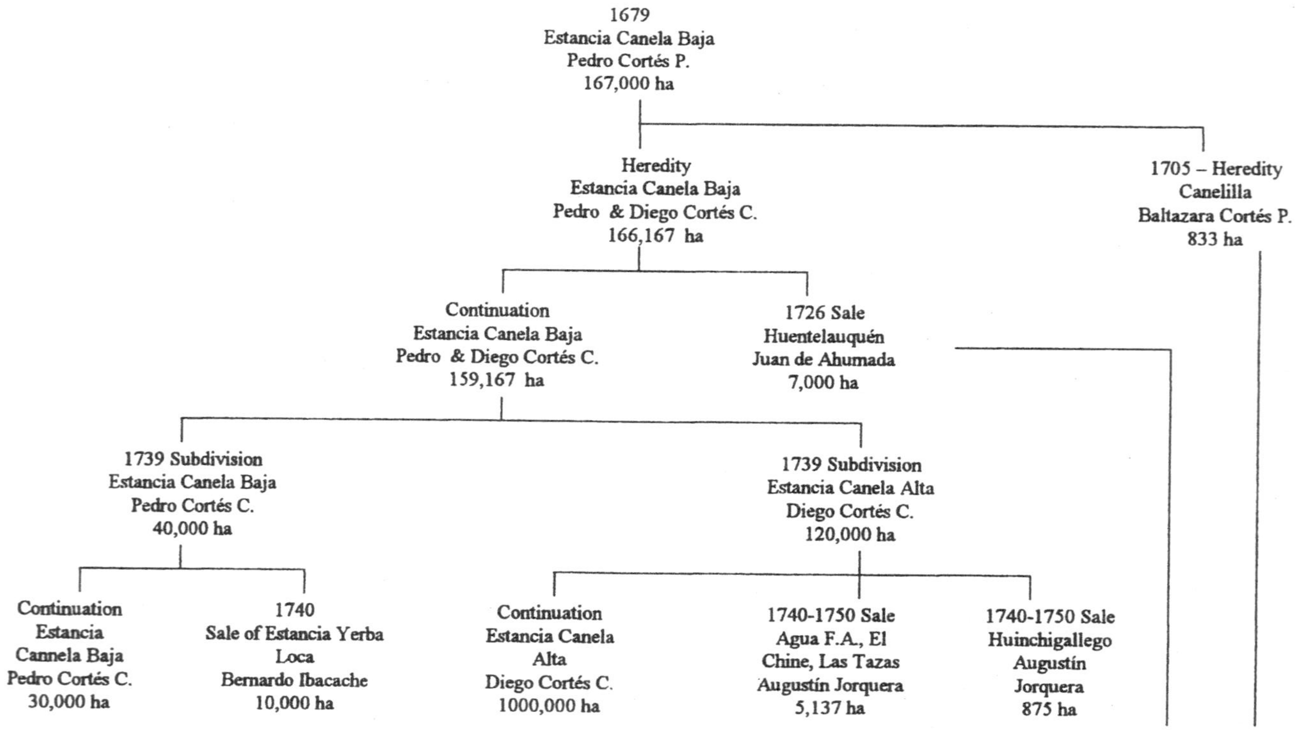

```
1679
Estancia Canela Baja
Pedro Cortés P.
167,000 ha
│
├── 1705 – Heredity
│   Canelilla
│   Baltazara Cortés P.
│   833 ha
│
└── Heredity
    Estancia Canela Baja
    Pedro & Diego Cortés C.
    166,167 ha
    │
    ├── 1726 Sale
    │   Huentelauquén
    │   Juan de Ahumada
    │   7,000 ha
    │
    └── Continuation
        Estancia Canela Baja
        Pedro & Diego Cortés C.
        159,167 ha
        │
        ├── 1739 Subdivision
        │   Estancia Canela Alta
        │   Diego Cortés C.
        │   120,000 ha
        │   │
        │   ├── 1740-1750 Sale
        │   │   Huinchigallego
        │   │   Augustin Jorquera
        │   │   875 ha
        │   │
        │   ├── 1740-1750 Sale
        │   │   Agua F.A., El
        │   │   Chine, Las Tazas
        │   │   Augustin Jorquera
        │   │   5,137 ha
        │   │
        │   └── Continuation
        │       Estancia Canela
        │       Alta
        │       Diego Cortés C.
        │       1000,000 ha
        │
        └── 1739 Subdivision
            Estancia Canela Baja
            Pedro Cortés C.
            40,000 ha
            │
            ├── 1740
            │   Sale of Estancia Yerba
            │   Loca
            │   Bernardo Ibacache
            │   10,000 ha
            │
            └── Continuation
                Estancia
                Canela Baja
                Pedro Cortés C.
                30,000 ha
```

Historical Formation of the Agricultural Community Canela Baja

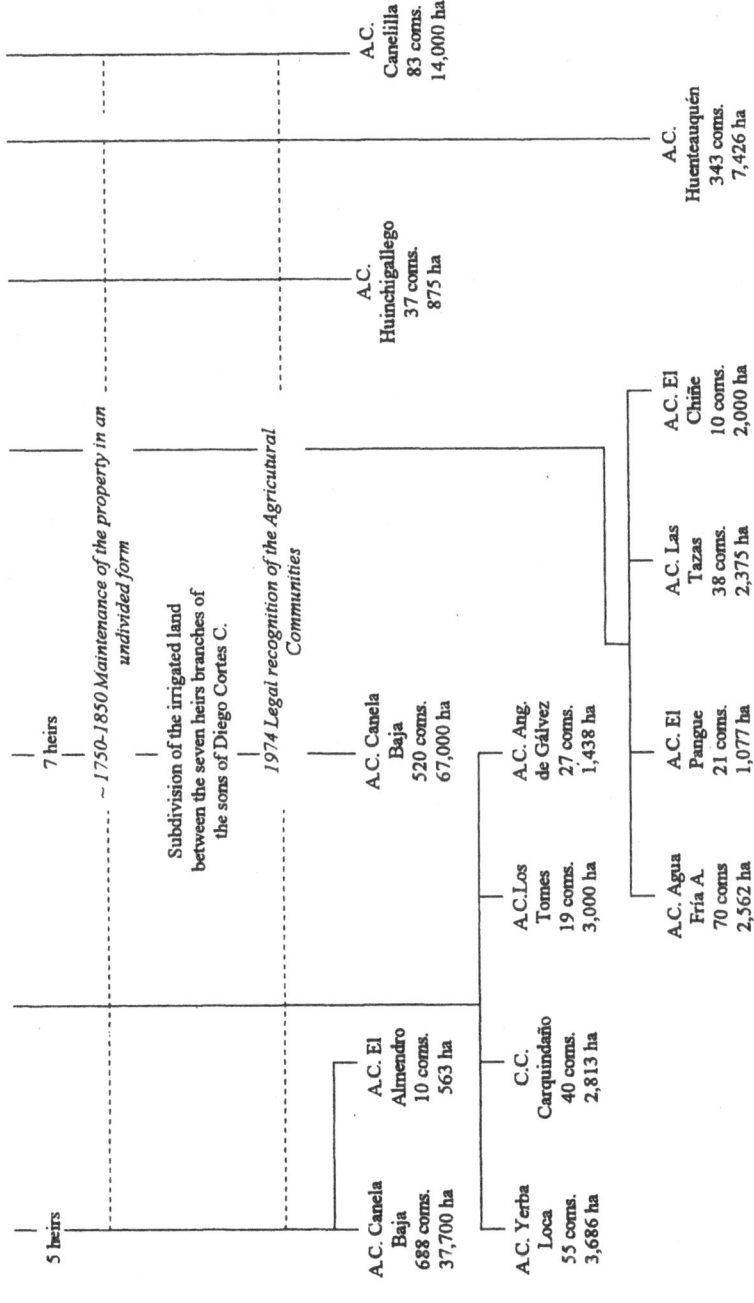

A.C. stands for Agricultural Community.
Coms. stands for comuneros.

Let me do a short exercise on the basis of the number of children. If it assumed that by the middle of 1700s, Pedro Cortés Castillo's 4 heirs from the *estancia* Canela Baja each had an average of 4 children, that Diego Cortés Castillo's 9 heirs from the *estancia* Canela Alta also had 4 children each, and the same for Agustín Jorquera's 6 heirs, these 19 children should by the second quarter of the century produce 76 children. These, in turn and with the same average of 4 children should, by the beginning of 1800s produce 304 other children. By 1825, these 304 children should in their turn produce 1,216 new children. This exercise shows that the demographic pressure upon a defined and finite land area, was already a fact during the first half of 1800s. The saltpetre mines of what is today northern Chile will become the salvation of the superfluous labour force from the second half of 1800s onwards.

In 1979, two and a half centuries later, the community of Canela Alta has 520 *comuneros* with 67,000 ha, and Canela Baja 668 *comuneros* with 30,700 ha, according to the communities' own data. It is obvious that due to the increase of the population, each community should have a larger number of *comuneros*, but emigration has been the safety valve for this pressure (see Chapter 2). The nucleus communities are still the largest agricultural properties of the commune, in comparison to the other agricultural communities and also, more importantly when compared to the *fundos*. Their area constitutes 60% of a total of 162,772 ha for the 24 agricultural communities. They also concentrate 48.9% of a total of 2,431 *comuneros* for the 24 agricultural communities.

During four centuries, the land of the *estancia* La Canela of about 180,000 ha has given rise to 14 of the 24 agricultural communities in the present-day commune of Canela. From the original *estancia*, which Diego Cortés Peréz inherited in 1679 came, not only the agricultural communities of the Canela Area (Canela Baja, Canela Alta, Canelilla and Angostura de Gálvez), but also the present-day agricultural communities of the Canela Riverside Area (Carquindaño, Yerba Loca, Los Tomes and El Almendro); part of the Area Agua Fría (El Pangue, Agua Fría Alta, Las Tazas and El Chiñe); as well as part of El Choapa (Huentelauquén, Huinchigallego). These 14 agricultural communities today cover 128,944 ha and 1,558 *comuneros*, based on the data from IREN 1977 and they may vary from those given by the communities themselves and other sources (see Table 2.6).

Dealing with my reconstruction of the agrarian structure over time, I would consider that, with the exceptions of some lacunae, most of my

Historical Formation of the Agricultural Community Canela Baja

calculated figures come close to the present-day land distribution. I will now briefly examine the case of the *estancia* Mincha as well as that of the *estancia* Conchalí and Chigualoco.

The *estancia* Mincha and the *estancia* Conchalí and Chigualoco

The case of Mincha is developed here not only because it belongs to the Canela commune but also because it further supports my thesis that the semi-communal land ownership of the agricultural communities has its origin in the colonial *mercedes de tierra*. The case of Conchalí and Chigualoco, part of which also belongs to the commune, is different to the *estancia* Mincha but similar to El Totoral and illustrates the other land development path in the commune, the continuation of these properties as private *haciendas*.

Alonso García de Ramón, the same governor who granted the *mercedes de tierra* La Canela and El Totoral, in 1600 and 1605, granted two other *mercedes de tierra* in the same zone, which later on became the *estancias* Conchalí and Chigualoco, and Mincha. The historical development of these two *mercedes* also came to determine the land tenure structure in the Canela commune. While the *estancia* Mincha gave place to several agricultural communities, the *estancia* Conchalí and Chigualoco became several *haciendas*. In spite of the fact that both *mercedes* were granted by the same governor, it became clear later that there was a border conflict between them.

According to Cañón (1964:34), the *merced* Conchalí was granted to Don Gerónimo Pizarro Cajal and Mincha to Juan de Ahumada in 1605. The *merced* Conchalí and Chigualoco was granted to the *conquistador* Francisco Hernández Ortiz (Villaroel *et al*, 1988:74). Francisco Hernández Ortiz was General grand master and married to one of Pedro Cortés Monroy's daughters, María Cortés y Tobar (Villaroel *et al*, 1988:73). He died before 1619. His son was Cristóbal Fernández Pizarro, born in 1601. He died in 1656. He had several important military and bureaucratic positions, among them Magistrate (*Corregidor*) of Santiago in 1655 (Fuentes *et al*, 1984:206). Judging from the historical archives documents, Cañón's version is wrong:

Communal Land Ownership in Chile

Alonso García Ramón, governor /---/ of the province of Chile, having in consideration the much and good that you Captain Francisco Hernández Ortiz have done to its Majesty in the war of this kingdom /---/ without any remuneration, I have for good, in its Royal name and as such its governor of giving grant /.../ of the lands that exists from the Conchalí river to the Chuapa river and the road from the sea to Mincha... (ANCH, Colección *Real Audiencia,* 1710, Doc. no. 4, Vol. 2714, pieza 2, 'Bartolomé Rojo con Cristóbal Pizarro, Mayordomo de la Santa Iglesia Católica de esta ciudad sobre la posesión de las tierras que compró de la Santa Iglesia pertenecientes a la estancia de Mincha, Partido de Quillota, Chuapa', folio 69 to 106 (or 1 to 30 verso). (See also Villaroel *et al,* 1988:73 and Cañón, 1964:34; Gerónimo Pizarro Cajal who, according to Cañón, received the *merced,* was grandson of Francisco Hernández Ortiz.)

Nowadays, the *estancia* Conchalí and Chigualoco corresponds to the *haciendas* Conchalí, Agua Amarilla, Millahue and Huentelauquén. Of these, Millahue (27,620 ha) and Huentelauquén (3,707 ha), the highest valued in the commune, are now part of the Canela commune and belong to one owner, Carlos Víal Espantoso.

The Ahumada who received Mincha was Captain Juan Alonso de Ahumada (Villaroel et. al., 1988:74). I stress this because there was another Juan de Ahumada, an *encomendero,* who received the land, which became the famous *estancia* Choapa, one of the biggest in colonial Chile and neighbour to the Mincha. The *hacienda* Choapa was one of the largest and richest estates in Chile. It included the land, which was later on divided into 14 large *haciendas.* These stretched over the entire Choapa valley, from the confluence of the River Illapel, to the mountains including the Illapel valley. It stretched from the junction of the rivers to the tributary Aucó (El Arenal), including the land on which the city of Illapel stands, and along the coast it included the *hacienda* Cavilolén, which embraced the present *fundos* El Mollar, La Puntilla, Las Vacas and Palo Colorado. Apart from these estates, it embraced in the Choapa valley; Cuncumén, Chillepín, Tranquilla, Coirón, Llimpo, Las Casas (Santa Rosa), Tahuinco, El Tambo, Limáhuida, Las Cañas, Chuchiñí, Peralillo, Pintacura, and in the Illapel valley: Bellavista, El Peral, Cuz-Cuz, La Aguada and Quillaicillo (Villaroel *et al*, 1988:74).

According to Cañón, the *estancia* Mincha included the land situated on both sides of the Choapa river to the east of Huinchigallego, stretching from the Millahue ravine to the south, to the limit of Pedro Cortés Monroy's (Riberos?) land to the north, northeast and west. Finally, to the east, the Mincha embraced all land as far as the junction of the rivers, supposedly the rivers Choapa and Illapel.

When, in 1726, Juan de Ahumada bought the Huentelauquén area from Pedro Cortés (Castillo), he became the owner of the northern banks along the River Choapa, from its confluence with the River Illapel to the sea (ANCH, AN Illapel, Vol. 4, 1775-1844, 'Venta Pedro Cortez a Juan de Ahumada', folio 42). This sale, according to Cañón, took place in 1626 and the vendor was Pedro Cortes Monroy (Riberos?). Adding the bought part, the *estancia* Mincha must then have comprised 30,000 ha or more. The Mincha *estancia* was, during 1660-1680, in the hands of Pedro de Ahumada, son of Juan Alonso de Ahumada (Cañón, 1964:42). Pedro de Ahumada rented Mincha for a period of eighteen years to Marquis Francisco Bravo de Saravia, the first Marquis de la Pica and owner of the *hacienda* Illapel. The marquis kept 5,000 goats on it (Villaroel *et al*, 1988:74). In 1704, the *estancia* was in the hands of Juan de Ahumada, son of Pedro de Ahumada (Cañón, 1964:42). That year, according to Cañón (1964, 42), the *estancia* Mincha was put up for auction at the request of several plaintiffs headed by the Cathedral Church. The owners had failed to pay the annuities they owed, both to the Cathedral Church of Santiago and to the Convent *Nuestra Señora de las Mercedes*.

The Church was involved in various ways in the Chilean agrarian economy. Through the encumbrances and liens, known as *capellanías, censos, obras and pías*, placed on property, the Church warranted funds. Not unexpectedly, due to the strong religious feeling of the people at that time, the encumbrances and liens were established by the landowner himself, often on his deathbed, placing a perpetual lien on the property:

> Such encumbrances were widespread and over the years many estates came to be burdened for up to a third or even half of what they were worth. The foundations were cumulative and usually perpetual. They could be paid off but rarely were; and as property changed hands the obligations went with the land (Bauer, 1975:119).

The *capellanías* and *censos* implied a drain on rural revenue for the landowners, and often resulted in intricate legal situations when property passed to another owner. The annuities had to be paid, whether the years were good or meagre, and even if the Church's recourse in case of non-fulfilment were slow, it does seem as if payments were regularly kept up. If not, as the case of Mincha shows, the Church took over the property. In

1865, through a series of laws and with some decades of the colonial era behind, the landowners were liberated from these obligations (Bauer, 1975:120).

After a frustrated public sale on the 30th of December 1709, the Cathedral Church of Santiago, as the major plaintiff, became the owner of the *estancia*. The same day it was divided into three *estancias* and sold to three different people; Captain Agustín Jorquera, Captain Diego de Valencia and Second Lieutenant Bartolomé Rojo (Villaroel *et al*, 1988:74-75). The Church kept the part of the Paynequelén tributary (Cañón, 1964:42-45).

The estancia Mincha under Second Lieutenant B. Rojo

Second Lieutenant Bartolomé Rojo bought the land that today corresponds to the communities Mincha Sur, Norte and Las Barrancas (Cañón, 1964:42-45). These properties presently cover approximately 5,625 ha. The family name Rojo continues to be one of the most common, both in the community Mincha Sur and in Mincha Norte. It is interesting to quote the information concerning the boundaries of Bartolomé Rojo's land because of the trials caused by its delimitation of the southern banks of the River Choapa. The borders were:

> ... *from one part and the other of the said Choapa river,* the Guelchuguallén ravine, to the Runi ravine, on the north side which, border on the captain Agustín de Jorquera's land and they are delimited by the hillock that comes down from the Guayecura hill, to the right of the Mincha hill and the Guayecura hill water falls that flow down into the Runi ravine which, borders on the captain don Diego de Valencia and the Salvia ravine which is included in this land and the water falls from the hillock that face Tunga which flow down into the river, delimiting the right to the Runi ravine which belongs to the said captain Diego de Valencia and to the south this land borders on the Pyniquelén ravine to the top of the Wolf hill... (Villaroel *et al*, 1988:75; emphasis added).

In 1710, Bartolomé Rojo found himself involved in a trial with the owner of the *estancia* Chigualoco, María Magdalena de Arqueros, married to Gerónimo Pizarro Cajal, over the land south of the River Choapa. As we have seen, this transfer was already included in the handing over of the *mercedes*, but apparently not actualised until a century later. More

Historical Formation of the Agricultural Community Canela Baja

information concerning this trial can be found in: ANCH, Colección *Real Audiencia*, 1710, Doc. no. 4, Vol. 2714, pieza 2, 1710, 'Bartolomé Rojo con Cristóbal Pizarro, Mayordomo...', folio 70 to 106 (or 1 to 30, verso). This extensive document provides an important source for the information regarding the transcription of the handing over of the *merced* Conchalí and Chigualoco to the Captain Francisco Hernández Ortíz by the Governor Alonso García Ramón.

The dispute was carried into this century when the *comuneros* of Mincha Sur and Tunga Sur claimed their rights granted by the Crown (Villaroel *et al*, 1988:73,75). According to Cañón (1964:34), the dispute between the *comuneros* of Mincha Sur and the *hacienda* Huentelauquén in force during the 1960s, a case that I will also mention in Chapter 8, was also a consequence of the former one.

The estancia Atelcura under Captain A. Jorquera

According to Cañón, Captain Agustín Jorquera bought the land that today corresponds to Atelcura and Agua Fría Baja:

> ... alongside from mayten [three] to Captain Diego Cortes [Pérez] land which they call Guenchuguallego [Huinchigallego] and across from the southern part towards the north from the hillock that comes down from the high hill of Gueyecure springs to the Atelcura ravine to the slope of the Augustinillo ravine and on the mentioned north side from the said maiten springs to the Atelcura ravine whose /---/ and Cuytuto place and all the falls that flow down into the Guenchuguallego ravine with the main hill of Pangue which delimits the mentioned land and to the south from where the Gueyecure hillock ends straight to the Mincha hill fall to the Atelcura ravine which borders on the land that the said Bartolomé Rojo buys (Cañón, 1964:44).

Based on the date, 30th December 1709, this Captain Diego Cortés should be Diego Cortés Pérez and not his son Diego Cortés Castillo, even though the first died some months earlier (17th July 1709). In addition, as far as I am aware, his son Diego was not a captain.

This land comprises, according to Cañón, the current seven communities of Atelcura, Agua Fría Baja, El Potrero, La Capilla, La Leona, Cabra Corral and Las Paredes. Today these communities total approximately 12,000 ha. The land of Agustín Jorquera, which also includes El Arrayán, came to be called *estancia* Atelcura (Villaroel *et al*, 1988:75). El Arrayán is today a *fundo* of 17,786 ha. Situated to the east of the community El Potrero, El Arrayán today seems to fall outside the limits of the Commune. These properties together currently total almost 20,000 ha.

The estancia Tunga under Captain D. de Valencia

The Captain Diego de Valencia bought the land, which today corresponds to Tunga Sur and Norte, now belonging to the Commune of Illapel. Together they cover 11,625 ha, the area of Tunga Sur being 5,250 ha and Tunga Norte, 6,375 ha (IREN: 1977:27).

Agricultural communities sprung from the Mincha estancia

The twelve agricultural communities that developed from the *estancia* Mincha today total approximately 29,250 ha. This excludes the area of the *fundo* El Arrayán, because I have not been able to verify whether or not it actually was a part of Agustín Jorquera's land. Excluding both Tunga Norte and Sur, which today no longer belong to the Canela commune, the remaining ten communities that were formed from the *estancia* Mincha add up to approximately 17,625 ha, at present with a total of 463 *comuneros*. These are from the Area Agua Fría, Agua Fría Baja and El Potrero; from the Atecura Area, Atelcura, La Capilla, La Leona and Cabra Corral; and from the Choapa Area, Las Paredes, Barrancas, Mincha Sur and Mincha Norte (IREN, 1977(2):26-27).

Historical Formation of the Agricultural Community Canela Baja

Figure 7.4 The sub-division of *Estancia Mincha*: 1605-1979

A.C. Stands for Agricultural Community
Coms. stands for comuneros

```
                                    1605
                              Estancia Mincha
                              Juan de Ahumada
                                 30,000 ha
                                     |
                                   1709
                            Auction Estancia Mincha
      ┌──────────────────────────────┼──────────────────────────────────┐
      │                              │                                  │
Estancia Tunga              Estancia Mincha                    Estancia Atelcura         Paynequelén
Diego de Valencia           Bartolomé Rojo                     Augustín Jorquera         Santiago Cathedral Church
   11,625 ha                   5,625 ha                           12,000 ha                    ? ha
      │                              │                                  │
    1979                           1979                               1979
      │                              │                                  │
 ┌────┼────┐              ┌──────────┼──────────┐      ┌────────┬───────┼────────┬──────────┬──────────┐
 │         │              │                     │      │        │       │        │          │          │
A.C. Tunga  A.C. Tunga   A.C. Mincha Sur   A.C. Mincha Norte  A.C. Las
  Sur         Norte       131 coms.         75 coms.      Barrancas
137 coms.   137 coms.     3,437 ha           625 ha       10 coms.
5,250 ha    5,250 ha                                      1,563 ha

A.C. Atelcura   A.C. Agua    A.C. El Potrero   A.C. La Capilla   A.C. La Leona   A.C. Cabra      A.C. Las
71 coms.        Fría Baja    28 coms.          32 coms.          7 coms.         Corral          Paredes
2,812 ha        70 Coms.     2,250 ha          500 ha            125 ha          40 coms.        18 coms.
                4,800 ha                                                         1,250 ha        375 ha
```

PART 3
CONTEMPORARY HISTORY

8 The Agricultural Community Canela Baja and the Struggle for Espíritu Santo

Struggles over ownership of property are important and interesting because they are so often at the crux of tensions in social relations and subsequent upheaval and social change (Fowler, 1993:V).

Introduction

This Chapter aims to reconstruct the struggle for the land of the ex-*fundo* Espíritu Santo, a part of the agricultural community Canela Baja that was seized during the 1800s. This struggle serves, firstly, to illustrate that the peasants are not passive recipients of 'modes of production' but real actors; that the peasantry can through local resistance, adaptive strategies and voluntary organisation, induce changes that affect their existence. Through this example, I will try to stress a perspective that focuses on the dynamics of rural society (Calderón, 1985; Campos, 1985) where the peasants actively defend their land.

Secondly, this example of the seizure of community land is one of several, which illustrates that however marginal the land, the struggle for its ownership - between landowners and/or capitalists and the peasants - is not, as for example, García (1973:99) believes, uncommon in the zones of poor land. How could it be otherwise when landlords and peasants share the same natural environment? However, according to García, because the agricultural communities and the *minifundia* in Latin-America are, in general, to be found in 'zones of refuge' (i.e. marginal land), they no longer withstand the pressure of the *latifundia*'s hunger for land. The view that the small peasantry survives because the landlords are not interested in the marginal land occupied by the small peasantry is also to be found in the Latin-American discussion from the 1950s onwards (Borde and Góngora, 1956; Baraona *et al*, 1961; Rivera, 1988(a), etc.). Both Borde and Góngora and Baraona *et al*, have also supported the other: that the *latifundia* tries to pre-empt the land of the *minifundia* (Chapter 1). As the agricultural communities are commonly included within the *minifundium*, the former view can be considered valid for the agricultural communities as well.

Feder (1978:44) with whom I agree here has a different opinion. According to him, landlords are not only interested in the poor and marginal land of the *minifundia*, but their expansionism is a deadly threat to it, for many reasons. Land concentration is a necessity for the expansion of capitalist agriculture. Although production costs are higher on poor land, the price of the land increases all the time due to population growth, and the demand for agricultural products grows. The longer the process of modernisation of agriculture, the more remunerative it is to bring poor land under production. According to Feder, it is possible to maintain that modernisation is a way of utilising poorer resources, although this process has its limits.

Thus, capitalism is on one side interested in putting under its dominion that land which still is not independent of its quality, to whom it belongs and its form (whether private or communal). On the other, the peasantry try to keep its land with all the means at their disposal. Theoretically, the small peasantry's non-transition from a formal to a real subordination under capitalism is commonly explained, implicitly or explicitly, almost exclusively in relation to capitalism's needs and dynamics. It is argued for example, that capitalism accommodates agricultural petty production (Alanen, 1991:325), that capitalism reinforces pre-existing non-capitalist modes of production, or even creates new ones (Kay, 1980:115-116); that the small peasantry is even 'necessary' to capitalism (Astorga, 1985:102), etc. Referring to the modes of production in Latin-America, Kay writes that these:

> emerge as a result of the expansion of capitalism in Western Europe. They emerge from the disarticulation, transformation and reintegration of the pre-colonial modes of production to the emerging capitalistic world system and subordinated to it (Kay, 1980:115-116).

From there, according to this author, the use of the concept of 'dependent' modes of production, are those that may be capitalist or not. He argues on the basis of the Latin-American societies that:

> these non capitalist social relations were created by the centre and form an integral part of the capitalist world system (Kay, 1980:18).

Thus, according to this logic, the non-capitalist mode/s of production in Latin America are born or created jointly by the capitalist world system. They obey the development of world capitalism without necessarily adopting capitalist relations of production. The capitalist mode of production is imposed as such, but it bases its own development on the subordination and subsistence of pre-capitalist relations of production.

I would suggest that no matter how marginal the land, the struggle for its ownership between *latifundistas* and *comuneros* has not been uncommon in the zone studied here. The case of Espíritu Santo as an example of the seizure of land by the *latifundistas* in the Commune of Canela is not unique except for the violence involved in the conflict. Among the documents that the *comunero* O. Ollarzú (deceased) lent me is a letter from a lawyer from Illapel, in which he reports to Ollarzú of a trial pursued by the *comuneros* of Mincha Sur (present agricultural community in the Commune of Canela) against the *hacienda* Huentelauquén for the seizure of community land, which had happened several decades previously:

> the owner of the Hacienda Huentelauquén, whose name I can no longer remember, inscribed in 1908 Huentelauquén annexing the comuneros' estancias Mincha Sur and Tunga Sur. In 1948, as the partner of the lawyer, Don Luís Escala Coo, in the name of the comuneros of Mincha Sur we initiated a case for the recovery of land against the hacienda Huentelauquén and even though this case has still not been decided, several well-known jurists, among them /---/ believe that the case will be decided in favour of the comuneros of Mincha Sur (Firma (Signed) H. Soto Vicencio, Illapel 17 de Diciembre, 1959).

The mentioned lawyer L. Escala Coo was co-owner of the *fundo* Las Palmas in 1942.

As Pascal explained in respect to another characteristic zone of *latifundia* and agricultural communities, the history of the Valley of Hurtado consists:

> of more than one hundred years of repeated legal conflicts and violence. Its history involves much truth, but also much myth (Pascal, 1968:69) (Commune of Río Hurtado, Limarí Province, Region IV).

Like this author I also want to:

> ... collect the facts and the myths [these also being facts] because that is how the present comunero knows these events (*Ibid*).

Dealing specifically with the character of the struggle for the land, there seems to be an unwillingness or lack of capacity, to recognise its relationship with the defence for the form of semi-communal land itself. For example, Borde and Góngora are reluctant to recognise the agricultural communities as a specific type of social organisation (see Chapter 4). CIDA (1966:137) points out that in respect to these conflicts, the internal organisation of the agricultural communities, above all in their struggle and conflicts with the *haciendas*, corresponds more to a resource in the struggle for survival than to a form of economic management. Where can the line be drawn between the strategies for survival and economic management?

These conflicts have, without doubt, contributed not only to the cohesion and strengthening of the community links, but also to a collective consciousness in the defence of their interest against the *latifundistas*. In this way, the struggle for the land is a contributing element in the crystallisation of the communal land ownership as a form of economic management. The struggle for Espíritu Santo, as an example of the struggle for land between communities and *haciendas*, is an important device in the understanding not only of the effects these conflicts have on the agricultural communities for their legal recognition, but also of the law and the political establishment's resolving of a long discord between the communities and the *latifundia* in the Norte Chico.

A short background

The history of the conflict over the seized land of the sub-area Espíritu Santo, sometimes active sometimes latent, was long and passed through various phases. It began at the end of the nineteenth century and ended in the 1970s with the recovery of the land of the *fundos* land by the Canela Baja agricultural community.

Although what happened to the now ex-*fundo* Espíritu Santo is, with a few exceptions, quite unknown beyond the limits of the community, it is still very fresh in the collective memory of the agricultural community

Canela Baja's *comuneros*. This is even truer in the case of the *comuneros* of the Espíritu Santo sub-area, not only because of the seizure, but also because it turned into an armed confrontation. Although of limited scope, it resulted in the murder of one of the *comuneros*' leaders and the death of another.

In spite of the fact that the illegal sale from which Espíritu Santo evolved as a *fundo* took place in 1853, the legal case and struggle for it began only at the end of the nineteenth century, J. D. Amenábar being the owner of the *fundo*. The background, relating to the period before Amenábar, is only concerned with the two first sales of the *fundo*.

Amenábar, a native of Ovalle (the present capital of Limarí Province, Region IV) was the third owner of the *fundo* since it's first illegal sale in 1853. On this date, J. A. Guerrero, 'an old owner' (Cañón, 1964:38) of the sub-area Espíritu Santo, illegally sold the property to B. Ossa (Illapel's RP, 1912, folio 9, no. 21). Either Guerrero or another person with this family name appears in the *comuneros* list of Espíritu Santo from 1893 (Repertorio del Conservador, Illapel, 1893, folio 56 verso. no. 61. Regulación de los *comuneros* de Espíritu Santo). The *comuneros* maintained that the transaction was illegal because the land was part of the indivisible property of the community Canela Baja. Therefore, Guerrero needed the authorisation of all the *comuneros* owners to sell it.

This is not to say that the agricultural communities were legally recognised and inscribed specifically under the form of semi-communal land ownership. It may be interesting to recall here a quotation from the *comunero* O. Ollarzú, dealing with the legal situation of the communities before they were legalised, in order to contextualise the situation of Espíritu Santo:

> on the land belonging to any one of these communities /---/ the dry land on the hills and hillocks and on some plains that lack water, is *undivided property*, common goods or common land and *the comuneros only have individual title deeds registered*, either in their own name or that of their ascendants, for the small irrigated plot which constitutes their hijuela and which gives him access to the common goods or estancia, giving him his status as comunero. *The communities do not have a registered title deed for the common goods in the name of the community, nor in the name of the comuneros* (emphasis added) (Letter of Legal Consultation (*s.a.*), written by Oscar Ollarzú).

Although these properties had during the 1800s, been crystallising in a semi-communal form, from the point of view of the existing legal framework, they could not be considered as other than private, which in fact they were historically. As we shall see in Chapter 10, an analysis of the documents of land sales during the 1800s and the beginning of the 1900s will clearly show that the terms of *estancia, fundo* or even *hacienda* are used as synonymous of community, referring to land that belongs to various owners, in undivided form. So is the case of Espíritu Santo, also named as *estancia* by the *comuneros* in 1893. This shows that these communities were still conceived as *fundos* or *haciendas* in the sense of large landed properties, and that these terms have been kept from a previous period when these properties belonged to a single person or family. The variety of terms used in order to denominate the land property makes it clear that the old terms are still utilised for the new form. This has partially its explanation in the fact that there was no place in the laws of the Chilean Republican, itself at that point not very old, for forms of properties other than the private, being the only recognised form. The Mapuche communities created by the state itself were an exception. The legal access to land was established in the country with the imposition of the Code of Civil Laws (1847) and the Regulation of the Conservatory of Real Estate (1857).

Given this context, the lawsuit concerning Espíritu Santo (to which the *comuneros* responded but which, was initiated by Amenábar) could not be argued in any form other than that of a private property, no matter who initiated the lawsuit. Seeing it from the perspective of the *comuneros*, their land constituted as a unit, a private property of many families, no matter that internally these properties were constituted both of semi-private and communal land. It is also interesting that from the legal point of view, the same argument is valid for the lawsuit in the second period, begun in the 1960s, when the long process of legal recognition of the communities started in the country. In other words, the fact that the communities were not legally recognised as a form of communal or semi-communal land does not mean that they were completely unprotected as property.

The *fundo* remained in the hands of the Ossa family for three decades. In 1884, the property was sold to E. Eastman who kept it for five years, selling it in 1889 to Amenábar, with whom the conflict started. From this point on, the history of the struggle to recover the land of the *fundo* is somewhat confused, myth being mixed with reality, the oral tradition with the scarce written tradition. On several occasions there are even conflicting dates. This is not only true in relation to the *comuneros*' own stories, but also Cañón, Aracena and CIDA, who sometimes diverge in their versions of the story. These three versions cover only the period up to the 1960s, the present reconstruction being a contribution to the written epilogue of this story. For both the periods before and after the 1960s, I have reconstructed the history of this conflict by collecting the oral memories of some of the *comuneros* who actively participated in the recuperation of Espíritu Santo at the beginning of the 1970s and who served as qualified informers on the above-mentioned versions and historical documents (see Chapter 1).

Cañón's, Aracena's and CIDA's version

The conflict started in 1890 with Amenábar when he visited the *fundo* after he purchased it. He found that several *comuneros* were living there and that it formed part of a community (Cañón, 1964:38). Amenábar, unlike the two previous owners, was probably the first owner to effectively take possession of the *fundo* and to try to oust the peasants from the *fundo*. Judging from the scarce information from the *comuneros* for the period before Amenábar, Ossa and Eastman, who bought the *fundo* in 1853 and 1884 respectively, apparently never took possession of the *fundo*, and used it only as pasture for their livestock and/or rented it to other farmers who used it to that end.

Seeing his land occupied, Amenábar filed a lawsuit against the *comuneros* before the Court of Ovalle, which did not possess jurisdiction over this land, as it in fact was under the jurisdiction of Illapel (present capital of the Choapa Province, Region IV). The *comuneros* responded to the litigation before the latter Court, which favoured them. Amenábar did not respect the verdict and sent a representative with police and peonages to Espíritu Santo, where an armed confrontation occurred. During the incident, B. Silva, the leader of the *comuneros,* was killed.

In 1896, the judge at Illapel was replaced by one who sided with Amenábar and his brother, who as a *comunero* (S. Jorquera (deceased), of the Canela Baja sub-area, oral interview, May 1988) later pointed out, were Conservatives. The Amenábars also received the help of the Governor of Illapel, who granted them the assistance of the police to evict the *comuneros*. In different armed confrontations, successive leaders of the *comuneros* were killed while the survivors fled, leaving Espíritu Santo vacant for the Amenábars (Cañón, 1964:38).

During this period the Chilean political scene was characterised by the conflict between the Liberals and Conservatives, which ended in the coup d'état of 1891 against Balmaceda (1886-1891). Even if I am not certain about whether this scenario had a direct influence on the conflict of Espíritu Santo, I am inclined to believe that it had. I suspect that the new judge in Illapel had a role in this new scenario.

About this period, the local priest of the Mincha Parish wrote in the book of baptisms:

> 1891 - fatal year - war!! Civil war!! The whole nation is against the President Balmaceda because of him disowning or disrespecting the Constitution and the Law. The Constitutionalists won (AP Mincha, Bautismos (1889-1894), folio 144).

According to Aracena's version, the people sent by Amenábar first notified B. Silva that he should leave the land of Espíritu Santo, which Silva refused to do. Three days later the representatives of Amenábar returned with more police and peonages, to attempt to eject Silva. As Silva offered resistance, he was beaten up, handcuffed and taken prisoner. On the way to Ovalle Silva was killed by Rivera, one of the policemen from Ovalle.

The rest of the *comuneros* decided to continue with the litigation. They brought it before the higher Court of La Serena (present capital of Region IV), which supported them. The Amenábar brothers asked for the decision to be nullified, alleging that only one of them had been notified. Later, with the help of the new judge of Illapel, and also of the Governor, G. Gómez, who gave them the support of the police, they sent a gang to Espíritu Santo to evict the *comuneros*. According to Aracena (1964:157), this judge, whose name he does not indicate, was because of his misdeeds, later dismissed from his post by President Ibañez (1927-1931/1952-1958).

On the 3rd of March 1896 a date which, with reason, Aracena notes:

> should have been stamped on the revolutionary annals of the country, as the first cry for agrarian freedom by the poor peasants (Aracena, 1941:157).

the armed forces under the command of Rivera, who had murdered Silva, arrived in Espíritu Santo. They notified J. de D. Ogalde, the new representative of the *comuneros*, that they had to leave the place. Ogalde

The Agricultural Community Canela Baja

and the other *comuneros* resisted, starting an exchange of gunfire in which Ogalde was killed. Given the strength of the resistance that the *comuneros* put up, Rivera and his men fled pursued by the *comuneros*, among them a brother of Ogalde. The gang split up, leaving their weapons and horses behind and hid in the mountains, arriving three days later in Illapel. In spite of this, the *comuneros* were later expelled (Aracena, 1941:156-7).

It is not clear from Aracena's account whether the *comuneros*, as Cañón claims, put up an armed fight against the new eviction attempts to which they were subjected, and if there were more deaths on either side. I am inclined to think that this was not the case given that at least the descendants of the new victims would have remembered. From what I can establish from Aracena's version, only Silva and Ogalde among the *comuneros* were killed. This was confirmed by other *comuneros*, who claimed that two members of the police (a sergeant and a constable) were also killed.

According to CIDA (1966:136-137):

> at the end of the last century [nineteenth] the mentioned community [Canela Baja] lost a great part of its territory in an unclear judgement from where resulted the hacienda Espíritu Santo which during some time was rented to the community and then sold to a third person, in 1890. The purchaser asked and obtained the support of the public forces to evict the comuneros. In 1890 the leader of the community was killed in a gunfight; later on was also his successor as well as the lieutenant of the purchaser. After a brutal repression the surviving comuneros moved to Canela Baja. In this way a community has become a hacienda and in this case under the same name: Espíritu Santo. The families that now live in the fundo have no relation with the expelled comuneros of 1890 [emphasis added].

According to this, the land of Espíritu Santo was rented to the community. The lessor was not mentioned. This does not agree with the *comuneros*' version, since according to them it was rather the community who rented the land. But this version does not seem to be correct either. First, if Eastman was the owner of Espíritu Santo before Amenábar, it should have been Eastman who was the lessor. For the same reason Espíritu Santo did not become a *hacienda*, as postulated by CIDA in 1890, which it already was prior to that date. Secondly, it was not the community that became a *hacienda* but only a part of it, i.e., Espíritu Santo, since the community was Canela Baja. It is correct however, that the *hacienda* already had the name

Espíritu Santo. According to a document presented by Silva, the murdered leader, in 1891 to the judge of Illapel when the brothers Amenábar petitioned for the inscription of the *hacienda* in their name, they declared that they had bought it under that denomination (Registro of Interdicciones y Prohibiciones, Illapel, 1891, no. 4, folio 4, verso, Título de prohibición de inscribir un título de propiedad ubicado en la estancia del Espíritu Santo, subdelegación de la Canela de este departamento y anotado en el repertorio bajo no. 50) (Article of prohibition of the registration of property located in the Espíritu Santo Estancia, sub-delegation of La Canela in this department and recorded in the Index under no. 50).

CIDA declared as well that the *comuneros* who lived in the *fundo* in the 1960s had no relation with the *comuneros* of 1890, which is not so clear. An analysis of the actual family names of the *comuneros* of this sub-area shows rather the contrary. Of the actual 125 *comuneros* of Espíritu Santo, 42.3% (53 *comuneros*) have the same family names as the *comuneros* from the end of the nineteenth century. In other words, of the thirty-three family names registered by me for the actual 125 *comuneros* of Espíritu Santo, nine (27.3%) names are to be found that correspond to the total of fourteen family names of the seventeen *comuneros* registered in 1893 (see Table 8.1).

The comuneros' version

In the collective memory of the present *comuneros* of the agricultural community Canela Baja, the incidents involving Espíritu Santo only started with the conflict with Amenábar. They know little of Ossa and Eastman, the two previous owners of the *fundo*. According to the *comuneros*, Amenábar, before becoming the owner of Espíritu Santo, rented it as pasture. The 80 years old J. Muñoz claimed:

> Espíritu Santo belonged to Canela, in about 1880, more or less, here the community rented to Mr. Amenábar of Ovalle this part, which at that time was grazing, for the cattle. After they became the owners they did not want to give it back and in 1886 a legal struggle began which resulted in deaths when the people defended their land (J. Muñoz, *comunero* from the agricultural community Canela Baja, co-owner of the present *fundo* Puerto Oscuro and former Mayor of the commune, recorded interview, 22 May 1988).

According to G. Castillo, a *comunero* from the Espíritu Santo sub-area, before Amenábar:

> what was here before was comuneros, because I remember that my father told me the story that Mr. Bernardo Silva was the leader who arranged the community system in Espíritu Santo, therefore I know that it was community land and was seized. I remember how the seizure occurred, the Amenábars rented a block of land only in Espíritu Santo, then they extended it /.../ to more than 3,000 hectares and it was this that caused the conflict. I remember that they told me and I read something of the story of when they killed Mr. Silva, they used some kind of trick, something to do with the courts and they sent some prisoners from the jail in Illapel. They tried to get him to leave the other comuneros with the intention of going to Ovalle, that the conflict was arranged, but it was the other way round and they killed him /.../ the other lot of people who came from the jail formed a revolution with the comuneros. The comuneros then carried on and went too far so that justice did not take note of the original conflict but punished the comuneros, many of whom fled into the hills and suffered there day and night (G. Castillo, recorded interview, 1 May 1988).

The now deceased S. Jorquera, a *comunero* from the Canela Baja sub-area, indicated that:

> The Amenábars brought large animals, horses, cows... they were Conservatives. They did not pay Bernardo Silva, the representative of the community, for pasturage /.../ Bonifacio Contreras, the Judge of Illapel and Teodoro Ceballo Illapel's public notary, arranged the title of sale for Amenábar. Casimiro Cortés, a very wealthy man, with a lot of properties, was named by the court to take the possession of Espíritu Santo for the Amenábars. Juan de Dios Ogalde was the representative of the comuneros when they came to take the land away, they sheltered in his house and Ogalde, a sergeant and a constable were killed. The representative of the Notary, a certain Rivero, got away pursued by the comuneros (S. Jorquera, *Ibid*).

When in September 1891 Silva sought via A. Cuevas, to the judge of Illapel (Registro de Interdicciones y Prohibiciones, Illapel, 1891, no. 4, folio 4 vers), the suspension of the registration of the title of Espíritu Santo made by D. and C. Amenábar before the CBR (Conservatory of Real Estate) of Illapel, he declared that:

according to the title that I here present, I possess *indivisible* with other comuneros the inheritance Canela Baja... (emphasis added).

He declared as well that neither the Amenábars nor those who sold the land, which the Amenábars claimed to have bought with the name Espíritu Santo, possessed legal title giving them ownership because the land was part of the community Canela Baja.

Three years later, on the 5th of September 1893 and with Silva now deceased, the 17 *comuneros* from Espíritu Santo, among them Silva's widow, requested the inscription of the title over Espíritu Santo at the Conservatory of Illapel. The Repertory of the Conservatory declares that it omitted:

the fixation and publication of the placard prescribed by the Regulation of the Conservatory, because the title is inserted previous to this date (Repertorio del Conservador, Illapel, 1893, no. 61, folio 56, verso Regulación).

The document does not indicate on which date the insertion of the title was made. It was probably before 1891 the date when Silva requested the suspension of the registration of the title over Espíritu Santo made by the Amenábars. As we have seen, Silva declared that according to the title he possessed, he and the other *comuneros* had indivisible possession of the inheritance Canela Baja and that neither the Amenábars nor those who sold the land, possessed legal title giving them ownership over Espíritu Santo. From this I can suppose that it was the community who, based on the legal title, could claim property rights over Espíritu Santo.

According to the document, the *comuneros* performed a written contract where they established the rules for the administration and the possession of the community. It also included the form in which they decided to conduct the trial against the Amenábars. The contract specified that Espíritu Santo was a part of the La Canela *estancia*. The said contract, from which I have constructed the following list, specified the percentage of rights each *comunero* possessed, the percentage each must contribute towards the court costs, the number of possession rights ('*lluvias*') and the number of animals on the community's common land.

It also indicated that while the court case with Amenábar lasted, all the products of the community would go towards the costs of the case. If these were not enough, each *comunero* would have to personally contribute

The Agricultural Community Canela Baja

an amount proportional to the percentage of land owned. By the mutual agreement of the other *comuneros*, Silva's widow, V. Barraza, remained exempt from contributing to these costs. R. Saavedra, the *comunero* with the most property rights within the community apart from Silva's widow, remained bound to carry out the defence of all the cases without payment. In spite of these efforts to safeguard the land they had inherited since the 1700s, the *comuneros* finally lost it.

Table 8.1 List of the *comuneros* of Espíritu Santo, 1893

Name of comuneros	% of rights	% of judicial contribution	No. of possessions (*lluvias*)	No. of animals on common land*
Ventura Barraza	20	0	3	150
Reinaldo Saavedra	30	-	4	200
Benito Lemus	10	20	3	200
Borjas Contreras	10	5	3	80
Manuel A. Montenegro	3	-	2	35
José A. Pizarro	3	10	2	50
Celestino Contreras	3	5	3	80
Estanislao Astorga	2	5	1	20
Segundo Andrade	3	5	1	50
Ceferino Carvajal	2	5	1	10
Lorenzo Contreras	2	4	1	30
Pedro Juan Rojas	2	9	1	30
Juan de Dios Vega	2	5	1	30
Pantaleón Robles	2	3	1	20
Juan de Dios Ogalde	2	6	1	30
Catalino Ogalde	2	5	1	30
José María Codoceo	2	4	1	30
Total	**100**	**91**	**30**	**1,075**

Source: The author, based on Repertorio del Conservador, Illapel, 1893, no. 61, folio 56 verso. Regulación...
*It is specified and understood that these animals are cattle, horses and mules, from which it follows that this limitation was not valid for sheep and goats. Those *comuneros* who had more large livestock than that laid down, had to pay 10 cents per head per season.

Table 8.2 The *fundo* Espíritu Santo, 1853-1972

Owner	Place of residence	Occupation or profession	Area (ha)	Years of ownership	Purchase price (Chilean $)	Sold to
Comuneros of Espíritu Santo	Espíritu Santo	Comuneros	-	- 1853	-	
In 1853 Juan A. Guerrero, comunero of Espíritu Santo illegally sells part of Espíritu Santo to Blas Ossa						
Blas Ossa	Ovalle	-	-	1853 -?	100,000	
Blas Ossa's son's widow	-	-	-	? - 1884	-	E. Eastman
E. Eastman	-	-	-	1884 - 1889	-	J. D. Amenábar
J.D. Amenábar	-	Stock breeder	-	1889 - 1899	-	L. & E. Lahaye
J. Toyos	Ovalle	-	-	1901 - 1912	-	F. Barrios
F. Barrios	Ovalle	-	-	1912 -?	-	
H. Vicuña	Ovalle	-		1931 -		
H. Vicuña E. G. & G.Vicuña H. Barrios	-	-	-	1940	-	L. Olavarría S. D. Daveggio L. J Cambisse F. M. & O. Ollarzú

Table 8.2 (continued)

L. Olavarría S.	Valparaíso	Merchant	¼		
D. Daveggio L	Valparaíso	Merchant	¼	1940 - →	500,000
J. Cambisse F.	Esp. Santo	Merchant	¼		
M. & O. Ollarzú	Canela	Merchants & comuneros	¼	1940 - 1948	Olavarría, Daveggio & Cambisse
L. Olavarría S.	Valparaíso	Merchant	¼	1940 - 1959	25,000
D. Daveggio L	Valparaíso	Merchant	¼	1940 - 1959	
M. J. Cambisse F.	Esp. Santo	-	¼	1940 - →	J. Cambisse F.
J. Cambisse F.	Esp. Santo	-	10,000	1940 - 1972	25,000,000
					1972, expropriation of Espíritu Santo by BN

In 1972 J. Cambisse returns 8,000 of 10,000 ha of Espíritu Santo to the agricultural community Canela Baja. His two sons keep 2,000 ha in the capacity of comuneros.

- These dates do not appear in the documents
Sources: The author based on various sources specified in the text

The *fundo* Espíritu Santo under private ownership

During the period from the middle of the 1890s to approximately 1950, the dispute over Espíritu Santo appears to have been dormant. However, to put it in the words of Bengoa (1988:148):

> ... it is neither possible nor legitimate to think that because there is submission there is no contradiction. The acceptation of the subordination from the slave or the serf's side does neither eliminate the social contradiction, nor the consciousness of it.

After that, for a time, it stopped, resulting in the eviction of the *comuneros*, I had not realised from the *comuneros'* history that problems had arisen regarding the legal ownership of the *fundo*. For this reason, and as Table 8.2 (above) shows, the history of the *fundo* from 1895 to 1950 only reveals the frequent transfers between different private owners, mainly by purchase. In this respect, this part of the history of Espíritu Santo does not differ much from that of the examined *fundos* El Totoral, Puerto Oscuro and Las Palmas, which also were frequently sold. This can be compared, for example, with Tables 6.1, 6.2 and 6.3.

It is not known whether, from the *comuneros'* side, there have been new legal efforts to recover Espíritu Santo during the period between 1895-1950. The problem, however, remained latent, becoming manifest again when Cambisse became the owner of the *fundo*. The latency can be deduced from an application for the registration of the property title of Espíritu Santo, dated 1912. It specified that Toyos, the vendor, would take charge of any litigation, which arose in relation to the property. It shows that the parties involved in the transaction were aware of the legal problems that hung over the *fundo*. According to the previously mentioned record, the vendor bonded himself:

> to the indemnification conformed to the law and consequently whatever litigation regarding the property matter of the contract of sale, will be exclusively at the vendor's own risk, who will be affected by and responsible for the consequences of the lawsuit (Illapel's RP, 1912, no. 21, folio 9).

As Table 8.2 shows, J. D. Amenábar who bought the *fundo* in 1889 and with whom the conflict began kept the *fundo* under his control for a decade. In 1899, he sold it to L. and E. Lahaye. The *fundo* remained in the Lahaye's hands for less than three years, being sold in 1901 to J. Toyos. Toyos, a Spaniard living in Ovalle, in turn owned the *fundo* for 12 years. He had the owner's house built, which still exists today (O. Ollarzú, *Ibid*). In 1912 Toyos sold the *fundo* to F. Barrios, a native of Ovalle. In a document of 1922 it appears that in 1921, in Ovalle, the property of Barrios' widow was divided. One of her sons, M. Barrios Ugalde took over the Espíritu Santo *fundo* (Illapel's RP, 1922, no. 128, folio 69). However, in 1929, in another document 'H. Vicuña and other' appear as the owners of the *fundo* (Rol de Avalúos, Comuna de Mincha, Dirección General de Impuestos Internos, Sociedad Imprenta y Litografía Universo, Valparaíso, 1929:35). Judging by the fact that the *comuneros* of Espíritu Santo connect Barrios and Vicuña as co-owners of the *fundo*, I can understand that since the decade of the 1930s, H. Vicuña became, along with the Barrios family, co-owner of the *fundo*. From the surnames of the vendors that follow and because of the sales, which I discuss below, I can also deduce that the families were related.

In 1940 three owners, H. Vicuña Escobar, Gustavo Vicuña Barrios and Graciela Vicuña Barrios sold the *fundo* to five people (Illapel's RP, 1948, no. 228, folio 144). In 1945, L. A. Barrios Ugalde, whose surnames suggests that he was another of Francisco Barrios sons, sold his rights to Espíritu Santo to Graciella Vicuña Barrios (Real Estate Register of Illapel, 1948, no. 63, folio 42 verso). Judging from this fact, it is probable that Hermógenes Vicuña Escobar, Gustavo Vicuña Barrios and Graciella Vicuña Barrios, had only been the owners of part of Espíritu Santo. That was because Graciela Vicuña Barrios bought, after the sale of the *fundo* that took place in 1940, certain rights of the *fundo* from L. A. Barrios Ugalde, one of the sons of Francisco Barrios. However, this son is not mentioned in the document according to which his brother took over Espíritu Santo in 1921, due to the partition of the family's property. I am unaware of what happened to the part that Graciella Vicuña Barrios bought, as I could not figure out in the property list of the commune a holding, which could correspond to her part.

Three of the five who bought the *fundo*, L. Olavarría S., J. Cambisse F. and D. Daveggio, were merchants from Valparaíso. The other two buyers were a *comunero* and merchant from Canela Baja, M. Ollarzú and his son O. Ollarzú; the latter also being one of my informants. The price of the *fundo* was 500,000 *pesos*, of which each of the first three paid a quarter, the last quarter being paid by M. Ollarzú and his son. In 1948, M. and O. Ollarzú sold their quarter of the *fundo* to the other three owners with whom they had bought the property in 1940 (Illapel's RP, 1948, no. 229, folio 145). Eleven years later in 1959 (Illapel's RP, 1959, no. 125, folio 91) Ollavarría and Daveggio sold their respective parts to Cambisse, the third owner. With this purchase, Cambisse, originally from Italy, became the sole and final owner of the *fundo* until 1972 (O. Ollarzú, *Ibid*).

The resurgence of the conflict

Sixty years after the end of the conflict with Amenábar and with Olavarría, Daveggio and Cambisse as co-owners of Espíritu Santo, the 1950s saw the reactivation of the conflict between the owners of the *fundo* and the peasants. I ignore what actually happened during the approximate period of between 1890 and 1950. According to the *comuneros'* accounts most of the owners of the *fundo* rented it to stock farmers who, in their turn, rented the land to them. Thus, the owners of the *fundo* were not only absentee landlords, but did not even bother exploiting the land via managers.

It is possible that the explanation for this phenomenon can be found in the latent legal problem over the ownership of the *fundo*. The owners avoided the possibility of coming into direct contact with the peasants by reducing land exploitation to pasture by leasing it to someone, who in their turn rented it to the peasants. If there was a problem, the peasants had to deal with the leaseholder, who could then plead that he was not the owner. In this way, the leaseholders served the owners as a 'containing wall' to the demands of the peasants. While having them as sub-tenants the owner of the *fundo* also avoided having to pay Social Security for them.

Within this context, perhaps it is not surprising that Cambisse who, unlike the previous owners lived on the *fundo* and took charge of it personally, entered into a dispute with the peasants. The situation became very similar to that of Amenábar, who although apparently never living in the *fundo*, started to have problems with the *comuneros* when he took effective possession of the *fundo*.

Judging from the information received form the *comuneros*, I can deduce, however, that the struggle they started then, at least during the 1950s and 1960s, was not directly over the legal ownership of Espíritu Santo, but about the exploitation they suffered under Cambisse. As Castillo

The Agricultural Community Canela Baja

from Espíritu Santo, told me, the problems with Cambisse began because of the difficult situation in which they lived:

> Cambisse charged us too much /.../ we were working only for him and we didn't have the means to run our homes. The fight sprang from there although it didn't only come from there /.../ it had many passages this struggle, it was a long struggle, but as I said a short time back, when 1954 came, I was returning from the María Elena [Saltpetre worker office of Region II] industries, with enough fighting spirit, because there one learns these things amongst the heat of the workers /.../ so I, seeing that there was a lack of organisation here, joined with them and we eliminated some of the vices that stopped us from uniting. Then we began the struggle and we refused to give the accounts. For example they assembled us in September to collect the animals that were in good condition /.../ well the gentleman took the animals to Valparaíso by truck and in that way Mr. Juan Cambisse, R.I.P. made a lot of money. When we saw this, we began to step up the struggle, we united more, and between the years 62 to 64, we carried on the struggle without respite, and we refused to pay him because we had acquired information about the fact that the land had been seized /.../ therefore it was an insult to the community. I investigated in some books about when it was and found out that it happened in 1890 with the Amenábars. From this we became certain that the land had been seized, and I should emphasise that we suffered many reprisals from the Mr. who said he was the owner of the land (G. Castillo, *Ibid*).

According to the same *comunero*, the matter reached the Illapel Court:

> I remember that once when we were taken with notification to the Illapel Court and I was representing my father and Mr. Cambisse had a lawyer /.../ and we were three peasants /.../ the other two that accompanied me had very little experience in defending themselves in court, but I had gained some knowledge of this and I made them [the Court] see our poverty because they told us that we grew a lot, and we filled our storerooms with cereals, wheat and other things and that we did not pay because we did not want to. I said, Your Excellency, I ask the court to send a commission and we will open our doors wide open for them to see the wealth we have according to Mr. Cambisse... (*Ibid*).

Not all the peasants refused to pay. Those that did were according to Castillo, the majority:

...of course there were other people that as always followed the patron, that did not bend themselves and said that Mr. Juan Cambisse is the owner and must be paid, for the simple reason that ignorance must be that /.../ in the end /.../ there always remained about 8 people who never stopped paying him (*Ibid*).

Along with other *comuneros*, Castillo remembers that Cambisse:

... had a grocery and a mill /.../ we grind wheat into flour but the mill was not good enough to grind flour fit for a human being and he also had the habit of putting in impurities and only being there one or two days a week (*Ibid*).

Cambisse also had, in addition to the grocery, a liquor store. He transported the merchandise from Ovalle to his property by truck along a road he made through the Las Palmas *fundo* with the help of the peasants.

Several *comuneros* from Espíritu Santo remember that Cambisse, unlike the previous owners of the *fundo*, who rented it and lived in Ovalle, lived on the *fundo* and personally managed it. This is confirmed by Castillo, who reported that Cambisse had also a house in Valparaíso (the present capital of Region V):

... but /.../ his residence was here /.../ in reality Mr. Cambisse was attached to the land and he cared more as he had earned so many pesos from us, one cares for where one earns money, but he earned it by exploiting us, not by legal means (*Ibid*).

While Castillo emphasised that the people who worked and lived on the *fundo* were not *inquilinos* but tenants, which meant that Cambisse had not to pay Social Security for them, some other *comuneros*, however, referred to themselves under that time as *inquilinos*. Considering that various *comuneros* pointed out that Vicuña and other owners of the *fundo* before Cambisse used the same system of exploitation as Cambisse, I can assume that the peasants were tenants under Cambisse and subtenants under the landowners before him. The difference being that the owners before Cambisse rented out the *fundo* through intermediaries, who in turn rented the land to the peasants, while Cambisse did it directly.

The *comuneros* paid for the land that they used, for the pasture of their animals and for the houses they lived in, many of them dating from the previous century and constructed by their ancestors. The payment for the pasture was by livestock, and varied according to the type of animal. It was greatest in the case of cattle, horses and mules and least in that of sheep (15%) and goats (10%).

By the characteristics of the system of exploitation that Cambisse used, although the peasants were tenants they nevertheless undertook some tasks, which were normal for *inquilinos* of the *fundos*. For example, they, or one of the members of their family had, in addition to the payments due as a tenant, to work 15 days per year on the *fundo* when the owner required it. If the peasant did not have the disposable labour to work the 15 days per year, he could pay someone to take his place. In this sense I could say that a peasant of Espíritu Santo did not differ very much from an *inquilino* but for one exception.

The Social Security (CIDA, 1966:6) consider *inquilinos* to be those agrarian workers to whom the patron gives an adequate house for them and their families, a piece of land, pasture for the animals, etc. and who, in return, are obliged to work in the *hacienda* or to send somebody else in their place (see Chapter 4). For Gómez *et al* (1981:34), the *inquilino* belongs to the group of peasants that have access to productive resources and has a double role, according to which:

> on one hand, is an entrepeneur of its own productive royalities and by the other, receives part of the salary in money and another in consumption royatities.

In this last sense, the peasants of Espíritu Santo would differ from an *inquilino* in that they did not earn a salary. This difference defines them more as tenants than *inquilinos* since they, on the contrary, had to pay the patron of the *fundo* in order to gain access to their productive resources. In other words they were, in comparison with the *inquilinos*, doubly exploited.

The end of the conflict and the recuperation of Espíritu Santo

Although the *comuneros*' struggle during the 1950s and the 1960s was over their exploitation by Cambisse, the problem of the legality of ownership of the *fundo* seems to underlay the claims the *comuneros* made to him. During the 1970s this problem again changed into a new attempt to recover the *fundo,* the new struggle activating the old one. The recuperation of the *fundo* was finally achieved during Allende's government and ratified under Pinochet. Although the process of legal recognition of the agricultural communities had started in a slow and staggering manner during the 1960s, the 'phantom of communism' of Allende's socialist coalition government during that period should have put wind in the sails of the *comuneros* aspirations for recovering the *fundo*.

According to Castillo, in 1970 in co-operation with E. Cortés, a *comunero* from the Canela Baja sub-area and then President of the *Junta* of *Comuneros*:

> ... then we passed on the fundo to Bienes Nacionales [National Estates] and so we won. It was Bienes Nacionales that decided that the land should go to the community after a summons with the Illapel Judge. They gave Mr. Cambisse a time limit to present his documents to the court and he had nothing to present, except on the last day when he came but without any legal documents (G. Castillo, *Ibid*).

The problems with Cambisse did not end when the *fundo* was transferred back to the community. Cortés, who at the time worked as the head of a squad of 42 people from the Road Service (Vialidad) on the construction of a road in the Espíritu Santo sub-area, told me that in 1972 a large group of people became organised. They took an excavator from Road Service and opened the gate where Cambisse still collected the toll from the *comuneros* for taking their livestock to Los Corrales, a part of the Espíritu Santo sub-area.

According to Cortés, the original route in agreement with the plans of Road Service would go through the northern part of the river Espíritu Santo to avoid passing through Cambisse's property (E. Cortés, oral interview, 7 March 1988). They built the road as far as the school of Los Corrales, passing instead right in front of the *fundo* owner's house. Cambisse called out the police from Canela Baja who threatened to shoot, but did not. The road was built in one month and people worked voluntarily, including women and children, alongside the workers from Road Service.

Apparently the coup of 1973 interrupted, although only temporarily, the legal negotiations over the transfer of the *fundo* to the community. According to Muñoz who, because of the coup, was dismissed from his post as Mayor and also to Cortés, who was imprisoned for a short time:

The Agricultural Community Canela Baja

... when we were almost there, that is close to recovering everything that had been stolen from the community, along came the Coup d'état and we couldn't do anything more, but then as we had already given notice, the [new] authorities knew all this.

When Muñoz says '... close to recovering everything that had been stolen...' he is referring to the land that El Totoral, Las Palmas and Puerto Oscuro had, according to the community, taken from them. Only Puerto Oscuro did not give back any part (J. Muñoz, *Ibid*).

Finally, in 1974, during the Pinochet regime with the indemnification of the community, the land of Cambisse's *fundo* was, after its expropriation, integrated into the agricultural community Canela Baja. According to Castillo:

... in the year 1974 the titles were handed over, the indemnification of the community, I remember it was in the community of Monte Patria, on Gabriella Mistral's birth place, they [the authorities] handed over 52 legal [community recognition] titles to the communities (G. Castillo, *Ibid*).

It is important not to confuse this expropriation with those performed by CORA up to the coup d'état of 1973, as a result of the agrarian reform. This expropriation came via mediation by the Office of BN, after it was proved that Espíritu Santo's land historically belonged to Canela Baja.

The re-incorporation of Espíritu Santo into the community was not free of problems. According to P. Velázques, the lawyer of BN of Ovalle, at the moment of the indemnification of the agricultural community Canela Baja, a large number of Espíritu Santo's *comuneros* wanted to set up a separate community (P. Velázques, oral interview, 1 March 1988). The Office of BN was against this idea, which was also strongly opposed by the *comuneros* of Canela Baja, some of them having also participated in the struggle.

Of the two sons of Cambisse, who were left with 2,000 ha, according to information received from the *comuneros*, one lives in Valparaíso and the other in the USA. Although absentee owners, the sons of Cambisse are in fact *comuneros*. In the agricultural community Canela Baja's own list of *comuneros*, there still appears the name of J. Cambisse, now deceased, as a *comunero*. This list was used in the official list when the indemnification of the community's property title started. From this I can assume that neither of his sons has, as yet, bothered to register the property in his name.

Although this property, or *hijuela*, is part of the agricultural community Canela Baja, both in the property list of CIREN from 1983, and the Internal Tax payments list, still figures as a *fundo* (CIREN, 1983:242, Número de avalúo 222-10). It appears still with 10,000 ha in the name of the deceased, J. Cambisse.

A watchman now occupies the *fundo's* house. He told me that he did not receive a salary for his services, though that is what the sons of Cambisse had promised, but he cultivated part of the land in lieu of payment. Another *comunero* of the sub-area, who also worked a part of the land as co-partner, claimed to have been entrusted with looking after the fences.

Some 8,000 ha of land, including 125 peasants, were returned from Espíritu Santo to the community, according to the *comunero* P. Carvajal (P. Carvajal, *comunero* from the sub-area Canela Baja, co-owner of the present *fundo* Puerto Oscuro, several oral interviews between 1988-1990). With the indemnification of the community in 1974, El Totoral and Las Palmas *fundo*s also returned some land to the agricultural community Canela Baja: 2,500-3,000 ha and 3 peasants from El Totoral and some 200 ha with 25 other peasants from Las Palmas. During the early 1970s, before all these returns including that of Espíritu Santo, the agricultural community Canela Baja must have had some 18-19,000 ha with some 515 *comuneros*. With the integration of all these new lands and peasants, the area of the agricultural community Canela Baja rose to 30,700 ha with 668 *comuneros*. This area agrees quite well with my estimation for the *estancia* Canela Baja of Pedro Cortés Castillo at around 1740 (see Chapter 7).

According to CIDA (1966:130) in 1963 the community had only 6,095 ha and 335 *comuneros*. This low figure does not correspond to my appraisals for that time. Indeed, CIDA emphasises that its data are highly uncertain due to the scarce knowledge existing in the 1960s about the communities of Norte Chico. Besides which, all data must be accepted with caution because even actual data, supposedly more reliable, does not coincide if one compares diverse official sources. According to Cañón (1964:27), in 1964 the community had 11,600 ha. It seems clear that the community could not have had, as pointed out by CIDA, only 6,095 ha in the 1960s. In that case, with the new land (10-11,000 ha.) that was returned to it, the community should now have approximately 20,000 ha and not the 30,700 ha that it has today.

The Agricultural Community Canela Baja

Considering that the new integrated land, not including that of Espíritu Santo, corresponds to the modification of the borders of the *fundos* El Totoral and Las Palmas and that the borders with the neighbouring communities have not, according to my knowledge, been modified, the difference of ca. 10,000 ha must come from the land the community had before its legal indemnification.

Summary

The history of the Espíritu Santo *fundo* can be divided into two parts: that which refers to the *fundo* while it was in the hands of different private owners, and that which refers to the *comuneros*' struggle to recover the land of the *fundo*.

In respect of the first part, it shows that during the time that the *fundo* was in private hands, it was frequently transferred between different owners, usually by sale. With the exception of those part owners of the *fundo* from Canela Baja, the others were all from outside the community, the majority of them from Ovalle, as were the first owners. The partial owners from Canela Baja, the Ollarzú, correspond to the then wealthiest family, not originally from the community, as the first Ollarzú arrived to the zone at the second half of the nineteenth century.

During over a hundred years, the *fundo* changed hands 7 times, from 1853, when Guerrero illegally sold Espíritu Santo to Ossa, until 1940, the date when the Society of Valparaíso and Canela Baja bought it. This does not include the sale by the Ollarzús to the other three owners and then by Olavarría and Daveggio of their respective parts to Cambisse in 1959. Including these, and without counting the first illegal sale from Guerrero to Ossa, during 75 years (between 1884 and 1959), the *fundo* underwent ten commercial transactions. Of all the owners, only Ossa and Barrios left the *fundo* to their descendants who later sold it. Cambisse's sons were also left the part that BN gave to Cambisse after the expropriation.

The constant transfers that the *fundo* underwent while being in private hands shows that for many of its owners, the *fundo* was a source of rent within a letting system and an object of commercial transaction. That is in opposition to a means of agro-pastoral production. In this way, the *fundo* Espíritu Santo does not differ much from the cases of the *fundos* El Totoral, Las Palmas and Puerto Oscuro that I have analysed.

As for the history of the *comuneros*' struggle for the land of the Espíritu Santo, it shows that even if the conflict remained dormant for a long time, finally, after more than 100 years, justice was done due to the strong fighting spirit of at least part of the *comuneros*. As a result of this, through the intervention of the Office of BN on behalf of the agricultural community Canela Baja, the conflict ended with the recovery of the *fundo* from the hands of private landowners and its reincorporating into the community.

It seems important to me to highlight a relevant aspect in the *comuneros*' struggle, which began in the 1950s. It is partially deduced from the reports of those that took an active part in the fight. It concerns the importance it has in the personal history of some of the protagonists, their experiences as workers in the nitrate fields and copper mines in the north of Chile, and their obvious political leanings to the left. This is particularly clear in Castillo's story which relates that after returning from the north of Chile to Espíritu Santo in the 1950s, they organised the struggle against Cambisse using his experience as nitrate worker:

> ... I was returning from the María Elena [Saltpetre worker office of Region II] industries, with enough fighting spirit, because there one learns these things amongst the heat of the workers /.../ so I, seeing that there was a lack of organisation here, joined with them and we eliminated some of the vices that stopped us from uniting (G. Castillo, *Ibid*).

This relationship between a clear left-wing tendency and the experiences acquired by the emigration of the *comuneros* to the north of Chile is also evident in the case of Muñoz. He told me, emotionally, that as a child in the nitrate fields, he had known L. E. Recabarren, the forerunner of Chilean socialism. From the end of the nineteenth century, the migration in the community goes, traditionally, to the copper mine of Chuquicamata and to the saltpetre mines which are mostly located in Region II of Antofagasta, at a distance of more than 1,000 km. from Canela Baja. Similar to Castillo and Muñoz, Cortés also had experience as a worker in the nitrate fields and in the copper mines of Chuquicamata. All of these people are still active, both in politics and in the organisation of the community. Cortés was in 1988 President of the *comuneros'* Junta, for the second time. It is not a coincidence that Cortés was elected by the *comuneros* as President of the Junta just at the time of Allende's government and again in 1988, the year when Pinochet's regime started its downfall.

The Agricultural Community Canela Baja

The left-wing political tendency is not only common to the *comuneros,* who had a leading role in the struggle to recover Espíritu Santo, but also among many of the *comuneros* of this sub-area. According to my survey (1988), this sub-area has the second highest representation of the left (31%) in the community. Simultaneously, according to the same survey, some 50% of those surveyed in this sub-area had emigrated at one time or another.

The 31% of left-wing representation in Espíritu Santo and other sub-areas should however be higher than that. The survey was done some months before the Plebiscite of 1988 by which Pinochet intended to stay as the head of the country. In the survey, a third of those surveyed preferred to declare as independent, probably due to the uncertain political situation and former repression.

Regarding the period prior Pinochet, according to the *comunero* P. Carvajal, in the 1973 election of the Mayor of the Commune the communist and socialist parties had 61.8% of the total of 2,065 votes with 46.4% and 15.4%, respectively. The previously mentioned J. Muñoz was elected. In the same year in the election of senators, the *Unidad Popular*, which represented Allende's supporting coalition, obtained 66.1% of the total of 3,610 votes in the Commune. Excluding Mincha as an electoral district and taking only Canela, the *Unidad Popular* obtained 68.1% (sic!) of the total of 2,298 votes (Registros Electorales, Senadores, 1973:11-12).

Already in democracy, and after 25 years of dictatorship, in the communal election of Mayor in June 1992, a candidate of the Communist Party, Norman Araya, got the first place with 1,000 votes, followed by a candidate of the Christian Democratic Party, Héctor Jorquera, with 705 votes. Because of the process of election of Mayors left by Pinochet, in spite of the difference in votes, both candidates have equal support of the six elected Municipal counsellors (three each), forcing them to divide the post as Mayor, two years each (MC, 1992). Araya was the only elected communist Mayor in the country.

In the last Mayoral communal election in October 1996, the Communist Party got 42.9% of the votes, followed by an *ad hoc* created coalition called Independientes Progresistas with 21% (Information from La Moneda (Government House) via Internet source http://www. elecciones96.cl /cgi-reporte/conscomuna. 04/25/97. Reporte por Partidos). Norman Araya, the Communist Party candidate was thus, elected once again, this time with 1,997 votes of a total of 4,912, whereof 48.9% men and 51.1% women (Information from La Moneda (Government House) via Internet source, http://www.elecciones96.cl/cgi-reporte/conscomuna. 04/25/97: Reporte por Candidatos). Together with the Socialist Party (9.9%), the Communist Party took 52.8% of the votes.

The relationship between the political tendencies of the *comuneros* and emigration is also reflected by the fact that in Espíritu Santo are to be found the few unions that exist, not only in the community, but in the Commune. According to information gathered amongst the *comuneros* of the sub-area Espíritu Santo there are two organised unions; 'El Amanecer' (The Dawn) in Los Corrales with 30 members, and 'Buena Esperanza' (Good Hope) in Alhuemilla. At the time of the survey two more unions were getting together: 'Nuevo Porvenir' (New Future) and 'Nuevo Amanecer' (New Dawn). The other organised union, 'Flor de Mayo' (May Flower), to be found in the community Canela Baja is in the Poza Honda sub-area and has 25 members.

All these unions go under the name *Sindicato de Trabajadores Agrícolas Independientes* (Union of Independent Agricultural Workers) (Nómina de Organizaciones Comunitarias, Secretaría Municipal, Comuna de Canela, September 1992). They play more of a role as a pressure group than negotiation, directed to the government as they are not employees, but consider themselves, although poor, as free peasants, i.e., they are their own bosses.

All these events, the struggle for the *fundo*, the way it came about, the leftist political tendencies, the organisation of unions and, no less important, the myths, have given the *comuneros* of Espíritu Santo the reputation of being 'bad people' (that is communists), 'people who have knives and guns', as a *comunera* from Canela Baja described them.

9 Fundos and Communities Ending the 1900s

This chapter is divided into two sub-chapters; one local, specific to the *fundo* Puerto Oscuro and one, more general about the legal recognition of the agricultural communities. Although each sub-chapter deals with one process, they will have common ground, i.e., of being the indirect product of the changes initiated by the agrarian reform in Chile as from the 1960s. While the first describes the progression of Puerto Oscuro from a private property into mainly *comunero* hands, the second refers to the agricultural communities' difficult progress into legality. In reconstructing these two minor processes, I will be bringing up-to-date the history of both the former *hacienda* El Totoral and of the communities, both initiated during the 1700s.

The present-day *fundo* Puerto Oscuro

Introduction

The history of El Totoral shows, retrospectively, several facets of the changes that have affected private land ownership during the last decades, which will be focussed upon in this chapter. Of the three rural landed properties *(fundos)* that resulted from the subdivision of the *hacienda* El Totoral at the end of the nineteenth century (El Totoral, Las Palmas and Puerto Oscuro), I have chosen to follow the later course (post Allende) of the *fundo* Puerto Oscuro, or Society Pereira, Cortés, Brito and Co. Ltd. (see Chapter 6).

Due to the changes arising from the agrarian reforms of the early 1970s and the new agricultural policies after 1973, through the application of Friedman's economics, perhaps as an unintended consequence, the *fundo* Puerto Oscuro was acquired by a group of people, mainly composed of *comuneros* from the Canela Baja community. This way the *fundo* came to represent, once again, private property under a new form of ownership.

This 'new' legal form of ownership, called *Sociedades limitadas de secano* (Limited dry-land societies) (Rivera, 1988(a):227) are organised formally as limited societies which, in fact, is not new as a legal form. It is new, however, for the *fundos*.

The organisation of the *fundo* resembles, in some aspects, the agricultural communities, as it is a shared property intended to be maintained as an undivided land unit, which is the property of multiple owners who, as other societies of limited responsibility, are organised formally by a system of shares. I would suggest that the commonality, or keeping the property as one undivided unit on a permanent basis as a way of organising the *fundo*, reveals the material conditions on which these rural properties exist as the main reason for that. This is the semi-mountainous non-irrigated land, which if divided into *minifundium* would be uneconomic. Commonality appears here as the best management solution for the resource, i.e., as a way of avoiding the *fundo* falling apart into many small properties.

Predominantly owned by *comuneros* today, who themselves had long considered that a part of the *fundo* historically belonged to the community, it is perhaps not wrong to think that the agricultural communities with their long tradition has in some way transplanted part of its characteristics to former *fundo* land. Until the agrarian reform, this represented the traditional *latifundium's* private ownership, whose main characteristic was the monopoly over land.

Certainly, the way the new owners of the *fundo* have organised the society, has been possible not only because the law allowed the formation of these societies of limited responsibility, but also indirectly, because at the same time, semi-communal land ownership as a form has been legally recognised. In this way the *comuneros*, being aware that their own organisation has become legalised, have won strength to undertake new compromises.

However, there are also differences regarding the organisation, at least in theory, of the *fundo* that remains more a corporation than a co-operative (Stevenson, 1991:43; see also Chapter 10). Whereas the former remains more of a modern enterprise, the latter better corresponds to the spirit of the agricultural communities. Nonetheless, if the communities influence the *fundo*, this could also influence the communities, especially regarding the exploitation of the land.

Fundos and Communities Ending the 1900s

How Puerto Oscuro came into the peasants' hands

The part of the expropriated ex-*fundo* Puerto Oscuro, which after the dissolution of the *asentamiento* passed during Pinochet's government to CONAF in 1978, was sold off by this institution in 1979. With the auction of the expropriated lands on the part of the State through CONAF, the *comuneros* of the area had for the first time, although in instalments and under mortgage, access to purchase. Up to the agrarian reform, the lands of the *fundos* were principally the monopoly of private landowners. During the agrarian reform, which distributed the expropriated land to landless peasants in the first instance, the *comuneros* remained excluded from this process.

When CONAF sold off Puerto Oscuro in 1979, it was acquired by a group of 86 members native to the commune, the majority of them being *comuneros* from the agricultural community Canela Baja. Among them there were also some nine ex-*inquilinos* of the expropriated *fundo* (Desiderio Collao, recorded interview, 4 March 1988). Collao (deceased) was an ex-*inquilino* of the *fundo*, a member of the present and also a *comunero* of the agricultural community Canela Baja).

Although the property continued to be known, even in official documents as Puerto Oscuro, its legal name after this purchase became, in accordance with the names of some of the society's members, the Society Pereira, Cortés, Brito and Co. Ltd.

With respect to how the idea of buying the *fundo* by the *comuneros* came about and how it was organised, Joel Muñoz, a *comunero* from the agricultural community Canela Baja and a present day member of the *fundo*, tells us that:

> the idea to buy the fundo came from extensive meetings of the comuneros where it was said that as we had already got back Espíritu Santo and [part of] Las Palmas, we should try to buy Puerto Oscuro /.../ The idea came from the fact that the comuneros considered that all the water streams from the ravines that fell to this side [of La Canela's river] belonged to the community... (Recorded interview, 22 May 1988. Muñoz was the Mayor of the Commune until the coup of 1973).

Muñoz highlights two fundamental points of dispute here that have always been present in the struggle between the *fundos* and the agricultural communities; those of land and water.

The *comuneros* were awarded the *fundo* for the sum of 10,600,000 Chilean *pesos* ($), equivalent to 16,554 *Unidades de Fomento* (UF) at $640 per UF (Fórmula Solicitud de Resciliación Parcial de Contrato, Piñeiro and Ruíz-Tagle, 1985, Estudio Jurídico, Santiago, Courtesy of Pedro Carvajal). The members paid one tenth of the price in cash at the time of purchase, the remainder being mortgaged with CONAF.

CONAF, which had acquired the *fundo* from CORA for $213,244 (the equivalent of 443 UF at $481 per UF), sold the *fundo* only one year later at a much higher price than it had paid for it. According to Muñoz, the property went up in price at the time of sale:

> ... in the sale there were four interested persons, but only one fought; because of this the price went up, one interested party, who had the information because he had been shown around on the land and he knew that it was good, began to bid until it got to $10,500,000. He didn't make another bid and we ended up [with the *fundo*] /.../ It was organised by shares, whoever was interested and had money joined /.../ taking one share was not accepted, only two or more shares were allowed /.../ not every body had money /.../ others took more, 4, 5, 8 and up to 17 shares... (Joel Muñoz, *Ibid*).

In the same way as other *fundos* of the commune, which were sold off, the *fundo* Puerto Oscuro was organised through the system of shares, which in total reached 280. These were distributed individually at the time of sale in accordance with the economic capacity of each member. The 86 members of the *fundo* at the beginning (1979) had been reduced by 29% (25) by 1989. Various members were not able to afford the payments in UF of their respective shares. The value of the UF, which is adjusted daily in relation to the IPC (Retail Price Index), had risen from $640 in 1979 to $6,427 on 9 October 1990. This indicates that during these 11 years the rise in the value of the UF was about 1000%.

The 48 shares of the 25 members, who had withdrawn had been commonly absorbed by the society. The remaining 61 members own 232 shares out of the total of 280. Of these 232 shares, 25% (58) are owned by 6.5% (4) of the members (Nómina de socios que subscribieron la escritura de sociedad Fundo Puerto Oscuro, 24 de Mayo de 1987. Courtesy of Pedro Carvajal). These four members have at least 12 shares, none more than 18 shares.

The 48 shares that have become the economic responsibility of the society as a whole are paid for, principally, out of the rent of grazing rights for livestock (cattle and equines) that the *fundo* sells. According to Pedro Carvajal, another member of the *fundo* and also a *comunero* of the community, in 1988 the *fundo* had some 540 cattle that paid for grazing rights, as well as 130 cattle of its own. By belonging to the society the members had the right to pasture only six big animals (cattle and equines). If a member had more than this he had to pay, at market rates, 1,000 *pesos* monthly for each extra animal, the same being valid for non-members of the *fundo*.

During ten years (1979-1989), the *fundo* functioned as a system of individual exploitation. According to the ex-manager of the *fundo*, Carlos Rocco, during this time approximately 30% of the members individually contracted between 30 and 40 temporary workers to bring in the harvest. Some 40% of the members worked the land themselves and some 30% used the system of sharecropping.

After 1989, the members of the *fundo* began to substitute the individual management of the land with a system of exploitation as a society oriented principally to the raising of livestock. With this purpose the members of the *fundo* put forward with the help of agricultural experts, an ambitious plan for the development and exploitation of the *fundo*.

Taking into account, that the area of the *fundo*, on the one hand, consists mainly of non-irrigated land, and, considering, on the other, the ecological history of the *fundo*, the said plan considers associated cattle-breeding as the ideal exploitation for this land. It has the advantage of permitting the rotation of lands for pasture, which would permit, in its turn, the re-afforestation of the eroded fields. The society proposed profound changes in the future system of exploitation with the aim of achieving the following objectives:

- maintain and improve the existing natural resources;
- create an agricultural enterprise for raising and fattening of Hereford cattle as they are the most appropriate for a property with semi-desert characteristics, gradually replacing the wheat sowing with permanent or semi-permanent meadows in order to continue to increase the livestock;

- change the system of individual exploitation to a joint system of management in which the interests of the group are given precedence over individual interests;
- establish a system of rational management and of adequate investments for the signalled objectives (Plan de desarrollo y Explotación del Predio 'Puerto Oscuro', courtesy of Carlos Rocco).

With respect to the exploitation of livestock it was hoped, according to the plan, that by 1997 there will be 1,498 head of cattle. The initial investment of the first purchase of 200 cows and 4 Hereford bulls was estimated in 1988 at 21 million *pesos*. For the future financing of the project it was recommended that credit from the Banco del Desarrollo (Development Bank) be used (Ibid). According to conversations with some members of the *fundo*, in 1989 they had been able to increase the number of cattle from 130 (in 1988) to 200.

With reference to forestation, according to the document, the society made an agreement with CONAF. By 1987, they had forested 2,048 ha with *Atriplex Nummularia* and 50 ha with *Atriplex Repanda* (both Australian species), with 698 ha remaining to be forested, according to the prevailing agreement for the years 1988 and 1989. There is also an agreement with CONAF for some sowing and small fruit and forestry plantations.

It should be pointed out that CONAF is the organisation that subsidises forestation of land in the country through bonuses established in DFL 710, accomplishing in this way one of the functions for which it originally was set up. Paradoxically, and as the members of the *fundo* recognised, by reducing the costs of forestation subsidised by CONAF, they have been able to pay part off the debt owed to CONAF with money that CONAF has given to the forestation of the *fundo*. Although I was not told how the costs of forestation were reduced, it is not difficult to understand that it was by paying poor salaries to the forestry workers, composed of labour from the community, principally the landless children of *comuneros*.

In spite of the advances achieved up to 1989 in the number of cattle and in forestation, the situation for the members of the *fundo* has nevertheless, become worse, threatening the future of the enterprise. There are three factors, which contributed to this situation. Firstly, the purchase of the *fundo* using the system of UF and its payments until 1991 meant a gradual individual impoverishment for the members of the *fundo*. To this can be added the difficult climatic conditions of 1985-1987 (see Chapter 3), which made it even more difficult to gather the economic means to pay the debt. Secondly, the society still had to pay $34 millions in UF. Thirdly, and no less important, the access to credit from the Banco del Desarrollo, recommended by the plan to buy cattle in 1997, was not possible while CONAF would not agree to lift the mortgage which weighed so heavily on the *fundo*, something it did not do until 1989.

As a result of part of the described situation, in 1985 the society appealed to CONAF for a partial annulment of the contract, pointing out that after this date they would find it impossible to keep on paying the dues. As reasons for partially annulling the contract, they argued, firstly, that the *fundo* was bought for three times CONAF's valuation of it. That is that while CONAF considered the minimum price for the auction of the *fundo* to be 3,220,000 Chilean pesos ($), the equivalent of 5,028 UF, the members paid $10,600,000 (Fórmula Solicitud de Resciliación Parcial...).

They declared that by May 1985 they had paid $27,565,192, with another $34,275,314 remaining to be paid, a total of $61,840,506, not counting the adjustable amount corresponding to the 5 following years in which they must pay the remaining $34 million. They argued that, according to an actual valuation that they had undertaken for application to CONAF, the commercial value of the *fundo* in May 1985 was only $17 million or 6,390 UF (at $2,660 per UF). Having already paid $27 million by this date, they declared that the society had paid a sum of some $10 million in excess of the total commercial value of the *fundo*.

They also pointed out that the 1990 valuation of the *fundo* for the Internal Tax Service (SII) was only $9,438,351 (Certificado de Avalúo 54, Illapel, 9 de Febrero de 1990. Courtesy of lawyer Hector Piñeiro Cuevas). They maintained, moreover, that the *fundo* was sold by CORA to CONAF in a way that was at odds with the arrangements considered legally valid for the transfer of the lands of the Agrarian Reform to the peasants (Fórmula Solicitud de Resciliación Parcial...). As they indicated in a later document, CORA transferred the *fundo* to CONAF:

> ... disregarding the peasants working on the land, and all option to purchase it in accordance with the process of agrarian reform to which the fundo was expropriated (Carta a su Excelencia, El Presidente de la República Patricio

Aylwin de Héctor E. Piñeiro Cuevas, abogado, representando a la Sociedad Pereira, Cortés, Brito y Compañia, 4 de Octubre de 1990).

Supported by these facts, they stated that the property was paid for, with a favourable balance to the society. Because of this, they asked CONAF to modify the price, establishing an amount of 11,237 UF, already paid by the society, and that:

> ... the said obligation should be considered as paid and therefore the mortgage should be lifted along with the prohibition to encumber and sell which weigh on the fundo and that was established in favour of CONAF... (Fórmula Solicitud de Resciliación Parcial...).

CONAF on its part offered, as a solution to the society, to re-negotiate the debt. The society would keep less than half of the property, while they would keep the rest, a solution, which the society did not accept. On the 3rd November 1986, however, the contract with CONAF was modified, with the declared aim of making it easier for the society to service the debt. The society promised to pay CONAF, a balance of 5,928 UF at a fixed annual interest rate of 2%, replacing the previous compound rate of 8%. The said total would be paid in 10 equal, successive, annual shares of 660 UF, including the 2% interest between the years, 1987 and 1996. The society fulfilled its payments for the first three years but was incapable of carrying on paying due to difficulties derived from drought.

Hopeful of the new political situation in the country, the society again appealed to CONAF in 1990 as well as the new President of the Republic, Patricio Aylwin (Carta a su Excelencia, El Presidente...), for the debt to be written off, something which they did not achieve. In 1992 the society again sought improved conditions asking that CONAF reduce the debt by 50% with the promise that they would pay the remainder in cash on the 30th June 1992. CONAF accepted the agreement, previously accepted by the Ministry of Agriculture that was in favour of the agreement. The rest of the debt was established as 2,478 UF or something more than $21 million. Two thousand UF or $17,012,420 had already been paid by the society in May of the same year.

On the 30th June the other 478 UF or $4,165,317 was cancelled. With this CONAF lifted the mortgage along with the prohibition to encumber and sell which the *fundo* had since 1979 (Repertorio 217, Escritura de Modificación de Contrato de Compra-venta. Cancelación

Alzamiento de CONAF a la Sociedad Pereira, Cortés, Brito y Compañia, Santiago 30 de Junio, 1992:1-4, Notaría de Santiago, R. Galecio G.). The society finally became the sole owner of the *fundo* although at the cost of considerable sacrifice. The total price paid for the *fundo* was more than 60 million *pesos* although the purchasing price was only 10 million.

Report of the 90s

Notwithstanding the serious difficulties, the society of the *fundo* Puerto Oscuro had in reaching the final 1992 agreement with CONAF, freeing the *fundo* from mortgage and obligations, its short history demonstrates the serious intentions that the new owners had with respect to the *fundo* and its exploitation.

The new owners not only organised themselves in order to acquire the *fundo*, but they also did so in order to defend their interests before CONAF, for which they hired a lawyer. No less important was the organisation concerning the exploitation plans of the *fundo*, for which they contracted not only a technical agriculturist as manager, but also agricultural experts who drew up the development plan. Apart from the onerous total price which was finally paid for the *fundo*, the high costs of contracting experts shows that perhaps for the first time in the *fundo's* history, efforts are being made to make it function as a modern cattle enterprise with rational management and concrete objectives.

In theory, if it succeeds in the long term, this enterprise could be an example worthy of being emulated by the agricultural communities of the area. Except for a greater erosion of their lands, the endowment of natural resources of the majority of the agricultural communities of the commune do not vary considerably from that of the *fundo* Puerto Oscuro. In their favour is the fact that they already owned their lands. This prevented the need for onerous borrowing, which, through the system of UF has resulted in many peasants loosing their land in the country.

To establish a system of joint exploitation within the agricultural communities, however, it will be necessary for the *comuneros* to abandon the long and deep-rooted practise of individual exploitation, for which they are characterised. Again in theory, the fact that many *comuneros* are at the same time members of the *fundo* should contribute, providing that the *fundo* brings economic success - to a gradual change in the mentality of the *comuneros*. It would bring forth a substitution of the present individual exploitation of the land for a more rational and joint exploitation. This would be a step forward which should contribute to raising the prevailing standard of living in the agricultural communities, above all because a unified organisation should be able to obtain loans for any future development plan, something which is difficult for individuals.

I have said, however, in theory. The reality is usually different, above all when dealing with the struggle for land, which as a resource is limited. My visit in 1992-93 showed me that it is not all peace and hope between the members of the *fundo* (the majority of whom are *comuneros*) and a family of *comuneros* who are not members. There exists between them, at this time, a pending case with respect to the boundaries of their properties. According to the present formulation of the boundaries of Puerto Oscuro it has limits:

> ... to the east with property of the community of Canela Baja and the estero [small river] Canela Baja which separates it from the communities Canela Baja and Yerba Loca... (Repertorio 217, ... *Ibid.*:2).

The formulation of these boundaries in a bill of sale of the *fundo* from 1919 is, however, somewhat different. It lists the boundaries of the *fundo* as:

> to the east, the ravine of Canela, from where it meets the ravine of Espíritu Santo, until the boundary with the middle hijuela of the fundo El Totoral (Repertorio 217, ... *Ibid.*:2).

The second clause of the same bill of sale points out, likewise, that the sale of the *fundo* includes:

> ... the rights to the water in the river of La Canela and all the rest which corresponds to the fundo for its irrigation (*Ibid*).

If we go even further back, in a document from 1858 it is stated that the limits of El Totoral (the name of the *hacienda* before being divided into three smaller *fundos*) is:

> ... to the east, the Espíritu Santo, the estero of the Canela and Guile (ANCH, AN Illapel, Vol. 15, Doc. no. 279, reverse 72 to folio 73).

Fundos and Communities Ending the 1900s

The uncertainty concerning the boundaries between these two properties comes from the 1700s, although until now has not gone as far as to a potential legal trial. In the exchange of land between Francisco de Aguirre and Pedro Cortés (Pérez) somewhere between 1679 and 1709 (see Chapter 5), the former ended up with the coastal strip, corresponding to the *hacienda* El Totoral (now the *fundos* El Totoral, Las Palmas, Las Palmeras, La Alcaparra, Puerto Oscuro and the reserves EL Totoral and Puerto Oscuro), and the latter with the hydrographical bed of the River La Canela (Cañón, 1964:34) (see Chapters 5 and 7).

Cañón argues that since the boundaries between these properties were never exactly established at the end of the nineteenth century and the beginning of this, the three *fundos* (El Totoral, Las Palmas and Puerto Oscuro) that came from the *hacienda* El Totoral, went from the highest summits to the edges of the river, which comprise the present-day boundary. Cañón (1964:34) also affirmed that the natural boundary would be the tops of the highest mountains.

Following this author, the lands at present in dispute would therefore be within what in theory should belong to the community. At present, the boundaries establish something different. If we examine the last two definitions of the boundaries of the *fundo*, corresponding to 1858 and 1919, we can come to two different conclusions with respect to the eastern boundaries of Puerto Oscuro.

It is one thing to say 'up to the ravine' and another to say 'up to the rivulet or river'. Even though in Spanish America ravine (*quebrada*) is also synonymous with small river or rivulet (*estero*), both meaning tributaries, a *quebrada* is understood in Chile as a smaller tributary than the *estero* (Pequeño Larousse, España, 1989:738). *Quebrada*, which by definition also means 'A narrow opening between two mountains,' helps to clarify the picture (Ibid).

If we understand *quebrada* as 'a narrow opening between two mountains,' which is a tributary, its boundaries would be marked by the summits of the highest range. If we say, on the other hand, 'up to the rivulet or river' it signifies going beyond the highest mountaintops and going down to the edge of the river or rivulet. For the *comuneros*, and as Cañón has also claimed, what traditionally marks the boundary between two rural properties are the water streams from the highest summits, also the *quebrada*.

As evidence of this tradition and definition before the society bought Puerto Oscuro, the agricultural community Canela Baja tried to recover part of the land belonging to Puerto Oscuro now in dispute. That happened between 1970-1974, at the same time as the ownership title of the agricultural community Canela Baja was being indemnified. The *comuneros* tried to ensure that Puerto Oscuro, as the *fundos* El Totoral and Las Palmas did, give back the waterfalls by altering the boundaries from west to east from the highest mountaintops to the riverbed of La Canela.

The owner of the *fundo* up to the time of the expropriation, J. A. Echavarría, was apparently negotiating to give back this part of the *fundo*, but they did not reach an agreement. Then came the coup of 1973, which interrupted the negotiations. In any case, according to the *comuneros*, Echavarría was showing good will (Juvenal Montoya, a *comunero* of the agricultural community Canela Baja, oral interview, 5 February 1993). It is against this background that Muñoz' words about how the idea of buying the *fundo* among the *comuneros* came about can be better understood. I repeat them here:

> The idea to buy the fundo came from extensive meetings of the comuneros where it was said that as we had already got back Espíritu Santo and [part of] Las Palmas, we should try to buy Puerto Oscuro... (Muñoz, *Ibid*).

In other words, since they could not get the part of Puerto Oscuro that the *comuneros* considered belonged to the community by negotiations, the last option was under the reigning circumstances after the coup of 1973, to buy it.

The sale of the *fundo* by CONAF in 1979 opened the possibility to buy the whole *fundo*. This was done by those who managed to get organised, who believed this to be a good idea and who also had the economical means to buy the required minimum of two shares.

The land or *hijuelas* in dispute between the *fundo* and the Valencia family are in an area, which the *fundo* considers, in accordance with its boundaries, as its own (part of the western edge of the River Canela seen from Canela Baja). The Valencia family bought these lands at the beginning of the century from the Infantes. According to the directory of the *fundo*, the Valencia family does not have the documents, which would accredit the legalisation of the sale, although the Valencias claim that they do. It will be a matter for the law to determine the result if they decide to go to trial.

Fundos and Communities Ending the 1900s

As far as I could see, the issue has caused annoyance among the *comuneros*, and not all of those who at the same time are members of the *fundo*, seem to agree in the dispute with the Valencias. Many *comuneros* probably have mixed loyalties and a conflict of interest, being members of the *fundo*, and *comuneros* of the community.

As the ownership title of the agricultural community Canela Baja and its boundaries was indemnified in 1974, it is difficult but perhaps not impossible for the community to ask for a rectification of the boundaries with respect to the *fundo* Puerto Oscuro. Some *comuneros*, according to Juvenal Montoya (mentioned above), seem to have discussed this when noticing the ambition of some of the *fundo's* owners. A measure of this kind, however, would create a profound division between *comuneros* who belong to the same collective, but until now nothing can be anticipated in this matter. A great impediment will be the problem of legal costs to the community without the guarantee of success, the same being valid for the *fundo*. This case is presently dormant.

The agricultural communities coming into legal recognition

The development of capitalism has created everywhere in the world the private, individual appropriation of the land (Stavenhagen, 1979: 66).

Introduction

This sub-chapter describes the agricultural communities coming into legal recognition from the 1960s onwards, as well as the modification of the relevant laws up to the 1990s, which finally lead to a full recognition, at least in comparison with the previous decrees. The legalisation of the agricultural communities is relevant in several aspects. Firstly, it exemplifies a paradoxical process; that of the legal recognition of the agricultural communities, which appears as more surprising against a context that in general terms, we could call the modernisation of the agrarian structure (see Chapter 2).

We will see how in this process of legal recognition the state, through its different instances, plays a central role in securing the semi-communal form of land ownership for the agricultural communities. At the same time, through its intervention, it destroys the social institution of the *latifundium*, a form, which like the agricultural communities has its roots in the colonial period. The legal recognition of the agricultural communities is also interesting because it shows that this process follows in its own way, independently and in spite of the different governments in power. Lastly, but not least, it is also interesting because it shows how the legislation finally recognises these communities for what they historically and traditionally have been and, how to a great extent, their own usage and customs have prevailed and have been transmitted through generations since colonial time.

The lack of legal status of the agricultural communities

Paradoxically, the agricultural communities, in spite of their stability and the fact that their origin can be traced as far back as to the second half of the 1700s, did not have a defined regulation for their land ownership within the country's legislation until the second half of the twentieth century. In spite of the existence of several forms of land ownership in Chile the only legally recognised form, up to the 1960s, was private ownership, represented on one extreme by the large *latifundia* and on the other by the *minifundia* or small peasantry, with all the other categories of private land ownership in between.

During the second half of the twentieth century, the winding road to legitimacy for the agricultural communities has lead them around many bends, from being unrecognised up to the 1960s, to a full recognition in the 1990s. It was a thirty-year long process. To understand the legal-juridical evolution of the agricultural communities, we have to roughly distinguish between two situations which, although related are of different kinds; one is the country's own Constitution, the other the decree-laws dictated by different governments, each of them with their own policy. I will mention them briefly to contextualise the agricultural communities way to legalisation.

The explanation for the lack of legal rights during the long existence of the agricultural communities can be found, as some authors have pointed out, fundamentally, in the Chilean Constitution (Baraona *et al*, 1961; Solis de Ovando, 1989). According to Baraona *et al*, the Chilean legislation has not recognised or looked sympathetically on collective property, in spite of its existence in several forms throughout in the country.

As CIDA indicates, the legal property regime in Chile was characterised, until 1925, by an almost total freedom in the possession and

Fundos and Communities Ending the 1900s

usufruct of property for those who had the monopoly of the land in the country. Article 582 of the Chilean Civil Code defines the right to property as:

> ... the dominance on a corporal thing to enjoy and have it arbitrarily, not being against the law or other persons right (CIDA, 1966:11).

Article 10 of the Chilean Constitution reaffirms this right, indicating that it was to:

> ... assure to all the inhabitants of the Republic the inviolability of all the properties, without any distinction and that nobody can be deprived of its property or part of it or from the right that he may have to it, but by virtue of a judicial judgement or of expropriation by cause of public usefulness qualified by a law... (CIDA; 1966:11).

It can be repeated here that the method of getting legal access to land was established in the country with the dictation of the Code of Civil Laws (1847) and the Regulation of the Conservatory of Real Estate (1857). The Code of Civil Laws established the obligation to register the property, its constitution and transfer in the Register of the Conservatory of Real Estate. Thus, the guarantee of the legal possession of land was established formally (IREN, 1978, Vol. 1:22). However, from the Constitution of 1925, was introduced for the first time, certain concepts about the social function of land (CIDA, 1966:11). In that respect the Constitution of 1925 says that:

> ... the exercise of right to property is subject to the limitations or rules that demand the maintenance or the progress of the social order and, in such sense, the law will be able to impose on it obligations or servitude of public usefulness in favour of the interests of the State and of the public health (CIDA, 1966:11).

Legal and socio-political background to the recognition

The second situation in the agricultural communities' legal-juridical development concerns five different governments and their respective policies from the 1960s onwards: Alessandri's liberal government (1958-1964); Frei's Christian Democrat government (1964-1970); the coalition government of Unidad Popular, led by the socialist Allende (1970-1973); Pinochet's military dictatorship (1973-1990) and the coalition government of Concertación Democrática, led by the Christian Democrat Aylwin (1990-1994). It is noteworthy here that once the process of recognition of the agricultural communities started, it continued forward, independently of the political colour of the regime in power.

However, the legal and socio-political background to the agricultural communities is given by the initiation of the recognition of the peasantry's democratic rights in the country through different laws. These rights and laws came, then in one way or another, to contribute to the legislation of the agricultural communities. The more general political background to this process is to be found, partially, in the pressure USA put on the Latin-American governments to redistribute the land through agrarian reforms, thought of as a way to refrain from the potential menace represented by the victory of the Cuban Revolution. The USA, at the Inter-American Conference of Punta del Este, Uruguay exerted this pressure in 1961.

Recognition of the peasantry's legal rights in Chile are identified in the laws listed below:

- the peasant-co-operative law (*Ley de cooperativas campesinas*) DFL 326 from 1960 (Rivera, 1988(a):206), during Alessandri's liberal government (1958-1964);
- the (first) Agrarian Reform Law 15.020 from 1962, also passed during Alessandri's liberal government;
- the (second) Agrarian Reform Law 16.640, authorised by the Christian Democrat Eduardo Frei's government (1964-1970) in 1964, finally passed in July of 1967 (Cortázar and Downey, 1977:688);
- law 16.625 from April 1967 gave rural workers the right to unionise and strike, also authorised by Eduardo Frei's government (Cortázar and Downey, 1977:694). Incidentally, as a direct result of this law, between 1964 and 1970 the unions grow from 22 to 488 and the number of members grows from 1,700 to almost 130,000 (Cortázar and Downey, 1977:694);
- law 17.626 from February 1972 that gave the right for illiterates to vote, the majority of them being peasants and people from the rural areas, was passed during Salvador Allende's government. (Source: Servicio Electoral, Calle Esmeralda 615, Santiago, Chile, Centro de Información, Ximena Pérez, informant, telephone interview, 4 February, 1998).

Although indirectly, Allende's government had an important influence on the whole process of the legal recognition of the agricultural communities and especially in how things developed in the Canela commune.

The agrarian reform and unionisation of the peasants had an indirect effect on the agricultural communities and their *comuneros*. The agrarian reform affected them indirectly because the distribution of land was aimed at peasants without land, mainly the *inquilinos* (tenant farmers) of the expropriated *fundos,* not those who owned land, which was the case of the *comuneros*. Likewise, the right to join the union was primarily aimed at rural employees (the *comuneros* worked their own land), although the possibility to join existed for the *comuneros* as well.

When the illiterate part of the population obtained the right to vote, it benefited the *comuneros* politically, directly and indirectly. Directly since there is a high percentage of illiterates among them who now got the right to vote for the first time. It also benefited the *comuneros* directly, in that among them there was a relatively high proportion who sympathised with the left wing, and the right to vote gave them political influence for the first time.

From the point of view of resources, both the agrarian reform and the right for illiterates to vote, favour the *comuneros* indirectly. During the years of Allende's government, a radicalisation of the agrarian reforms of the previous governments resulted in a voluntary devolution of land by several landowners to some agricultural communities in the commune of Canela. However, this devolution did not prevent several *fundos* in the zone from being expropriated during the Allende administration at the beginning of the 1970s.

The peasant-co-operative law also benefited the agricultural communities in an indirect manner. According to Baraona *et al* (1961:130), the agricultural communities entered legal recognition first:

> ... through 'the back door', and by making use of the existence of the legal provisions concerning co-operatives of small-scale producers.

As Baraona *et al* wrote about the community of Valle de Putaendo, the enrolment of the agricultural communities was done:

> ... in the name of particular individual owners of the common lands; the property is not registered in the name of a legal institution: the community (Baraona *et al*, 1961:131).

From what has been said above, one cannot assume, however, that the agricultural communities reaped the fruit of someone else's struggle, so to speak. On the contrary, if they began to achieve some recognition it was because they actively pursued and fought for it. This struggle also involved taking advantage of any crack in the law and the political conjuncture. As an example of the effort made by the agricultural communities to achieve legal recognition, it can be mentioned that in 1954, in Ovalle:

> ... a provincial congress was held where the legal recognition of the communally owned land of the 'comunidades' in the province of Coquimbo was requested (Huizer, G., 1966:4).

Beginning of the long winding road to legitimacy

According to IREN (1978, Vol. 1:34), the agricultural communities started to have 'legal existence' during 1962 in connection with the dictation of the Agrarian Reform Law 15.020, which would regulate their legal situation. The said law establishes in Article 40 that:

> ... for the provinces of Coquimbo [today Region IV] and Atacama, [today Region III] the President of the Republic will dictate dispositions that will tend to constitute the property on the rural lands owned in common by different landowners, on which the number of comuneros is clearly greater than the productive capacity of the property, so that the respective family groups can provide for their essential subsistence needs.

In order to fulfil the mentioned dispositions, the DFL 19 was passed in 1963 (DFL stands for *Decreto con Fuerza de Ley* or Decree with Legal Power or with Force of Law. The modification was published first in 1968). This authority was again, granted to the President of the Republic in 1967 and that same year the DFL 5 appeared, modifying and extending the DFL 19. According to the DFL 5, indemnification is the same as:

> ... the establishment of the property belonging to the communities, the indemnification of their title deeds and their organisation. It means, through this process, it is intended not only to regularise the title deeds, but also to provide the communities with a kind of administrative organisation to keep all their economic activities in order (IREN, 1978, Vol. 1:34).

Of the 162 agricultural communities registered by IREN in the Norte Chico up to 1977, that is fourteen years after the DFL 19 of 1963, only around 30% (50 communities) were indemnified and registered in the Conservatory of Real Estate (IREN, 1978, Vol. 1:34). The other 112 communities were in the following situation: 8 were in the process of a judicial sentence; 47 had only the maps; 34 had had their application of indemnification accepted; 19 had not presented antecedents or application and finally, there were 4 communities for which the situation was unknown (IREN, 1978, Vol. 1:34).

The indemnification of the communities was, and still is, of vital importance as it permits the agricultural communities to be treated as legal entities, besides being an essential condition to obtain credit and different kinds of development aid. Although the majority of the agricultural communities of Region IV have indemnified their title deeds during the 1990s, what CIDA pointed out in 1966 continues to be valid for the communities today, in the sense that many *comuneros* have not regularised their legal status through title deeds and other formalities (CIDA, 1966:41).

According to CIPRES (1992:15-16), in 1992 there were a total of 200 agricultural communities in Region IV. Of these, 165 were legally recognised and four were in the process of indemnification. 31 were *de facto* communities and of them, 27 were qualified to apply for indemnification. The first 169 communities had, in 1992, a total of 14,884 registered *comuneros*.

Despite the fact that the legislature during the Frei administration 'recognised' the agricultural communities, the type of recognition demonstrated that Chilean law continued to be lackadaisical towards the form of communally or semi-communally owned land characterising the agricultural communities. This became obvious through various factors that turned the, above-mentioned, law into something both contradictory and highly paternalistic. Firstly, the agricultural communities are still defined in the same way as in Article 40 of the Agrarian Reform Law from 1962. Agricultural communities were considered as:

> ... those rural lands owned in common by different landowners, on which the number of comuneros is clearly greater than the productive capacity of the property so that the respective family groups can provide for their essential subsistence needs (DFL 5, 1967, Artículo 1°, Diario Oficial..., 17 de Enero de 1968).

Before going further, let me draw attention to two things: Firstly, it is interesting to note, as the *comunero* Pedro Carvajal writes in a letter, that the term community is applied to the land and not to the people (letter from Pedro Carvajal to the author, dated in Canela, 13 of November 1995). Secondly, the emphasis of this definition is not on the semi-communal ownership of the land belonging to the agricultural communities, but on their poverty derived from the low productivity of the land. As Solis de Ovando has commented in respect to this, the reason for the common management of the land is not the low productivity of the land, but the type of agrarian economy which characterises those agricultural communities, i.e. mainly goat rearing, which due to the constant need for new pasture, requires vast extensions of land thus avoiding the traditional subdivision of the land. In a critical study of this law, Solis de Ovando (1989:22) asks, "Why give the agricultural communities legal recognition for reasons different from those which would justify their persistent and prolonged existence?" According to him, with this type of recognition the legislature establishes an institution, which is understood as being completely exceptional, given that the idea of communally owned rural property is not accepted within the framework of the laws of the country:

> ... from this perception of community property comes an attitude opposed to accepting that the laws of indemnification are not really 'creating' a juridical situation but rather are admitting the existence of communities with a long tradition, which the said laws come to grant legal status which legally recognises their existence, determines their internal rights, and tutelary them from the State administration (Solis de Ovando, 1989:22-23).

Strangely enough, the law concerning the agricultural communities, apart from the peculiar definition of the very concept of agricultural communities and quite against legal practice, which recommends a definition of the juridical key concepts, does not contain a definition of the concepts involved in the law. For this reason, the lawyer Solis de Ovando distinguishes four key concepts in his study of this law, defining them as follows. The common property is:

> ...all the land belonging to the agricultural community. It belongs to the agricultural community as a legal entity and not to the comuneros individually. The common property constitutes the object of domain of the

community or the condominium of the comuneros. It is the property that the comunero shares 'with others' (Solis de Ovando, 1989:51-52).

From the moment the community is indemnified according to the regulations, established in the DFL 5 from 1967, the location, range and delimitation of the common property is established and it is registered in the Real Estate Register of the local Conservatory of Real Estate. Common land is:

> land which is situated within the common property and which can be used by all comuneros, individually or jointly, without exclusions (Solis de Ovando, 1989:52).

The last statement, according to the DFL 5 of 1967, does not imply that the General Board of *Comuneros* cannot claim their right to a regulation of common land use in order to preserve the property. Of the single or individual usage (*goces singulares*):

> It is that part of the common property whose usage is assigned to the comuneros individually, excluding the others (Solis de Ovando, 1989:52).

Of the *comunero's* shares or rights:

> It is the participation that the comunero has, as proportion, over the community's goods and rights. The comunero's shares or rights are equivalent to the shares owned by the members of a company. That is the fundamental object for all the other rights: to the common land and to the individual usage, to the extent that these rights depend on the shares that the comunero has in the community and thus should stand in proportion to the same (Solis de Ovando, 1989:54).

Once the share has been established (this is done during the indemnification of the community) it can be transferred or negotiated, but the proportion it represents in the community can never be altered. As Solis de Ovando indicates (1989:55), the legislator ignored the dynamic instilled by the communitarian life when he transformed the *comunero*'s fee in a static relation with the community. Moreover, the original DFL 19 from 1963 limited the territorial area to the regions of Atacama and Coquimbo. Nevertheless, in the revision of the 1967 law this stipulation was removed, from which it can be deduced, according to Solis de Ovando (1989:25), that they extended it to the whole country. In spite of this only the communities of Region IV have, in practice, been indemnified. It is considered by this author, there are no signs that communities with similar characteristics, of the highlands of the Norte Grande (Regions I and II of Tarapacá and Antofagasta respectively) for example, are doing the same (see Chapter 1).

The law, which took effect in June 1993, was special not only for its peculiar definition of the agricultural communities, but also because it was clearly tutelary and contradictory. The person who exercised the tutelary role, representing the State, was the lawyer of the Office of National Estates. According to law, the communities are constituted on their own initiative, applying at the Office for titles within the Department of Land and National Estates. Once the application is accepted, in its judicial and extra judicial dealings, the community must grant patronage and authority to the lawyer of the Office of National Estates (Solis de Ovando, 1989:27). This disposition continued in the law from 1993, with the difference that the mentioned tutelary duty is now delegated to the head of the Division for Constitution of Real Estates of the National Estates' Ministry. As far as I understand, this disposition is valid only for as long as the indemnification of the agricultural community continues.

However, in the DFL 5 from 1967 Article 18 this tutelary duty reached beyond the community's constitution, towards the power of the General Boards. Having carried out the inscription of the property, in the name of the community, before the Real Estate Register of the corresponding Conservatory of Real Estate, and registered the statutes of the community, as well as elected the board, the community became fully constituted and registered. Consequently, and according to the law, the community:

> ... will behave in its relations as a legal entity with private rights distinct from those of the comuneros which it is composed of, capable of exercising rights and contracting obligations and of being represented judicially and extra judicially... (Solis de Ovando, 1989:32-33).

Notwithstanding this (Article 27), there was also Article 16, which gave an indication of the paternalistic nature of the law, in that the lawyer of the Office of National Estates, who will have the right to express his opinion, must assist the General Boards of the community, ordinary or extraordinary. To this end, the community was able to notify the lawyer in

Fundos and Communities Ending the 1900s

writing with respect to the date and time for the board meeting. If the lawyer did not attend the meeting, the Board was able to send the decisions to his office within 15 days, or face the nullification (sic!) of the accords (Solis de Ovando, 1989:36).

While the control on behalf of the State extended further than the initial legal constitution of the communities, the State created a kind of permanent intervention in the communities (Solis de Ovando, 1989:37). There was a contradiction in the fact that the law established that a community might act as a legal entity with private rights in its relations with a third party. However, at the same time it could insist that the community could not make fundamental decisions through its General Board without the presence of the ministry's lawyer (Solis de Ovando, 1989:37).

In what is referred to as the modifications of the law introduced by the Pinochet administration (Ley 18.353, Diario Oficial..., 26 de Octubre de 1984), Article 25 is particularly important. It allowed the legal inscription of the *hijuelas* or *goces singulares* on the part of the *comuneros* through the Legal Decree 2.695 of 1979, from which they had previously been excluded. The Law Decree 2.695 of 1979 declared precisely in its Article 8 that its orders were not valid for the agricultural communities (Solis de Ovando, 1989:105). Those who could have recourse in the last mentioned law were the *comuneros* who had *goces singulares*, according to the logic that the occupation or cultivation of *goces singulares* meant that it was considered the property of the *comunero*. Through this inscription the *goces singulares* stopped being community property (Solis de Ovando, 1989:39).

In order to clarify this, it should be said that the *comuneros* could register their *hijuelas* even prior to Pinochet's modification of 1984. What is new is that with the modification of Article 25 they could do this supported by a law, which stated that once it had been registered the property ceased to belong to the community, thus turning the *comuneros* into proprietors of their *goces singulares*. It is obvious that this new procedure would undermine the very foundations of the community.

This also resulted in the Board losing its ability to distribute the *goces singulares*. Through their legal registration, these *goces singulares* became an exclusive right of the *comuneros* (Solis de Ovando, 1989:43). This is clearly contradictory with the Article 18, which establishes that the General Board of *comuneros* may, if necessary, designate or redistribute the *goces singulares* or the *hijuelas* (for the construction of an urban centre, a school, a football field, cultural centres, electric installation). In this particular issue it remained unchanged according to the modifications from 1984.

These modifications also introduced a change in Article 42, concerning the transfer of the *hijuelas*. Article 42 from 1967 established a:

> term of five years – counted from the constitution of the Community – after which the comuneros could voluntarily transfer their rights to *another* comunero or to the community (Solis de Ovando, 1989:93; emphasis added).

Once the five-year term has passed:

> ... they can only be transferred *to a natural person, whether or not a comunero*, or to the same Community (Solis de Ovando, 1989:93; emphasis added).

In the new Article 42, the term was reduced to two years including transfers to the community. After the term of two years, the specifications are the same as cited before.

Article 42 (prior to the modifications introduced during the Pinochet administration) is among those that have caused suspicion among the *comuneros* given that to a certain degree, it subjected the *hijuelas* to market forces. I could observe, whilst in the community during 1989, a fear that people from outside the community would begin to buy *goces singulares* coming up for sale. This would break up the common interests and customs of the community, as well as the traditional maintenance of the land among the descendants of its first owners.

According to my knowledge, in the case of the agricultural community Canela Baja, some people from the area who are former emigrants and children of *comuneros* have bought *hijuelas* in the community. This way, the descendants of previous *comuneros* have been re-integrated into the community, reassuring the continuation of the property within the same families. Other emigrants have become reincorporated into the community not as *comuneros*, but by buying houses in the villages.

Although Article 42 exposed the communities to the interest of private buyers from the outside who wanted to acquire land, in the particular case of the community Canela Baja this possibility appears unlikely due to the lack of irrigation. However, it is a real threat in the case of communities with better agricultural land, above all for communities in the area of the rapidly increasing fruit production in Region IV. This is particularly valid for the Limarí province, the only one in Chile to have three reservoirs and an interconnected system that assures water supply to the farmers in the area, even during droughts of three to four years. The reservoirs La Paloma, Recoleta and Cogotí distribute water to irrigate 40,000 hectares and the whole system accumulates a thousand million cubic meters of water, which comes from the Andes. This system has made the permanent cultivation of grapes for exportation possible, while before having access to the interconnected irrigation system the production consisted of tomatoes, beans and various kinds of vegetables, together with grapes for the distillation of liquor. The construction belongs to the State but the water belongs to the people who have bought shares and who are organised in Vigilance Groups, Water Communities and Associations of Canals (Albina Sabater, Revisa El Domingo, El Mercurio, 21 de Enero, 1990, 1.205, "Reales Lagos de Artificio").

The hunger for irrigated land does not constitute the only threat to the communities. The increasing interest on the coastal sectors in holiday resorts for the swelling upper-middle class of the country constitutes another. The recent sale (1995) of a part of the coastal sector by the agricultural community Huentelauquén to a private society is an example of that. Here, the small amount of 352 ha was sold for one million dollars to Alfredo Larraín S. A. (Courtesy of Héctor Jorquera, *consejal* (counsellor), letter from the 20th of July, 1997). With this, the most popular beach of the Canela Commune 'Agua Dulce' remains situated within this new private property, where a tourist-complex is to be built. Even though this caused much irritation among the inhabitants of the Canela commune and other neighbouring communes, the decision to sell belonged to the *comuneros* of the Huentelauquén agricultural community itself. This was under the cover of the most recent legislation that Article 49 permits the alienation of part of the community, now without the authorisation of the Ministry of National Estates.

It is important to stress that the increasing interest on the coastal sectors also involves the *fundos* near the coast. In 1997, the reserve El Totoral was also sold, though apparently only a part since according to Héctor Jorquera, approximately 350 ha were sold of the total of 3,000 ha.

The price was about 1,375 million dollars (Ibid). These sales will bring new revenue to the commune through licences for construction, trade and traffic. There will also be new sources of employment but, at the same time, the price of land will go up especially in the private sector.

Returning to Article 42, one thing is clear. The law, when restricting the sale of rights to individuals, at least protects the territorial property of the agricultural communities from private companies and similar buyers getting into the community itself. The former example of the beach is different, since it means that a part of the community is alienated, conforming thus a new and separate property.

According to the new law of 1993 the *goces singulares*, once inscribed in the Conservatory, cease to be private property. This is something that should mitigate the *comuneros'* fear, since it means that the *hijuelas* are now less subjected to market forces due to the fact that the indisputable proprietor of all the land is now the agricultural community.

However, before the new law in 1993, the *comuneros* were aware of the dangers imposed by some of the statutes of the law and the communities organised themselves at various levels, both local and provincial, in order to defend their interests and obtain help from the government. A result at a provincial level is the *Comuneros'* Association of the Province of Choapa. According to Diego Alzamora, President of this organisation, they had a meeting in Santiago in 1990 with the ministers of Agriculture, Public Works, Planning and National Estates. During this meeting they asked for the road that joins Illapel with Canela to be widened in order to create new sources of employment in the area. They also asked for the construction of a dam in the zone, something that would provide them with water for irrigation (Gabriela Gayani, La Nación, Segundo cuerpo, 11 de Noviembre, 1990:8-9).

Even if this association has succeeded in achieving certain benefits, they were not able to obtain a modification in the 1993 law of Article 42, which permits the sale of rights to people who are not *comuneros* and which has caused resentment among the *comuneros*. The *Comuneros'* Association of the Province of Choapa, as well as the unions play the role of pressure groups petitioning the government rather than negotiating bodies against the employees (see Chapter 8).

Even the modification of Article 24 introduced during the Pinochet administration, made the communities vulnerable. The DFL 5 of 1967 prohibited the sale, total or partial, or to encumber the common land and the right to use the community's water without the consent of all the *comuneros* (Solis de Ovando, 1989:56). This part of the article does not change with the 1984 modification, but it does make it possible to delegate the faculty of all the *comuneros* to the General Boards. At this meeting, the agreement must be decided upon by two thirds of the *comuneros*, representing not less than 70% of the total of the inscribed rights.

Since the modification of Article 42 permits a *comunero* to have a maximum of 10% of the total of the inscribed rights, the required 70%, necessary to carry the agreements, could in theory be represented by a limited number of *comuneros*. The decision to modify the statutes only requires the agreement of an Extraordinary General Board meeting where the agreement can be carried with a low quorum and low representation.

According to information given by the *comuneros*, Pinochet introduced another modification into the law, according to which the number of *comuneros* could decrease but not increase. That is not exactly what the law says, although the effect was that only one of the children of a *comunero* could take his place when he died. Besides, this decree (Article 38) was brought into statute prior to Pinochet. Although this measure caused considerable discontent among the children of the *comuneros*, it only legalised a practise, which has been exercised within the communities whereby the *hijuelas* cannot be further subdivided.

Traditionally, given that the individual plots are meagre and unable to feed all heirs, especially when these form their own families, the majority of them leave the community. According to custom, the son or daughter who remains with the parents is the one who inherits the *hijuela*. This is not necessarily the eldest of the heirs. It can, in fact, be the youngest one with whom would also rest the responsibility not only of the property, but of the old parents. In this sense the inheritance will be a reward for the efforts of the heirs who remained in charge.

According to Article 38, in the adjudication of the right:

> ... preference will be given to the legitimate, natural or adopted child over age who is living and working on the property. Between several with the same preference it will be applied according to age, starting with the eldest (Ley 19.233, Diario Oficial..., 5 de Agosto de 1993:2).

In spite of the fact that this only confirms an old custom, the children of the *comuneros* were opposed to Article 38 as they felt discriminated. In 1991 some *comuneros* and their children organised themselves to protest against this measure.

In relation to the former Article (38), it should be mentioned that the law of 1967 constitutes an exception in regard to the regulations of the succession rights. The Civil Code establishes in its Article 1317 that:

> ... none of the co-legatee of a universal or singular thing will be forced to remain in the *indivision* (Solis de Ovando, 1989:62; emphasis added).

Article 37, however, establishes the opposite regulation thus trying to avoid a division, which affects the integrity of the rights in the community.

It is also interesting to mention that the legislation of the agricultural communities emanates directly from the executive power and lacks, in the words of Solis de Ovando (1989:17-18), a 'legislative history'. A relevant aspect of this law is that it is the legislator who has introduced a form to gain possession of land through a prescription. The general tendency is that, through the inscription a new, different property results for each of the heirs.

The 1993 changes to the law: more than a modification

The end of the Pinochet administration and the coming to power in 1990 of the political coalition Concertación Democrática, led by Patricio Aylwin, means the beginning of a new phase for the agricultural communities: that of a legal recognition, which can be considered to be more in order than the previous ones. Law 19.233, modifies the DFL 5, 1968 from the Ministry of Agriculture, which contains the legal normative for agricultural communities (published in Diario Oficial /.../, 5 de Agosto de 1993:2). Although the majority of the 60 articles, which make up the law for agricultural communities remain unaltered, when modified in 1993 the changes introduced are enough to consider it as qualitatively different from the previous version. Here I will only discuss a few articles that I consider relevant in relation to the DFL 5 of 1967 and some of the modifications from 1984.

Parting from the same definition of the agricultural communities, there is first of all a substantial change surrounding the new law. According to the new text (Article 1):

> ... [An] Agricultural Community is the group of proprietors of a common rural land which they inhabit, exploit and cultivate and who organise themselves in accordance with this legal text (Ley 19.233, Diario Oficial /.../, 5 de Agosto de 1993:2).

We can observe that this new definition, as opposed to the previous one, does not include the relationship between the number of *comuneros* and the productive capacity of the property. The emphasis of the new article lies on the group of proprietors who share common land.

As with the previous law, the one from 1993 establishes in Article 1 that once the property has been registered in presence of the corresponding Conservator of Real Estate, the agricultural communities:

> ... will be able to execute their rights and acquire obligations and to be represented judicially and extra judicially.

However, since parts of the earlier Article 16, which contradicted the mentioned rights, are derogated, the obligatory presence of a lawyer and his right to vote disappears. Now:

> The meetings of the General Board ordinary or extraordinary may take place with the assistance of a lawyer, if the members of the meeting so request, to inform the comuneros about legal norms that may affect them and to serve as a spokesman in contacts with the ministry, when dealing with problems of its concern (*Ibid.*:3).

Excluded from the text is also Article 16 concerning the lawyer's attendance at the meetings of the communities. With it, the law loses much of its paternalistic nature and the type of permanent intervention that the State created in the communities.

Also new is the specification in Article 16 that each and every *comunero* will have the right to one vote, from which can be deduced that an increase in the number of rights or shares per *comunero* does not give them the right to additional votes.

Continuing with the new Article 1 it contains, as opposed to the previous law, the definitions of a *comunero*, a *goce singular* and the common land.

The Article 1 points out that *Comuneros*:

... are the *title holders* of the common land that appears on the list which is elaborated according to this legal text (*Ibid.*:2; emphasis added).

The *goce singular*:

> ... is a determined portion of *community owned* land which is assigned to a comunero and his family in order for them to exploit and cultivate it on a permanent and exclusive basis (*Ibid.*, emphasis added).

A '*lluvia*' is:

> ... a determined portion of *community owned* land which is assigned to a comunero and his family for a limited period of time (Ibid., emphasis added).

The common land is the rest or:

> ... that part of the community property on which there is no goce singular or lluvia (*Ibid.*).

From what can be read from the clauses above, it is very clear that both the *goces singulares* and the '*lluvias*' are, unquestionably, community property. Both are distributed by the community to each *comunero*; the *goces singulares* on a permanent basis and the '*lluvia*' for a limited period of time. In other words, the *comuneros* make individual use of the plot, but do not privately own it.

The new law establishes that the *comuneros* are owners of:

> ... the right or share over the common property... (Article 1 bis c).

This right gives them access to the usage of the community goods, which are:
- the common land, as determined by the General Board of *Comuneros*;
- the *goces singulares* which are assigned to them by the General Board of *Comuneros* in an exclusive and permanent way; and
- the rights to use water that belongs to the community by registration, the rain water that falls or is collected on the common land and that which corresponds to springs that begin, flow through or end on that same land (*Ibid.*).

In agreement with the new Article 1, cited above, part of Article 25 is excluded. The modification in 1993 introduces, again, the exception from the law of 1967, which indicated that the agricultural communities could not have recourse to the Law Decree 2.695 of 1979. In Article 8 this law excludes the agricultural communities. This established that the occupation or cultivation of a *goce singular* meant that it was considered as the property of the *comunero*.

Furthermore it eliminates the specification, which stated that when a *comunero* registered a *goce singular*, it ceased to belong to the agricultural community. For the same reason, the contradiction pointed out by Solis de Ovando is removed, in the sense that the legislation established that the General Board of *Comuneros* may, if deemed necessary, designate or redistribute the *goces singulares* or *hijuelas*. The legal inscription of the *hijuelas* or *goces singulares* on the part of the *comuneros* resulted in the Board losing its ability to distribute these *goces singulares*, since through their legal registration they ceased being community property.

The part of the Article 42, which concerns the transfer of the *hijuelas* to persons who are not *comuneros*, has not been changed in the modifications of 1993. What is changed here is that:

> the rights which the comuneros can obtain, added to the shares they already own, or the third parties must not exceed the 3% of the registered rights (*Ibid.*:3).

This earlier percentage was 10%. With the introduction in Article 42 of a maximum of rights per *comunero*, the law established manifestly a limit in regard to the concentration of rights. With the reduction to 3%, this restriction is further reinforced. This impediment for concentration is fully in accordance with the specificity of the agricultural communities, since it would go against the characteristic which constitutes its specificity; the common property. In the agricultural community Canela Baja there exist 668 rights, also a number equal to the number of *comuneros*. The 10% meant that a *comunero* could have a maximum of 67 rights. With the 3%, valid from 1993, the most that a *comunero* can accumulate are 20 rights. Unfortunately, and according to Pedro Carvajal, there is no list over the number of rights each *comunero* has. Thus it is not possible to see how the total number of rights, and with them the *goces singulares*, are distributed, but they should be divided quite equally amongst the *comuneros*. According to my own interviews, there are a few families that have several *goces singulares* distributed between several different agricultural communities.

For those cases where the community has to sell the rights of some *comuneros* because, for example, they have failed to pay their fees, these rights will be put up for auction. It is also established that only children of *comuneros* who appear on the community's list can buy these rights. This is valid on all occasions when the community acquires shares or rights to any title. If no buyer comes forward at the auction, the community can appropriate these rights for itself for two thirds of the opening price. This should always be done before a civil judge from the commune. If no child of a *comunero* can or wants to take over the rights that the community has put up for sale, there exists the alternative of dividing these rights proportionally between all of the *comuneros*.

With this new specification in Article 42, which gives preference to children of *comuneros* when it comes to buying rights that the community has put up for sale, it seems to me that to a certain extent, this compensates the fact that the *comuneros* can individually sell their rights to a third party who is not a *comunero*.

With the introduction of the definitions in the new Article 1, the law loses, in principle, the ambiguity by which it was formerly characterised in regard to who owns what. Furthermore, with these new definitions, the classification of the agricultural communities as entities with both semi-communal and semi-private land, as it has been described by CIDA, disappears.

However, things are not that simple, due to an exception to Article 1 bis c, included in Article 18, letter c, that somehow actualises the former classifications by the CIDA. Let us examine this. The re-modified letter c in Article 18, which concerns the attribution of the General Board when it comes to the distribution of *goces singulares*, specifies that:

> the prior original existing *goces singulares* will not be affected by the new community regulation ...

which means that it only concerns the distribution of new *goces singulares* and '*lluvias*'.

Firstly, this implies that a *de facto* situation is accepted of what traditionally constituted an agricultural community prior to its legal recognition. Secondly, as I see it, this actualises the classifications by

Fundos and Communities Ending the 1900s

CIDA of semi-communal and semi-private in respect to the different forms of land tenure inside the agricultural communities.

In spite of the fact that it is the community as a whole who is the proprietor of the *goces singulares*, in case the new law does not extend this regulation to those cases prior to the modification of the law (1993), those *comuneros* who find themselves in the said situation, which is the majority, are in reality the virtual 'proprietors' of their *goces singulares*.

Hence it is possible to classify these two forms as semi-private and semi-communal, as has been done by CIDA. Semi- and not altogether private, due to the fact that the *goces singulares* are not only traditionally accepted, but today also legally subject to some regulation, and not, therefore, entirely private. Since the *'lluvias'* are also to be found on the communal property, the community taken as a whole is semi- and not fully communal.

Table 9.1 Land ownership in an agricultural community of Region IV from 1993

Type of exploitation	Duration	Ownership	Denomination
Agricultural exploitation	Permanent	Semi-private: A. Land granted by the community	*Goce singular*
	Determined period	B. Land granted by the community	*'Lluvia'*
Pastoral exploitation	Temporary	Communal: A. Undivided property of all *comuneros*	Common land
		B. Undivided property belonging to several communities	Common enclosures

Source: The author, made on the basis of Figure X-9 from CIDA (1966:131)

In Table 9.1 (above), I try to summarise the land ownership form in the agricultural communities on the basis of the modifications of the law in 1993.

Communal Land Ownership in Chile

Epilogue with a happy ending?

If the agricultural communities *de facto* survived until the 1960s, the new times with its political changes gradually deepened their unsteady legal recognition in such a way that the law of 1993 *de jure* has come to reassure their existence. This may not have been the specific aim of this law, but in spite of the possible ambiguities it may still contain, it reaffirms the agricultural communities within a context acknowledged within agriculture as an accelerated advance of capitalism.

Paraphrasing Solis de Ovando, the agricultural communities are now legally recognised as communally owned rural property for the same reasons that have justified their persistent and prolonged existence. The regime has formalised rules and regulations for a customary property rights system of land tenancy, securing its existence through legislation.

Does it constitute a paradox that the modern state, through its legal apparatus, sanctioned the existence of a customary property right in the context of an advanced development of market relations? Is in this case, the state acting against the interests of the market? I would suggest here that the empirical process of the legal recognition of the agricultural communities in Chile shows another conception about the state than that of:

> radical analysts who tend to see the state as instrument of domination for the economically dominant group in society (Dzorgbo, D. Bright, 1997:11).

It shows rather a Weberian conception of the state, a state as:

> a set of organisations invested with the authority to make binding decisions for people and organisations juridically located in a particular territory and to implement these decisions using, if necessary force (*Ibid*).

Therefore the communal form appears here as its own. Its persistent existence depends first of all on its own capability, no matter how precarious or marginal this might be, of being as real as private property, and therefore having its own place, needs and demands, to the rest of the system, including the state. If so, it cannot be strange that the estate legalises the agricultural communities, a form that is as old as private property in the country. If by so doing, the state is at the same time taking political responsibility against its own citizens, avoiding part of the exodus of the rural people to the cities and ultimately benefiting itself politically and also capitalism in the long run, these are consequences - unexpected or expected - of several processes where the economic is only one among others.

10 The Common Denominator

Introduction

As Silverman (1986:24) states:

> If the initial stages of a study are concerned with narrowing down the research problem, the concluding stage is a good time to broaden out once again.

Therefore, in this chapter I will try to answer the question, "What is the form of communal land ownership?" I will do this through a formal definition, distinguishing it from both private property and open access. In this way, I will recapture with the help of Stevenson, what I have pointed out as the common denominator, the form of communal land ownership. I will return to why I chose Stevenson for this.

Firstly, I will summarise the thesis and then analyse the development process of land ownership in the Canela commune mainly discussed in Part 2. After that, the postponed Swiss case and English open field system will be briefly developed together with agricultural communities of Norte Chico. Belonging to a Third World country, they paradoxically, show more similarities with the two European cases, regarding origin and emergence, than with the examples from South Africa and Mexico.

This investigation was divided into three parts. In the General Introduction we moved in the present, contextualising the study object, nationally and regionally, geographically and socio-economically. The purpose of this study was presented to investigate the historical origin, emergence and present reproduction of semi-communal land ownership of the Norte Chico region in Chile through the specific case of the agricultural community Canela Baja and its colonial predecessor, the *estancia* La Canela. I suggested that Chile's Norte Chico was peculiar within a national, Latin-American and even world context, not only because of its current land structure, which mixes semi-communal land ownership with private ownership in the *latifundium* and *minifundium,* but also because it presents the development during colonial time of semi-communally owned property out of the *latifundias* private property. Although as a form, as old as the *latifundium*, semi-communal land ownership was not legally recognised until quite recently.

However, communal land exists in different parts of the world. On a global level, examples from Switzerland, South Africa and Mexico, belonging to three different continents, confirmed the generality of the form. Nonetheless, different socio-political contexts and material conditions at the same time confirmed some differences particularly in the way they originated.

Therefore, an analytical distinction between the form and its historical development was made. While the form stands for the general, history stands for the particular. While the form became our sociological common denominator, history became the field where the differences between some examples of communal land ownership showed up. Dealing with the form, the most basic characteristic of communal land ownership was, as suggested, the co-ownership of land on a permanent basis as a managerial resource solution, combined with private land possessions. The exploitation in both economic spheres was mostly individual. This is to say, what is communal is the ownership of the land, rather than its exploitation, or to express it with Lewis' (1960:27) words the, "land holdings are worked individually rather than collectively".

Dealing with the historical development of the form, some instances were the product of a 'spontaneous' process, while others were imposed from above. In respect to origin and development, the agricultural communities of Norte Chico differed from other both Chilean and non-Chilean concrete forms of communal land ownership. Through a brief contrast with other agricultural communities, I suggested that while the semi-communal property of the agricultural communities of the Norte Chico, similar to the present Swiss and the extinct English systems, were the result of a long 'spontaneous' historical process, the Mexican *ejidos,* and the reserves of South Africa, as well as the indigenous agricultural communities of the South of Chile were imposed forms created by laws.

In Chile, semi-communal land ownership shared a common origin in the colonial *mercedes de tierras* with both the *latifundium* and the *minifundium* – forms that together make up the Norte Chico's land tenure structure.

To contextualise my subject, I described the present-day land tenure structure in Chile in Chapter 2, including a short historical retrospect, as well as the results of the last decades agrarian reforms. I situated my study within the greater social structure of the commune, including its present land structure and its population, mainly made up of the population of agricultural communities.

Chapter 3 comprised the physical description of the Canela commune where the agricultural community Canela Baja and the former *hacienda* El Totoral are located, permitting us to understand the conditions in which the *comuneros* live. Using this context as background, a factual characterisation of the form was presented, i.e., how the semi-communal land ownership of the agricultural communities was mainly organised until 1993.

As a whole, Part 2, the Historical Past, took us to the colonial period and embraced both the developing of the Chilean agrarian structure as well as that of my case. Chapter 4 over-viewed the colonial formation of land tenure in Chile, trying to put the Norte Chico within the 'national' framework. Terms related to the Chilean and Latin American agrarian structure were discussed as *mercedes de tierra, encomienda, estancia, hacienda and fundo*. I developed the historical precedents and endurance of the small property in Chile, and discussed the problem of the origin of the semi-communally owned land property in the Norte Chico. I contrasted how different authors have explained the formation of the agricultural communities or, what I defined as the conversion of private property into semi-communal, as well as those elements that would explain the continuity of other properties in private ownership. In connection, I developed my own theses of the origin and formation of the agricultural communities by contrasting them with private property.

Chapters 5 to 7 dealt specifically with the historical case study. I attempted to reconstruct the two main paths of socio-economic development dealing with land tenure formation since colonial time in the Canela Commune, private and semi-communal property. Since the *estancia* La Canela, constituting almost the entire geographical area of the Canela commune, became many distinct landed properties, in reconstructing its historic development my contribution to the local history went beyond that of the agricultural community Canela Baja. Through the history of Espíritu Santo, in Chapter 8, the struggle for land between the *latifundia* and the agricultural communities was shown and reconstructed, specifically dealing with Espíritu Santo. If for the latter some scarce references existed, a history about El Totoral and its resulting *fundos* was, however, entirely missing.

In Chapter 5, through a common introduction for El Totoral and La Canela, I empirically support my argument that what today constitutes both *fundos* and agricultural communities in the commune of Canela have a common origin, the past colonial *mercedes*. Reserved as they were for the highest colonial social strata, this fact served me to deny that the agricultural communities arose from land given to low-rank soldiers.

Following the history of El Totoral and its subdivisions, I illustrated in Chapter 6 the development of private property in the Canela Commune. Empirically I showed a process in which the property of *haciendas* and *fundos*, today seven in total, were constantly transferred between different owners during almost a century.

Chapter 7 attempted a reconstruction of the diverging development path of ownership of semi-communal land of the agricultural community Canela Baja out of the colonial *estancia* La Canela, resulting in fourteen agricultural communities. In that chapter, I supported my thesis that the agricultural communities, as opposed to the *haciendas* and *fundos*, are characterised by a hereditary maintenance of the land since colonial times, between the descendants of the original proprietors of the land. Even the case of the *estancias* Mincha, and Conchalí and Chiagualoco was briefly developed, giving further support that the semi-communal land ownership has its origin in the colonial *mercedes de tierra*. Showing a parallel developing process to the one represented by La Canela and El Totoral, respectively, Conchalí and Chigualoco, different to the *estancia* Mincha, but similar to El Totoral, illustrate the other development path: the continuation of these properties in a private form, being still *haciendas* today. In contrast, ten agricultural communities developed from one *merced de tierra* later to become the Mincha *estancia*.

Part 3, returned us to the present, giving an account of the latest transformations in the Canela commune as a result of the changes that took place in the national context, dealing with both the *fundos* and the agricultural communities, as well as with the conflicting relationship between them. This is illustrated through the struggle for the land of Espíritu Santo that, as seen, ended successfully in the 1970s on behalf of the agricultural community Canela Baja and its *comuneros*.

The reconstruction of this struggle, in Chapter 8, permitted me to reject the argument that poor, or marginal land, is not of interest for landlords or capitalism. This example shows that the peasantry actively defended their land; that the peasantry can through local resistance, adaptive strategies and voluntary organisation, provoke changes that affect their existence.

Chapter 9 dealt with two different minor processes, both indirect products of changes initiated by the agrarian reform in the Chilean agrarian structure as of the 1960s. While the first describes the coming of Puerto Oscuro as a private property, into mainly *comunero* hands, the second refers to the agricultural communities' slow process of legalisation. Describing these in Chapter 9, both the history of the former *hacienda* El Totoral and that of the communities, initiated sometime in the 1700s, came to an end. In other words, I tried to close a history initiated 300 years before. It is now time to analyse this historical process more closely.

Contributing elements

I will try to identify some key elements that resulted in two patterns of agrarian development, the *latifundium* and the agricultural communities. From the historical reconstruction of my case study, I will contrast some of them, on one side, against my own theses. On the other side they will be contrasted against the studies about the Norte Chico's agricultural communities, in particular, as well as against the studies on the Chilean agrarian structure, in general.

The reconstruction of the process of transition from private land ownership to the form of semi-communal from the 1700s forward was examined in Chapter 7. The variety of terms used in the colonial period in order to denominate the land property until the beginning of the twentieth century shows that land ownership was a process in definition, neither smooth nor linear. The land sales documents are revealing in that respect for part of this period. Therefore, an analysis of the terms used during part of this long process is necessary.

Estancias, comunidades, fundos and haciendas

Analysing the eighteen sales of land specified in Table 7.1, and sales like those that follow below, it is possible to draw two conclusions. When, on one hand, those properties that evolved into semi-communal land of the agricultural communities, the most commonly used terms are *estancia* and *comunidad* (community). In other cases they are denominated as *fundos,* even as *haciendas.*

When, on the other hand, those properties that did not evolve into agricultural communities are mentioned, the terms *hacienda* and *fundo* are preferred. Yet the term *estancia* also appears sometimes. Dealing in first place, with the agricultural communities:

- in a sale of 1863, it is mentioned that the purchased piece of land had rights to the *estancia* Fasico (present day sub-area of the agricultural community Canela Baja) and that its boundary to the north was the *estancia* of the same name (ANCH, AN Illapel, Vol. 23, RP, 1863, folio 59, Doc. no. 8. "Transacción entre Manuel Godoy, como comprador y Toribio Bacho y Gregorio Carvajal, como vendedores");
- in the next century, in a payment adjudication of 1922, a *hijuela* located in La Higuerita is mentioned, with rights to the *estancia* Canela Baja, while the borders that are named to the south is the *comunidad* Canela Baja ("Haber de doña Manuela Olivares y Vicencio Cortes", 10 de Enero, 1922, courtesy of José Antonio Cortés, *comunero* of Canela Baja). In the same document another *hijuela* is mentioned located in the *fundo* Canelilla (presently an agricultural community) and with rights to the same *estancia.*

When within an agricultural community land is sold in the form of *hijuelas,* mentioned also in the common word land (*terrenos*), little distinction is made between the terms *estancia* and *bien común* (common goods or wealth) to indicate the rights to which the purchase of the *hijuelas* gives (see Table 7.1). The right to the *estancia* is then always associated to the *hijuela* property. It is clear that the terms *estancia, fundo* or even *hacienda,* are used as synonymous of community, referring to land which belongs to various owners in undivided form.

The use of these terms shows that during the 1800s and the beginning of the 1900s, these communities were still considered as *estancias, fundos,* or *haciendas,* and that these terms have been kept from a previous time when these properties originally belonged to one person or family.

Dealing secondly with those large landed properties, which did not evolve into agricultural communities, the terms *hacienda* and *fundo* are the common ones. However, as late as 1925, the term *estancia* was also used as synonymous to *fundos,* as the fifth and last example below shows. That *hacienda* and *fundo* are preferred terms can be observed in the cases of the *haciendas* El Totoral, Limáhuida, Peña Blanca, Durazno and Quelón. The last three were owned by the marquis of Huana and Piedra Blanca. The *hacienda El* Durazno and part of El Quelón belong, nowadays, to the community Canela Alta:

- in a sale of 1843 (Table 7.1), it is said that Tomas Ibacache sold to Francisco Cortés 50 *varas*:

    ... of lands with estancia rights situated in the Ranchitos in Canela Abajo [present day agricultural community] that border in the east to the estancia Carquindano [present day agricultural community] in the south to the Leones's lands, in the west to the *hacienda* El Totoral and in the north to the lands of the Corteses (ANCH, AN Illapel, Vol. 11, 1843, folio 139; emphasis added);

- in 1849, Ramón and Juan Antonio Montes mortgaged with Santiago Lira the *hacienda* of Limaguida and the *estancia* Gallardo, with the rights they had in Huentelauquén. As borders of the *estancia* Gallardo, the *hacienda* El Totoral is named to the north (ANCH, AN Illapel, Vol. 15, Doc. no. 11, 1849, verso folio 3 to 4);
- in 1861, Francisco Cortés Monroy, as owner, gave authorisation to Manuel Antonio Gonzáles to ask for the devolution of the *haciendas* Peña Blanca, Durazno and Quelón because of the ending of the rental contract he (Francisco Cortés Monroy) had with José Manuel Vásquez (ANCH, AN Illapel, Vol. 26, Doc. no. 37, 1861, verso folio 43 to 44);
- in a sale of 1863 it is mentioned that the borders of the *fundo* to the north is the *estancia* Espíritu Santo (presently a sub-area of the agricultural community Canela Baja) (ANCH, AN Illapel, Vol. 23, Register of property of 1863, folio 49, Doc. no. 1. 'Transacción entre Lorenzo Codoceo y Simona Trigo y su esposo Miguel Bugeño como vendedores');

The Common Denominator

- in a 1925 document of the sale of rights to the *fundo* Talinay, it is mentioned as *estancia*. About its borders, it is said that to the east is the *fundo* Los Tomes (present day agricultural community of the same name, which constituted a *fundo* until the 1973) (Courtesy of José Antonio Cortés, *comunero* of Canela Baja) (Sale of rights of Talinay, Clodomira Rojo, AN Illapel, Vol. ?, 1925, Doc.no. 368, folio 289).

For the sake of clarity, I will repeat here what these terms historically stand for in Chile. As shown in Chapter 4, *estancia* frequently used as synonymous with *hacienda*, predates this term and *fundo*. Having its origin in the colonial *mercedes de tierra*, and *pastos* (grass), or *asientos* (settlements), in the strict sense of the term, *estancia* concerns uncultivated rural land, dedicated to livestock.

Hacienda refers to those properties where agriculture was introduced alongside livestock. From the middle of the 1800s, the term *fundo* began to be imposed, without completely substituting *hacienda* or *latifundio*, another term used as synonym to *hacienda* and *fundo*.

The new term *fundo* refers to those properties, which resulted from the '*hijuelación*', or division, of the *haciendas*, from whence the term *hijuela* originally came. With the hereditary division of the *haciendas*, *fundos* became an intermediate form of property between the *haciendas* and the smaller family based forms (the *minifundia*).

This helps us to understand why the terms *estancia, hacienda* or *fundo* until the beginning of the twentieth century were still used in land sales within Canela Baja and Canela Alta. It depends, on one hand, on the fact that these properties were *estancias* in the literal meaning of the world, i.e., mainly aimed to cattle raising and, on the other, on the private character these properties - intended or not - acquired, evolving from *mercedes*. As Borde and Góngora (1956:145) have already indicated, the diverse forms of agricultural property in Chile, with the exception of property at the urban periphery (*chacras)*, all have their roots in the *hacienda* and its transformations; the *haciendas* having their precedents in the *estancias* and these again in the *mercedes*.

Within the studied context, it remains clear that what today in the Canela commune, on one side, constitutes several agricultural communities, were originally colonial land grants, part of which, like El Totoral, on the other side, evolved into *haciendas*. In the specific cases of the agricultural communities Canela Baja, Canela Alta and the *hacienda* El Totoral, they came from what apparently were two colonial land grants, which became one property. Later, via an exchange of properties, it became two different properties again. But while the *estancia* El Totoral, as well as those *fundos* that arose from it, today seven *fundos* in all remain private property, the *estancia* La Canela, on the other hand, evolved into fourteen semi-communal owned agricultural communities. The same historical process is valid for the colonial *estancias* Conchalí and Chigualoco, and Mincha, respectively.

Establishing that these properties had their origin in the colonial land grants, however, does not explain why they became two different forms of land ownership. The idea that the agricultural communities were land grants given to low-rank soldiers, as postulated by Santander (*s.a.*:1), among others, should so far have fallen, at least in theory, by its own inconsistency and by the fact that land grants (*mercedes de tierras*) were only given to the most outstanding social personages of colonial society. Therefore, to affirm that the *mercedes* were given to low-rank soldiers involves a contradiction (see Chapter 5).

The conqueror Pedro Cortés Monroy and his descendants came to belong to the highest social strata. I have to return to the particular examples since they are aimed at supporting some of my theses. The case of Pedro Cortés Monroy confirms that to be rewarded with *mercedes* and *encomiendas* was no easy task, involving decades of struggle, not only on the colony's battlefront without remuneration, but even in the sovereign's Court.

So neither can I say that Pedro Cortés Monroy, as a designator of land grants was a low rank soldier, or only at the beginning of his career, nor can I say that this was the case of the other conquerors who received land grants in the area. The *conquistador* Francisco Hernández Ortiz, granted Conchalí and Chigualoco, was as specified General Grand Master and Juan de Ahumada, granted the *merced* of Mincha, was captain (Villaroel et al., 1988:73-74). So too, was the case with the *encomendero* Juan de Ahumada, who became the owner of the famous *estancia* Choapa. He was lieutenant *corregidor* (Spanish magistrate) three times, and three times Mayor of the city of Santiago. When he died, he had over 20 rent paying Indians and 62 slaves (Villaroel *et al*, 1988:66, 72).

Specifically regarding the case of La Canela, the fact that Diego Cortés Pérez, as well as his sons, occupied a lower social position than his paternal half-brother (the marquis of Huana and Piedra Blanca) has obviously nothing to do with the idea that the land, which today constitutes agricultural communities, were *mercedes de tierras* given to low-rank officials. Diego Cortés Pérez, great-grandson of the conqueror Pedro Cortés Monroy, born out of wedlock, was sergeant major.

The two sons of Diego Cortés Peréz apparently moved to the *estancia* La Canela sometime during the first decades of the 1700s. Why they moved to La Canela is something I cannot account for. It is curious, since they had the property El Chañaral, apparently of better land quality, but on the other hand, they also had the gold mine of Espíritu Santo. However, and more important, the time they moved to La Canela coincides with the Norte Chico's economic crisis, when wheat export to Peru begins to decrease. According to Carmagnani (1963:36), from being a wheat exporting region, the Norte Chico experienced a deficit, so that in 1724 it was forbidden to take wheat outside the zone, the neighbouring zones of Copiapó and Huasco excepted. In 1740, the crisis was such that the ration of wheat to the Indians was reduced with one third.

If there is a relationship between this economic crisis and the emergence of the agricultural communities, which I consider plausible, then this case would support Albala *et al*, (1967:13) and Castro and Bahamondes' (1983:1-2), hypothesis on the effects of the economic crisis upon the agrarian structure in the Norte Chico. I can also add the interference of six epidemic outbreaks during 1700-1744 and the earthquake of 1730, which was followed by a cycle of bad years in agriculture (Pinto, 1980:38-39; 44). The epidemic outbreaks were in 1705, 1718, 1720, 1724, 1731 and 1740. Those from 1718 and 1724 were of typhus and dysentery and those from 1710 (sic! 1720?) and 1740 of smallpox (Pinto, 1983:119, 44). According to Pinto, who follows Carmagnani, there were three difficult periods for agriculture in the Norte Chico; 1705-1706, 1715-1716 and 1729-1735. The last period was considered to be the worst of the century.

However, at the same time during the first half of the 1700s, the production of gold increased considerably, especially in the margins of the River Choapa and Petorca (Pinto, 1983:42). This could have attracted land speculators. It may also have been a reason for the sons of Diego Cortés Pérez to move to La Canela, since they also had the gold mine of Espíritu Santo.

This period of economic crisis, as well as of gold rush, would coincide with the period up to the 1750, which I defined as relatively active in sales and exchanges of land for this area. This resulted in new *estancias* (Chapter 7). The numerous small land sales registered after 1750 had, however another character, resulting not in new *estancias*, but in a redistribution of the main properties among the existing families. From the history studied, I can only deduce that other elements could have contributed to the sons of Diego Cortés Peréz settling in La Canela. Excepting the El Chañaral farm, of which I know nothing, that these sons inherited, considering that the wealth that Diego and Pedro Cortés Castillo inherited from their father was mainly land (*estancia* La Canela) and livestock and not money, it seems that they decided to take possession of it by taking residence there. It is uncertain of what happened to the mine of Espíritu Santo. Because of its location it should have been within the borders of Canela Baja *estancia* that remained in the hand of Pedro Cortés Castillo, but neither he nor his wife left testaments, where we could have obtained some information about the mine. The decision to move to La Canela could have had its starting point in the economic crisis and perhaps in the meagre chances of a military career with uncertain economic rewards in colonial society.

Probably in order to raise some capital, before dividing La Canela into two *estancias*, the brothers sold two parts, Talinay and Huentealuquén, to Lieutenant Juan de Céspedes and Captain Juan de Ahumada, respectively. Later, the brothers again sold parts of their *estancias*. All these sales took place before 1750.

These factors may not only have forced them to settle on the inherited land, but even to sell of part of it in order to raise some capital, probably to exploit the gold mine of Espíritu Santo. Both Ibacache and Jorquera, who respectively bought land from the *estancias* of the Cortés' brothers, were captains, as was Pedro Cortés Castillo. Diego, the other brother, does not appear in any records as having occupied any military rank or other position within the colonial bureaucracy. Through the sale of parts of the *estancia* La Canela before and after it was divided between the brothers Cortés Castillo, and their later hereditary subdivision and further sales, the land of the original *estancia* La Canela was gradually populated. In this way new families were included, whose surnames, along with that of Cortés, exist to this day.

The surnames of the owners of the *haciendas*, have on the other hand, not been maintained to the same extent as in the agricultural communities, where the relationship between the original owners and the present-day owners of the land is quite clear (see Appendix 1).

Different factors explain the fact that the surnames of the *haciendas'* owners have not been maintained in the region. The first reason is, the non-settlement and/or absenteeism of the owners on their land during the 1600s and 1700s. As postulated in my second thesis (Chapter 4), the non-settlement of the landowners, absenteeism or residence depended on their positions within the bureaucratic-military hierarchy and/or their socio-economic status within colonial society. In other words, the higher their social position within the colonial society, the lesser the interest in residence and direct exploitation of the properties. Without settlement, no local demographic growth and, therefore, less or no subdivision of the properties, at least in comparison with those that were settled, preserving their character of large private properties. Consequently, the lower the position of the owners within the bureaucratic-military hierarchy or, the lower their socio-economic status, the stronger was their interest in settling and exploiting the land they possessed.

Francisco de Aguirre y Cortés, the owner of El Totoral, was the great-great-grandson of the *conquistador* Francisco de Aguirre on the paternal side, and great-grandson of the *conquistador* Pedro Cortés Monroy on the maternal side, and belonged to one of the wealthiest families of La Serena's colonial society. He and his descendants had an innumerably list of important posts in the colonial bureaucracy. He was Spanish magistrate (*corregidor*) of La Serena in 1685 and town councillor (*regidor*) in 1689 and 1693. His grandson José de Aguirre y Gallardo was also Spanish magistrate in 1751 and in 1753 Mayor of the same city. The mayor of La Serena was also José Ignacio de Aguirre y Lisperger in 1732, the son of Francisco de Aguirre y Cortés. The son of the former, Miguel de Aguirre y Lisperger was mayor of La Serena in 1718, and Spanish magistrate, in 1748 (Retamal *et al*, 1992:128) (see also Chapter 5).

The owners of the other landed properties, which became *haciendas* in the Canela Commune, also held important posts in the colonial hierarchy. Considering, that these people were first of all colonial bureaucrats and soldiers, it is improbable that they were also active agriculturists living in their landed properties. The parochial archives, examined to account for the sparse population in the commune at the end of the 1600s and beginning of the 1700s, reinforced my thesis about these people not living in their properties. I also demonstrated, empirically, that neither Pedro Cortés Pérez, nor his ancestors lived in the present Canela commune. He was buried in La Serena alongside his ancestors.

A second factor, which explains that the surnames of the *haciendas'* owners have not been maintained in the region, is the constant transfer of ownership between diverse owners during the 1800s and 1900s. A third factor during the same period was the long tradition of absenteeism, which came to form part of the idiosyncrasy of the owners of the *haciendas* in Chile. My empirical study of El Totoral shows quite clearly the existence of both factors. Absenteeism then as a phenomenon would just be a continuation of the non-settlement of the 1600s and 1700s. Without settlement, with absentee and diverse landlords due to the constant transfer of property, no demographic increase in the area and, consequently, the discontinuance of their family names.

In opposition to the *haciendas*, the establishment of the owners on their land is the primordial element or factor contributing to the initial formation of the agricultural communities. This is largely because it was followed by the demographic increase of their descendants over a land area that, contrary to the population, did not increase.

The economic crisis during the first decades of the 1700s may have played an important role in the formation of the agricultural communities when wheat export to Peru started to decrease, as suggested by Albala *et al*, (1967), and Castro and Bahamondes (1983). While the strong landowners managed to keep their large *haciendas,* the weaker ones had to divide their land, sell and/or sell, the latter becoming the agricultural communities.

The agricultural communities would thus be the result of the relative division, settlement or selling of those large landed properties that could not stand the economic crisis. I mean relative division, because as we have seen, the properties succeed in remaining, to a great extent, large properties. This says more about the formation of the agricultural communities from the 1700s, than about the eventual settlement of the landowners on their *mercedes de tierras* during the 1600s, when these were granted.

However, during the 1700s, these two factors - the effects of the economic crisis and the gradual emergence of the agricultural communities - may have been related. If the owners of the land or their descendants had still not settled on their properties, or had been absentees, the effects of the economic crisis may have forced them to live on their *haciendas* or *estancias*.

It is primarily the direct establishment of the landowners onto their properties, and, eventually, their low social status, that was decisive for the formation of the semi-communal owned agricultural communities (see Chapter 4). This is not to say that the form of semi-communal land ownership arose from those lands given to the low-rank soldiers. Hitherto we have dealt with the question of the origin or starting point of the agricultural communities. However, the formation of the agricultural communities, once the land became occupied or settled, should now be considered.

In my first thesis, I also put forward the view that for the formation of the semi-communal land ownership of the agricultural communities two more factors were necessary. These were the demographic increase of the old proprietary (on the same quantity of land) and the specific geographical conditions of the Norte Chico with its semi-arid environment and prevalence of hilly and unirrigated land. According to Gastó *et al*, (1986:71) the Norte Chico region presented some substantive differences with other arid Mediterranean areas:

> One of them lies in the presence of the Andes mountain chain, where the rain is abundant, thus constituting a valuable hydrographical basin, from which forms numerous irrigated valleys of high productivity. *This permits the integration of the dry land with the irrigated and the utilisation of the draining water in the dry land.* The proximity of the Andes also stimulates *the transhumance* of the cattle from the occident, of Mediterranean climate and winter growing on the meadow land towards the mountain, of cold climate and summer growing of the pasture (emphasis added).

Once the land was occupied, due to the demographic increase and pressure on the land, the scarce flat and irrigated land was fenced, denoting the character of private property (*hijuelas*):

> As in the course of human evolution the density of settlement increases not only because the number of individuals in a given territory increases but also because, partly as a consequence, the number of interactions between individuals increases, there is a need for specialisation of activities so as to increase productivity. Specialisation is required if a greater number of interacting individuals are forced to assure their livelihood on a given territory (Coser, Introduction in Durkheim, 1984:XVI).

The fencing of the hilly and dry lands, on the other hand, in combination with a specific type of exploitation specialising principally in goats, would have been uneconomic, since this would have reduced the pasture area so necessary for the goats, since they graze over great distances. The hills become communal property (*campos comunes*). Goat rearing, within each owner's individual fenced dry area, would have been impossible.

This process of dividing the flat and irrigated land into small strips not only defined its private character but kept the hilly and irrigated lands undivided in a permanent way, thereby defining their common character. This shows the existence of a (previous) common understanding or agreement between individuals about the best way to manage and preserve existing natural and economic resources.

The use of the hilly and dry land as common land was originally due to the traditional transhumance or nomadic livestock, conditioned by a Mediterranean region between valley and mountains. As Borde and Góngora (1956) have shown for the Valle del Puangue, this tradition was common in Chile before the *haciendas* began to fence the land with the advent of agriculture (see Chapter 4). In this sense, the use of common pastureland within the properties that became agricultural communities represented the continuity of a tradition, which precedes them, but that was accentuated with the fencing the lands of the *haciendas* at the end of 1700s.

The prevalence of hilly and semi-arid environment throughout the Norte Chico and hence in the *haciendas*, becomes decisive however, if we add the factor of the establishment of the landowners on their respective properties. The demographic development of the population and the inherent process of the subdivision of the flat and irrigated land, at a time when the fencing of the *haciendas'* land was started, followed this process.

The formation of the private property of the *haciendas*, or of the semi-communal nature of the agricultural communities is thus not necessary related to the quality of the land (irrigated-non irrigated/hilly-valley). The origin of the agricultural communities is to be found mainly and principally, in the establishment of the former owners (or/and their inheritors) in their respective properties (see the first thesis, Chapter 4), this eventually relating to the low social status they occupied within colonial society. This settlement would have been accentuated by the economic crisis.

The formation of one or other type of property is not necessarily related to the size of the property. The large *haciendas*, with the fencing of their lands, had not displaced the smaller ones. It is important to note that the *estancia* La Canela for example, once El Totoral became another property, was much larger than the *estancia* El Totoral and continues to be so. I would suggest here that the fencing of the *haciendas'* land, which ended during the last part of 1700s, was to the detriment of those that had become populated, which continued being private. Limiting the traditional use of common pastures was not necessarily done to the detriment of those smaller properties. In this way, while the *haciendas* - generally owned by absentee landlords - continued alongside agriculture, with the exploitation of cattle, those properties that were settled as a result of the demographic increase, had reduced their pastures.

The demographic pressure exerted on the scarce flat and irrigated land necessitated the regulation of what belonged to each of the inheritors, of the families of the former owners. They have simultaneously, implicitly or explicitly, an understanding or agreement about leaving the grazing land undivided, i.e., as common. So while, with their fencing and legal registration, the *hijuelas* consolidated their character of private property inside the agricultural communities, the grazing land consolidated its character of common property in a parallel form but without being legally recognised, since the law does not accommodate that form of ownership. We can see here a coincidence in the time the *hijuelas* start to be registered, in 1855 in the case of Canela Alta, and the dictation of the code of civil law referred to above.

In this way, my argument contradicts the idea, sustained among others by Cañón, that because the flat land was valuable it was fenced, whereas the hills, implicitly not so valuable, were not fenced and remained more or less in abandonment.

By defining a part of the land as valuable, even the rest becomes defined, but this does not necessarily mean that it is not as valuable. Thus, a parallel and simultaneous process of definition takes place for both types of land. Having thus considered that it is the mountainous landscape that propitiates a grazing economy, the area being consequently defined more by cattle *estancias* than agriculturist *haciendas*, it is hard to imagine that its owners would have considered the hills without value. 'Without value' perhaps for agricultural purposes, but hardly for cattle-raising. On the contrary, to avoid its scattering, or *minifundisation*, it must have appeared as a suitable solution for this environment. So while the fragmentation of the irrigated land was caused by an existing tradition of dividing and defining what belonged to the heirs of the inherited land, the non-scattering of the hilly and dry land, as a resource organisation, is the one that appears as the 'novelty', organised within one property of many owners. I would suggest that *the greater the division of the flat land, the greater the necessity to maintain the hills undivided.*

However, although the agricultural communities are constituted both by semi-private and communal properties internally, seen from the outside they constitute one unit, a property of many families. In this way, the partial conversion of certain properties into agricultural communities could neither comply, as a report indicates to the fencing of the land in the area, nor be a product of a change in land tenancy. According to the development plan for the present-day *fundo* Puerto Oscuro, formulated by agricultural experts, mentioned in Chapter 9, the erosion in the zone is due to the fact that with a change in the tenure of land:

> ... formerly constituted by nomadic stock farmers who moved from the sea to the mountain, according to the seasons the fields began to be sown and enclosed. This forced the peasants to sow on the hilly land and thus restricted the movement of livestock, having to keep the livestock in the same place for longer periods, as well as to the excessive felling of tress and bushes. For these reasons, the peasants gradually preferred to rear goats because of the lower initial investment, the more rapid return on the investment and their rusticity. Since goats, if they were allowed, would graze over vast territories, the men obliging them to live on small areas to be near during the milking time, caused serious erosion (Plan de Desarrollo y Explotación del Predio "Puerto Oscuro" (*s.a.*) courtesy of Carlos Rocco, former agricultural technician and manager of the *fundo*).

The fencing of the land, reducing the pasture areas, accentuated the common use of the hilly and non-irrigated land on those properties, which were kept indivisible or in common form.

Summing up the analysis of the historical process, I would say that the semi-communal land ownership of the agricultural communities began to crystallise as a form of land ownership during the second part of the 1700s, as a result of the intervention of various elements. Among them, I have considered:

- the break up of the land into several units through sales;
- further hereditary subdivision of the land;

- the contribution of the specific ecological environment;
- type of economy (cattle extensive in the hills and agriculture intensive on the irrigated land);
- the fencing of the flat and irrigated land; and
- the further preservation of an earlier tradition of communal lands within the resultant properties due to economic rationale.

In conclusion, I would say that this very long process clearly shows in the case study how the agricultural communities of Chile's Norte Chico are the result of a spontaneous historical process, where the recognition of the form was made long after the form had persisted. To show in the same way, exactly how and in what order different elements contributed to that formation is more difficult. I have finally tried, however, to connect plausible circumstances confronting the specific case with those regional socio-economic phenomena during the colonial time.

The English open field system, the Swiss grazing commons and the agricultural communities

I will now contrast the process of formation of the agricultural communities with two European examples; the English open field system and the Swiss system. I will follow Stevenson's *Common Property Economics: A General Theory And Land Use Applications* (1991). Stevenson's book is relevant here because it constitutes a recent empirical and conceptual study about a living example of communal land ownership, which is to be found in Europe, a continent where capitalism cannot be said to be a recent phenomena, as could be argued for Third World countries. Theoretically, he distinguishes between open access and common property, by which he arrives to a formal definition of communal land ownership that fits in very well with my case study. This is a factor, which further supports not only the generality of the form but is also analogous to the historical processes to some extent.

Stevenson compares the forms of common property with private property in the present alpine grazing land in Switzerland, but reduces his empirical study to the German speaking part. He also points out the similarities between the Swiss case and the feudal English open field system, restricting the last to the particular area of the Midlands. One of

Stevenson's merits consists of extending the form of communal management resource to other natural resources, especially those of open access, as an alternative to private property. This way, he shows the validity of the form to other spheres of socio-economic life, which appears as relevant in this 'globalising era'. As Stevenson's contribution on common land initially is derived from the field of economics, his empirical comparison between common and private property, using econometric models, falls outside the focus of this dissertation. The question of the efficiency of common property as economic system, in comparison with the private, is certainly both theoretically and empirically relevant, especially for resources that potentially may be managed under common property in the future. Applied to already existing forms of common property, it can be considered quite irrelevant, as the question of their transformation into another system is not at stake. Dealing with the comparison between common and private property, it could be pointed out that if part of the landed commons has emerged due to specific material conditions, these being unsuitable for private management, it might be true that they do not:

> work ideally, but at least it works. Under the same conditions private property might not work at all (Stevenson, 1991:222).

Even though common property may be not perfect, neither is private property.

Material or geographical variations in our sociological common denominator, communal land ownership, are many. This form occurred in the English Midlands of the past and in the present Swiss mountainous land. The form, however, remains mostly the same. We have within one institution, the communal land, and also the individual possessions; the exploitation of both economic spheres being mainly individual, as opposed to collective (see the already examined examples in Chapter 1).

In the now defunct English open fields system, crop cultivation occurred mainly under individual tenancy, intermixed with and complemented by, grazing on common property (Stevenson, 1991:56). The arable land was divided into long narrow strips, which was held by a peasant in feudal tenancy, left unfenced. Hence, the name 'open fields'. The harvest was individual, some aspects of the farming being either co-operative or individual. There was also a community control of cropping, about which Stevenson does not elaborate, but that somehow implied that the peasants cultivate the land co-operatively, using for example animals and crop rotation organised by common rules.

The large, undivided common land for grazing comprised common pasture of stubble, fallow, meadow, waste, and balks in the open fields. Much of the township's land underwent common grazing during one season or another. The waste, land beyond the arable land, was grazed in common during the summer. English meadows, was land reserved to grow hay in spring and, after the hay harvest, were opened to common grazing. The arable land was subjected to common grazing of the haulm after harvest. During the year it was left uncultivated, and grazed by tethered animals on any balks or common ways while it was in crop. In both the Swiss and the English system, arable land was destined for grazing during certain seasons. Of this English system, the waste can, according to Stevenson (1991:144) be compared with the Swiss alps and the meadows with the Swiss May-fields or forealps.

Let me now take the Swiss system, which not only represents a living example of communal land ownership, but also several variations of the same. The Swiss system shows, according to Stevenson, three general levels of pastures in ascending latitude; the village level, the forealps (Mayfields) and the alpine grazing areas. While the first two are most often privately owned, the third can be private or common (1991:86-87). Stevenson concentrates on the last level, the common-owned alpine grazing areas, this being, according to him, the true alpine grazing areas. The word alp originally comes from alpine pasture and in German means 'grazing area in the mountain' while in English it became another word for mountain.

The alpine grazing areas are covered with snow during winter and with forage in spring and summer, not being apt for agriculture, except for grazing (Stevenson, 1991:86). Interestingly, in the third level of pastures, historically two different forms of ownership have arisen side-by-side, determining in some cases private land ownership and communal in others, in spite of having a common geographical base. The pattern of usage in this area is that the cattle change altitude to take advantage of new forage, as it appears when the warm season advances (transhumance). This system has a simple economic rationale. By using the mountain grasslands, the farmers can support more animals than if they used only the pasture of the valley. Utilising this system, the Swiss mountain areas support approximately 30 per cent more animals than if they were not used at all (Stevenson, 1991:86-87).

Topographically, the alpine grazing areas have much in common with the *veranadas,* or summer grazing areas of the Andes in Chile and on the Argentina side. The common land of the agricultural communities is mainly composed of hills, similar to the fore alps. So while the common land of the agricultural communities corresponds to the local own grazing areas, the *veranadas* mainly remain located outside their own physical institution. However, there are also some agricultural communities that have their own *veranadas*. The *veranadas,* as with the Swiss case, can also be private or state-owned. In the Choapa province, there are examples of both private and communal. The private belonged, at least until the 1970s, to many *hacienda* owners, the *veranadas* embracing both sides of the Andes beyond the Chilean limits (Aranda, 1971:131). In addition to their own cattle, the owners of the *veranadas* hire part of it out to other cattle owners (middle, small and *comuneros*).

In other words, this system of transhumance to the *veranadas* in the grassland of both the Chilean and Argentinean Andes is used, not only by the private property of the *haciendas* and *fundos*, but also by the agricultural communities. This means that both property forms, private and semi-communal, combine their own pasture system with that of the *veranadas*.

The economic relevance of the mountain grasslands has been pointed out, among others, by Almeyda (1948:10; see Chapter 4). According to Aranda (1971:5), the *veranadas* of Region IV are estimated between 100,000 and 150,000 ha, the meadowlands being 950,000 ha. In the region, in a period of 10 years (1959-1969), 33.4 % of the total goat bulk and 28.2% of the ovine cattle was brought to the *veranadas* (Aranda, 1971:29-30). Thus, there is a close similarity between the Swiss case and Chile's Region IV regarding the economic relevance of the mountain grasslands.

Common property can be organised in different ways. In the alpine grazing areas there are different systems of common property; the main ones being the share rights, the community alps, Korporations and property alps. Dealing with the first three, their origin can be traced as far back as the Middle Ages, as is also the case with private property (Stevenson, 1991:115).

Although these four different systems of common property, because of the high geographical location, are topographically like the *veranadas* in

The Common Denominator

Chile, with respect to the way they function, all of them have some common features with the communities of Region IV. This is in aspects that deal with different conditions to be able to belong to the system and also relative to their internal operating as a social organisation. Moreover, I would suggest that the agricultural communities of Region IV constitute a compendium of many characteristics of the four Swiss cases. Let me briefly describe these four systems of common property and compare them with the agricultural communities.

The *share rights alps* limit entry by requiring users to possess grazing rights. In the archetypal, or classical form, a right allows its owner to graze one animal unit, usually equal to one cow (Stevenson, 1991:89). These rights are perpetual, and they are transferable by rental or sale. The share rights system both limits access for outsiders who may want to enter and defines grazing rights among users within the group. In terms of operation, this system is best illustrated, in my case, by the first written regulation of the *comuneros* from Espíritu Santo from the end of the nineteenth century (see Chapter 8, Table 8.1). However, there was no exact correspondence between number of rights and number of animals on the common land. The moment the contract was made, it seems that the limitation in the number of animals was established according to their factual possession at the time. Those who had more, had to pay extra for every unit of animal, yet there was a clear correspondence between number of rights and number of animals on the common land, in the sense that those who had more rights had generally more animals. This also points at the social differentiation of that time between *comuneros*. The present situation in most communities is not very different from the referred one, where there is a lot of flexibility concerning the number of animals. If nothing else, nature itself regulates, through periodic drought, any exaggerated increase in the number of goats and other animals. The rights in the agricultural communities of Chile Region IV are perpetual, but also transferable by rental or sale.

The second major common right system in Switzerland, called *community alps*, are alpine grazing areas owned by communities or townships. In most cases, the primary requirement for use is residency in the townships. In some cases, 'citizenship' in the community is required, this being a stringent requirement based on the citizenship that every Swiss national has in the particular township, from which his or her ancestors came. Even this system has similarities with the agricultural communities of Region IV in terms of ownership, the right to the common land given by the relative possession of cultivated land (the *hijuelas*). *Hijuelas* are mostly inherited.

Korporation alps represent the third major right system in the Swiss Alps. Korporation means 'corporate body of citizenship':

> The 'citizens' of the Korporations are members of families with certain surnames – the old families of the districts in which the Korporations were founded. Rights to use the Korporations' alps are limited to those families. The Korporations are umbrella organisations that each owns many alps (Stevenson, 1991:90).

This system too shows clear resemblance with the agricultural communities of Region IV. Those who own the agricultural communities today are descendants of the old colonial families who owned this land. Therefore, the colonial lineage is one of the main historical characteristics of these communities. So, if the Swiss Korporations are made of member families with certain surnames, so it is with the agricultural communities (see Appendix 1).

Property alps represents the fourth system of limiting entry based on land ownership in the valleys, this being a rather rare form of rights determination in Switzerland. The number of common use rights is here tied to the ownership of particular parcels near the village. If the parcel ownership is transferred, the alp rights automatically follow. If the land is divided by sale or inheritance the number of rights transferred to each new owner is proportional to the hectares that each new owner receives. In this way, entry to common use alps is limited to those who have correspondent property interest in the valley, and overall use is limited at carrying capacity (Stevenson, 1991:90).

If this system is rare in Switzerland, it is quite common in Chile's Region IV, where land ownership (*hijuelas*) in the valleys is an essential requirement to be a *comunero*. By being a *comunero*, a person has rights to common land, and *comuneros* are those who possess a *hijuela*, or strip of land, in the valleys - exceptionally, there are also some *hijuelas* in the hills. There are also some *comuneros* who lack *hijuelas*, the community permitting them to keep their rights to the common land. However, as in the property alps, if the ownership of the *hijuela* is transferred, the rights are automatically transferred to the new owner.

The Common Denominator

I will now examine some differences between the three referred cases. Comparing the Swiss example with the Midland open fields system, the first noticeable difference is in geographical, or material conditions (Stevenson, 1991:144). While the open field system was organised around growing crops, the Swiss system is dominantly pastoral. The pastoral economy was important, but complementary, in the English system. In the Swiss Alps, however, arable land is limited, the mountains favouring a pasturing economy (Stevenson, 1991:143). The agricultural communities of Region IV are not homogeneous, some more agricultural than pastoral, and vice versa, depending principally on the local natural environment and access to irrigation (see Chapter 3). However, considering as a whole the area where the agricultural communities are located, their climate and physical conformation, I would suggest that, due to the scarcity of arable land, as well as the complementary importance of livestock production for the economy of the *comuneros*, the agricultural communities are in material conditions in between the English and the Swiss, being rather agro-pastoral than just mainly agricultural or pastoral.

Another difference between the English and the Swiss case regards the rights to the system. In the English system this was property or predial-related, or bounded, whereas the Swiss rights are personally related, through residency, citizenship, family lineage or the holding of share rights (Stevenson, 1991:145-6). What gives the status of a *comunero* are the *hijuelas*, the rights to the common land are predial-related, the *comuneros* being exchangeable, the rights passing to a new person if the *comunero* sells an *hijuela*. At the same time, we cannot disregard the importance of lineage; as *comuneros* are mainly those who are descendants of the old family owners.

I will also suggest another important difference, socio-political in character, between the English system and the Swiss grazing commons and the agricultural communities of Chile's Region IV. The open field system operated within a feudal structure. The peasants held land in feudal tenancy, the lords being the owners (Stevenson, 1991:144), the relationship between them being rather antagonistic and vertical. During the enclosure movement, the rights to the commons was disputed between the lords and the peasants, but the interests of the lords prevailed, resulting in the disappearance of common grazing in England by the end of the 1800s (Stevenson, 1991:151; Marx, 1983, Vol. 1:676).

387

In Switzerland, in spite of the feudal system, the holders of land and common rights, granted under feudal contracts, gradually came to regard their land as absolute domain (Stevenson, 1991:151). In England this happened only for the arable land. In Chile's Region IV, the commoners were, even before legalised, co-owners of the land, no lord, Crown or State, having claiming rights to their land. That is, excepting those properties, mainly *haciendas*, with disputes over common borders with the communities. What is more, this is an important historic difference as the land of the agricultural communities of Chile's Region IV, belonged to the *comunero* ancestors. This is not to deny that there may be cases that resemble the Swiss case, where the appropriation of the land was the result of a gradual process.

This third difference is related to another important one, also pointed out by Stevenson, regarding the legal system regulating the commons in both countries. This also relates to my own empirical cases. In his words, in the English system:

> ... basic agricultural rules were never codified but rather were generally accepted precepts based on use from time out of mind. The rules that began appearing in manorial court rolls in the thirteenth century were changes in, additions to, or presentments of fines for violation of the unwritten rules. Over time, a long list of bylaws collected in the manorial courts rolls from the annual court meetings, without the original set of bylaws ever being written down /.../ This contrasts with the situation in Switzerland, where complete sets of alps regulations have been kept at least since the eighteenth century. The Swiss system, however, may have advanced farther than the English system ever did simply because the former system has lived longer (Stevenson, 1991: 151).

As in the English case, in the agricultural communities of Chile's Region IV the rules that ordered the organisation were not codified until the second part of the twentieth century, the rules organising the community system being rather generally accepted precepts based on use 'from time out of mind'. That is one of the most common expressions to be found in the old archival documents, as in the indemnification of the property titles of the agricultural communities in the 1970s.

Similarly in the English case, before the agricultural communities of Chile's Region IV became recognised, some land litigation with the *latifundia* must have revealed the problem for the Courts, latent or manifested, dealing with their land rights, as the case of Espíritu Santo showed. As with Switzerland, where, according to Stevenson, complete sets of alps regulations have been kept at least since the 1880s, Espíritu Santo gave in the Canela commune, the first formal written example of internal regulation, born out of the result of the dispute over who were the owners of these lands.

Some of the precedents left by the litigations, as the litigations themselves understood as social conflicts between divergent social groups, could have been of importance later in the process of legal recognition of the agricultural communities. There are also clearer similarities with the Swiss case here, because the internal, informal and implicit codification and practices among *comuneros* constitute the main basis for the formal law about the agricultural communities.

To summarise, I would stress once again that the agricultural communities of Chile's Region IV have historically much in common with the Swiss and the English common land systems. This is principally due to them being the result of a long process whose main feature was spontaneous and historically as old as those of the private property of the *hacienda*. Even this process of the emergence of both private and common property has a parallel in the Swiss example. According to Stevenson (1991:115), in Switzerland, three out of four of the common alpine grazing areas (share rights, community and Korporations alps) have their origin in the same period as private property, the Middle Ages.

Hitherto, I have contrasted Stevenson's two examples of communal land ownership with the Norte Chico's agricultural communities. But what about the origin and emergence of these forms? Examining the reasons for calling common property, as such, Stevenson gives a brief historical perspective. There are two reasons for denoting this property as common, one historical and one that I would call semantic. This distinction implies an analytical distinction between form and history. Let me begin with history.

Common property in history

According to Stevenson, common property does not represent a lower stage of development belonging to prehistory. It still reproduces successfully in Switzerland as he shows. Nor has common property represented a system of open access. It seems that open access was rather scarce, historically, including hunting and gathering societies. Bearing in mind the confusion between communal land ownership and open access, Stevenson indicates that far from causing over-exploitation, prehistoric hunting and gathering societies regulated land on communal basis with the help of several institutions, the possible reason being preservation of the resources on a sustained productive basis. Among these institutions are, according to Stevenson (1991:46-47):

> tribal heads, closed seasons, social taboos on marriage and lactation, and fission of tribal groups.

Quoting Gordon (1954) who, according to Stevenson (1991:61), began the modern theoretical debate on open access resources:

> property rights in some form predominate by far, and, most important, their existence may be easily explained in terms of the necessity for orderly exploitation and conservation of the resource. Environmental conditions make necessary some vehicle which prevent the resources of the community at large from being destroyed by excessive exploitation. Private or group land tenure accomplishes this end in an easily understandable fashion.

As an institution, common property manifests itself in different ways, and it can manage different types of goods or resources, including public goods (Stevenson, 1991:54-56). Resources used under common property can be complementary to other forms of resource ownership. An example is the English open fields system. Here crop cultivation occurred mainly under individual tenancy intermixed with and complemented by grazing under common property (Stevenson, 1991:56). Therefore, and within the referred historical context, English common grazing of the Midlands in the late Middle Ages, rather than being a maladaptation, may well have been the most efficient production method alongside individual cropping on the arable land (Stevenson, 1991:47). This method of the open field system of England was used across northern Europe for centuries, in a system where the capital inputs as cows and other livestock remain private, but the land is under group control (Stevenson, 1991:62,68).

Stevenson also distinguishes, as I did for the agricultural communities (see Chapter 4), between historical origin - 'roots' in his words - of common property and the reasons or factors, which may help explain its emergence or development, even though they are interwoven.

The factor that leads to the emergence of the system of common rights seems for Stevenson (1991:150) to be demographic. Both the Swiss and English systems probably had their origin in the immigration of Germanic people into these regions in the early middle ages (around the fifth century). In England the inter-commoning declined as the population doubled in the twelfth and thirteenth centuries.

The English common system, or perhaps the first embryonic forms of common property, apparently sprang from previously open access to land. Very early, all members of a community had equal rights to use. Due to demographic pressure and the subsequent diminishing resources, open access was turned into exclusive rights (Stevenson, 1991:47), those belonging to other communities being apparently excluded; still the borders of the pastures between communities not being very clear. This happened, according to Stevenson, during pre-feudal and feudal times, before the population growth of the twelfth and thirteenth centuries, when apparently, a more distinct form of common property took form.

Following Stevenson, the historical roots of this system of common property are to be found, *grosso modo*, in three periods in England; prior to the Anglo-Saxon invasion, during the Anglo-Saxon invasion itself (fifth and sixth centuries), and in the seventh and eight centuries and the Norman invasion of the ninth century. During the first, there were common pasture rights. During the second, the inter-commoning on the wastes introduced by the Anglo-Saxons, extended the former existing common pasture. The inter-commoning was the common pasture of several villages on the wastes beyond the villages. Even the inter-commonings are to be found in the agricultural communities of Chile's Region IV, known under the name common fences or enclosures (see Chapter 3). The Anglo-Saxons practised an extensive pastoral economy in the wastes and forests, and a primitive agriculture in rectangular plots. During the third period, the Anglo-Saxon villages underwent a process of nucleation, but at the time of the Norman invasion, there was still common waste beyond the villages and the inter-commoning continued, apparently, until the twelfth and thirteenth centuries. Then, the inter-commoning started to decline as a result of population growth. The villages made clearer borders between themselves; the common wastes became the possession of particular communities. According to Stevenson (1991:150):

this period parallels the breakup of the mark in Switzerland, when individual communities claimed rights to particular alps and other common property resources.

These land regions that were held in common, were called the marks (Markgenossenschaft). As a system, the Germanic people that invaded the Swiss alpine region between the fourth and eleventh centuries introduced them in a similar way as they did in England (Stevenson, 1991:115-116). The Swiss case, however, is different. Here the reclamation of common land emerged from collective land clearing. Thereafter, the newly cultivated land was divided proportionally to what people already had (Stevenson, 1991:150).

Briefly, as a more or less well defined form of property belonging to particular communities or villages, the main explanation for the emergence of common property seems to be the demographic pressure over resources. Now, the explanation for the emergence of common property as a form or as an agricultural system within the communities themselves is, probably, to be found in the field of economics. This, I would add, in conjunction with the physical environment. Even the described process for the case of England where, with time, the common rights were strengthened, has a parallel in Chile. The common land as a system was imported from Spain. It was not until the introduction of agriculture, side by side with cattle-raising, that, slowly but surely, common pastureland ceased, the lands being fenced even in the mountains (see Chapter 4). Common land persists, however, within defined properties, those that became the agricultural communities, as the only way to raise cattle on a land where it could not have been done on an individual basis.

Since the 1960s, the property rights and institutional schools of economics have debated the emergence of common property, its efficiency and stability (Stevenson, 1991:67). Obviously, the discipline of economics is not alone in its interest for the emergence, effectiveness and solidity of common property and, although the question of efficiency belongs more to the discipline of economics, the other questions are interdisciplinary. The so-called property rights paradigm explains the emergence of common property due to economic circumstances:

> Its main idea is that new private property rights in objects emerge when the benefits of claiming rights exceed the cost of negotiating and enforcing those

The Common Denominator

rights. The value of assets and the cost of protecting assets vary over time, because of change in technology, relative factor scarcities, tastes and preferences, governmental regulation, and so forth. As these values and costs change, the marginal benefits and marginal costs of defining property rights shift, so that agents gain or lose interest in defining and enforcing rights in the assets (Stevenson, 1991:67-68).

Following Dahlman, Stevenson (1991:68) emphasises the importance of the material conditions, i.e., the resources and social characteristics (cost of exploitation) as defining for the form of property, not only private property, but property in general:

> ... characteristics of the resources, economies of scale involved in the technologies to exploit them, and other economic factors affect the property rights structure. Depending on resources and social characteristics, one incentive system yields a better economic outcome than another. Hence, actors choose different property rights systems, depending on their efficiency characteristic, to manage different resources.

The emergence of common property as an agricultural system within the communities is explained by varying optimal scales in the medieval era. Since the cultivation, realised in arable individual plots, was family based, and livestock production showed a comparatively greater scale, this family-centred production, did not manage to exploit a cattle grazing economy on a large scale, leaving the large grazing lands to be used in common. In contrast, the arable land was divided:

> into small strips, some just fractions of an acre, to fit the technological capabilities available in crop cultivation (Stevenson, 1991:68).

This explains, according to him, the existence and efficiency of common property in grazing.

It is interesting here to see the similarity between the so-called 'property rights paradigm' and Cañón's twofold argument between flat-irrigated-valuable land and hilly-dry-unworthy land for the emergence of the agricultural communities in Chile. There are also similarities between Stevenson's explanations and those offered by Borde and Góngora, and Baraona *et al*. I do not consider it necessary to repeat their arguments here (see Chapter 4). Compared to Stevenson's historical explanation, I would say that in dealing with the agricultural communities the Chilean authors, especially Baraona et al., it is easier to identify the implicit sequence in which the explanations are brought together. However, there is a fundamental difference. While Stevenson recognises in common property a special institution of resource management, Borde and Góngora do not. Baraona *et al*, on the other hand, takes a middle position between Stevenson and Borde and Góngora. Solis de Ovando is here, compared to the named Chilean authors, a clear exception in the 1980s, because he goes in the same direction as Stevenson (See Chapter 9 dealing with Solis de Ovando). Moreover, because Stevenson recognises in common property a specific institution for resource management, he is able to systematise theoretically the specific conditions that constitute the core of this ownership form, differentiating it both from private property and open access. So too, does Solis de Ovando from the juridical field for the Chilean agricultural communities. However, before I go into Stevenson's formal definition, it is necessary to understand his semantic meaning of common property.

The semantic meaning of common property

The reason for denoting common property, to indicate an institution of shared ownership, lays according to Stevenson, in the meaning of property itself and its distinction from non-property. Property in an object form entails rights and duties, the class of rights called property rights, both for property holders and for those who are not, or:

> ... the absence of rights and duties means that the institution of property does not exist /.../ open access exhibits the complete absence of ex ante (prior to capture) rights and duties, and therefore it constitutes the total absence of property (Stevenson, 1991:49).

In contrast:

> common property, on the other hand, as the word 'property' implies, involves ex ante rights for the rights holders, even if they are multiple rather than single, and duties for non-property holders (Stevenson, 1991:49).

Property rights are important for the discussion about common property, according to Stevenson. In other words, there is a relationship - legal or ethical - between persons where four pairs or correlates, which are invariable linked, are to be found. The property rights in the form of the correlate right/duty are the first pair. The other three are liberty (privilege)/no right; power/liability, and immunity/no power:

> The power/liability correlates refer to the situation in which one party has the *power* to change the rights, duties, liberties, powers or immunities of another person at will... [i.e., testament]. The heirs' *liabilities* lie in the fact that they must respect their changed legal status toward the bequeathed goods (Stevenson, 1991:50; emphasis original).

A right:

> ... is a claim by one individual or institution (the right holder) on another (the duty bearer) for an act or forbearance, such as if the act or forbearance is not performed, it would be morally or legally acceptable to use coercion to extract compliance or compensation in lieu of it (Stevenson, 1991:49).

A duty, as the complement, or correlate, to a right:

> ... is the obligation of the duty bearer to perform the act or forbearance. Thus, if one agent has the right to expect an act or a forbearance from another, the other necessarily has the duty, in a moral or legal sense, to act or forbear (Stevenson, 1991:49).

The second pair is also relevant for common property. A liberty, or privilege:

> ... is a legal or ethical freedom to perform or not to perform an act without any duty incumbent on another person. It also means that others have no right to require the person at liberty to act or forbear from the act; that is, others hold *no right* as the correlate to the person's liberty (Stevenson, 1991:50; emphasis original).

The described property rights are involved in common property, but not in open access:

> Whereas rights are relationships between persons, property rights are specifically relationships between persons regarding use of a thing – whether corporal or incorporeal (Stevenson, 1991:50).

A person's property rights are defined by a combination of rights, duties, liberties, powers, immunities and liabilities defining, at the same time, how others are required, morally or legally, to behave in respect to the object of property. The list over all these rights, duties, liberties, powers and immunities and that define the degree of ownership is long, being:

> ... the right to possess; the right to personal use; the right to manage (i.e., to decide how and by whom a thing shall be used); the right to income through forgoing personal use and allowing others to use a thing; the powers to alienate, consume, waste, modify, or destroy a thing; an immunity from expropriation; the power to bequeath; the rights regarding term of ownership; the duty to forbear from using the thing in ways harmful to others; the liability to expropriation for unpaid debt; and rights and duties regarding their reversion of lapsed ownership rights (Stevenson, 1991:50).

It is, precisely, the existence of customs, or practices, of these rights, duties, etc., that make property different from non-property, distinguishing also one type of property from another. Consequently, without the relationship right/duty, as in an open access resource, there is no property and, therefore, no owners either:

> common property on the other hand, *is property*. It has a definable set of users who have the right to exclude others from possession use, and enjoyment of benefits. Excluded persons have the duty to observe the rights of the included user to extract the resource. Furthermore, in a well-functioning situation, the users have certain rights and duties among themselves with respect to possession, use and enjoyment of benefits from the resource (Stevenson, 1991:51, emphasis added).

In the concept of property itself, and its requisite of well-defined rights and duties, is to be found, as Stevenson (1991:52) stresses, an implicit, but clear distinction between common property and open access, in the sense that while common property does represent property; open access does not. According to Stevenson, there also exists something he calls limited open access, which is also different from common property. In limited open access, as for example, in common oil and gas pools, the user has the exclusive right to extract the resource, but not the exclusive right to a certain amount of the resource extracted. This can be exploited at the free decision of the user and if only their number is limited, but not the rate of exploitation, this can go beyond the optimal level. In comparison with open access, here the over-exploitation may be less extreme. This situation, however, remains excluded from common property as here property rights between users and non-users and among the users themselves are defined in order to avoid over-exploitation. This is a reason why common property constitutes an alternative to limited open access in order to reach optimal resource extraction in the case where this is limited (Stevenson, 1991:52-53).

Recapturing the common denominator: the form of communal land ownership

For Stevenson, common property, or *res comunes,* is a form of ownership of its own, a resource management institution neither inferior nor superior to private property, but in between this and open access. Stevenson does not only plea for common property as a form of its own, but also as a reasonable alternative for those resources that due to physical attributes and cost exploitation are less suitable to be managed privately. According to Stevenson (1991:69):

> ... physical attributes and the costs of exploitation render common pool resources unsuitable for division into individual units on the one hand and unworkable for sole ownership on the other.

Also:

> common property is a preferred solution to open access when the resource is unamenable to being split into individually controlled units, the control cost of sole ownership are prohibitive, or the technological characteristics of production (e.g., economies of scale) favour it over private property. It may be also preferred when social and cultural factors favour a group over an individualistic solution (Stevenson, 1991:76).

As an institution, common property has not only been ignored but often confused with open access, and the differences deserve to be understood. Open access, to which the famous 'tragedy of the common' refers, but which should rather, according to Stevenson (1991:63), be called the 'tragedy of open access', consigns the usage or exploitation of resources without any control on the amount extracted, often leading to over-exploitation and mismanagement. In common property, in opposition, both resource access, and the amount extracted are under the management of the group that controls the property. Open access has been defined:

> ... as depleteable, fugitive resources that are open to extraction by anyone, whose extraction is rival, and whose exploitation leads to negative externalities [effects] for other users of the resource (Stevenson, 1991:31).

The rivalry in production indicates that the extraction by one agent precludes the possession of another on the resource. The depletability, or exhaustion, indicates that there is not only a rivalry in exploitation, but that this exploitation can reduce the resource to zero, dealing both exhaustible resources (oil and minerals) as those renewable (fish and trees). The fugitive nature of a resource in an open access system means that the resource must be 'reduced to ownership by capture'. The negative externalities, or effects, can be symmetric or asymmetric. The first refer to when the exploitation of one agent on the resource result in negative effect to all other users, whose exploitation also result negative in the former, the negative effects being reciprocal (fisheries, wildlife, open grazing land, groundwater, unregulated wood and forest and common oil and gas pool). Asymmetric externality takes place when the economic decision of the actor on production or consumption influences the others, while the activities of the latter does not affect in the former like for example, when, the pollution of a factory affects the water quality of another village (Stevenson, 1991:8-9).

For common property, Stevenson systematises in seven points the necessary and sufficient conditions, which constitute the core of the formal definition of this ownership form. Each condition is necessary for the resource managed under common property. Together, the conditions are sufficient for common property, because open access and private property do not exhibit at least one of the conditions. In developing these conditions, when similarities and dissimilarities with both open access and private property arise, they are stressed by Stevenson.

We shall see how the institution of the agricultural communities of Chile's Region IV will encounter all the conditions for common property specified by Stevenson, and even surpass them. These will be brought into the discussion in a parallel form. In one way or another, I have considered most of these conditions through this dissertation, especially in Chapters 3 and 9. I will not repeat them here in detail, but will rather, for the sake of coherence, refer to them following Stevenson. However, simplistically, I will mostly refer to the agricultural communities as defined in Chapter 9 after the 1993 modification of their law. This law finally recognised the agricultural communities for what they have been traditionally, the legal concepts answer, to a great extent, to the spirit of the old, local, socio-economic agrarian institutions. Following Solis de Ovando (1989), I considered several of the conditions here systematised with Stevenson.

Stevenson's *first condition* is that common property is a form of resource ownership where the resource unit has well defined borders by physical, biological, and social parameters, or by a combination of them. This condition answers to the question, "What is the resource?" While the resource subjected to ownership is physically tangible, being the one that the group manage together, as a social institution common property is intangible:

> The institution cannot exist without the resource that it controls (Stevenson, 1991:40).

For example, the Swiss grazing land is defined by social convention of property lines, which can also be defined by the interaction of physical bounds as a mountain ridge.

In the agricultural communities of Chile's Region IV, the resource unit is the land, which has well defined physical borders, based on social and traditional conventions. These often coincide, as in the Swiss case, with mountain ridges. The institution is the agricultural community and the resource is the land. The institution is intangible; the land is not.

Stevenson's *second condition* for common property is a well-defined group of users, the commoners, distinct from persons excluded from resource use. Simply 'we' and 'they' or user and non-user, are the two groups with a relationship to the resource. The first group consists of an identifiable, countable number of commoners or users. The second group comprises all those who do not have the right to use it. In contrast, in a situation of open access, everyone is a potential user (Stevenson, 1991:41). Private property also meets the second and fourth points of the definition of common property (Stevenson, 1991:57).

The *seventh condition* can also be brought in here, as it is partially associated with the second condition, the well-delineated group of rights holders may, or may not, coincide with the group of users, as the rights holders may rent their rights (Stevenson, 1991:44).

In the agricultural communities of Region IV there is, prior and posterior to their legalisation, a well-defined group of users (the *comuneros*) which is the identifiable and countable group of people registered in every community whose relationship to the resource, the land of the community, is of joint or co-ownership. What is more, once the community has become indemnified and the number of its *comuneros* established, their number can decrease but not increase.

The agricultural communities of Region IV met the seventh condition. Those who are *comuneros* are not necessarily identical with the person that uses the land, as many *comuneros* are in fact absentees.

Stevenson's *third condition* for common property is that multiple users participate in resource extraction. This means that the common property is utilised by two or more people, excluding being run by a single person, a characteristic otherwise still associated with private property (Stevenson, 1991:41). The agricultural communities of Region IV met this condition of common property too, the number of users being 668 in the case of the studied community Canela Baja. Not all of them claim their rights to use the common land effectively, this right being latent.

As a *fourth condition* for common property Stevenson suggests that there exist, explicit or implicit, well-understood rules among commoners regarding their rights and duties to one another in respect of resource extraction. Of these rules, the most important is, because it distinguishes common property from open access, the existence of methods to control who may take how much of the resource. This is not to say that right to use is synonymous of equal amount of the resource. In common property, what the users have is coequal rights, sharing oscillation in availability of the resource proportionally according to each user's basic rights to use, or historical pattern of use (Stevenson, 1991:45). Under common property, the rules and conventions always appeal to some authority higher than the individual user or any sub-set of users. Other rules may include how rights are transferred, financial obligation of the users to the group, work requirement and how the rules themselves are changed. The rules may be formal and explicit, or informal and implicit, and the latter may precede the formal rules. The Swiss Alps exemplifies this (Stevenson, 1991:41-42).

The agricultural communities of Region IV meet even this condition. Its most formal expression is the specific law about the agricultural communities themselves, and the written statutes that every community has. These statutes, or well-understood rules among *comuneros,* regarding their rights and duties to one another in respect to resource extraction, existed explicitly in many communities before legalised, and implicitly in many others. These statutes serve as a basis for the law of the communities, this being an example where, as with the Swiss case, the informal and implicit rules preceded the formal ones, or where the formal law codifies an already existing informal rule.

However, the statutes and their application, vary from community to community, some of them having more common land and resources than others in relation to number of *comuneros.* However, the statutes mostly restricted the number of animals to pasture, controlled the opening of the fences of the *lluvias* after the *comuneros* has stopped using them. They also controlled the distribution of the *lluvias,* and very important, the distribution of the water for irrigation, measures for conservation of the soil, etc. (Estatutos de la comunidad, 1970).

Dealing with the question of authority, the rules and conventions of the statutes always appeal to the Junta of the community and this is elected democratically by the *comuneros.* In other words, as Stevenson, points out, the rules appeal to a body that is higher than the individual users or any subset of users. The other rules of the statutes as well as those from the law include how rights are to be transferred, financial obligation of the users to the group, work requirement of the *comuneros* for the community, as well as how the rules themselves are to be changed. In this and other cases, the rules establish even the concrete percentage of votes needed for every type of decision to be taken, depending on the importance of the matter to be voted (see Chapter 9).

The agricultural communities of Region IV not only met all the conditions for common property specified by Stevenson, but even more. I would suggest that this is so because there is a limit regarding the maximum number of rights a *comunero* can concentrate in the agricultural communities. This is not just another rule, but in full agreement with what is one of their major features, the common property. If it were allowed to be concentrated in a few hands, it would cease to be common (see Chapter 9).

Stevenson's *fifth condition* for common property is that users share joint, non-exclusive entitlement to the *in situ* or uncaptured resource, prior to its capture or use (Stevenson, 1991:40). Under private property the *in situ* resource can be said to belong to a particular, real or legal, person, as well as the physical unit itself. Under common property, instead, the resource is uncaptured or fugitive. Under common property, neither the resource *in situ* nor the physical unit can be associated to a particular user as its owner, the commoners having expectations to certain amounts of the resource.

The joint entitlement condition means that the commoners have simultaneously *ex ante* (prior to capture) claims to any particular unit of the resource. Only by capturing the resource, does it become the exclusive ownership of the user (Stevenson, 1991:42-43). Or:

> the owners of common property resources possess a *potential* benefit, contingent upon capture or efforts to use the resource (Stevenson, 1991:55).

The agricultural communities also met Stevenson's fifth condition for common property, the users sharing joint, nonexclusive entitlement to the in situ resource prior to its use. Unlike private property, the *in situ* resource, the land, can neither be said to belong to a particular, real or legal person, but to a collective of persons, i.e., all the *comuneros* registered in that community. Nor can the physical unit itself, the land, be associated to a particular user as its owner, belonging thus to all the *comuneros*. What the *comuneros* have, are expectations on certain amounts of the resource, such as the right to particular possessions in common land (whether *lluvia* possession or ground), as well as to all the other resources found in the common land: medicinal herbs, wood for fuel or construction, wild animals, and last but not least, the pasture itself. Once a *comunero* have got the disposition (temporally) right, for example, to a *lluvia*, its use is exclusive.

The *sixth condition* for common property is that commoners compete for the resource and, thereby, impose negative externalities or effects on one another. This fact does not exclude the co-operation among them for common goals dealing with the resource. This, specifically, differentiates common property from a corporation, where two or more users start an enterprise to exploit a resource, joining their capital and skills in order to get a common return. In common property, collective ownership of buildings, equipment or other input also exists, but some inputs and/or outputs remain in the ownership of the individual commoners. Therefore, as Stevenson suggests, the model for common property is to be found more in a co-operative than in a corporation:

> competing users under common property come together *to co-operate* rather than *to become corporate* (Stevenson, 1991:43, emphasis added).

In the idea that user's extraction produces negative effects for the other users, common property is similar to open access. The difference lies in the extent to which the effects are generated, these being controlled in common property by the well-defined group of users and well-understood rules (conditions two and four). The aggregate effects, as it is with open access, may be reciprocal or non-reciprocal. The reciprocal effects are most likely to happen when the users have similar reasons for exploiting the resource; the non-reciprocal when the reasons are diverse. However, Stevenson limits his discussion of common property to the reciprocal externalities, because including the non-reciprocal would have complicate his analysis (Stevenson, 1991:43-44). Open access met points five and six of the definition of common property (Stevenson, 1991:57).

The sixth condition for common property is also to be found in the agricultural communities. The *comuneros* compete for the resource, imposing negative reciprocal effects on one another. It concerns for example, whether they pasture more animals than the environment allows, wood extraction, farming in *lluvias* in excessive altitudes, by not opening the *lluvias* when these are no longer cultivated, using more irrigation water than allowed, etc. In other words, there is rivalry in the use of all the resources. This rivalry does not mean that the *comuneros* are unable to co-operate with each other. In fact they very often co-operate for common goals to the benefit of the community, as for example in the re-afforestation of the communities.

The *comuneros* of the agricultural communities of Region IV come together to co-operate, but after performing the common tasks, each of them goes back to activities of his/her own. Although there is collective ownership of buildings, as the co-operatives for cheese production, both the input and output remain in the ownership of the individuals. It is important, however, that the negative effects remain under control, to say the least, by the reciprocal effects themselves as well as through rules, statutes, the law and by the social control of the *comuneros* themselves.

Now, when we have come that far, I can finish this dissertation, rounding up the discussion by taking Stevenson's (1991:46) synoptic definition of common property as:

> ... a form of resource management in which a well-delineated group of competing users participates in extraction or use of a jointly held, fugitive resource according to explicit or implicit understood rules about who may take how much of the resource.

Dealing with our common denominator, the communal form, I think that Stevenson, presents in his book a position that succeeds to apprehend the specificity of it, emerging as just another form of ownership, and of organising resources and production, no less rational or inferior to the private. It appears as well as a reasonable alternative for resources under open access.

Stevenson's approach allows another conceptualisation, where semi-communal land ownership is not reduced to vestiges of the past, or to the small peasantry. It helps to understand that the agricultural communities are not a dispersed amount of individual peasants but a community, and that this community is given by what the private, individual, small peasant lacks: the co-ownership of land. In this conceptualisation, common property arises not only with power as an institution of its own, but also as an institution that historically is as old as private property.

The fact that common property is marginal compared to private property does not mean that we are witnessing the last vestiges of a form dying out. On the contrary, as we have seen, it still exists here and there, all over the world, in spite of capitalist expansion. Moreover, perhaps because of the further advancing globalisation, common property may appear as a real alternative in solving urgent environmental problems. This form of natural resource management institution could perhaps be expanded beyond the agricultural world, to include some of those precious natural resources on which the survival of future generations depends, for example the oceans and the air.

The significance of semi-communal land ownership, specifically, is perhaps best understood if we put it within the bigger world context of dry land (regardless of ownership form) to which the agricultural communities of the Norte Chico belong. The Smithsonian Institute and United Nations Environment Programme, give us the following information; 40% of the planet's total land surface corresponds to dry lands, agriculture being still the main productive activity in them (http://drylands.nasm.edu:1995/drylands.html, visited on 17 March 1998). Dry lands are among the most productive ecosystems, and economically important. They serve as the world's breadbasket and more than one billion people live there. Seventy five percent of the world's food supply consists of five crops; potatoes, manioc, wheat, maize and rice, all of them being grown in the dry lands.

Dry land ecosystems play a major role in global biophysical processes. This by reflecting and absorbing solar radiation, maintaining an equilibrium of atmospheric constituents, and sustaining biomass and bio-diversity. Therefore, the interaction of humans and nature in these areas has a global-scale influence. Dry land problems such as soil degradation, loss of bio-diversity, and the effects of changes in climate, threaten the dry lands and us all. Sustainable socio-economic development and sound environmental management is in the interest of all.

The traditional dry land heritage and wisdom of dry lands people is jeopardised by the day-to-day struggle for survival:

> Traditional dry lands cultures are a repository of knowledge accumulated during centuries of responding to climate variation /---/ Many traditional land use systems successfully insure food supply and access to water under variable and adverse conditions. A rich base of knowledge and skills has been refined through generations of living in the dry lands, providing a hedge against a difficult climate and the ability to optimise the use of scarce resources (The Smithsonian Institute and United Nations Environment Programme. Source: http://drylands.nasm.edu:1995/drylands.html, visited on 17 March 1998).

Primary Sources and Literature

Archivos Judiciales (AJ), (Judicial Archives)

ANCH AJ La Serena, Legajo no. 15, pieza no. 18, 1696, "Pedro Cortés con Diego Cortés".
ANCH AJ La Serena, Civiles, Legajo no. 79 (1685-1726), 1691, "Pisarro Cajal, Jerónimo con Francisco de Aguirre. Derecho de tierras".
ANCH AJ La Serena, Civiles, Legajo no. 117 (1733-1765), 1733, "Aguilera Santiago contra los herederos de Diego Cortés. Derecho de tierras".
ANCH AJ Ovalle, Legajo no. 1, pieza 4, 1739, "Sobre derecho de tierras en Tabalí".
ANCH AJ Illapel, Legajo no. 5, pieza 4, caratulado no. 23, Civil, 1855, "Francisco Cortez Espinosa y otros contra Lino Paez y otros sobre derechos de unos terrenos".

Archivos Notariales (AN), (Notaries Archives)

ANCH AN Illapel, Vol. 1 (1751-1814), 1754, "Testamento Marcela Valencia" [viuda A. Jorquera].
ANCH AN Illapel, Vol. 1 (1751-1814), "Testamento Justo Cortés".
ANCH AN Illapel, Vol. 1 (1751-1814) 1844, "Testamento Pascuala Cortés".
ANCH AN Illapel, Vol. 3 (1826-1843), "Testamento Diego Cortés" [Castillo].
ANCH AN Illapel, Vol. 3 (1826-1843), 1832, "Venta de J. M. Ibacache a Pascuala Gallardo".
ANCH AN Illapel, Vol. 3 (1826-1843), 1837, "Venta Pedro Cortez a Pedro Zamorano".
ANCH AN Illapel, Vol. 4 (1775-1844), 1726, "Venta Pedro Cortez a Juan de Ahumada".
ANCH AN Illapel, Vol. 6 (1800-1833), 1805 (Pedro J. Cortés vende a José Valencia) (When the documents have no names, their matters are given in parenthesis).
ANCH AN Illapel, Vol. 6 (1800-1833), 1834 (Ambrosio Ibacache vende a Nicolás Cortés).
ANCH AN Illapel, Vol. 11 (1840-1843), 1841 (Francisco Cortés vende a Felipa Pizarro).

Primary Sources and Literature

ANCH AN Illapel, Vol. 11 (1840-1843), 1843 (Lorenzo Cortés y J. M. Beza y S. Bugeño, representando a su esposa, venden a Tomasa Bugeño).
ANCH AN Illapel, Vol. 11 (1840-1843), 1843 (Venta Tomas Ibacache a Francisco Cortés).
ANCH AN Illapel, Vol. 12, 1842 (Cornelio Cortés vende a Felipa Pizarro).
ANCH AN Illapel, Vol. 13, 1845 (J. A. y Lorenzo Cortés venden a Miguel Bugeño).
ANCH AN Illapel, Vol. 15, Doc. no. 11, 1849 (Hipoteca hacienda Limaguida y estancia de Gallardo).
ANCH AN Illapel, Vol. 15, Doc. no. 279, 1858 (Hipoteca hacienda El Totoral por Mariana Montt).
ANCH AN Illapel, Vol. 16, 1850 (Prudencia y María del R. Ibacache venden a Cipriano Cortés).
ANCH AN Illapel, Vol. 17, 1853 (María del R. Ibacache vende a Cipriano Cortés).
ANCH AN Illapel, Vol. 23, 1860 (Fermín y Prudencio Gallardo venden a José Vicencio).
ANCH AN Illapel, Vol. 23, Doc. no. 14, 1865 (Hipoteca hacienda El Totoral por Mariana Montt).
ANCH AN Illapel, Vol. 23, RP, Doc. no. 14, 1861 Partición (hacienda El Totoral entre Mariana Montt y hermanos).
ANCH AN Illapel, Vol. 23, RP, 1863, Doc. no. 1, "Compra-venta entre Lorenzo Codoceo y vendedor Simona Trigo y esposo Miguel Bugeño".
ANCH AN Illapel, Vol. 23, RP, 1863, Doc. no. 12, "Transacción entre Teodoro Chávez y Mariana Bacho como vendedores y Bartolo Paz como comprador".
ANCH AN Illapel, Vol. 23, RP, Doc. no. 8, 1863, "Transacción entre Manuel Godoy, como comprador y Toribio Bacho y Gregorio Carvajal, como vendedores".
ANCH AN Illapel, Vol. 26, Doc. no. 37, 1861 (Poder de Francisco Cortés Monroy a Manuel Antonio Gonzáles para que reclame las haciendas El Durazno, Peña Blanca y Quelón).
ANCH AN Illapel, Vol. 33, 1866 (Juan Cortés vende a Pedro Pablo Cortés).
ANCH AN Illapel, Vol. 34, 1867 (Isidoro Cortés vende a Vicente Tabilo).
ANCH AN Illapel, Vol. 35, 1868 (Cruz Cortés vende a Felipe Lemus).
ANCH AN Illapel, Vol. 35, 1868 (J. J. y Bonifacio Cortés venden a Juan Bugeño).
ANCH AN Illapel, Vol. 35, 1868 (Isidoro y Manuela Cortés venden a Juan Bugeño).
ANCH AN Illapel, Vol. 36 (*s.a.*) (Jorge Vicencio, Fermín Prudencio, Paulina y Francisco Gallardo venden a José del C. Vicencio).

ANCH AN Illapel, Vol. ? no. 201, 1856 (Felipa Pizarro, María Pinto, Juan Bugeño, Juan Montenegro, Cipriano Cortés, Juan Reyes Olivares, Mariano Galleguillos y Juan de la Rosa Cortés venden a José Vicencio).

ANCH AN Illapel, Vol. ? no. 368, 1925 (Venta derechos sobre Talinay, Clodomira Rojo).

Private Family Document, 1922, 10 de Enero, "Haber de doña Manuela Olivares and Vicencio Cortes".

Real Audiencia (Real Audience)

ANCH Colección Real Audiencia, 1710, Doc. no. 4, Vol. 2714, pieza 2, "Bartolomé Rojo con Cristóbal Pizarro, Mayordomo de la Santa Iglesia Católica de esta ciudad sobre la posesión de las tierras que compró de la Santa Iglesia pertenecientes a la estancia de Mincha, Partido de Quillota, Chuapa" (Bartolomé Rojo with Cristóbal Pizarro, major-domo of the *Santa Iglesia Católica* of this city over the possession of the land that he acquired from the *Santa Iglesia* belonging to the *estancia* of Mincha).

Registros de Propiedad del Conservador de Bienes Raíces, Illapel (1874-) (RP of the CBR or Property Register of the Conservatory of Real Estates)

RP, 1889, no. 22 (Inscripción Hacienda El Totoral).
RP, 1890, no. 62 (Inscripción Fundo o Hijuela Puerto Oscuro).
RP, 1890, no. 63 (Inscripción Fundo o Hijuela El Totoral).
RP, 1890, no. 64 (Inscripción Fundo o Hijuela Las Palmas).
RP, 1912, no. 12 (Inscripción contrato de arrendamiento del Fundo Las Palmas).
RP, 1912, no. 21 (Inscripción Fundo Espíritu Santo).
RP, 1912, no. 155 (Traslación del dominio *Fundo* Puerto Oscuro).
RP, 1913, no. 15 (Inscripción Fundo El Totoral).
RP, 1920, no. 114 (Inscripción Fundo Puerto Oscuro).
RP, 1921, no. 84 (Inscripción Fundo Puerto Oscuro).
RP, 1922, no. 128 (Inscripción Fundo Espíritu Santo).
RP, 1926, no. 60 (Inscripción de escritura disolución sociedad sobre Fundo Puerto Oscuro).
RP, 1929, no. 15 (Inscripción Fundo El Totoral).
RP, 1929, no. 70 (Inscripción Fundo Puerto Oscuro).
RP, 1929, no. 127 (Inscripción Fundo Las Palmas).
RP, 1934, no. 114 (Inscripción Fundo Las Palmas).
RP, 1938, no. 159 (Inscripción Fundo El Totoral).

Primary Sources and Literature

RP, 1939, no. 14 (Inscripción Fundo Las Palmas).
RP, 1940, no. 25 (Inscripción Fundo Las Palmas).
RP, 1940, no. 26 (Inscripción Fundo Las Palmeras).
RP, 1940, no. 153 (Inscripción parte Fundo Las Palmas).
RP, 1941, no. 151 (Inscripción Fundo El Totoral).
RP, 1942, no. 75 (Inscripción Fundo Las Palmas).
RP, 1942, no. 178 (Inscripción Fundo Las Palmeras).
RP, 1944, no. 40 (Inscripción Fundo Las Palmeras).
RP, 1948, no. 63 (Inscripción derechos Fundo Espíritu Santo).
RP, 1948, no. 228 (Inscripción Fundo Espíritu Santo).
RP, 1948, no. 229 (Cesión de derechos de Espíritu Santo).
RP, 1950, no. 366 (Inscripción Fundo El Totoral).
RP, 1959, no. 125 (Inscripción Fundo Espíritu Santo).
RP, 1964, no. 73 (Inscripción Fundo Puerto Oscuro).
Registro de Interdicciones y prohibiciones (Register of Interdictions and Prohibitions), Illapel, 1891, no. 4. Título de prohibición de inscribir un título de propiedad ubicado en la estancia del Espírutu Santo, subdelegación de la Canela de este departamento y anotado en el repertorio bajo no. 50 (Article of prohibition of the registration of property located in the Espíritu Santo Estancia, sub-delegation of La Canela in this department and recorded in the Index under no. 50).
Repertorio del Conservador, Illapel, 1893, no. 61, Reglamento de los comuneros de Espíritu Santo (Regulation of the *comuneros* of Espíritu Santo).
AJ, Santiago de Chile, 2 de Enero de 1920, "Venta Infante Carlos y otros a Lorenz Ernesto", no. 15, folio 14, B.P. 10c. C. 18813.

Archivos Parroquiales (AP) (Parochial Archives)

AP Parroquia Iglesia La Merced, La Serena Defunciones y Matrimonios (Deaths and Marriages), 1661-1733.
AP Parroquia San Vicente Ferrer, Mincha, Bautismos (Baptisms), 1889-1894.
AP Parroquia San Vicente Ferrer, Mincha, Defunciones (Deaths), 1694-1797.
AP Parroquia San Vicente Ferrer, Mincha, Matrimonios (Marriages), 1689-1796.

Other documents

Carta a su Excelencia, El Presidente de la República Patricio Aylwin de Héctor E. Piñeiro Cuevas, abogado, representando a la Sociedad Pereira, Cortés, Brito y Cía, 4 de Octubre de 1990 (Letter to His Excellency, the President of the

Republic Patricio Aylwin from Héctor E. Piñeiro Cuevas, lawyer, representing the Society Pereira, Cortés, Brito and Co.).
CBR of Illapel, 1986, Comunidades Agrícolas Comuna de Mincha.
Certificado de Avalúo Puerto Oscuro del SII, no. 54, Illapel, 9 de Febrero, 1990 (Certificate of Evaluation of SII).
CIREN: Lista de Propiedades Agrícolas Comuna de Canela, 1983 (List of Properties in the Commune of Canela).
CONAF: Certificado de Clasificación de Terrenos de Aptitud Preferentemente Forestal Fundo Puerto Oscuro, no. 53340/269, 12 de Junio, 1987 (Certificate of Classification of land of Suitability Preferably Forest).
CORA, Consejo de: Acuerdo Expropiación fundo Las Palmas no. 1775, Artículo 4, 25 de Abril de 1972 (Expropriation agreement).
CORA: Resolución de Devolución Fundo Las Palmas, no. 1731, 26 de Abril de 1976, Oficina de Cambios de Tenencia de la Tierra: no. 2843 (Resolution of devolution of Fundo Las Palmas, Office for Changes in the Tenancy of Land).
CORA, Secretaría de Consejo: Acuerdo Expropiación Fundo Puerto Oscuro, CHC/COW/amb. A/C no. 1773, 22 de Abril de 1972 (Expropriation agreement).
CORA, Secretaría de Consejo: Documentos relativos a la expropiación del fundo Puerto Oscuro CHC/COW/amb. A/C no. 3551, 12 de Julio de 1972 (Documents relative to the expropriation of Puerto Oscuro).
Diagnóstico Plan de Desarrollo Comunal, 1985: Municipalidad de Mincha, Canela.
Diario Oficial (Official Newspaper): 17 de Enero de 1968, D.F.L. 5, 1967, modifica, complementa y fija texto refundido del D.F.L. 19 comunidades agrícolas.
Diario Oficial (Official Newspaper): 26 de octubre de 1984, Ley 18.353, modifica el D.F.L. 5, 1967 del Ministerio de Agricultura que contiene la normativa legal de las comunidades agrícolas.
Diario Oficial (Official Newspaper): 5 de Agosto de 1993, Ley 19.233, modifica el D.F.L. 5, 1968 del Ministerio de Agricultura que contiene la normativa legal de las comunidades agrícolas.
Fórmula Solicitud de Resciliación Parcial de Contrato a CONAF, Santiago, 1985, Piñeiro and Ruíz-Tagle, Estudio Jurídico (Form Petition for the Partial Rescission [nullify] of Contract).
Internado Canela Baja: Lista de Internos Internado Canela Baja, 1987 (List of boarding pupils, Student Household of Canela Baja, 1987).
Lista Comunidades Agrícolas con Número de Comuneros, Comuna de Mincha, 1979.
Lista de Patentes de Vehículos, 1980-1987, Municipalidad de Canela.

Lista Patentes Comerciales, 1987, Municipalidad de Mincha-Canela, Segundo semestre.
Ministerio de Obras Públicas: Informe Climatológico, Dirección de Aguas del Ministerio de Obras Públicas para la IV Región Provincia de Choapa, Estación Illapel, 1985-1987 (Ministry of Public Works: Climatological Rapport, Direction of Waters from the Ministry of Public Works for Region IV, Province of Choapa, Station Illapel, 1985-1987). Cortesía de Antonio Castillo.
Municipalidad de Canela, 1992, Resultados Elecciones Municipales, 26 de Septiembre de 1992.
Nómina de Organizaciones Comunitarias, 1992, Secretaría Municipal, Comuna de Canela.
Nómina de socios que subscribieron la escritura de sociedad Fundo Puerto Oscuro: 24 de Mayo de 1987 (List of the members of the Society *Fundo* Puerto Oscuro).
Personajes que se han destacado en la Comuna de Mincha..., O. Ollarzú (*s.a.*), manuscrito.
Plan de Desarrollo y Explotación del Predio "Puerto Oscuro" (*s.l., s.a.*) (Plan for the development and exploitation of the property "Puerto Oscuro").
RCCBR, 1983, Rol de Cobro-Contribuciones de Bienenes Raíces del SII, Comuna de Canela, Abril (List of the Roll of Collection-Contributions of Real Estates).
RCCBR, 1987, Rol de Cobro-Contribuciones de Bienenes Raíces del SII, Comuna de Canela, Abril (List of the Roll of Collection-Contributions of Real Estates).
RCCBR, 1988, Rol de Cobro-Contribuciones de Bienes Raíces del SII, Comuna de Canela, Junio (List of the Roll of Collection-Contributions of Real Estates).
Registros Electorales, Elección de Senadores, 1973.
Repertorio no. 217, Escritura de Modificación de Contrato de Compra-venta. Cancelación Alzamiento de CONAF a la Sociedad Pereíra, Cortés, Brito y Cía., Santiago 30 de Junio, 1992, Notaría de Santiago, R. Galecio G. (Scripture Modification of Purchase and Sale Contract, Cancellation, Lifting CONAF to the Society Pereira, Cortés, Brito and Co.).
Reseña histórica y panorámica de Canela y Mincha (s.a.), O. Ollarzú, manuscrito.
Rol Anual de Contribuciones de Bienes Raíces del SII, 1995, Comuna de Canela, Predios Agrícolas, Noviembre (List of the Roll of Contributions of Real Estates, Canela Commune, Agricultural Estates).
SAG: Acuerdo Expropiación fundo El Totoral, Resolución del 25 de April de 1972, Rol no. 219-2, folio no. 3.616 (Publicado en el Diario Oficial el 15 de Mayo de 1972) (Expropiation agreement, published in the Official Diary of May 15, 1972).
SAG: Documento relativo a las causales de expropiación Fundo Las Palmas SAG, Rol no. 221-5, Folio 3.617 (document related to the causes of expropriation fundo Las Palmas).

SNGM, 1986, Rol de Concesiones Mineras de Exploración.
SNGM, 1986, Rol de Concesiones Mineras de Explotación Constituídas.

Letters (cartas)

Letter to O. Ollarzú from H. Soto Vicencio, Illapel, 7 de Diciembre, 1959.
Letter of Legal Consultation, (*s.a.*) written by Oscar Ollarzú.
Letter from María Eugenia Barrientos H., Conservator of the National Archive, Chile, no. 058, Santiago, 5 de Septiembre, 1994.
Letter from J. A. Bustamante, CIREN's Executive Director. Authorisation letter to reproduce IREN's maps. Santiago, 7 de Agosto, 1995.
Letter from Pedro Carvajal, Canela, 13 de Noviembre, 1995.
Letter from Héctor Jorquera Valencia, consejal (counsellor) for The Christian Democratic Party for 1996, 20 de Julio, 1997.

Newspapers, Television and Internet

Bright Edges of The World, 98/03/17.
http://drylands.nasm.edu:1995/drylands.html.
El Mercurio, 1990. *Reales Lagos de Artificio*, Albina Sabater, Revisa El Domingo, 21/01/90, no. 1.205.
La Moneda. *Reporte por Partidos y Reporte por Candidatos*.
http://www.elecciones96.cl/cgireporte/conscomuna. Site visited, 25th April 1997.
La Nación, 1990. *Comuneros de Choapa, Vivir en la Sequía*, Gabriela Gayani, Segundo cuerpo, domingo 11, Noviembre de 1990, 8-9.
Ministerio de Agricultura (Government House), 07/22/97, http:// www. minagri.gob .cl/ minagri/ sag/sag.html
Revista Análisis, 1990. *Canela, capital de la pobreza,* Ivan Badilla, Año XIII, no. 357, 12-18/11/90.
Revista Cauce, 1987. No. 21, Semana 21-27 Septiembre.
Televisión Nacional, 1988. *Informe Especial*, 25/08/88.

Primary Sources and Literature

Qualified Informers

Deceased (last actualised: middle of 1998)

Arenas Héctor, *comunero* agricultural community Canela Baja, sub-area Espíritu Santo. Oral interview, 10th March 1988.
Astorga Miguel, *comunero* agricultural community Canela Baja, merchant and member of the new *fundo* El Totoral (after its action by CONAF). Oral interview, 27th June 1988.
Collao Desiderio, *comunero* agricultural community Canela Baja, former *inquilino fundo* Puerto Oscuro and former member of the *fundo* Puerto Oscuro or Sociedad Pereíra, Cortés, Brito y Cía. Recorded interview, 4th March 1988.
Echavarría E. J. A., part owner *fundo* Puerto Oscuro to its expropriation 1972. Several oral interviews between 1988-1990.
Ibacache Eugenia, *comunera* agricultural community Canela Baja. Oral interview, 5th March 1988.
Jorquera Samuel, *comunero* agricultural community Canela Baja. Oral interview, 21st May 1988.
Montenegro Laura, *comunera* agricultural community Canela Baja. Oral interview, 8th March 1988.
Ollarzú F. Oscar, *comunero* agricultural community Canela Baja, former Mayor Commune of Mincha, merchant and also former owner *fundo* Espíritu Santo. Several oral interviews between 1988-1990.
Valencia Rigoberto, former secretary Mincha Municipality. Oral interview, 4th March 1988.

Alive in 1988

Carvajal Pedro, *comunero* agricultural community Canela Baja and member of the *fundo* Puerto Oscuro or Sociedad Pereira, Cortés, Brito y Cía. Several oral interviews between 1988-1995.
Castillo Guillermo, *comunero* agricultural community Canela Baja, sub-area Espíritu Santo. Recorded interview, 15th May 1988.
Cortés Emiliano, *comunero* agricultural community Canela Baja, twice President of the *Junta de Comuneros* agricultural community Canela Baja. Oral interview, 7th March 1988.
Cortés José Antonio, *comunero* agricultural community Canela Baja, sub-area Canela Alta. Oral interview, January, 1995.
Guamán Orlando, Police stations Chief, Canela Baja. Oral interview, January 1988.

Montoya Juvenal, *comunero* agricultural community Canela Baja. Oral interview, 5th February 1993.
Moya R., Owner of the *fundo* Las Palmas. Telephone interview, 14th October 1990.
Muñoz Joel, *comunero* agricultural community Canela Baja, twice Mayor Mincha commune and present member of the *fundo* Puerto Oscuro or Sociedad Pereia, Cortés, Brito y Cía. Recorded interview, 22nd May 1988.
Pérez, Ximena, Servicio Electoral, Centro de Información, Calle Esmeralda no. 615, Santiago, Chile. Telephone interview, 4th February 1998.
Rocco Carlos, agricultural technician, former manager of the *fundo* Puerto Oscuro or Sociedad Pereíra, Cortés, Brito y Cía. Oral Interview, 26th January 1988.
Velázquez Patricio, lawyer Office National Estates, Ovalle. Oral interview, 3rd March 1988.
Zavala, Ana. Lorenz's relative. Telephone interview through Edith Valencia Ollarzú, 19th November 1990.

References

AAWW, 1984. *La Repitencia en los Cuartos Años Básicos 1982 en la Comuna de Mincha*, Depto. de Educación, Facultad de Humanidades, Universidad de La Serena.
Admassie, Y., 1995. *Twenty Years to Nowhere, Property Rights, Land Management and Conservation in Ethiopia*, PhD Dissertation, Repro-C HSC, Department of Sociology, Uppsala University.
Alanen, I., 1991. *Miten teoretisoida maatalouden pientuotantoa (On the Conceptualization of Petty Production in Agriculture)*, PhD Dissertation, Jyväskylä Studies in Education, Psychology and Social Research 81, Finland, University of Jyväskylä).
Albala, L., Ruíz R. & Pascal, A., 1967. *Relaciones de Poder en una Localidad Rural: Análisis Histórico-social de la Localidad de Valle de Hurtado,* (Bachelor Thesis), Escuela de Sociología, Facultad de Filosofía y Educación, Santiago, Universidad de Chile.
Almeyda A. E., 1948. *Pluviometría de las Zonas del Desierto y las Estepas Cálidas de Chile*, Santiago, Editorial Universitaria.
Amunátegui, S. D., 1898. *Un Soldado de la Conquista de Chile*, Santiago de Chile, Imprenta Cervantes.
Anrup, R., 1984. Totalidad social: unidad conceptual o unicidad Real? *Revista de Extensión Cultural,* no. 20, sede Medellín, Universidad Nacional de Colombia, 1985, 6-23.
Anrup, R., 1990. *El Taita y el Toro: En Torno a la Configuración Patriarcal del Régimen Hacendario Cuzqueño*, Depto. de Historia, Universidad de

Primary Sources and Literature

Gotemburgo/Instituto de Estudios Latinoamericanos, Universidad de Estocolmo.
Aracena, L. A., 1941. *Ensayos Económicos, Políticos y Sociales*, Santiago, Imprenta Helvecia.
Aranda, X., 1971. *Un Tipo de Ganadería Tradicional en el Norte Chico, la Transhumancia*, Depto. de Geografía, Universidad de Chile, Santiago.
Archetti, E., 1978. Una visión general de los estudios sobre el campesinado, *Estudios Rurales Latinoamericanos*, Vol. 1, Enero-Abril, Bogotá, Colombia, 7-25.
Astorga, E., 1985. Más campesinos, más proletarios: Elementos para reinterpretar la acción institucional en el campo, *Revista Mexicana de Sociología*, no. 3, Julio-Sept., México, 99-113.
Baraona, R., Aranda, X. & Santana, R., 1961. *Valle de Putaendo: Estudio de Estructura Agraria*, Instituto de Geografía, Universidad de Chile, Santiago, Editorial Universitaria, S. A.
Barrios, B. J. E., 1949. El conquistador Francisco de Aguirre y su descendencia, *Revista de Estudios Históricos*, no. 1, Instituto Chileno de Investigaciones Genealógicas, Santiago de Chile, 6-54.
Bauer, J. A., 1975. *Chilean Rural Society from the Spanish Conquest to 1930*, Cambridge, Cambridge University Press.
Bengoa, J., 1988. *Historia Social de la Agricultura Chilena*, Vol. 1, Santiago, Ediciones Sur.
Bobbio, N. & Matteucci, N., 1986. *Diccionario de Política*, 2 Vols., México, Siglo XXI Ed.
Borde, J. & Góngora, M., 1956. *Evolución de la Propiedad Rural en el Valle del Puangue*, Santiago, Universitaria, S. A.
Bourdieu, P., Chamboredon, J-C. & Passeron J-C., 1976. *El Oficio de Sociólogo*, España, Siglo XXI.
Bovin, M., 1995. Pastoralists, Droughts, and Survival in West Africa, *Dimensions of Development with Emphasis on Africa*. Nordiska Afrikainstitut, Uppsala, Negash, T. & Rudebeck, L. (eds.), Uppsala University, 238-245.
Brante, T. & Norman, H., 1995. *Epidemisk Masspsykos eller Reell Risk? En Sociologisk Studie av Kontroversen Kring Elöverkänslighet*, Symposiun, Stockholm.
Braudel, F., 1981. *El Mediterráneo y el Mundo Mediterráneo en la Epoca de Felipe II*, Vol. 1, México, Fondo de Cultura Económica.
Bunge, M., 1975. *La Ciencia, su Método y su Filosofía*, Buenos Aires, Ed. Siglo XXI.

Calderón, F., 1985. Pensando esas culturas, *Revista Mexicana de Sociología*, no. 3, Julio-Sept., México, 139-159.
Campaña, P., 1985. Una propuesta metodológica para el estudio del campesinado, *Agricultura y Sociedad*, Grupo de Investigaciones Agrarias, Academia de Humanismo Cristiano, 1/85, Sept., Santiago de Chile, 35-42.
Campos, L., 1985. Transición capitalista y formas de producción agrícola, *Revista Mexicana de Sociología*, no. 3, Julio-Sept., México, 21-40.
Cañón, P., 1964. *Las Comunidades Agrícolas de la Provincia de Coquimbo Frente a una Refoma Agraria: el Caso de Mincha*, (Bachelor Thesis), Escuela de Agronomía, Santiago, Universidad de Chile.
Cardoso, C. F. S., 1982. Severo Martínez Pelaes y el carácter del régimen colonial, *Cuadernos de Pasado y Presente*, no. 40, México, 83-109.
Carmagnani, M., 1963. *EL Salario Minero en Chile Colonial, su Desarrollo en una Sociedad Provincial: El Norte Chico 1690-1800*, Santiago, Ed. Universitaria.
Castro, M. & Bahamondes, M., 1983. Un aporte antropológico al conocimiento de los mecanismos de subsistencia de las comunidades de la IV Región, Chile, Primer encuentro científico sobre el medio ambiente chileno, Vol. 2, Organiza: *CIPMA*, Sede: Universidad de La Serena, 56-60.
Castro, M. & Bahamondes, M., 1986. Surgimiento y transformación del sistema comunitario: Las comunidades agrícolas, IV Región, Chile, *Ambiente y Desarrollo*, Vol. 2, no. 1, mayo, 111-126.
Castro, M., (s.a.). *Desertification and poverty: agropastoral communities of Chile's arid lands*, Department of Anthropology, University of Chile.
Charon, J. M., 1998. *Symbolic Interactionism. An introduction, an interpretation, an integration*, New Jersey, Prentice Hall.
Chayanov, A.V., 1966. *On The Theory of Peasant Economy*, Illinois, Richard D. Irwin, INC.
CIDA, 1966. *Chile: Tenencia de la Tierra y Desarrollo Socio-económico del Sector Agrícola*, Santiago.
CIPRES Consultores Ltda., 1992. *Diagnóstico para la regularización y saneamiento de las comunidades agrícolas de hecho de la IV Región, Informe Final*, Agosto, Mimeográfo, Santiago de Chile.
CONAF, 1981. *Proyecto Desarrollo Forestal de un Sector Arido Cálido en Chile*, GCP/INT/363/SWE-Chile, Canela de Mincha, IV Región.
Cortázar, R. & Downey, R., 1977. Efectos redistributivos de la reforma agraria, *El Trimestre Económico*, Vol. XLIV (3), no. 175, Julio-Septiembre, México, 685-713.
Cortés-M, C. R., 1991-1992. El conquistador Pedro Cortés de Monroy y su descendencia: Trayectoria de un linaje de más de cuatro siglos en Chile, *Revista de Estudios Históricos*, Instituto Chileno de Investigaciones Genealógicas, Año XLIV, no. 36, Santiago de Chile, 161-258.

Cunill, P., 1975. La temprana sementera urbana chilena y los comienzos del deterioro ambiental, *7 Estudios*, Universidad de Chile, Santiago, 59-80.
Diccionario Enciclopédico Planeta, 1984.
Dieterich, H., 1978. *Relaciones de Producción en América Latina*, México, Ed. de Cultura Popular.
Dirección General de Impuestos Internos, 1929. *Rol de Avaluos de la Communa de Mincha*, Valparaíso, Sociedad Imprenta y Litografía Universo, Abril.
Djurfeldt, G., 1990. Livsformer i Landtbruket. Produktions-och levnedsförhållanden i ett jordbrukssociologiskt perspektiv, *Arbejdspapir no. 2, Sociologisk Institut*, Köbenhavns Universitet, 1-66.
Djurfeldt, G., 1994. *Gods och Gårdar, Jordbruket i Sociologiskt Perspektiv*, Arkiv förlag, Lund.
Durkheim, E., 1984. *The Division of Labour in Society*, London, Macmillan Press.
Dzorgbo, D. B., 1997. *The African states and underdevelopment*, working paper presented at the Department of Sociology, Uppsala University, Sweden, on the 9th December.
Feder, E., 1977-1978. Campesinistas y descampesinistas: Tres enfoques divergentes (no incompatibles) sobre la destrucción del campesinado, *Comercio Exterior*, Vol. 27. no. 12, México, diciembre 1977, 1439-1446, and Vol. 28, no. 1, enero 1978, 42-51.
Fowler, C., 1993. *Unnatural Selection. Technology, Politics, Law and the Rationalization of Plant Evolution*, PhD, Dep. of Sociology, Uppsala University, Repro-C HSC.
Fuentes, J., et al, 1984. *Diccionario Histórico de Chile*, Santiago de Chile, Ed. Zig-Zag.
García, A., 1973. *Sociología de la Reforma Agraria en América Latina*, Buenos Aires, Amorrotu Ed.
García, X., et al, 1986. Influencia de algunos factores no genéticos como fuentes de variación en la producción de leche de cabras criollas de la zona mediterránea árida de Chile, *Avances en Producción Animal*, no. 11 (1-2), Facultad de Ciencias Agrarias y Forestales, Universidad de Chile, Santiago, 77-85.
Gastó, J., Contreas, D. & Cosio, F., 1986. Degradación y rehabilitación de la zona mediterránea árida de Chile. Estudio socioeconómico de un caso, *Ambiente y Desarrollo*, CIPMA, Centro de Investigación y Planificación del Medio Ambiente, Vol. II, Mayo, 69-102.
Gómez, S., 1981. Transformaciones en un área de minifundio: Valle de Putaendo. 1960-1980, *Documento de Trabajo, Programa-FLACSO*, Santiago de Chile, no. 106, enero, 1-241.
Gómez, S., 1989. Políticas estatales y campesinado en Chile (1960-1989), *Documento de trabajo Programa FLACSO-CHILE*, no. 409, Junio, Santiago de Chile, 1-26.

Gómez, S., 1990. Cambios en la cultura campesina en Chile, 1965-1990. Algunas notas, *Documento de Trabajo, Programa-FLACSO*, Serie Estudios Sociales no. 4.

Gómez, S., Arteaga, J. M. & Cruz, M. E., 1981. Cambios estructurales en el campo y migraciones en Chile, (Estudios de casos), Vol. 1-5, *Documento de trabajo, Programa FLACSO-Santiago de Chile*, no. 128.

Góngora, M., 1970. *Encomenderos y Estancieros. Estudios acerca de la Constitución Social Aristocrática de Chile después de la Conquista, 1580-1660*, Santiago de Chile, Ed. Universitaria S. A.

González, L., 1972. *Pueblo en vilo: Microhistoria de San José de Gracia*, Centro de Estudios Históricos, Nueva Serie 1, Colegio de México.

González, L., 1995. *El Oficio de Historiar*, Vol. 1, Ed. Clío, México.

Gramsci, A., 1980. Notas críticas sobre una tentativa de ensayo popular de sociología, *Cuadernos de Pasado y Presente*, no. 19, México, 95-150.

Havnevik, K., 1997. The land question in Sub-Sahara Africa, *IRD-Currents*, Dept. of Rural Development, Swedish University of Agricultural Sciences, Uppsala, 4-9.

Hendricks, T. F., 1990. *The Pillars of Apartheid. Land Tenure, Rural Planning and the Chieftancy*, PhD., Acta Universitatis Upsaliensis, Studia Sociologica Upsaliensia, 32, Uppsala.

Huizer, G., 1966. *Rural organizations in Chile: preliminary notes and observations especially on the Peasants Unions in the Valley of Choapa*, April, Mimeograph, reproduced by the University of Wisconsin's Land Tenure Center, Chile (Biblioteca GIA).

IGM, 1981. *Atlas Regionalizado de Chile*.

INE, 1982. *Localidades Pobladas, XV Censo Nacional de Población y IV de Vivienda-Chile*.

INE, 1985/86. *Estadísticas Agropecuarias*, Año agrícola 85/86.

INE, 1986/87. *Estadísticas Agropecuarias*, Año agrícola 86/87.

INE, 1992. *Localidades Pobladas, XV Censo Nacional de Población y IV de Vivienda-Chile*.

IREN-CORFO, 1977-1978. *Estudios de las Comunidades Agrícolas IV Región*, Santiago. This study embraces 16 books and a final rapport, Diagnóstico Integrado (Vol. 1, 1978): (1) Bibliografía, (2) Catastro, (3) Caracterización Climática, (4) Hidrología, (5) Geología Regional, (6) Geomorfología, (7) Recursos Mineros, (8) Agrología, (9) Uso y Manejo Actual del Suelo, (10) Vegetación, (11) Infraestructura y Servicios Esenciales, (12) Diagnóstico Socioeconómico, (13) Descripción del Predio Corral de Julio, (14) Evaluación de Programas de Desarrollo y Experiencias Silvo-agropecuarias, (15) Plan Piloto de Transferencia Tecnológica, and (16) Comercialización.

Primary Sources and Literature

Jonsson, U., 1992. The paradox of share tenancy under capitalism: a comparative perspective on late nineteenth- and twentieth-century French and Italian sharecropping, *Rural History*, 1992:3, 2, Cambridge University Press, 191-217.

Jonsson, U. & Pettersson, R., 1989. Friends or Foes? Peasants, Capitalists, and Markets in West European Agriculture, 1850-1939, *Review Fernand Braudel Center*, Vol. XII, no. 4, 535-571.

Lewis, O., 1960. *Tepoztlán: Village in México*, USA, Holt, Rinehart and Winston, Inc.

Kaplan, O., 1948. *Geografía de Chile*, Santiago, Instituto Geográfico Militar.

Kay, C., 1980. *El Sistema Señorial Europeo y la Hacienda Latinoamericana*, México, Ed. Era.

Keller, C., 1956. El Norte Chico en la época de la formación de la República, *Revista Chilena de Historia y Geografía*, no. 123, Años 1954-1955, Santiago de Chile, 15-49.

Krantz, L. (*s.a.*). Mercadeo, Intermediación y Estratificaciones en las Sociedades Campesinas: un caso de México Central, *Estudios Rurales Latinoamericanos*, Vol 4, no. 1, 89-112.

Mahan, V. & Gónzales J. G., 1994. *Breve Diagnóstico Socieconómico de la Comuna de Canela*, Universidad de Chile, Departamento de Historia, mimeográfo.

Mann, S., 1990. *Agrarian Capitalism in Theory and Practice*, The University of North Carolina Press.

Marx, K., 1983. *Capital*, Vol. 1, Moscow, Progress Publishers.

Mellafe, R., 1981. Latifundio y poder rural en Chile de los siglos XVII y XVIII, *Cuadernos de Historia*, Depto. de Ciencias Históricas, Universidad de Chile, Diciembre, 87-108.

Mostny, G., 1985. *Prehistoria de Chile*, Santiago de Chile, Editorial Universitaria.

Pascal, A., 1968. *Relaciones de Poder en una Localidad Rural: Estudio de Caso en el Valle de Hurtado, Coquimbo*, Santiago, ICIRA.

Paz, O., 1983. *El Ogro Filantrópico*, España, Seix Barral.

Pequeño Larousse Ilustrado, 1989. España, Ed. Larousse.

Pinto, R. J., 1983. *La Serena Colonial: La ciudad y Sus Valles Hace Dos Siglos.*, Universidad Católica de Valparaíso, Ediciones Universitarias.

Pucciarelli, A., 1985. El dominio estatal de la agricultura campesina. Estudio sobre ejidatarios minifundistas de la comarca lagunera, *Revista Mexicana de Sociología*, no. 3, Julio-Sept., México, 41-57.

Retamal, J., Celis, C. & Muñoz, J. G., 1992. *Familias Fundadoras de Chile (1540-1600)*, Santiago de Chile, Ed. Universitaria, S. A.

Rivera, R., 1988(a). *Los Campesinos Chilenos*, Serie GIA/3, Santiago de Chile, Grupo de Investigaciones Agrarias.
Rivera, R., 1988(b). *Introducción a la Historia Agraria de América Latina* (draft), Santiago de Chile, Grupo de Investigaciones Agrarias, Nov.
Santander, A. (s.a.). *Comunidades Agrícolas IV Región: Proposición de una Estrategia para Erradicar la Extrema Pobreza Asegurando Protección y Conservación del Medio Ambiente, Perfiles de Planes y Programas de Desarrollo*, CEDECOM, Santiago, Chile.
Schnore F. L., 1967. *Community in Sociology: An introduction*, N. J. Smelser (Ed.), New York, Wiley International Edition.
Seyler, H., 1983. *Hur Bonden Blev Lönearbetare: Industrisamhallet och den Svenska Bondeklassens Omvandlig*. Arkiv avhandlingsserie 17, Lund.
Silva Lezaeta, L., 1904. *El Conquistador Francisco de Aguirre*, Santiago de Chile, Imprenta de La Revista Católica.
Silva Lezaeta, L., 1953. *El Conquistador Francisco de Aguirre*, Fondo Histórico y Bibliográfico J. T. Medina, Santiago de Chile.
Silverman, D., 1986. *Qualitative Methodology and Sociology. Describing the Social World*, Great Britain, Gower.
Solis de Ovando, J., 1989. *Normativa Legal de las Comunidades Agrícolas, Estudio Crítico del D.F.L. 5 de 1967 del Ministerio de Agricultura con sus modificaciones posteriores*, JUNDEP/Programa Rural (s.l.), Ed. Antártica S.A.
Stavenhagen, R. (Ed.), 1970. *Agrarian Problems and Peasants Movements in Latin America*, USA, Anchor Books Edition.
Stavenhagen, R., 1979. *Las Clases Sociales en las Sociedades Agrarias*, México, Ed. Siglo XXI.
Stevenson, G. G., 1991. *Common Property Economics: A General Theory and Land Use Applications*, Cambridge, Cambridge University Press.
Thayer Ojeda, T., 1939. *Formación de la Sociedad Chilena y Censo de la Población de Chile en los años de 1540 a 1565*, Vol. 1, Prensa de la Universidad de Chile.
Thompson, P., 1980. *Det Förgångnas Röst: Den Muntliga Historieforskningens Grunder*, Södertälje, Gidlunds.
Vansina, J., 1989. *The Social Science Encyclopedia*, London, Edited by A. Kuper and J. Kuper, Routledge.
Vega, J. X., 1987. *Constitución de la Gran Propiedad Agraria en el Partido de Coquimbo: Un Estudio Socio-económico a través de la Familia Cortés Monroy, 1557-1817* (Bachelor Thesis), Depto de Ciencias Sociales, Facultad de Humanidades, Universidad de La Serena, Chile.
Villaroel N. L., et al, 1988. *Illapel, Cuidad de los Naranjos*, Municipalidad de Illapel.
Warman, A., 1976. *... y Venimos a Contradecir: Los Campesinos de Morelos y el Estado Nacional*, México, D. F., Ed. Casa Chata.

Warman, A., 1985. Notas para una redefinición de la comunidad agraria, *Revista Mexicana de Sociología*, no. 3, Julio-Sept., México, 5-19.
Wonnacott, T. & Wonnacot, R., 1977. *Introductory Statistics*, Ed., New York, John Wiley & Sons.

Appendix 1

Present surnames in the community Canela Baja

According to my third thesis regarding the agricultural communities they are, as opposed to the *haciendas* and *fundos*, characterised by hereditary maintenance of the land property between the descendants of the original proprietors of the land since colonial times. That the present-day *comuneros* of the agricultural community Canela Baja are descendants of the Corteses, who inherited La Canela during colonial time, becomes quite clear when we examine their surnames. This reveals that Cortés continues to be the most common surname both in the community Canela Baja and Canela Alta.

Of the total of 88 paternal surnames registered for the 668 *comuneros* of the community Canela Baja, only the name Cortés reaches as high as 13.3% (89 of 668 cases) of the total. Although this percentage cannot be considered statistically significant, none of the other surnames exceeds 6%. 10.6% (70 of 668 cases) of the *comuneros* also have the surname Cortés as a maternal surname. Of this total, 18.6% (13 cases) have it both as a maternal and paternal surname, something which demonstrates that marriage between relatives is common.

Of the total of 668 *comuneros*, 7.5% (50 cases) have the same maternal and paternal surname, independently of whether the surname is Cortés or something else. In Los Rulos, sub-area of the agricultural community Canela Alta, between 80 and 85% of the *comuneros* has, according to the teacher Patricio Ollarzú, the surname Araya (sic!).

Although the percentage frequency of each of the 10 surnames varies between the 8 sub-areas, the name Cortés is in first or second place in four of them. Notwithstanding that the 10 surnames of Table A1 comprise only 11.4% of the total of 88 surnames, it has to be pointed out that 30.6% (27 cases) of these 88 surnames correspond, according to key informants, to names alien to the zone or the community.

Appendix 1

Table A1 List of the present ten most common surnames among the *comuneros* of the agricultural community Canela Baja

Surname	% of the total of 668 *comuneros*	Number of *comuneros* with each surname
1. Cortés	13.3	89
2. Castillo	5.8	39
3. Olivares	5.1	34
4. Contreras	4.9	33
5. Barraza	4.8	32
6. Pérez	4.5	30
7. Roble	4.5	30
8. Pereira	4.2	28
9. Leyton	3.7	25
10. Pinto	3.6	24
Total		364

Source: The author.

Table A2 List of the present two/three most common surnames among the *comuneros* of the agricultural community Canela Baja by sub-areas

Sub-areas	Two most common surnames	No. of cases	% in respect to the total per sub-area	Total *comuneros* per sub-area
1. Canela Baja	Pereira and Cortés	43	26.7	161
2. Canela Alta	Olivares & Vicencio	29	40.3	72
3. El Chircal	Cortés & Leyton	26	45.6	57
4. Poza Honda	Robles & Pérez	23	31.5	73
5. Espíritu Santo	Barraza & Araya	35	28.6	125
6. Jabonería	Castillo, Cortés & Bugeño	26	36.7	71
7. Fasico	Cortés & Leyton	35	41.7	84
8. Las Palmas	Robles and Bugeño	10	40.0	25

Source: The author.

Communal Land Ownership in Chile

Some of the names have tended to disappear among the *comuneros*, for example: Collao, and Muñoz. Even though the surname Collao is not alien to the community, the only person with that surname is a *comunero* who is a former *inquilino* of the expropriated *fundo* Puerto Oscuro and who became a *comunero* thanks to a donation from a Canela Baja's *comunera*. However, the remaining 25 names only correspond to one *comunero* each, supporting the idea that some of them do not originally belong to the community. These are; Arancibia, Cambisse, Díaz, Echeverría, Estay, Gallegos, Garay, Gonzáles, Guerrero, Henríquez, Jofré, Macaya, Marambio, Martínez, Michea, Morales, Navarro, Nuñez, Ossandón, Plaza, Saglie, Sánches, Villalobos, Villalón and Zarricueta.

Among these names foreign to the community are for example the names Morales, Michea, Saglie, Cambisse, etc. People with the surname Morales arrived in the community during the depression of the 1930s, coming from the saltpetre mines of northern Chile to the gold panning of the Espíritu Santo sub-area. According to O. Ollarzú (Personajes... manuscript, s.a.), his father Miguel E. Ollarzú V. brought 450 unemployed saltpetre workers in 1932 to exploit several gold pannings. The person by the name Michea in the Espíritu Santo sub-area is from Argentina. The name Saglie in Canela Baja belongs to descendants of an immigrant from Saudi Arabia who arrived in the 1920s and whose original name was Manzur Sahlie. The name Cambisse corresponds to the two sons of the former owner of the ex-*fundo* Espíritu Santo, who is originally from Italy. However, neither of them live in the vicinity (source: List of *comuneros* of the community, 1979).

Appendix 2

Short description of the survey

The reason for conducting my own survey was to get information about the socio-economic conditions of the *comuneros*. Since there were no reports that would have given me relevant information on this matter, I considered it necessary to carry out a survey in the community to learn how the *comuneros* live beyond the limits of the main villages. I describe here only how I conducted the survey, leaving its complete analysis for another work. Even though the Municipality of the commune possesses information about poverty in the commune, this would hardly serve as information about the topics that I wanted to investigate. Besides, I was not given access to it. Other information like the one from the official census of INE, even though useful can be misleading (see Chapter 1).

Concerning the present socio-economic conditions of the *comuneros*, I was interested in seven major topics: (1) general statistics data (sex, age, school attendance, family structure, etc.; (2) means and relations of production; (3) relations of economic exchange; (4) complementary occupations, income and subsidies; (5) savings and the interviewees own evaluation of their economic situation; (6) emigration; and (7) political position and participation in social organisations. The inquiry comprised a total of 107 questions, the majority of which were open and later closed and re-codified in order to resume the collected information and facilitate understanding. The inquiry was processed using the program SPSS/PC+ of FLACSO-Chile (Latin-American Faculty of Social Sciences, seated in Santiago).

For the sample, I decided to take 30% (200 of 668) of the total number of *comuneros* who make up the community, considering it to be a relatively representative sample of the total population. Since the community embraces eight different geographic sub-areas, each of them with a varying numbers of *comuneros*, in order to ensure a geographically representative coverage, I applied a simple random sample. This was not applied to the whole-undifferentiated population but to each of the eight sub-areas, by which each individual in every sub-area was equally likely to be sampled (Wonnacott and Wonnacott, 1977:7,143). Thus for each sub-area, I wrote the number appearing in front of the name of the *comunero* on separate pieces of paper. The total numbers corresponding to each sub-area were placed in separate bags, from which I drew 30%.

I considered important to have all the sub-areas represented in order to see whether there were differences between them, either political or other. I have, for example heard that some sub-areas were 'reddish' (read communist). There are also differences between sub-areas as Canela Baja and Canela Alta are urban villages, and the rest not.

Being this commune, as many in Region IV, traditionally a migration community, of the 668 *comuneros*, several have emigrated, leaving a lesser number still living in the community. According to figures from the Conservatory of Real Estate, absenteeism among the 24 agricultural communities in the commune of Canela would be approximately 23.6% and 17.8% for the area of Canela.

I did not take the sample from the number of *comuneros* effectively settled on their land because the exact figure is not known. The list (from 1979) of the community registers by sub-areas all the *comuneros* with rights and not those who effectively live there. I consider that by taking the sample from the total number of *comuneros* registered, the result of the inquiry would later show the approximate percentage of absenteeism inside the community. Taking 30% of each of the sub-areas into which the community is subdivided (see also Figure 1.2, which does not exactly with the specified sub-areas, but also shows many others), the number of *comuneros* to be interviewed for each sub-area is listed in Table A3.

Considering that the community does not possess a current list over *comuneros*, there were cases in which chosen *comuneros* appeared in the list as deceased. I decided to leave them, supposing that their place had been taken by a heir (spouse, child or other). I also made a second list containing 20% more *comuneros* for each sub-area. These were to be used as reserves in the case of those originally chosen being unable to participate. In the cases where, as occasionally occurred, neither the *comunero* of the original list nor his supposed substitute from the reserve list were able to participate, a new substitute was found by interviewing a *comunero* from the same vicinity who had not previously participated, even though this was not probabilistic sampling, but both the inaccessible terrain and geographical distance between households did not allow another solution. The interviewers were happy though to find a substitute at all, after perhaps two hours of walking to reach the place. Finally, of the total

Appendix 2

of 185 *comuneros* effectively interviewed, 12.9% (24 cases) correspond to substitutes who did not appear on either of the two lists.

Table A3 Sub-areas agricultural community Canela Baja and the sample

Sub-areas in the community Canela Baja	Total no. of *comuneros* per sub-area	The 30% sample	Total no. of *comuneros* to inquiry
1. Canela Baja	161	48.3	48
2. Canela Alta*	72	21.6	22
3. El Chircal	57	17.1	17
4. Fasico	84	25.2	25
5. Poza Honda	73	21.9	22
6. Jabonería	71	21.3	21
7. Las Palmas	25	7.5	8
8. Espíritu Santo	125	37.5	37
Total	**668**	**200.4**	**200 (29.94%)**

Source: The author
* This is a sub-area of the agricultural community Canela Baja and should not be confused with the agricultural community Canela Alta.

Because of the relatively high number of *comuneros* to be interviewed, the large geographical area to be covered, mostly by foot, the great geographical dispersion of the households, and the difficult nature of the terrain, I needed to carry out the surveys with the help of nine people, who were distributed following the natural order of the ravines in each sub-area. The interviewers were chosen from people of the area. They consisted of two university students who were studying to become social assistants, two students from a teaching college, three local, rural teachers, a primary school teacher from Santiago and a journalist. As should be more than clear to the reader, the procedure of sending the interviews by post or collecting information by telephone was completely out of the question.

Before starting the inquiry, I held three preparatory meetings with the interviewers. At the first meeting I explained the purpose of the inquiry, its contents and other details regarding instructions on how to carry it out. The second meeting was held to choose the *comuneros* who were to be interviewed and the third for ironing out details and doubts.

The interviews were carried out in two stages. In the first stage, interviews were carried out over a period of 6 days, starting on the 14th of

February 1988. We started from the sub-area of Espíritu Santo, the most distant of the sub-areas from the village of Canela Baja. It is also the area from which we were to interview the second largest number of *comuneros*.

In both the first and second stage we failed to interview the 8 *comuneros* of the sub-area Las Palmas. During the second stage, which we began on the 1st of May, although some of the *comuneros* from Las Palmas were to assist in the celebrations of that day, none of them came. I decided, therefore, to interview six *comuneros* of Espíritu Santo, in the same place, I repeat, well aware that this was not ideal from the point of view of being representative, but these had, at least, certain factors in common with the *comuneros* of Las Palmas. Apart from the geographical closeness, they had been incorporated into the agricultural community Canela Baja in 1972.

In order to complete the total quota, I chose two additional *comuneros* from the sub-area Canela Baja at random. These interviews were carried out on the 2nd of May 1988. On the same day I also managed to interview some of those who had previously refused and with whom I now completed the 200 interview cases, as I had originally intended. The total number of *comuneros* interviewed remains, however, 185 and not 200 because for 15 cases the interview was not pertinent. I call these cases 'special cases', but on these I will not elaborate in this investigation.

Appendix 3

Other services in the commune of Canela

Road infrastructure and transportation

Roads. The North Pan-American Highway crosses the Commune of Canela lengthwise for some 60 km, going through the agricultural communities of Huentelauquén and Angostura de Gálvez. At 280 km from Santiago, the road that carries until Combarbalá diverts, crossing the urban villages of Canela Baja and Canela Alta. The road from the Pan-Americana Highway to Canela has been paved in 1998. The commune's road infrastructure is of 550 km, including the trunk road that carries to Combarbalá and other secondary roads. These join the various localities of the commune. Their use is often temporary and their operation depends on the rainfall that during the winter bursts the banks of ditches, ravines, rivulets and rivers, if abundant.

Old cattle-troop trails. The old cattle-troop trails are of special importance when others are out of operation, since the people of the interior can only transport themselves with help of animals. Although the collective transport has increased, there is no daily service. Therefore, the use of horses, mules and even donkeys has not been displaced totally, maintaining the old cattle trails in good shape since the time of the colony.

Public transport. The existence of the North Pan-American Highway dates only from 1950s. A few decades ago, the most common means of transportation were the trucks, which transported, separately or together, animals, commodities and people. The first bus route began at the beginning of the 1960s, joining Canela Baja with Illapel. Presently there is one direct collective transportation enterprise from the city of Santiago to Combarbalá, passing on its route through Huentelauquén, Angostura de Gálvez, Canela Baja and Canela Alta. As an alternative to the local buses there are bus routes to the north that also pass the commune's coastal sector. In this case, other transportation must be used to get to the interior. Many of the local commune's passengers, making the tour to and from

Santiago prefer this alternative, even though it costs more, because it is quicker. A ticket from Santiago to Angostura de Gálvez costs some 3,000 *pesos*. From there to Canela Baja, a taxi costs 1,500 *pesos*, and the same or more from Canela to the localities of the interior. The intra-commune collective transportation only joins the villages with some localities of the interior and their frequency is once or twice a week. From Canela Baja there are daily buses to Illapel and Ovalle.

Registered public and private transport. In 1987, five buses and seven taxis were registered in the Municipality (Lista de Patentes de Vehículos, 1980-1987, MC). Private vehicles have increased considerably in the two last decades. The total of licenses granted by the MC was in 1987, 212. Of this total, 79 corresponded to private cars, 74 to pickup trucks, 44 to trucks, one of tow and two agricultural tractors. Not all the licenses corresponding to private cars belong to owners living in the commune, some of them belong to people of the commune who have emigrated, but register their cars in the commune because it is cheaper than in other communes.

Post office and telephones

Until December 1997, the commune depended on five public telephones located in the urban villages Canela Alta, Canela Baja, Huentelauquén and Mincha Norte and that of the Municipality. These five telephones directly benefited some 2,000 persons (in the villages) and the rest of the commune indirectly. In 1998 came not only tarmac road, but also the installation of both private and publics telephones and faxes, only in the villages, the rural areas are still excluded from these services. Calls for the local people had to be done through the messenger system, that is to say, a messenger was sent to tell the person about him/her being called. This system is still used for the majority of the people as only part of the population has the resource to buy private telephones.

There are mail agencies in the four urban villages. There is no delivery of letters to domicile; they have to be collected directly at the post office. People of the interior who come down to the villages take correspondence with them for the rest of the people. Until the 1960s, correspondence was transported from Illapel twice a week during spring and summer; more rarely during winter. At present, mail is brought by public transportation from Illapel six days a week. The commune does not have a telegraph service. There was one until 1977 which was

Appendix 3

'rationalised', leaving the commune with the nearest telegraph in Los Vilos.

Access to mass media

In the urban village Canela Baja there is a kiosk where it is possible to buy the capital press and magazines of various types. The most popular newspaper is La Tercera, though not many people buy this or other newspapers (see Table A4). Most of the people, also those with small resources, have radio, often a treasured keepsake from the mines of the North. The radio is the only contact with the outside world in the most remote localities. The bands that are reached are those of the own Region IV and mainly those of Region V. The television net covers the urban villages Canela Baja, Canela Alta and Huentelauquén. The main channels captured are no. 7 of *Televisión Nacional* (from 1978) and no. 13 from the *Pontificia Universidad Católica* (from 1983). Some other channels have in 1997/1998 been integrated as some satellite dishes have been installed. Most of the population of the urban villages has television sets, mostly black and white.

Table A4 Weekly sales of newspapers in the village Canela Baja

Newspapers	During week	Sunday
El Mercurio	10	25
La Tercera	15	25
Las Ultimas Noticias	10	20
Total % in respect to the villages total population*	4%	8%

Source: Courtesy of Marcelo Jorquera V., through Héctor Jorquera V., *consejal* (counsellor), letter from 20th July (1997)
* Population according to INE's census in 1982 (see Table 2.9).

For emergency cases, the intra-commune communication is by radio from the Municipality through nine stations located in the schools of the most distant sectors. There is no banking service in the commune. There are no cinemas, theatres or other entertainment, except football fields (34), which are to be found everywhere. Even women practice this sport. The traditional Chilean *rodeos* are also popular, mainly among men.

Services of order

The commune has one *Retén* of *Carabineros* (Police Station) located in Canela Baja, established in 1932. The station has a staff of six men who supervise the commune. Among the police's functions are to investigate the fulfilment of the alcohol law, to control offences of drunkenness, cattle stealing, aggressions and thefts, and to control the attendance at school of the children of school age. The police have one vehicle and some horses for their rounds. As can be expected in a rural zone, delinquency is not a great problem. According to Orlando Guamán, Chief of the Reserve, in the most distant rural areas the expansion of the schools with its rural teachers, the rounds of the medical staff, the organisation of Boards of Neighbours and the constant visits of the Church's priest, has contributed towards the control of social problems such as rape, incest and others. However, this does not mean that delinquency is totally absent. According to the police information, in 1986 and 1987 several offences were registered. These included accusations and arrests of various kinds; drunkenness, with 42 arrested in 1986 and 67 in 1987; mild aggression with 26 accusations, none arrested in 1983 and 12 accusations with four arrested in 1987; and quarrels with 13 arrested in 1986 and 10 in 1987 (courtesy of Orlando Guamán, police stations Chief, Canela Baja, 1987). Also common are, transgression, either of the Law of Licenses (clandestine businesses) with 15 cases both for 1986 and 1987, respectively; non attendance of children to school with 20 cases and 1 for 1986 and 1987, respectively, and traffic offences with 70 cases both for 1986 and 1987, respectively, are also common. There was even a case of rape accusation with one arrested occurred in 1986. I did not inquire more about this case. The high number of traffic offences do not correspond altogether to inhabitants of the commune, but to vehicles that circulate the part of the Pan-American Highway under the jurisdiction of the Canela commune.

Health services

The only rural medical practise in the commune is located in Canela Baja. Besides this practise, there are four rural posts and some ten medical stations without personnel. The medical staff of the practise visits these. By 1988, the commune has two medical staff, a matron, a university nurse and two paramedic auxiliaries. The practise also has two administrators, the ambulance driver and a cleaning assistant.

The building of the practise was set up, without at that time having a doctor, in 1966 and is a contribution of the *Canelinos* (Canela born people) who have migrated to the copper mine enclave of Chuquicamata, through the Sports Club of the *Canelinos* in the mine. The name of the practise 'The Copper' honours the mineral where many *canelinos* found stable and well remunerated jobs. However, only in the beginning of 1980 did the National Health Service begin to send recently qualified medical staff, those who accomplished their practical during two years. The doctors, after finishing their formal education must practice in the countryside before they chose their specialisation. When they arrive at the villages, they are just general practice doctors.

The building is 1,200 m^2 and had bed spaces until approximately 1979, when they were 'moved' to the Hospital of Los Vilos, by order of the military government. According to the Municipality, the theoretical requirements in the practise are of some 30 beds. Without these, the practise can only give basic attention, and cases for hospitalisation have to travel to the hospital of Los Vilos or Illapel and La Serena, depending on the type of services that the patient requires. The population of the sub areas Choapa, Atelcura and Agua Fría preferably attend the health services of Los Vilos and Illapel because they are nearer.

Educational services

The first school was created in the commune about 1850 and was only for boys. This and those to come, were created thanks to the efforts of the communities, who provided both the site and the construction, as well as housing for the teacher. The Municipality decided upon the salary for the teachers. Many services in the commune have been created thanks to the joint efforts of the communities. Such is also the case with the construction of many roads, churches, television antennas, cultural centres, sports and football fields, medical practise, post and stations, etc.

The examples of community spirit abound in the commune. The commune had a total of 36 basic schools in 1984. Of this, 27 are municipal and nine particular (subsidised). The number of pupils is just over 2,000 in the municipal schools and approximately 400 pupils in the particular schools. Both types of schools are split into those with one teacher (12), two teachers (13) and three or more teachers (9). 34 of the 36 schools are in the rural sectors. In 14 schools with one teacher, the teaching is common, although the pupils follow different levels.

The total number of teachers in the commune in 1982, amounted to 104, not counting the personnel of the kindergarten that counts five personnel attending 96 children. Only 54 of the 104 teachers were graduates, the private schools having no graduate teachers. At present, all non-graduate teachers are required from the end of the 1980s to attend the universities in Santiago, which began a special program for them, where they attended classes during the weekends in order to graduate.

In 1993 a secondary technical-agricultural school was also opened in Canela Baja, for which the community traditionally provided the site. This is the first secondary school in the commune. In 1982 there were 1,880 potential pupils (Diagnóstico... MM, 1985:54), the majority of whom were unable to follow the secondary level in any other commune, leaving to join the economically active population.

The last two courses of the basic level (seventh and eighth classes) are only taught in the urban villages of Canela Baja, Canela Alta and in Mincha Norte. The total population attending school is 2,425 (Diagnóstico... MM, 1985:66), while the total population of six to 14 years old is 2,569 (see Table 2.10). Thus, the coverage of basic education is approximately 94%. The coverage of pre-basic (kindergarten) level is 14% (with 65 children of a total of 478 in the age range between five to six years). The Canela Alta School also has a kindergarten. There are three boarding schools; two municipal in Canela Baja and Mincha Norte and one in Canela Alta. These offer complete board to a total of 156 pupils who study the seventh and eighth basic grades in the respective schools (AAVV, 1984:70). Most pupils are from localities further away who otherwise could not complete the basic cycle, given the large distances, and because the last level is only offered in Canela Alta, Canela Baja, and Mincha Norte schools. To give an idea of the social situation of the boarding pupils, I will take the case of the boarding school of Canela Baja for 1987. It has a total of 84 boarding pupils (53.8% of the total of the commune). Of this total 26.1% (22) are from Canela Baja, 14.2% (12) from El Totoral, 9.5% (8) from Carquindaño, 7.1% (6) from Los Tomes, 4.7% (4) from Yerba Loca, 4.7% (4) from El Almendro and 4.7% (4) from Poza Honda etc. (List of boarding pupils, Student Household of Canela Baja, 1987. Courtesy of Lina Castillo). Those pupils that are from Poza Honda, Cortadera and Espíritu Santo, for example, have to travel a distance of 40 km and more to arrive to their households. That is to say, for a large part of the boarding population who are not from Canela Baja, the distances that they have to go on foot are considerable if they do not find a vehicle to give them a lift along the road,

Appendix 3

something not so frequent on the roads of the most remote localities. Many pupils walk on foot for 5 hours each way during weekends. The pupils, who attend the corresponding schools of their localities, also have to go considerable distances since the schools are not always located near their homes.

Index

Absentee landowners 216, 225
Age distribution 86-87
Agrarian reform 14-17, 31, 35, 45, 57, 59, 60-63, 68, 70, 72, 78, 127, 140, 150, 176-177, 182, 215, 224, 227, 229, 233-236, 240, 244-247, 249, 323, 329-331, 335-336, 344-346, 348, 366, 368
Agrarian structure 6-7, 35, 41, 57-59, 60, 63-64, 66, 142, 152, 160, 170-171, 175, 214, 291, 342, 366, 368, 373
Agricultural communities 3-7, 9-16, 18, 20-24, 26, 28-37, 39-45, 52-53, 57-60, 63, 68, 70, 72-73, 76-78, 80-82, 90, 93, 95-97, 98, 103-106, 108-110, 113-117, 120-130, 133, 137, 142, 144, 150-153, 155, 157-171, 173-185, 186-188, 202, 210, 212-213, 214, 242-243, 245-247, 250, 274-278, 281, 285-287, 290-291, 296, 301-305, 322, 329-331, 337-338, 341-348, 350-351, 354-357, 359-363, 364-373, 375-381, 384-389, 391-392, 394, 401-405
Agro-pastoral 50, 123-125, 134, 243-244, 326, 387
Agro-pastoral economy 134, 243
Alessandri 34, 61, 228, 343-344
Allende 34, 39, 62, 215, 226, 229, 239, 246-249, 322, 327, 343-345
Almojarifazgos 143
Analytical distinction 9, 365, 389
Andes Mountains 98, 103, 139, 171, 353, 377, 384

Arable land 18, 60-61, 71, 95, 112, 123, 172, 234, 286, 382-383, 387-388, 390, 393
Asientos 153, 160, 167-168, 258, 371
Atacama Desert 4, 98, 106, 346, 349
Aymara Indian communities 7, 8, 21, 22, 24-25

Canela (Commune of) 3-4, 32, 36, 40, 42, 46, 51, 54-56, 72, 79-81, 84, 87-89, 93, 95, 98-99, 103, 109-114, 122, 155, 163-164, 167, 175, 177, 186-187, 199, 206, 208, 210, 212, 214, 228, 250, 254, 265, 278, 290, 296, 303, 345, 353, 364, 366-367, 371, 389
Canela Alta (Agricultural Community of) 32, 43, 73, 76-78, 80, 84, 86, 94, 96, 103, 105, 108, 168, 205, 250, 265, 277-278, 280, 290, 370, 372
Canela Baja (Agricultural Community of) 3, 32, 40-45, 49, 51-53, 55, 56-57, 64, 73, 76-78, 80, 84, 94-96, 98- 99, 103, 105, 164, 168, 189, 196, 212-213, 214-215, 223, 227-228, 234, 242, 250-251, 254, 262-265, 267, 271, 278, 280, 285, 301, 303-305, 310, 312, 319, 323-324, 328-329, 331, 339-341, 352, 359, 364, 366-370, 400
Castilian community system 160, 169-170
Cattle economy 139, 337

Index

Cattle raising 13, 95, 139-140, 143, 153, 166, 168, 173, 371, 379, 392
Cereals 101, 119, 121, 140, 143-145, 166, 319
Choapa (Province of) 3-4, 36, 76, 77, 82-85, 96, 99, 101, 119, 121, 167, 307, 354, 384
Colonial society 164, 178, 186, 195, 200, 259, 372, 374-375, 378
Common land 7, 13, 18, 76, 115, 116, 118-121, 128, 130, 157-158, 171, 305, 312-313, 346, 354, 357-359, 361, 378, 382-387, 389, 392, 400-402
Communal land ownership 3-5, 8-10, 12-13, 16-18, 21-22, 27-29, 32-35, 37, 39-40, 58, 98, 129, 159-160, 175, 210, 213, 214, 250-251, 279, 281, 286, 291, 304-305, 330, 364-367, 377, 380-383, 389-390, 397, 404
Comunero 5, 11-15, 18, 21, 24, 28, 33-34, 43-45, 50-55, 58, 61, 63-64, 72-73, 76, 78, 80, 82-86, 88-92, 94, 97, 101, 104, 110-112, 114-116, 117-126, 128-129, 172, 176, 179-181, 183-185, 200, 220, 227-229, 236, 240, 242-244, 246-247, 254, 264, 278, 280, 285, 290, 295- 296, 303-313, 316-328, 329-334, 337-341, 345-361, 366-369, 371, 384-404
Conservatory of Real Estate 42, 48, 285, 287, 306, 311, 343, 347, 349, 350

Desertification 105

Ecosystem 99, 106, 110
Ejido 11, 16-18, 20
Encomendados 135, 137, 162

Encomendero 134-135, 137, 168, 200, 202, 207, 292
Encomiendas 21, 29, 56, 133-138, 143, 151, 153, 160, 162-167, 170, 179, 187, 194-195, 200-203, 207, 216, 366, 372
England 388, 390-392
English open field system 364, 381-382
Erosion 103, 105-107, 337, 380
Estancia La Canela 3, 32, 39, 41, 56, 167, 186-187, 192-193, 196-199, 212, 219, 250-251, 253, 255, 258-259, 261-263, 265, 271, 281, 285-286, 290, 364, 366-367, 372-374, 379
Estancias 3, 29, 32, 39, 41, 56-57, 116, 138-143, 145, 165, 167, 171, 173, 175, 177, 186-187, 192-193, 196-199, 205-206, 210, 212-213, 219, 250-251, 253-256, 258-259, 261-265, 267, 270-279, 281, 285-287, 290-296, 303, 305, 310, 324, 364, 366-374, 377, 379
Estancias de ganado 138-139, 171, 173

Farming 112, 124, 279, 382, 403
Fishing 89-90, 92-93, 398
Forestation 8, 106, 128, 333-334, 403
Fragmentation 12, 39, 150, 154, 160-161, 165-166, 182-185, 213, 235, 285-286, 379
Frei 30, 34, 246, 343-344, 347
Fundo 4, 10, 12, 23, 32, 39, 42, 44, 50, 52-54, 56-57, 62-63, 78-81, 90, 123, 140-142, 144-145, 152, 154-155, 157, 188, 196, 211-213, 214-217, 220, 222-247, 250, 261, 267, 276-278, 281, 285-287, 290,

292, 296, 299, 303-307, 309-310, 316-318, 320-326, 328, 329-341, 345, 353, 366-372, 384

Goats 76, 93, 95-97, 99, 106, 111-112, 120-123, 128-129, 139, 143, 166, 172-174, 255, 293, 313, 321, 348, 378, 380, 384-385
Goces 117, 349, 351-352, 354, 357-361

Hacienda 3, 10, 12-16, 23, 29, 32-34, 37, 39-40, 42-44, 48, 54-58, 61-62, 78-79, 98, 123, 135, 137, 140-154, 160, 162, 165-166, 174-175, 177-183, 188, 194-195, 209-213, 214-218, 220-223, 229, 242-248, 250, 252-253, 264, 277-278, 280-281, 285-287, 291-293, 295, 303-304, 306, 309-310, 321, 329, 338-339, 366-372, 375-379, 384, 388-389
Hacienda El Totoral 32, 40, 43-44, 48, 54-57, 98, 144, 195, 212-213, 214-215, 218, 220-223, 229, 245, 247-248, 250, 264, 287, 329, 339, 366, 368, 370, 372
Hijuelas 15, 64, 79, 82, 104, 115-117, 119-123, 126, 127, 129, 142, 152, 167, 179-185, 212, 222, 238, 240, 276-279, 281, 305, 324, 338, 340, 351-352, 354-355, 359, 369, 371, 377, 379, 386-387
Historical development 6, 40, 159, 175, 179, 187, 291, 365
Housing 24, 73, 83, 85-86, 91-92

Inca Empire 150-152, 161
Industry 89, 93, 185, 218, 236, 319, 326

Inquilinos 14-15, 42, 54, 126, 144-151, 227-229, 240, 242-244, 246-247, 320-321, 331, 345, 424

Judicial archives 47-48, 270

Land concentration 153, 181, 245, 302
Land grants 3, 28-29, 115, 133, 138, 140, 150, 152, 164, 175-177, 361, 371-372
Land structure 6, 47, 51, 55-56, 60, 78, 133, 150, 215, 364, 366
Land tenure 4-6, 17, 19, 26-30, 41, 51, 55-57, 60, 63, 66-69, 73, 78, 115, 133, 138, 151, 156, 159, 165, 186, 291, 361, 365-366, 390
Landlord 14, 35, 37, 134, 144-145, 147-149, 162, 234, 238, 299-302, 318, 367, 376, 379
Latifundium 3-7, 9-17, 22, 28-29, 31-37, 39, 42, 56, 58, 61, 63, 68, 133-134, 137, 142, 144, 146, 174, 176, 181, 187, 216, 243, 285, 301, 303-304, 330-331, 342, 364-366, 368, 371, 388
Left-wing party representation 126, 185, 326-327
Lluvias 13, 24, 104, 106, 116, 117-121, 126, 129, 173, 240, 312-313, 358, 361, 401-403

Mapuche communities 7-8, 11, 20-26, 143, 201, 306
Medierîa 64, 145
Mercedes 3, 10, 16, 28-29, 33, 56-57, 133-138, 140, 143, 151-153, 159-160, 163-164, 166-167, 170, 174, 186-187, 198-205, 207-211, 250-252, 291-294, 365-367, 371, 372-373, 376

Index

Mercedes de tierra 4, 10, 28-29, 33, 56-57, 133, 135-139, 152, 159-160, 163-167, 170, 174, 179, 186-187, 200, 210, 250, 291, 365-367, 371-373, 376
Mestizo 24, 26, 145, 150-151, 162, 169
Mexico 4, 16-18, 49, 63, 126-127, 143, 204, 364-365
Migration 51, 162, 180, 183-185, 244, 326
Minifundium 4, 6-7, 9-17, 22, 24, 26, 29, 31, 35, 37, 39, 61-72, 116, 123, 133, 141, 144, 150-156, 174, 181, 245, 286, 301-302, 330, 342, 364-365, 371, 379
Mining 91, 93-94, 106, 133, 137, 142-143, 153, 160, 166-168, 171, 173, 185, 218, 244, 258

Nobility 140, 164, 203
Norte Chico 3-4, 7-9, 11-12, 18- 25, 28-34, 36-37, 40-41, 51, 56, 58, 60, 70-71, 98, 103, 106, 115, 122, 127, 133, 150, 155, 158-159, 161-166, 168-170, 173-174, 179, 186, 244, 286, 304, 324, 347, 364-366, 368, 373, 377-378, 381, 389, 405

Occupations 25, 50, 72, 82, 87-91, 93-94, 224, 230, 236, 425
Open access 5, 7, 9, 58, 364, 381-382, 390-391, 394, 396-400, 403-404
Open field system 364, 381-382, 387, 390
Ownership 3-14, 16-18, 20-22, 27-30, 32-35, 37, 39-41, 44, 48, 56-58, 63, 97, 98, 113-115, 117, 120-123, 125-130, 135, 138, 149, 152, 158-160, 170, 174-176, 178-179, 181-182, 187, 189, 201, 210, 213, 214, 223-224, 228, 230, 235-236, 246, 250-251, 279, 281, 286, 291, 301, 303-305, 312, 316, 318, 321, 329-330, 340-342, 348, 361-362, 364-368, 372, 376-377, 379-383, 386-387, 389-390, 394, 396-400, 402-405

Pastoral 50, 123-125, 134, 140, 142, 145, 243-244, 326, 361, 387, 391
Peasants 5, 7-8, 10-11, 13-18, 23, 26, 29, 31, 34-37, 39, 42, 55, 61-66, 68-72, 94, 97, 98, 125-127, 129, 135, 144-148, 150-152, 154-156, 167, 171, 185, 214, 216, 227, 234, 243-247, 301-302, 307-308, 318-321, 324, 328, 331, 335, 337, 342, 344-345, 367-368, 380, 382-383, 387, 404
Pechero 164, 203
Pinochet 34, 44, 51, 57, 60-62, 78-79, 215, 227, 229, 234, 241-242, 246-247, 322-323, 327, 331, 343, 351-352, 354-356
Piso 116-117, 120
Placillas 153, 160, 167-168
Population 18, 24, 26, 33-34, 40, 43, 53, 55, 61, 65-66, 72-73, 76, 78, 82-84, 87-88, 90-91, 93-94, 98, 111, 124-125, 134-137, 144, 150-151, 153, 156-158, 160-164, 167-169, 172-174, 258, 260, 278, 286-287, 290, 302, 345, 366, 375-376, 378, 391
Posesiones 116, 119-121, 129
Private ownership 29, 56, 126-127, 149, 160, 316-318, 329, 342, 364, 366
Private property 3-5, 7, 9, 15-16, 18, 20, 22, 27-29, 32-33, 37, 39, 41, 57-58, 63, 65-66, 72, 78, 90, 97,

111, 116-119, 122-123, 126-127, 129, 138-139, 152-153, 157, 160, 169, 174-175, 177-180, 182-183, 188, 200, 210, 212-213, 214-249, 250-251, 278-279, 306, 329, 353-354, 362-363, 364, 366-368, 372, 377-379, 381-382, 384, 389, 393-394, 397-400, 402, 404

Pueblos de indios 23, 137, 160, 162, 168-169

Region IV 3-4, 38, 68, 78, 83, 85-86, 93, 97, 99, 101, 113, 119, 122, 124, 153, 155, 158-160, 163, 165-166, 170, 183, 187, 199, 201-202, 243, 245, 303, 305, 307-308, 346-347, 350, 353, 361, 384-389, 391, 398-401, 403, 426, 431

Semi-communal land ownership 3-5, 9, 12-13, 16, 28-29, 32-35, 37, 39, 58, 98, 129, 159-160, 175, 210, 213, 214, 250-251, 279, 281, 291, 305, 330, 364-367, 377, 380, 404

Socio-economic factors 5, 12, 33, 39, 43, 45, 55, 57, 60-97, 116, 125, 166, 169, 170, 176, 178-183, 213, 228, 252, 364, 366, 375, 381, 399, 405, 425

South Africa 4, 7-9, 16, 18-21, 364-365

Subsistence economy 176, 181-185

Sweden 49, 60, 64-65

Switzerland 4, 365, 381, 385-386, 388-390, 392

Tenure 3, 5-6, 17-19, 23-24, 26-30, 41, 51, 55-57, 59, 60-97, 115-116, 122-123, 126, 133-185, 186, 291, 361, 365-366, 380, 390

Trade 88, 94-95, 143, 165-166, 353

Transhumance 139-140, 169, 171, 173, 377-378, 383